Intersecting Entrepreneurship, Internationalization, and Green Innovation

Muhammad Nawaz Tunio
University of Sufism and Modern Sciences, Pakistan

Aamir Rashid
City University of New York, USA

Muhammad Asif Qureshi
Muhammad Ali Jinnah University, Pakistan

Jawaid Ahmed Qureshi
Shaheed Zulfikar Ali Bhutto Institute of Science and Technology, Pakistan

Rizwana Rasheed
Iqra University, Pakistan

IGI Global
Publishing Tomorrow's Research Today

Vice President of Editorial	Melissa Wagner
Managing Editor of Acquisitions	Mikaela Felty
Managing Editor of Book Development	Jocelynn Hessler
Production Manager	Mike Brehm
Cover Design	Phillip Shickler

Published in the United States of America by
IGI Global Scientific Publishing
701 East Chocolate Avenue
Hershey, PA, 17033, USA
Tel: 717-533-8845
Fax: 717-533-8661
Website: https://www.igi-global.com E-mail: cust@igi-global.com

Library of Congress Cataloging-in-Publication Data

Names: Tunio, Muhammad Nawaz, 1984- editor.
Title: Intersecting entrepreneurship, internationalization, and green innovation / edited by Muhammad Nawaz Tunio, Aamir Rashid, Muhammad Qureshi, Jawaid Qureshi, Rizwana Rasheed.
Description: Hershey, PA : IGI Global Scientific Publishing, [2025] | Includes bibliographical references and index. | Summary: "This book explores the intricate relationships between entrepreneurship, internationalization, and green innovation. Through case studies, theoretical frameworks, and practical insights, this work aims to provide a comprehensive understanding of how these elements intersect and drive the future of business and sustainability"-- Provided by publisher.
Identifiers: LCCN 2024052891 (print) | LCCN 2024052892 (ebook) | ISBN 9798369392416 (hardcover) | ISBN 9798369392423 (paperback) | ISBN 9798369392430 (ebook)
Subjects: LCSH: Sustainable development. | Entrepreneurship. | International trade. | Technological innovations--Environmental aspects.
Classification: LCC HC79.E5 I628 2025 (print) | LCC HC79.E5 (ebook) | DDC 338.9/27--dc23/eng/20250108
LC record available at https://lccn.loc.gov/2024052891
LC ebook record available at https://lccn.loc.gov/2024052892

British Cataloguing in Publication Data
A Cataloguing in Publication record for this book is available from the British Library.

Table of Contents

Detailed Table of Contents

Over the years, academic literature has systematically linked internal locus of control to entrepreneurial accomplishments and motivation. This chapter presents a micro-level theory to explain the process of internalization of locus of control among entrepreneurs and working professionals under stress. When corporate entrepreneurs and professionals have self-efficacy to exercise control over their work outcomes, it impacts self-regulation and utilizing of cognitive skills, both of which lead to work behaviors that make it possible to internalize locus of control. Self-efficacy will trigger self-regulation and cognitive skills when there is a supportive external organizational environment, which nurtures an internal environment (within the professional) where self-efficacy can be high. Such an approach could serve to render stress more manageable, bolster productivity, and enhance the overall quality of entrepreneurs' and employees' work lives.

This research aims to analyze the model of entrepreneurial inclusive civic culture created and developed in the Agro ecological Park of Zapopan (PAZ). Based on the need to rescue vacant urban land use with the participation of residents residing in the surrounding colonies, social movements, civil society, and local government, they have designed and implemented actions to create PAZ (PEACE) as an area of green innovation. In addition to the cultivation of vegetables, vegetables, medicinal plants and decoration under relations of

The 21st century has brought many challenges for supply chains and their actors. Ever-changing customer demands, changes in the economic sphere, events that are shaking the world economy to its core, all force businesses to be as secure as possible. One of the best "weapons" that businesses have against unforeseen risks is to cooperate with each other at some level. The higher the level of cooperation, the greater the chances of jointly averting a threat or minimising potential damage. The aim of this study is to examine the extent to which companies prefer forms of cooperation. It illustrates how attitudes towards cooperation have changed over the past decades by using real-life examples. The study also examines the views of Hungarian companies: a group of experts has been formed to identify the most important factors influencing the choice of partners, in order to draw conclusions about the demand for partnerships among Hungarian companies in the 21st century.

The objective of this paper is to analyze the functioning of an integral model of entrepreneurship in green innovation business (GIB) that is currently emerging and in the process of internationalization. Therefore, this work aims to study the central perspectives of technology that are based on the phenomenon of entrepreneurship and thus develop a strategy that adapts to companies with an ecological basis to achieve internationalization. This article analyzes a particular company, which specializes in ecological biomineral organic fertilizer, where no chemical product is used to produce the composition, everything that is marketed is made up of a base of organic minerals and other organic compounds.

This chapter highlights the role of fsQCA in supply chain management operations, building on previous research. It develops a conceptual framework for sustainable supply chain management using fsQCA, analyzed through content and Pareto analysis. The study examines 75 publications from 19 leading journals (2015-2024). Results, presented as clusters, indicate fsQCA's frequent application in production strategies, sourcing, risk management, and sustainability within logistics operations. The analysis also offers new perspectives on fsQCA's applicability in other research areas and provides recommendations for future studies. The chapter identifies significant research challenges and factors for improvement. It advocates for developing new models for better global adaptation and execution of fsQCA within predefined frameworks, urging business managers and academics to consider these insights. Additionally, it calls for an in-depth analysis of how fsQCA can be applied to existing logistics structures.

This chapter explores the transformative potential of circular business models, focusing on Resource Sharing and Product-as-a-Service (PaaS). These models represent a shift from traditional linear approaches to a more sustainable, resource-efficient economy. The chapter examines key enablers such as technological advancements, regulatory frameworks, and evolving consumer behavior, while also addressing the challenges and risks associated with implementing circular practices. Strategic recommendations are provided to help businesses navigate operational complexities, financial barriers, and market dynamics. The future outlook highlights opportunities for innovation and growth within circular ecosystems, emphasizing the need for collaboration and adaptability. By embracing circular business models, companies can contribute to sustainability goals, enhance resource efficiency, and build a competitive edge in the evolving market landscape.

Circular economy startups are pivotal in advancing sustainable and equitable economic models. This chapter explores their social impact, focusing on key metrics that highlight their contributions to environmental sustainability, economic development, social equity, and consumer engagement. By examining environmental benefits, job creation, inclusion practices, and supply chain sustainability, the chapter provides a comprehensive analysis of how these startups drive positive societal change. Challenges in measuring social impact are also discussed, emphasizing the need for standardized indicators and robust data collection. The findings underscore the importance of effective metrics in demonstrating the value of circular economy practices and guiding future developments. This exploration is crucial for stakeholders aiming to understand and enhance the role of circular startups in fostering a more sustainable and equitable future.

Entrepreneurial Spirit and novelty are crucial for small and medium enterprises (SMEs) aiming to thrive, especially during economic crises. Gender differences among entrepreneurs may influence these dynamics. The present study investigates potential differences in the five aspects of individual entrepreneurial orientation and their impact on performance amongst 352 SME owners, analyzing male and female entrepreneurs. Using structural equation modeling (SEM) and multi-group analysis, the study finds that while all dimensions of Entrepreneurial Spirit are significant, risk-taking stands out as notably different between genders, with male entrepreneurs generally displaying a greater propensity for risk. Additionally, Entrepreneurial Spirit significantly enhances performance through novelty, with no substantial difference observed between male and female entrepreneurs in this regard. These insights contribute to understanding gender's role in entrepreneurial behavior and the relationship between novelty and SME performance.

Our chapter explores the operational management challenges and strategic responses of Shell Company, particularly in the face of increasing environmental pressures and global competition. The first section provides an overview of Shell's background and operational management issues. The second section discusses Shell's key operational strategies, including infrastructure location analysis, factor rating, cost-return analysis, product and process layout, and both internal and external system reforms. The third section identifies current management challenges and offers detailed suggestions for improving Shell's operational management. These suggestions include developing clear sustainable development goals, investing in green technologies, promoting carbon neutrality, enhancing stakeholder cooperation, improving employee environmental awareness, strengthening transparency and accountability, and establishing crisis response capabilities.

Fuzzy-set Qualitative Comparative Analysis (fsQCA) is a configurational method used in fields like business, marketing, and supply chain management. Despite its utility, its role in supply chain operations has been underexplored. This research aims to investigate fsQCA's application in these areas. The study includes a comprehensive literature review and a systematic and bibliometric analysis of 75 publications from 19 leading journals (2015-2024). The findings offer new insights into fsQCA's potential in various research areas and suggest future research directions. The study also identifies significant research challenges and highlights key perspectives for advancing this critical field.

Preface

In the ever-evolving landscape of the global economy, three distinct yet profoundly interconnected realms are reshaping the future of business and society: entrepreneurship, internationalization, and green innovation. This preface aims to elucidate the convergence of these domains and highlight their collective impact on sustainable development and economic progress.

The Role of Entrepreneurship

Entrepreneurship has long been celebrated as a driving force behind economic growth and innovation. At its core, entrepreneurship involves the identification and exploitation of new opportunities, often in the face of uncertainty. Entrepreneurs possess the unique ability to transform visionary ideas into tangible realities, frequently challenging established norms and creating novel solutions to pressing problems.

In recent years, the traditional notion of entrepreneurship has expanded beyond the confines of individual ventures and local markets. Today's entrepreneurs are increasingly engaged in addressing global challenges and leveraging technological advancements to create scalable impacts. This evolution reflects a broader understanding of the role that entrepreneurship plays not only in generating economic value but also in fostering societal change.

The Dynamics of Internationalization

Internationalization, the process by which businesses expand their operations and influence beyond domestic borders, is another critical dimension of modern entrepreneurship. The global marketplace offers unprecedented opportunities for growth, innovation, and cross-cultural exchange. However, internationalization also presents significant challenges, including navigating diverse regulatory environments, understanding cultural nuances, and managing global supply chains.

The intersection of entrepreneurship and internationalization is particularly compelling. Entrepreneurs who successfully navigate these challenges can tap into new markets, access a broader talent pool, and foster international partnerships. Moreover, internationalization can amplify the impact of entrepreneurial ventures, enabling them to contribute to global solutions and harness opportunities across different regions.

The Imperative of Green Innovation

As environmental concerns become increasingly urgent, green innovation has emerged as a vital component of sustainable development. Green innovation refers to the development and application of technologies, processes, and business models designed to minimize environmental impact and promote resource efficiency. This paradigm shift is driven by the growing recognition of the need to address climate change, reduce waste, and transition to a circular economy.

Entrepreneurs and international businesses are at the forefront of this green revolution. By integrating sustainability into their core strategies, they are not only responding to regulatory pressures and market demands but also setting new standards for corporate responsibility. Green innovation encompasses a broad spectrum of activities, from the creation of renewable energy technologies to the implementation of sustainable supply chain practices. Its integration into entrepreneurial ventures and international strategies is essential for achieving long-term environmental and economic goals.

The Convergence of Entrepreneurship, Internationalization, and Green Innovation

The intersection of entrepreneurship, internationalization, and green innovation represents a dynamic and transformative nexus. Entrepreneurs who embrace green innovation can differentiate their ventures in a competitive global market while contributing to environmental sustainability. Similarly, internationalized businesses that prioritize green innovation can leverage global networks to drive systemic change and influence industry standards.

This convergence is not merely a theoretical construct but a practical reality with profound implications. The successful integration of these three dimensions can lead to the emergence of new business models, the creation of sustainable value chains, and the advancement of global environmental goals. It requires a holistic approach that considers the interplay between entrepreneurial ambition, international market dynamics, and environmental stewardship.

Looking Ahead

As we delve into the following chapters, we will explore the intricate relationships between entrepreneurship, internationalization, and green innovation. Through case studies, theoretical frameworks, and practical insights, this work aims to provide a comprehensive understanding of how these elements intersect and drive the future of business and sustainability.

We invite you to embark on this exploration, guided by the belief that the integration of entrepreneurship, internationalization, and green innovation holds the key to addressing some of the most pressing challenges of our time. By examining these interconnections, we hope to inspire and inform a new generation of entrepreneurs, policymakers, and business leaders dedicated to creating a more sustainable and prosperous world.

Welcome to a journey at the forefront of innovation and global transformation.

Muhammad Nawaz Tunio

University of Sufism and Modern Sciences, Bhitshah, Pakistan

Chapter 1
The Model of Internalization of Locus of Control: A Grounded Theory Approach

Ambreen Ahmed
https://orcid.org/0000-0001-9946-8989
SZABIST University, Karachi, Pakistan

Afzal Ahmed
SZABIST University, Karachi, Pakistan

ABSTRACT

Over the years, academic literature has systematically linked internal locus of control to entrepreneurial accomplishments and motivation. This chapter presents a micro-level theory to explain the process of internalization of locus of control among entrepreneurs and working professionals under stress. When corporate entrepreneurs and professionals have self-efficacy to exercise control over their work outcomes, it impacts self-regulation and utilizing of cognitive skills, both of which lead to work behaviors that make it possible to internalize locus of control. Self-efficacy will trigger self-regulation and cognitive skills when there is a supportive external organizational environment, which nurtures an internal environment (within the professional) where self-efficacy can be high. Such an approach could serve to render stress more manageable, bolster productivity, and enhance the overall quality of entrepreneurs' and employees' work lives.

DOI: 10.4018/979-8-3693-9241-6.ch001

1. INTRODUCTION

Many corporate entrepreneurs and professionals seek strategies to navigate stress in the workplace. The prevalence of stress among professionals is widely acknowledged, with the World Health Organization characterizing it as a pervasive global health epidemic (Fernandez, 2016). The World Health Organization defines stress as being in a state of anxiety or tension because the demands of a situation are more than one's resources to fulfill them (Stress, 2023). It is a leading cause of poor health in the long run and results in millions of lost working hours (American Psychological Association, 2019). Indeed, stress arises when an individual perceives that the demands placed upon them surpass their available personal resources to meet them (Galor, 2014; Lazarus, 1990). Given the incessant demands of modern work environments, mastering stress management becomes imperative for maintaining productivity and ensuring entrepreneurial success. While organizational interventions play a crucial role in enhancing productivity, it is equally essential to complement them with personal coping strategies tailored to the needs of stressed-out entrepreneurs and professionals in management roles such as supply chain managers or human resource managers.

Certain personality traits play a significant role in shaping how individuals cope with demands within organizational settings. Among these traits, locus of control stands out as particularly influential (Cobb-Clark, 2015; Spector, 1982). The locus of control indicates a fundamental predisposition towards attributing the cause of desired outcomes, such as goal achievement or favorable results, either to internal aspects (internal locus of control) or external reasons (external locus of control). In essence, locus of control encapsulates a broad expectancy regarding the likelihood of receiving reinforcement. Better mental health of men as compared to women has been attributed to the locus of control (Churchill, Munyanyi, Prakash, & Smyth, 2020). The conception of locus of control stems from the Social Learning Theory (Cobb-Clark, 2015; Kormanik & Rocco, 2009; Rotter, 1954), which posits that a person's behaviors are influenced by their expectations of receiving reinforcement, the value they place on that reinforcement, and the situational context in which they find themselves (Kormanik & Rocco, 2009). When an action results in an outcome, it strengthens the belief that the same behavior or event will lead to similar consequences in the future. Consequently, one's orientation towards a particular locus of control is subject to change based on life experiences (Kormanik & Rocco, 2009).

Locus of control evolves gradually over time as individuals accumulate diverse life experiences, leading to the formation of enduring beliefs regarding their ability to exert control over their circumstances (Lefcourt, 2014; Reynolds, 1976). Individuals who tend to attribute outcomes to their own actions and enduring characteristics possess an internal locus of control, often termed internality (Manichander, 2014;

Rotter, 1964; Wang et al., 2010), and are commonly known as internals. Conversely, individuals who attribute outcomes to powerful others, luck, or chance rather than their actions exhibit an external locus of control, termed externality (Manichander, 2014; Rotter, 1954; Wang et al., 2010), and are referred to as externals. Moreover, certain demographic groups, including patients, genders, members of a race, social groups, political groups, and employees, may exhibit a shared locus of control predisposition (Kormanik & Rocco, 2009).

Locus of control emerges as an important factor in stress and coping mechanisms (Lazarus, 2014), with a discernible correlation existing between level of stress and locus of control (Bernardi, 2011; Wang, Bowling, & Eschleman, 2010). External locus of control (externality) demonstrates a positive correlation with level of stress (Evans & Coman, 1991; Jennings, 1990; Manichander, 2014), whereas having an internal locus of control (internality) has positive association with reduced felt stress (Manichander, 2014; Schafer & McKenna, 1991). Moreover, beyond direct correlations, locus of control has been observed to influence the relationship between job stressors and stress levels among salespersons (Roberts, Lapidus & Chonko, 1997).

In addition to its role as a moderator between stress level and other factors, locus of control exhibits direct correlations with crucial organizational factors. Within an organizational context, it is related to organizational level, salary, turnover intention, absenteeism, job performance (Wang, Bowling, & Eschleman, 2010), motivation (Cobb-Clark, 2015), supervisory style, complying with authority, effort, job perception, and level of job satisfaction (Ng et al., 2006; Padmanabhan, 2021; Spector, 1982); perceptions of the office environment, interpersonal relationships, and coping behaviors (Ng et al., 2006; Wang, Bowling, & Eschleman, 2010).

The locus of control has been related to entrepreneurial intentions (Uysal, Karadağ, Tuncer, & Şahin, 2022). The originator of the locus of control construct, Rotter (2021) has highlighted the development and application of the internal locus of control in the context of entrepreneurial accomplishments and motivation. Internal locus of control propels internals to be proactive, pursue goals despite formidable obstacles, and perceive that outcomes are the direct consequences of their own efforts. These are important beliefs for entrepreneurial performance, especially in today's rapidly evolving digital landscape. The domain-specific characteristic of work locus of control influences significant organizational factors, including absenteeism, job involvement, and job satisfaction (Shannak & Al-Taher, 2012), as well as affective commitment, continuance commitment, job-induced tension, role ambiguity, and burnout (Wang, Bowling, & Eschleman, 2010).

1.1 Importance of Internal Locus of Control

Employees characterized by an internal locus of control (internals) consistently report enhanced job satisfaction compared to their counterparts with an external locus of control (externals) (Padmanabhan, 2021; Shannak & Al-Taher, 2012; Mitchell, Smyser & Weed, 1975; Schafer & McKenna, 1991). Furthermore, internals tend to experience reduced emotional exhaustion due to their perception of having some degree of control over their surrounding environment (Whitebook et al., 1982).

Internalization, as conceptualized by Kelman (1958), represents a process of influence wherein an individual embraces external ideas and actions because they are inherently rewarding and align with their personal values. In the current study, internalization involves the complete assimilation of the belief that control over outcomes resides within oneself, leading to behaviors that reflect this conviction and integration into one's identity.

A thorough review of the literature on locus of control and its significance in coping with stress (e.g. Lefcourt, 2014; Roberts, Lapidus & Chonko, 1997; Roddenberry & Renk, 2010), highlighted a notable gap in understanding how to maintain an internal locus of control amidst stress or how to transform an external locus of control into an internal one among working professionals who encounter daily stressors. While studies have explored how control beliefs influence adaptation to stressful situations (Susan, 1984), there is limited research on strategies for internalizing one's own or another individual's locus of control during periods of stress in managerial roles as corporate entrepreneurs or supply chain managers. Recently Spector (2022) suggested interventions such as giving more autonomy and opportunities for decision-making, setting goals, making expectations clear, developing performance-based rewards, and facilitating stress management and problem-solving skill development for internalizing or developing an internal locus of control. However, the mechanism or process of internalizing locus of control while experiencing stress has yet to be examined.

The purpose of the current research study is to propose a micro-level theory that will explain the mental process of internalization locus of control among corporate entrepreneurs and working professionals under stress. The study will delve deeper into the internalization process under two distinct conditions: (i) the preservation of an already established internal locus of control, and (ii) the transformation of an external locus of control into an internal one.

The study holds significance on multiple fronts. Firstly, it has developed a micro-level theory elucidating the mechanism of internalization of locus of control in stressful situations. This contributes to the existing knowledge base by integrating the concepts of locus of control and stress into a cohesive theory of internalization. Notably, such a theory currently does not exist, making this research particularly pioneering and impactful. Secondly, top managers can implement this model to support their employees having an entrepreneurial orientation in internalizing locus of control. They can provide this support by creating an organizational environment that will make the entrepreneurs take control of their work life, increase their job satisfaction, enhance work performance, develop organizational commitment, and reduce absenteeism. Lastly, grounded in this theory, organizations and managers are encouraged to design job roles and allocate work assignments in a manner that empowers corporate entrepreneurs to feel more in control of control over their tasks. By doing so, stress levels can be mitigated, productivity enhanced, and the chances of the entrepreneurial ventures.

1.2 Research Question and Research Objectives

The main research question of the current study is:

What is the process through which professionals under stress internalize locus of control?

This research question is operationalized through the following research objectives:

1. Identifying the factors influencing locus of control under stress.
2. Identifying the factors contributing to the transition between internal and external locus of control, or vice versa.
3. Determine the reasons behind some professionals' ability to maintain an internal locus of control when experiencing stress.
4. Theorize the coping mechanism professionals adopt to manage stress by internalizing locus of control.

2. LITERATURE REVIEW

The locus of control constitutes a component of the broader concept known as core self-evaluation (Timothy & Joyce, 2001). An individual's core self-evaluation encompasses four key factors which are self-esteem, locus of control, emotional stability/low neuroticism, and generalized self-efficacy. These four factors represent some of the main antecedents of job performance, job satisfaction, and other work-related outcomes (Judge & Bono, 2001).

Locus of control is intricately linked to significant job attitudes, job-related outcomes, and behaviors. Internal locus of control is linked to higher levels of job involvement and an inclination towards participative management behaviors (Runyon, 1973). Internals are also more likely to hold higher ranks in organizational hierarchies (Pryer & Distefano, 1971), report more satisfaction with their jobs (Mitchell, Smyser & Weed, 1975), and change their behaviors more in response to feedback (McCarthy & Garavan, 2006).

However, it is important to acknowledge the potential downsides of having an internal locus of control. Cobb-Clark (2015) noted that those having an internal locus of control may prove more challenging to influence, persuade, or conform to expectations compared to their peers characterized by an external locus of control.

Locus of control demonstrates a moderating influence on numerous relationships within organizational contexts. For instance, it affects the association between job stressors and felt stress among salesperson (Roberts, Lapidus & Chonko, 1997). Additionally, locus of control influences the relationship between stress and associated coping mechanisms (Roddenberry & Renk, 2010).

A research conducted with customer service workers suggested that internal locus of control moderated the relationship of job satisfaction with turnover intention and organizational commitment. However, for individuals having an external locus of control, perceived organizational support had a bigger impact on job satisfaction and organizational commitment (Chiu, Lin, Tsai, & Hsiao, 2005). Similarly, locus of control has also demonstrated a moderating influence on the relationship between psychological empowerment and work performance (Li et al., 2015). These findings underscore the influential role of locus of control in changing various organizational outcomes and behaviors, highlighting its subtle influence as a moderating factor in diverse work environments.

Undeniably, developing a theoretical explanation for internalizing locus of control is essential considering its relationship with several desirable work outcomes and employee attitudes and behaviors (Cobb-Clark, 2015). On the other hand, having an external locus of control has been linked to reduced employee effort and a decline in work motivation (Cobb-Clark, 2015). Thus, it follows that developing a theoretical framework explaining how individuals may internalize locus of control is essential for enabling positive work outcomes and increasing employee motivation and engagement.

2.1 Determinants of Locus of Control

Cobb-Clark (2015) has suggested that organizational factors that can shape workers' locus of control are work environments, compensation schedules, and institutional arrangements (systems and policies for achieving organizations goals). As for individual personality traits, internals have been characterized as having more self-esteem, being active, assertive, and competent (Reynolds, 1976) dominant, tolerant, sociable. On the other hand, externals are characterized as dependent, less effective (Reynolds, 1976), anxious, less trusting, more suspicious, dogmatic, aggressive, low in confidence, and having a low need for approval (Joe, 1971). Some demographic variables are also suggested as determinants of locus of control. People in lower socio-economic classes were found to be more external than people in middle and upper socio-economic classes (Reynolds, 1976). In addition, members of minority racial groups (blacks) had a more external orientation than whites (Reynolds, 1976). Shannak & Al-Taher (2012) argue that gender is not a determinant of locus of control; however, research conducted in Jordan revealed that male university students tend to exhibit a more internal locus of control compared to their female counterparts (Serin, Serin, & Şahin, 2010). Moreover, marital status has been identified as a factor influencing the locus of control, with married employees demonstrating a higher degree of external locus of control in comparison to single employees (Shannak & Al-Taher, 2012).

Additionally, religious beliefs and commitment to worship have been found to exert an influence on locus of control (Shannak & Al-Taher, 2012). Furthermore, parental behavior and personality traits are regarded as antecedents of locus of control, contributing to the development of either an internal or external orientation (Joe, 1971). These findings underscore the multifaceted nature of factors shaping individuals' locus of control orientations.

2.2 General and Work Locus of Control

Locus of control is structured hierarchically, with the general locus of control at the top of the hierarchy (Chen, Goddard, and Casper, 2004). The general locus of control is the degree to which people believe that their personal decisions and actions, rather than external factors, are resulting in the rewards they receive (Levenson, 1981). The general locus of control is not limited to a certain context or situation. Occupying lower levels of the locus of control hierarchy are its sub-dimensions. These sub-dimensions are context-specific including health-related locus of control, locus of control in marital relationships, parental/guardian locus of control, and work-oriented locus of control (Wang, Bowling & Eschleman, 2010).

Global measures of the construct of locus of control have been used in research studies conducted in workplace settings (Martin et al., 2005). In addition, work-specific scales of locus of control are also commonly used and have been related to key outcomes such as job satisfaction and employee retention (Campagna, 2015). Moreover, Wang and colleagues (2010) have suggested the work locus of control (WLC) exhibits a stronger relationship with work-related outcomes compared to the general locus of control.

WLC indicates the degree to which individuals believe that work-related rewards and consequences are due to their own actions and decisions (internal locus of control) rather than due to luck, chance, or other external reasons e.g. boss or supervisor (external locus of control) (Wang, Bowling & Eschleman, 2010). Substantive research suggests that WLC has a stronger influence on overall job satisfaction, continuance and affective commitment, absenteeism, organizational level, job burnout, and job stress compared to the general locus of control (Campagna, 2015; Wang et al., 2010).

Substantive literature on WLC suggests that internal locus of control has a greater likelihood of resulting in desirable work outcomes, such as better task performance, constructive social interactions, and higher work motivation (Ng, Sorensen, & Eby, 2010). On the other hand, external locus of control has been linked to lower job satisfaction, higher employee turnover rates, lesser perceived organizational influence, and more job-related stress (Spector, 1988). These findings emphasize the need to use work-specific measures of locus of control in understanding its role in work settings and overall employee well-being.

Internal locus of control serves as a buffer against stress, according to Daniels and Guppy (1992). Internals experience less job stress than externals (Wang et al., 2010). In tense situations, internals are more likely to have confidence in their ability to affect the outcomes and try to influence them, whereas externals behave more passively and feel helpless (Shannak & Al-Taher, 2012). Internals stay focused on the challenge and divert their energy towards formulating and implementing measures to lessen the impact of the stress inducer, and try to find social support (Ng et al., 2006). Overall, possessing an internal locus of control reduces strain and helps to maintain mental and physiological well-being (Krause & Stryker, 1984).

2.3 Theoretical Underpinning

The proposed model for internalizing locus of control is based on logical relationships supported by established theories. The concepts and underlying logic used in these theories were borrowed for categorizing emergent focused codes into categories and for labeling categories.

In their two-process model of perceived control, Rothbaum, Weisz, and Snyder (1982) propose that individuals acquire a sense of control through two distinct processes. Firstly, individuals strive to adapt their surrounding environment to align with their needs, termed primary control. Secondly, individuals align themselves with their environment and adjust their behavior accordingly, termed secondary control. While exerting primary control by attempting to change the world can yield satisfying outcomes, it may also lead to disappointments. Conversely, aligning the self with the world is less likely to result in extreme highs and lows (Rothbaum et al., 1982). Typically, one's primary and secondary control processes are intertwined, with primary control preceding secondary control. For instance, negotiation may be followed by compromise. However, secondary control comes into play after one experiences failure in primary control endeavors.

Second, Heckhausen and Schulz's (1995) life-span theory of control posits that there are dynamic alterations between primary and secondary control processes throughout an individual's lifespan, from infancy to old age. Primary control behaviors involve efforts to alter the external environment to align with one's desires, while secondary control encompasses internal processes aimed at maintaining or enhancing primary control, or mitigating the effects of failed primary control attempts. In essence, secondary control mechanisms assist individuals in coping with setbacks and redirecting motivational resources toward adjusting actions and goals to reinforce primary control (Heckhausen & Schulz, 1995). This framework highlights the adaptive nature of control processes across different stages of life, emphasizing the interplay between efforts to influence the external world and internal strategies to manage and navigate challenges.

Lastly, Bandura's (1991) social cognitive theory of self-regulation elaborates on how individuals constantly adjust their thoughts, emotions, and actions to produce desired outcomes.

Integrating these frameworks provided a comprehensive understanding of the processes involved in internalizing locus of control across various contexts and developmental stages. However, a limitation of the concept of locus of control in the proposed model pertains to its nature as a generalized expectancy for reinforcement, as elucidated by Rotter (1975). This characteristic implies that only broad and general predictions of behavior may be inferred from the small data set collected, rather than definite predictions of actions. Similarly, the proposed model for the internalization of locus of control cannot suggest exact processes for individuals to perform in the internalizing locus of control but rather provide a broad framework for guidance. Consistent with Rotter's elucidation of the concept, the constructed theory has broadly hypothesized how locus of control may potentially be changed across various situations (involving professionals from different lines of work such as supply chain), without specifying exact steps for specific individuals in particular professions.

However, despite this limitation, the theoretical examination of locus of control remains beneficial. As a generalized set of expectations about outcomes, it can serve as a reliable predictor of actions when individuals have limited experience in a given situation to develop specific expectancies (Reynolds, 1976). Similarly, a micro-level theory for internalizing the locus of control in working professionals experiencing on-the-job stress can lay the groundwork for subsequent development and statistical verification of situation-specific and occupation-specific mechanisms for internalizing locus of control under stress.Top of Form

3. RESEARCH METHODOLOGY

3.1 Philosophical Underpinnings

The research design adopted for this study is primarily rooted in a qualitative-constructivist approach, utilizing the abduction research strategy, constructionism as the epistemology, and an ontological position of subtle realism (Blaikie, 2007). Grounded Theory, as articulated by Charmaz (2008), serves as the theoretical framework to elucidate the process through which stressed professionals can internalize locus of control, either by preserving an internal locus of control (if the locus of control is already internal) or by transitioning from an external to an internal locus of control. It entails developing an understanding of participants' constructions of social life as well as how the researcher participates in this construction. Constructionist grounded theory (Charmaz, 2008) doesn't oversimplify, blur differences, ignore variation, and adopt a neutral position during the research, which is the hallmark of objectivist approaches (which promote the views of an independent, external reality out there and an "observer" role of researcher). Rather, it promotes adopting analytic strategies that urge the researcher to focus on context, actions, and their interpretations to produce a theory with explanatory power and conceptual understanding. In other words, constructionist grounded theory approach promotes both explanation and understanding by focusing attention on *what* and *how* questions, which form the foundation for answering *why* questions (Charmaz, 2008).

The study is confronted with ontological concerns stemming from the unique locus of control possessed by each professional, shaped by individual experiences and life circumstances, and subject to change for reasons that may not be readily observable or articulated by every participant. Moreover, participants' perceptions of reality are usually shaped by their cultural beliefs. The reality constructed in this research was seen through the cultural lens of a subtle realist, as advocated by Blaikie (2007). It is important to understand that had the respondents belonged to a different culture, the reality constructed may have had different perspectives or outcomes.

As the aim of this study was to construct a model for internalizing locus of control, the preferred research strategy was abduction. Abduction allowed the researcher to explore the shared tacit knowledge among corporate entrepreneurs and professionals to develop a technical description and mechanism for internalizing locus of control under stress (Blaikie, 2007). Abduction facilitated the synthesis of existing knowledge to extract new insights about the process of internalizing locus of control.

Thus, in the current study, the researcher's role was that of co-constructor of reality with the research participants (Charmaz, 2008). The researcher took necessary precautions to maintain objectivity during the respondents' interviews. The first step was bracketing personal opinions so that they could be separated from the statements provided by the participants. Next, in designing the interview protocol, leading and loaded questions were avoided to minimize bias in the responses. By phrasing questions neutrally, participants were encouraged to freely express their viewpoints, and consequently, the researcher ensured the integrity and authenticity of the data collected. Lastly, reflexivity (Creswell, 2013) was incorporated into the analysis process by methodically reflecting on the data about participants' experiences. Systematic self-reflection about one's biases and their potential influence on data interpretation helped to ensure a rigorous and impartial analysis of the interview data. These three measures ensured a more authentic depiction of the participants' views and experiences about the internalization of locus of control during stressful situations.

3.2 Sampling Methodology and Research Setting

Theoretical sampling involves the selection of participants based on specific criteria stemming from theoretical considerations. In the current study, corporate entrepreneurs and professionals attempted a written stress test (Siegrist, et al., 2009) to measure their work stress level. The selection criterion was having a test score within the third quartile of the score distribution of all respondents.

This approach aligns with theoretical sampling, which aims to select participants who can provide rich and diverse perspectives relevant to the research question or theoretical framework under investigation. By focusing on individuals with higher levels of work stress, the study sought to gain insights into the experiences and processes associated with internalizing locus of control in the context of heightened stress. Therefore, only those who were experiencing higher levels of stress were recruited. Initially, eight participants were interviewed, and later two more were recruited to achieve theoretical saturation of the concept of risk. Two of these 10 participants were referred to by an earlier interviewee, which constitutes a snowball sampling strategy.

Given the absence of any theoretical explanation for maintaining an internal locus of control or converting an external locus of control to an internal locus of control under stress, the sampling strategy adopted in this study also utilized typical case sampling. This approach involved selecting participants who represented typically stressed professionals meeting all the remaining inclusion and exclusion criteria. By focusing on typical cases, the study aimed to elucidate the process of internalization of locus of control in a manner that is representative of the broader population of stressed corporate entrepreneurs and professionals. This enabled the identification of important themes and insights that were pivotal in the development of the proposed theoretical understanding for internalizing locus of control.

Finally, the third sampling strategy was purposive sampling. It was executed by inviting only those participants for semi-structured in-depth interviews who were expressive, articulate, and willing to openly share their views.

By following these three sampling strategies, 10 employed corporate entrepreneurs from managerial, supply chain, administrative, accounting, IT, and engineering professions were identified from a single metropolis. Subsequently, nine interviews were conducted in the researcher's office, and one was conducted in the interviewee's workplace.

3.3 Data Collection

The emergent theory was synthesized from the data collected systematically in several iterations.

Secondary data was collected through electronic resources, consisting of scholarly articles and books on locus of control and job stress. These sources were carefully examined and synthesized to inform the development of the interview protocol. By reviewing existing literature on locus of control and stress, the researcher gained valuable insights into theoretical frameworks, empirical findings, and methodological approaches relevant to the study. This enabled the researcher to design interview protocol questions that were aligned with the research objectives.Top of Form In particular, thoroughly revieing the literature facilitated the development of distinct core questions tailored for respondents assessed to have either an internal or external locus of control. As suggested by Charmaz (2000), substantive literature on locus of control and stress was thoroughly reviewed to synthesize and stimulate ideas, label theoretical concepts, merge concepts into emerging categories, and develop logical connections between categories.

Primary data was collected through semi-structured, in-depth interviews comprising of open-ended questions, augmented by probing questions and appropriate prompts. During the interviews, participants were encouraged to express their views freely. All interviews were digitally recorded to accurately capture the participants' responses and were later transcribed verbatim by the researcher.

This rigorous approach allowed the researcher to thoroughly explore the participants' experiences and views regarding the internalization of locus of control under stress, resulting in developing the underlying logic connecting the various key concepts involved.

3.4 Inclusion and Exclusion Criteria

All research participants were among the top 15 highest scorers on the criterion stress scale (Siegrist et al., 2009). This measure has been widely used for assessing work stress across occupations in several countries (Siegrist, *et al.*, 2009). For the current research, it was administered to a sample of 50 corporate entrepreneurs and professionals who met several specific criteria. Firstly, only those respondents who were working in the supply chain, managerial, engineering, administrative, or Information Technology professions in an officer-level or above position were selected. Additionally, they were required to possess at least a bachelor's degree in a relevant field of education. Furthermore, only those respondents who had entrepreneurial intentions and responsibilities in permanent positions in 9-to-5 jobs were shortlisted. In addition to these qualifications, selected participants were not from the teaching profession, although some of them had worked in support or administrative positions in primary-, secondary-, or tertiary-level educational institutions. Finally, respondents who consented to willingly disclose information and agreed to have their interview recorded were chosen for subsequent interviews.

By selecting corporate entrepreneurs and professionals who met the above criteria, the relevance and validity of the study findings were enhanced.

3.5 Method of Contacting Participants

A pool of 50 potentially stressed corporate entrepreneurs and professionals was developed as likely participants. The pool was generated through self-reporting, snowball sampling, and the researcher's professional network. The potential participants were given a self-administered test that had two measures. The first was a generic work stress scale (Siegrist, *et al.*, 2009) that was used as the criterion scale and the second was the Work Locus of Control Scale (Spector, 1988) to determine whether they had internal or external locus of control.

The work stress scale's responses were coded and summated. As suggested by J. Siegrist (personal communication, November 2, 2023), respondents falling in the third quartile of the score distribution were considered as the most stressed. The respondents had provided contact information on the stress questionnaire forms to make them reachable. Those in the third quartile were contacted by phone to be informed about their suitability for participation in the research, and those agreeing to participate were invited for interviews.

3.5.1 Data Collection Instruments

Potential participants were shortlisted for interviews on the basis of a criterion test of stress. A shorter version of a generic measure of work stress was used to determine if a professional is in a stressful work environment (Siegrist, *et al.*, 2009). This measure is useful for assessing work stress even across countries, and is recommended for use in research as well as practice (Siegrist, *et al.*, 2009). The original generic measure is based on the effort-reward imbalance model (ERI; Siegrist, 1996). This model depicts the relationship between effort put in performing the job and subsequent reward. The ERI model asserts that frequently effort made is not reciprocated with reward, which results in strong negative emotional reactions and sustained stress, which eventually affects mental and physical health (Siegrist, 1996).

The existing ERI questionnaire was translated into several languages. It has 23 items to represent three sub- scales which are effort, reward, and over-commitment. The rewards include wages, performance-related esteem, job performance, and promotional prospects. Workers can be over-committed due to psychological reasons or implied work pressure. The shorter generic measure has 16 items measured on a 4-point Likert scale. As reported by Siegrist, *et al.* (2009), the short generic measures' inter-item consistency for all three subscales is above .70, with effort .74, reward .79, and over-commitment .79, indicating acceptable inter-item consistency. Siegrist, *et al.* (2009) report that the short measure has discriminant validity in that effort, reward and over-commitment scores have statistically significant differences, as expected, between genders, occupational groups, socio-economic positions, and gender role orientations. Confirmatory factor analysis shows a good model fit of the theoretical structure with the data. The scale also has criterion validity (Siegrist, *et al.*, 2009), as the scores have correlation with appropriate health measures, indicating that the short measure of generic work stress is identifying employees who are at risk of poor self-rated health.

The core interview questions had to be phrased in different ways to participants with an internal and external locus of control; therefore, it was necessary to identify the participant's locus of control before the interview. For this, a 16-item Work Locus of Control Scale (WLCS; Spector, 1988) measured the locus of control of shortlisted participants who met the criterion of being stressed. It was self-administered by participants along with the stress test, but was coded only for those who were in the third quartile of the test score distribution. Higher scores on the Work Locus of Control Scale (WLCS) indicated an external locus of control, and lower scores indicate an internal locus of control. The WLCS is significantly correlated with job satisfaction, intention to quit, perceived influence of work, perceptions of supervisory style, and role stress. Inter-item reliability of the scale ranges from .75 to .85

(Spector, 1988). Therefore, Spector (1988) concludes that the WLCS may predict work behavior more accurately than general scales of locus of control.

A total of 13 short-listed respondents were invited, of which two were unavailable and one was not interested in participation because of his busy schedule. One interview was conducted per day, over a span of two weeks. For the 10 who agreed to give the interview, their responses to the WLCS were coded and scored to determine their locus of control orientation before the interview, so that they could be questioned accordingly

4. DATA ANALYSIS AND EMERGENT THEORY

The 10 short-listed participants selected for the study consisted of both males and females. Of the 10, four males and two females had an internal locus of control, whereas the remaining four males had an external locus of control. All the participants had at least 1.5 year of work experience and up to 12 years. Their ages ranged from 26 to 43 years. They were in the early mid-career or mid-career stage of their career life cycle.

4.1 Emergence of Concepts, Categories, and Linkages

The initial open coding of every interview transcript resulted in a new code for every idea. In some cases line by line coding was done, whereas in other cases a whole idea or chunk of data was coded. Later, the open codes that were similar in meaning or related to the same general idea were grouped under the same concept. For instance, in vivo codes such as "set clear priorities," "no procrastination," "clarify tasks," "start early," "put in extra time," "manage interruptions," "manage time," "do something every day," and "start early," that emerged from all transcripts were grouped under the concept of time management. Similarly, other concepts that emerged with more and more interviews were developed through constant comparison across interviews. These concepts were found to be related to the theoretical concepts of the Social Cognitive Theory of Self-Regulation (Bandura, 1991)

In this theory there are two mechanisms that motivate and regulate human behavior: self-regulation itself, and self-efficacy. The self-regulation mechanism is based on three sub-functions: (1) Self-monitoring one's performance, the condition under which it occurs, and its effects; (2) Judging and guiding one's actions on the basis of personal standards; and (3) Self-reactive influence, which involves setting standards and incentives to regulate one's courses of action, and affective reactions to one's behavior if it meets or doesn't meet one's internal standards (Bandura, 1991).

Self-efficacy is the other important mechanism of self-directedness. Self-efficacy beliefs have a strong role to play in how the three sub-functions of self-regulation mechanism operate. They impact how one self-monitors one performance as well as how one cognitively processes it, which eventually affects the outcomes of self-monitoring behaviors and cognitive processing (Bandura, 1991).

The model of internalization of locus of control that emerged from the data collected for this study is closely aligned with some of the categories and relationships depicted by the Social Cognitive Theory of Self-Regulation (Bandura, 1991). The concepts emerging from interview transcripts after constant comparison were part of both the major mechanisms of self-regulation, i.e. they were subsumed under two of the three sub-functions of self-regulation itself (self-monitoring and self-reactive influence), and self-efficacy. Thus, self-regulation was pegged as one of the theoretical categories of the model.

The concepts which emerged from the data and were subsumed under self-regulation's sub-function of self-monitoring are time management, self-motivation, maintaining emotional distance from work and coworkers, and self-control. The concept of self-reactive influence was formed by combining the concepts of creating incentives for good performance, doing whatever it takes to produce desired performance, and positive feelings about self.

Similarly, the concept of perseverance and self-aiding thought patterns were combined under the larger theoretical category of self-efficacy, which is the second major mechanism of self-regulation (Bandura, 1991).

Another set of concepts that explained how control of the situation was retained or seized emerged from the data, with the common nature of being abilities to do something well. These concepts were decision-making skills, analytical skills, problem-solving skills, learning, compartmentalization, focus, and attention to detail. These were combined into the theoretical category of Cognitive Skills (Michelon, 2016).

According to Social Cognitive Theory of Self-Regulation (Bandura, 1991), the self-efficacy mechanism affects cognitive processing. Thus, there is a link between theoretical category of Self-Regulation and the theoretical category of Cognitive Skills, and they mutually affect each other. The outcomes of both these categories were combined into the larger theoretical category of Work Behaviors.

Both internals and externals highlighted behaviors that they engaged in or would like to engage in to feel more in control of their work outcomes. These behaviors (or concepts) have been grouped into the theoretical category of Work Behaviors. These include: developing a positive working relationship with the immediate supervisor; nurturing coworker relationships; delegating work to subordinates; taking calculated risks; negotiating deadlines; exercising and/or acquiring authority; using supporting technology; formalizing operations; and demonstrating behavioral control at work (and at home).

While self-regulation and cognitive skills, positively impacted by self-efficacy, will result in the work behaviors needed to retain internal control or convert from an external to an internal locus of control, they need an external organizational environment that will support self-regulation, nurture cognitive skills, and promote work behaviors that result in internalization of control. In addition to such an external organizational environment, individuals need to have an internal environment within them that will allow them to take the "risk" of taking charge of their work life, without "fretting too much" over consequences. The presence or absence of these environments and their characteristics were clearly present in interview transcripts.

The theoretical category of external environment includes organizational context factors that support, nurture, and promote employee efforts to seize control of their work outcomes. The related concepts combined to form this category are: top management's direction and interest; supportive supervisor; smooth operations of all related departments; predictable work demands; authority commensurate with responsibility; SOPs and chain of command being followed; specialization; and culture of recognition and respect. In addition to these external organizational factors, internals insisted that "self-confidence," "trust in one's instinct," "good mood," and "work experience" will help to bring things under their control at work. These codes have been combined under the theoretical category of internal environment.

All themes/theoretical categories and their underlying concepts are shown in Table 1.

Table 1. Theoretical Categories

Theretcal Category	Self-regulation			Cognitive Skills	Work behaviors	External Environment	Internal Environment
	Self-efficacy	Self-monitor	Self-reactive Influence				
Subsumed concepts	Belief in one's ability to do the task	Time mgt	Creating incentives for good performance	Decison-making skils	Developing a positive working relationship wit the supervior	Top mgt direction and interest	Self-confidence
	Self-aiding thoughts	Self-motivation	Doing whatever it taks to produce desired	Analytical Skills	Nurturing coworker relationship	Supportive supervisor	Trust in one's insticts
	Perseverence	Maintiing emotional distance from work and coworkers	Positive feelings about self	Learning	Delegate work to sub-ordinates	Smooth operations of related departmenst	Good mood
		Self-control		Attention to detail; eye for detail; alert; mentally available; compartmentalize;	Take calculated risks	Predictable work demands	Work experience
				Problem solving skills	Negotiate deadlines	Authority commensurate with responsibility	
					Exercise and/or acquire authority	Culture of recognition and respect	
					Use supporting technology Formalize operations Demonstrate behavioral control	Specialization of wok	

4.2 Internalization Model of Locus of Control

The theoretical categories emerging from the data (in bold text) and their linkages, as gleaned from the data, as well as supported by the Social Cognitive Theory of Self-Regulation (Bandura, 1991), are pictorially depicted as the Model of Internalization of Locus of Control of stressed corporate entrepreneurs and professionals in Figure 1: Model of Internalization of Locus of Control of Stressed Professionals.

Figure 1. Model of Internalization of Locus of Control of Stressed Professionals

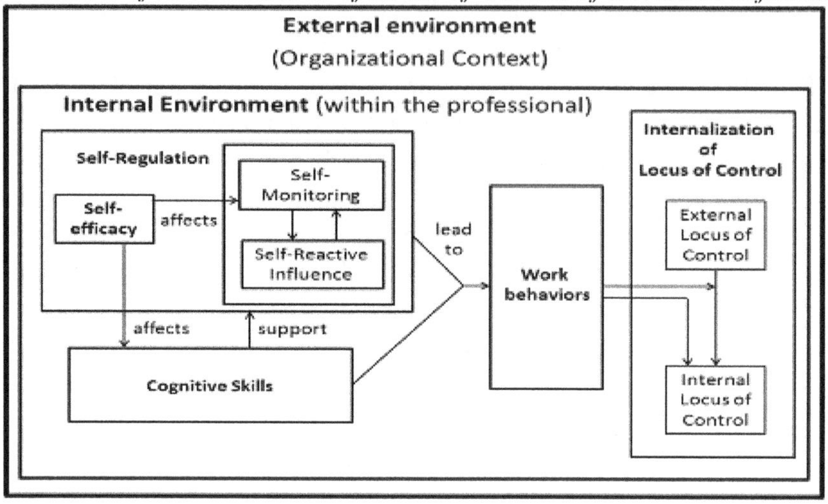

The professional's self-efficacy beliefs that she can control her work outcomes are nurtured by the external and internal environments. These self-aiding thoughts and perseverance[self-efficacy], despite being under stress, will spur her on to monitor and regulate her job performance, moods, emotional reactions (by maintaining emotional distance from work), and behavioral reactions to various stimuli [self-monitoring and self-regulation].

She will set personal standards for her performance and create incentives to motivate herself. She knows how she will emotionally respond to performing or not performing up to her own standards, so she will adopt different ways (time management, maintaining emotional distance from work and coworkers, and self-control) that will produce her desired outcomes [self-reactive influence]. The desired outcomes, among others, are feelings of self-worth because of her good work performance, and respect, appreciation, and recognition from others.

This self-regulatory mechanism will be supported by developing and utilizing cognitive skills, such as decision making skills, analytical skills, problem-solving skills, learning skills, paying attention to detail, compartmentalizing, and focusing on the tasks at hand. Well-developed cognitive skills will increase self-efficacy and enhance overall self-regulation.

Enhanced self-regulation and cognitive abilities will lead to, and make easier, various work behaviors. These work behaviors will make the stressed professional take control of his/her work outcomes.

4.3 Justification for Linkages Between Theoretical Categories

The linkages in Bandura's (1991) social cognitive theory of self-regulation provide justification and logic for connecting the theoretical categories of self-efficacy, self-regulation, and cognitive skills with work behaviors. Concepts that were combined to form the theoretical categories of external environment and internal environment clearly indicate that these two categories are context factors, and thus will surround the other categories.

4.4 Justification for the Completeness of the Model

The model does not include any other theoretical categories because the properties of all categories were saturated with 10 participant interviews. The sampling methodology employing (1) theoretical sampling, by using a criterion stress test to scientifically select potential participants experiencing overwhelming work demands and (2) purposive sampling that selected articulate and expressive participants who were willing to share information, also ensured that professionals who were able and willing to share information were recruited for participation in the study. Iterative and open-ended questions during the interviews also extracted pertinent and rich information. The researcher's reflective commentary in the form of initial and refined memos ensured that no important threads or themes were left unexplored during data collected and analysis.

4.5 Boundary Conditions and Assumptions

There are some boundary conditions for this theory of internalization of locus of control, beyond which it will not be applicable. It does not apply to work settings where centralized decision making is necessary for performance, such as on the battle ground, team sports, and highly coordinated work activities where everyone has to follow a preplanned course of action and seamlessly merge/integrate their results, e.g. design and construction of high-tech equipment and brick and mortar structures. The more a professional is responsible for a job from start to end, the more the applicability of this theory.

In addition, the corporate entrepreneur has to be educated and trained to some extent in her line of work to be able to feel capable of doing the task i.e. have the level self-efficacy need to strive for control, which is supported by actual expertise.

If the professional feels that she lacks the expertise and experience needed for a task, attempts to internalize locus of control may enhance her stress levels.

Lastly, a professional whose external locus of control is a means of coping with stress (because she finds solace in the belief that she can't be responsible for work outcomes that are in someone else's control or based on sheer luck), will not attempt to seize control. Thus, this theory is applicable for stressed corporate entrepreneurs who actually strive for control.

For the process outlined by the Internalization Model to be take place, the basic assumptions are:

1. The corporate entrepreneur has been working for some time and has the minimum training and knowledge to feel capable of bringing about desired work outcomes (self-efficacy).
2. The professional feels that she needs to control her work outcomes to reduce stress. The model will not work for those professionals who reduce their stress by thinking that the outcome is not under their control anyway, so why bother to take any action?
3. The corporate entrepreneur possesses the drive to grow further in her career and does not have a laid-back or indifferent predisposition to career progression.
4. The corporate entrepreneur possesses mental strength, despite being under stress, to plan and exercise self-regulation, engage in cognitive development activities, and perform work behaviors that lead to internalization of locus of control.

4.6 Theory of Internalization of Locus of Control

The theory of internalization of locus of control explains the process by which individuals can maintain an internal locus of control or transition from an external locus of control to an internal locus of control in response to work-related stressors.

When corporate entrepreneur and professionals have self-efficacy to exercise control over their work outcomes, it impacts self-regulation and utilizing of cognitive skills, both of which lead to work behaviors that make it possible to internalize locus of control. Self-efficacy will trigger self-regulation and cognitive skills when there is a supportive external organizational environment, which nurtures an internal environment within the professional where self-efficacy can be high.

5. DISCUSSION

The overall model, its theoretical categories and their constituting concepts are clearly supported by past research and literature on control.

The work behaviors that corporate entrepreneur can adopt to control their work life are reminiscent of the primary control concept of the Two-process Model of Perceived Control (Rothbaum, Weisz, and Snyder, 1982). In the Two-process Model, primary control entailed changing the surrounding environment to match one's own needs. Along the same lines, the Internalization of the Locus of Control Model suggests work behaviors to make the stressed professional feel in control of his/her work, and they include developing a positive professional relationship with the supervisor, nurturing coworker relationships, delegating work to subordinates, taking calculated risks, negotiating deadlines with other stakeholders, exercising existing authority (and acquiring more authority, if possible), using supporting technology, and formalizing operations. All these behaviors will bring about changes in the work environment. As suggested by the Two-process model, all these primary control work behaviors can produce satisfying results, but also disappointing setbacks, to deal with which secondary control kicks in.

The secondary control concept of the two-process model of perceived control (Rothbaum, Weisz, and Snyder, 1982) entailed aligning oneself with the environment to feel more in control. The Internalization Model's self-regulation (time management, emotional distance, self-control) and use of cognitive abilities (focusing, compartmentalizing, problem-solving, analyzing, deciding, learning), impacted by self-efficacy beliefs are ways of aligning oneself with the environment.

However, the difference between the two models is that in the two-process model primary control precedes secondary control, whereas in the Internalization Model, self-efficacy, self-regulation, and cognitive abilities lead to work behaviors. The logic behind this sequencing is that first one should believe that one can do the work, then motivate, incentivize, manage one's time, and exercise self-control, all with the aid of clear-headed cognitive processing, and then attempt to bring the environment under one's control by engaging in work behaviors.

There is nothing to stop one from engaging in this process iteratively. The work behaviors may in turn affect self-efficacy, and compel one to engage in improved self-regulation and develop cognitive abilities. Thus, as suggested by another control theory, the life-span theory of control (Heckhausen & Schulz, 1995), secondary control (self-efficacy, self-regulation, and cognitive skills) can help to cope with failure and direct motivational resources towards changing actions and goals throughout life to strengthen primary control (work behaviors).

In the Internalization of Locus of Control model, merging the concepts and labeling the theoretical categories, and the linkages of the concepts and relationship between the theoretical categories self-efficacy, self-regulation, and cognitive skills leading to work behaviors, closely matches the theoretical categories and linkages of the Social Cognitive Theory of Self-regulation (Bandura, 1991), lending it further credibility.

5.1 Contribution to Managerial Practice

The research conducted has made a significant contribution by developing a novel model outlining how corporate entrepreneur and professionals under stress can internalize locus of control. This model, subject to further testing and refinement, holds the potential to serve as a comprehensive theoretical framework for guiding the development of personal and organizational interventions aimed at facilitating coping behaviors that lead to desirable outcomes, such as entrepreneurial success, job satisfaction and job performance.

The proposed theory offers broad guidelines for corporate policy makers and human resources professionals in designing empowering job roles and formulating policies conducive to a supportive and responsive work environment. By fostering a sense of control over work-related tasks, career progression, rewards, and other desirable outcomes, organizations can cultivate an atmosphere where corporate entrepreneurs feel empowered and motivated to excel.

6. CONCLUSION AND RECOMMENDATION

The many benefits of a professional's internal work locus of control, such as better health due to lower stress (Roddeberry & Renk, 2010), desirable work outcomes (Cobb-Clark, 2015), job satisfaction and retention, continuance and affective commitment, and lower absenteeism (Campagna, 2015), can be reaped by corporate entrepreneurs as well as organizations. However, both the professional and as the organization will have to create an environment in which corporate entrepreneurs can regulate their work, and take certain steps to ensure that the supporting contextual factors exist for retaining or seizing control of work life.

Within this environment (and sometimes without), the professional has to believe in her ability to do the work, and will have to regulate her thoughts, emotions and actions to get it done. She will also utilize and develop her cognitive skills in this process. Better self-regulation and cognitive abilities will lead to work behaviors that will help to take control of the professional's work demands despite constant stress, which is the hallmark of contemporary work life.

6.1 Recommendations

The theoretical framework provides broad and actionable guidelines for organizational policy-makers, top-level managers, corporate entrepreneurs, line managers, and working professionals about what they can do to enhance job performance, job satisfaction, and commitment.

Top and middle managers can achieve these desirable outcomes by promoting an organizational environment that empowers employees, and by engaging in managerial practices that allow, support, and encourage the corporate entrepreneurs to take more control of their work outcomes.

Professionals themselves should harbor positive self-beliefs about their abilities, focus on their work, compartmentalize their various personal and professional demands, take effective measures to regulate their work, develop and utilize cognitive skills, and actively engage in work behaviors that give them control over their work outcomes.

6.2 Directions for Future Research

The theoretical and purposive sampling methodology adopted in this study resulted in highly stressed professionals being identified and interviewed, and intensive interviewing lead to detailed insights, which were assimilated and synthesized through rigorous analysis into a coherent model having literature support. However, this model remains to be tested under different contexts such as specific occupations, different age groups, highly stressful work environments, and different organizational contexts that do not meet the ideal of the nurturing external environment constructed in the model.

REFERENCES

American Psychological Association. (2019). *Stress in America 2019*. Retrieved February 18th, 2020, from https://www.apa.org/images/stress-america-2019_tcm7-264533.pdf

Bandura, A. (1991). Social cognitive theory of self-regulation. *Organizational Behavior and Human Decision Processes*, 50(2), 248–287. DOI: 10.1016/0749-5978(91)90022-L

Bernardi, R. A. (2011). The Relationships among locus of control, perceptions of stress and performance. *Journal of Applied Business Research*, 13(4), 1. Advance online publication. DOI: 10.19030/jabr.v13i4.5736

Blaikie, N. (2007). *Approaches to Social Inquiry*. Polity Press.

Campagna, K., Wilson, R., Callahan, S., & Jason, L. A. (2015). Women in recovery: Predictors of internal and external work locus of control. *Journal of Psychological Issues in Organizational Culture*, 6(1), 7–15. Advance online publication. DOI: 10.1002/jpoc.21169

Charmaz, K. (2000). Constructivist and objectivist grounded theory. In Denzin, N. K., & Lincoln, Y. (Eds.), *Handbook of qualitative research* (pp. 509–535). Sage.

Charmaz, K. (2008). Constructionism and the Grounded Theory Method. In Holstein, J. A., & Gubrium, F. J. (Eds.), *Handbook of Constructionist Research* (pp. 397–412). The Guilford Press.

Chen, G., Goddard, T. G., & Casper, W. J. (2004). Examination of the relationship among general and work-specific self-evaluations, work-related control beliefs, and job attitudes. *Applied Psychology*, 53(3), 349–370. DOI: 10.1111/j.1464-0597.2004.00175.x

Chiu, C. K., Lin, C. P., Tsai, Y. H., & Hsiao, C. Y. (2005). Modelling turnover incidents and their antecedents using the locus of control as a moderator: A case of customer service employees. *Human Resource Development Quarterly*, 16(4), 481–499. DOI: 10.1002/hrdq.1152

Churchill, S. A., Munyanyi, M. E., Prakash, K., & Smyth, R. (2020). Locus of control and the gender gap in mental health. *Journal of Economic Behavior & Organization*, 178, 740–758. DOI: 10.1016/j.jebo.2020.08.013

Cobb-Clark, D. (2015). Locus of control and the labor market. *IZA Journal of Labor Economics*, 4(1), 3. DOI: 10.1186/s40172-014-0017-x

Creswell, J. W. (2013). *Qualitative Inquiry and Research Design: Choosing among five approaches*. SAGE Publication.

Daniels, K., & Guppy, A. (1992). Control, information-seeking preferences, occupational stressors, and psychological wellbeing. *Work and Stress*, 6(4), 347–353. DOI: 10.1080/02678379208259965

Evans, B. J., & Coman, G. J. (1993). General versus specific measures of occupational stress: An Australian police survey. *Stress Medicine*, 9(1), 11–20. DOI: 10.1002/smi.2460090105

Fernandez, R. (2016). How to boost your resilience at work. Retrieved from https://hbr.org/2016/06/627-building-resilience-ic-5-ways-to-build-your-personal-resilience-at-work

Galor, S. (2014). Stress - An overview and the start of a few articles on the phenomenon. Retrieved from https://drsharongalor.wordpress.com/2014/11/02/stress-an-overview-and-the-start-of-a-few-articles-on-the-phenomenon/

Heckhausen, J., & Schulz, R. (1995). A life-span theory of control. *Psychological Review*, 102(2), 284–304. DOI: 10.1037/0033-295X.102.2.284 PMID: 7740091

Jennings, B. M. (1990). Stress, locus of control, and psychological symptoms among head nurses. *Research in Nursing & Health*, 13(6), 393–401. DOI: 10.1002/nur.4770130607 PMID: 2270304

Joe, V. C. (1971). Review of the internal-external control construct as a personality variable. *Psychological Reports*, 28(2), 619–640. DOI: 10.2466/pr0.1971.28.2.619 PMID: 4932156

Judge, T. A., & Bono, J. E. (2001). Relationship of core self-evaluations traits—self-esteem, generalized self-efficacy, locus of control, and emotional stability—with job satisfaction and job performance: A meta-analysis. *The Journal of Applied Psychology*, 86(1), 80–92. DOI: 10.1037/0021-9010.86.1.80 PMID: 11302235

Kelman, H. C. (1958). Compliance, identification, and internalization three processes of attitude change. *The Journal of Conflict Resolution*, 2(1), 51–60. DOI: 10.1177/002200275800200106

Kormanik, M. B., & Rocco, T. S. (2009). Internal versus external control of reinforcement: Q review of the locus of control construct. *Human Resource Development Review*, 8(4), 463–483. DOI: 10.1177/1534484309342080

Krause, N., & Stryker, S. (1984). Stress and well-being: The buffering role of locus of control beliefs. *Social Science & Medicine*, 18(9), 783–790. Advance online publication. DOI: 10.1016/0277-9536(84)90105-9 PMID: 6729538

Lazarus, R. S. (1990). Theory-based stress measurement. *Psychological Inquiry*, 1(1), 3–13. DOI: 10.1207/s15327965pli0101_1

Lefcout, R. S. (2014). *Locus of Control: Current trends in theory and research.* Psychology Press. DOI: 10.4324/9781315798813

Levenson, H. (1981). Differentiating among internality, powerful others, and chance. In Lefcourt, H. M. (Ed.), Research with the locus of control construct. vol. I: *Assessment methods* (pp. 15-63). New York: Academic Press. DOI: 10.1016/B978-0-12-443201-7.50006-3

Li, Y., Wei, F., Ren, S., & Di, Y. (2015). Locus of control, psychological empowerment and intrinsic motivation relation to performance. *Journal of Managerial Psychology*, 20(4), 422–438. DOI: 10.1108/JMP-10-2012-0318

Manichander, T. (2014). Locus of Control and Performance: Widening Applications. *Indian Journal of Research*, 3(2).

Martin, R., Thomas, G., Charles, K., Epitropaki, O., & McNamara, R. (2005). The role of leader-memberexchanges in mediating the relationship between locus of control and work reactions. *Journal of Occupational and Organizational Psychology*, 78(1), 141–147. DOI: 10.1348/096317904X23763

McCarthy, A., & Garavan, T. (2006). Post-feedback development perceptions: Applying the theory of planned behavior. *Human Resource Development Quarterly*, 17(3), 245–267. DOI: 10.1002/hrdq.1173

Michelon, P. (2016, December 18). What are Cognitive Abilities and Skills, and how to boost them? Retrieved from https://sharpbrains.com/blog/2006/12/18/what-are-cognitive-abilities/

Mitchell, T. R., Smyser, C. M., & Weed, S. E. (1975). Locus of Control: Supervision and work satisfaction. *Academy of Management Journal*, 18(3), 623–631. DOI: 10.2307/255692

Ng, T. W. H., Sorensen, K. L., & Eby, L. (2006). Locus of control at work: A meta-analysis. *Journal of Organizational Behavior*, 27(8), 1057–1087. DOI: 10.1002/job.416

Padmanabhan, S. (2021). The impact of locus of control on workplace stress and job satisfaction: A pilot study on private-sector employees. *Current Research in Behavioral Sciences*, 2, 100026. DOI: 10.1016/j.crbeha.2021.100026

Pryer, M. W., & Distefano, M. K.Jr. (1971). Perceptions of leadership behaviour, job satisfaction, and internal-external control across three nursing levels. *Nursing Research*, 20(6), 534–537. DOI: 10.1097/00006199-197111000-00014 PMID: 5210833

Reynolds, C. H. (1976). Correlational findings, educational implications, and criticisms of locus of control research. *Journal of Black Studies*, 6(3), 221–256. DOI: 10.1177/002193477600600301

Roberts, J. A., Lapidus, R. S., & Chonko, L. B. (1997). Salespeople and Stress : The Moderating Role of Locus of Control on Work Stressors and Felt Stress. *Journal of Marketing Theory and Practice*, 5(3), 93–108. DOI: 10.1080/10696679.1997.11501773

Roddenberry, A., & Renk, K. (2010). Locus of control and self-efficacy: Potential mediators of stress, illness, and utilization of health services in college students. *Child Psychiatry and Human Development*, 41(4), 353–370. DOI: 10.1007/s10578-010-0173-6 PMID: 20204497

Rothbaum, F., Weisz, J. R., & Snyder, S. S. (1982). Changing the world and changing the self: A two-process model of perceived control. *Journal of Personality and Social Psychology*, 42(1), 5–37. DOI: 10.1037/0022-3514.42.1.5 PMID: 7108745

Rotter, J. B. (1954). *Social learning and clinical psychology*. Prentice Hall. DOI: 10.1037/10788-000

Rotter, J. B. (1975). Some problems and misconceptions related to the construct of internal versus external control of reinforcement. *Journal of Consulting and Clinical Psychology*, 43(1), 56–67. DOI: 10.1037/h0076301

Rotter, J. B. (2021). Internal versus external control of reinforcement: A case history of a variable. *The American Psychologist*, 45(4), 489–493. DOI: 10.1037/0003-066X.45.4.489

Runyon, K. E. (1973). Some interactions between personality variables and management styles. *The Journal of Applied Psychology*, 57(3), 288–294. DOI: 10.1037/h0034723

Schafer, W. E., & McKenna, J. F. (1991). Perceived energy and stress resistance: A study of city managers. *Journal of Social Behavior and Personality*, •••, 271–282.

Serin, N. B., Serin, O., & Şahin, F. S. (2010). Factors affecting the locus of control of the university students. *Procedia: Social and Behavioral Sciences*, 2(2), 449–452. DOI: 10.1016/j.sbspro.2010.03.041

Shannak, R. O., & Al-Taher, A. (2012). Factors affecting Work Locus of Control : An Analytical and Comparative Study. *Jordan Journal of Business Administration*, 8(2), 373–389.

Siegrist, J. (1996). Adverse health effects of high-effort/low-reward conditions. *Journal of Occupational Health Psychology*, 1(1), 27–41. DOI: 10.1037/1076-8998.1.1.27 PMID: 9547031

Siegrist, J., Wege, N., Pühlhofer, F., & Wahrendorf, M. (2009). A short generic measure of work stress in the era of globalization: Effort–reward imbalance. *International Archives of Occupational and Environmental Health*, 82(8), 1005–1013. DOI: 10.1007/s00420-008-0384-3 PMID: 19018554

Spector, P. E. (1982). Behavior of organizations as a function of employee's locus of control. *Psychological Bulletin*, 91(3), 482–497. DOI: 10.1037/0033-2909.91.3.482

Spector, P. E. (1988). Development of the work locus of control scale. *Journal of Occupational Psychology*, 61(4), 335–340. DOI: 10.1111/j.2044-8325.1988.tb00470.x

Spector, P. E. (2022). Behavior in organizations as a function of employee's locus of control. *Psychological Bulletin*, 91(3), 482–497. DOI: 10.1037/0033-2909.91.3.482

Stress. (2023, February 21). World Health Organization (WHO). Retrieved January 29, 2024, from https://www.who.int//news-room/questions-and-answers/item/stress/?gclid=EAIaIQobChMI5Yzj2feBhAMVc6hoCR25mAVSEAAYASAAEgISFvD_BwE

Susan, F. (1984). Personal control and stress and coping processes: A theoretical analysis. *Journal of Personality and Social Psychology*, 46(4), 893–852. DOI: 10.1037/0022-3514.46.4.839 PMID: 6737195

Uysal, Ş. K., Karadağ, H., Tuncer, B., & Şahin, F. (2022). Locus of control, need for achievement, and entrepreneurial intention: A moderated mediation model. *International Journal of Management Education*, 20(2), 100560. DOI: 10.1016/j.ijme.2021.100560

Wang, Q., Bowling, N. A., & Eschleman, K. J. (2010). A meta-analytic examination of work and general locus of control. *The Journal of Applied Psychology*, 95(4), 761–768. DOI: 10.1037/a0017707 PMID: 20604595

Chapter 2

Entrepreneurship Fostering a Social Inclusive Civil Culture Model:

The Agroecological Park of Zapopan Case

José G. Vargas-Hernandez
https://orcid.org/0000-0003-0938-4197
Tecnológico Nacional de México, ITS Fresnillo, Mexico

Omar C. Vargas-González
https://orcid.org/0000-0002-6089-956X
Tecnológico Nacional de México, Ciudad Guzman, Mexico

Francisco J. González-Ávila
Tecnológico Nacional de México, ITS Fresnillo, Mexico

ABSTRACT

This research aims to analyze the model of entrepreneurial inclusive civic culture created and developed in the Agro ecological Park of Zapopan (PAZ). Based on the need to rescue vacant urban land use with the participation of residents residing in the surrounding colonies, social movements, civil society, and local government, they have designed and implemented actions to create PAZ (PEACE) as an area of green innovation. In addition to the cultivation of vegetables, vegetables, medicinal plants and decoration under relations of

DOI: 10.4018/979-8-3693-9241-6.ch002

INTRODUCTION

There is an increasing number of urban inhabitants that have migrated from their rural locations and have no other means of generating income which have contributed to have all added to elevated levels of poverty, especially among the households headed by women. Moreover, poor households in urban communities protect themselves from income risks by seeking and diversifying their sources of income such as formal employment and some informal small scale entrepreneurial activities, which only provide the necessary for subsistence and is not secure.

It has been historically evident the restrictions on creating and developing an entrepreneurial inclusive civic culture because the poor support from public, governmental, private or social organizations and institutions in terms of providing access to scarce resources and skill training.

The motivation to conduct this study springs from these needs and have different intentions. One is the global struggle for urban community development to address the main issues of global sustainable development goals in areas such as food, health, security, etc. The emerging sanitary, economic, social, political, and cultural crisis intersecting access to resources and skills with social inclusiveness, inequality and justice, economic growth and efficiency, and environmental sustainability.

The motivation of this study emerges from the question How do actor with diverse and compiling interests work out their differences to work on a community project? The rationale for undertaking this analysis is to identify to what extent community changes and transformations into a more oriented entrepreneurial inclusive culture can contribute economic, social, and environmental development.

Attached to this question are other important motivations: There is misleading wide-spread assumption based on the argument that community development is linear and continuous. This study intends to demonstrate the reality based on the assumption that community development in one domain may coexist with inequality in others. However, the study goes beyond to demonstrate that community development can be more harmonious in all domains if all the stakeholders involved have the intentions to overcome the determinants that are the obstacle by promoting changes toward a more entrepreneurial inclusive civic culture.

This study analyses the factors that successfully contribute to social transformation of a community through the creation and development of an entrepreneurial inclusive civic culture based on agro ecology and green practices in an urban space. The analysis highlights the empowerment of disadvantaged inhabitants to gain access to natural resources and skills to enable and sustain the implementation of an entrepreneurial inclusive civic culture in a community that allow them to gain economic growth, social inclusiveness and justice, and environmental sustainability.

This study has an impact on design and implementation of public policy and local governance, research and practice. It can be a guide to replicate the study and achieve the social and community benefits.

LOCATION AS A DETERMINANT FACTOR

The Zapopan agro ecological Park is in "Cerrada Santa Laura" within Santa Margaritas colony in the municipality of Zapopan, State of Jalisco. The located zones will be defined within the municipality of Zapopan. The population of Zapopan in 2015 according to Inter Census Survey was 1,332,272 people; 48.8 percent of men and 51.2 percent of women. Comparing the estimated population in 2015 with the population in 2010 it can be perceived that the population increased 7.1 percent in five years. It is estimated that in 2020 this population will increase close to 1,414,972 habitants. Nowadays 689,327 million, are men and 725,645 are women, representing 16.92 percent of the total population of Jalisco. In 2010 the municipality counted in total 234 localities. The municipal head of Zapopan is the most populated locality with 1,142,483 people, representing 91.9% of the population, followed by San Francisco. Tesistán with 5.0%, "La Venta del Astillero" (Sale of the Shipyard) with 0.5%,

"Fraccionamiento Campestre Las Palomas" with 0.4% percent and "Nextipac" with 0.3% percent of the municipal total. (IIEG, 2016).

Most of the existing buildings have electricity, but only a few have access to piped water and drainage. The constructions are made with timber, concrete, bricks and adobe. The municipality offers public lighting services, markets, trails, parking lots, cemeteries, roads, public toilets, public security, traffic, parks, gardens and sports centers. Regarding basic services, 94.8% of the installed infrastructure has potable water, 96.9% of sewage and 98.9% of electric energy. Most of the municipality of Zapopan (85.4%) has a semi-warm climate, half damp. The average annual temperature is 20.5 ° C, while the maximum and minimum average oscillates between 32.1 ° C and 8.4 ° C respectively. The climate of the municipality is temperate, semi-dry, with dry winters and dry springs. It is semi-warm with benign winter, it also has an average annual temperature of 23.5° C, and an average annual rainfall of 906.1 millimeters with rainfalls from June to October.

The lands of the municipality are mostly composed from rocks, basalt and tuff. The dominant soils have Eugic Regosol, Haplic Feozem and chromic Luvisol. The predominant soil is the Phaeozem (Feozem) with almost 50.6%, and it is presented in any type of land relief. It has a dark, soft, rich surface layer with organic matter and a lot of nutrients. Most of the land is only used for agricultural purposes. The municipality also has three characteristic forms of reliefs. In a higher percentage the injured zones are formed by a height of 1,500 to 2,000 meters, following the flat and semi-flat areas. The main elevations of the municipality are: "Las Colinas de La Col" (2,200 masl), "El Tepopote" (1950 masl), "La Mesa del Burro" (1,700 masl), "El Tule" (2,050 masl), "El Chapulin" (2,000 masl) high (1,990 masl), "El Colli" (1,950 masl), "El Chato" (1,800 masl), "El Masahuate" (2,100 masl), and the Lobera with (1,900 masl). The municipality of Zapopan registered the highest education levels in 2012 with 10.4 years as the average. Zapopan also has the lowest education gap (28.6%) and follows Guadalajara in concentration of the enrollment with 27.0% (Plan Estatal de Desarrollo Jalisco, 2013).

NATURAL RESOURCES AND ECONOMICS

The natural wealth of the municipality is represented by 11,400 hectares of forest, where pine, encino, creton, jonote, madroño, oak, oyamel and tepame predominate. Its mineral resources are deposits of marble, kaolin, feldspar, agate, tezontle, gravel and sand (clay). The vegetation of the municipality is conformed mostly by pine and encino; both species are in the forests of the municipality: "El bosque de la primavera", "Bosque de Nixticuil" and "Bosque del Centinela". The current fauna of the place, includes 106 species of animals such as white-tailed deer, puma, lynx, coyote, gray fox, badger, hare and raccoon, among others. Nearly 137 species of migratory and resident birds have been identified and can be observed hawks, eagles, herons, thrushes, quail, roadrunners, woodpeckers, etc.

Local crops include vegetables, fruits and seeds like corn, sorghum, zucchini, tomato, chickpea, avocado, mango and plum. Poultry, beef cattle, pig, sheep, goat meat and hives are also raised. A great industrial activity is developed. Companies like: Motorola and Coca-Cola, among others. According to (DENUE), the municipality of Zapopan by 2015 had 49,543 economic units and its sectors showed a predominance of economic service units, representing 47.3% of the total companies within the municipality (IIEG, 2016). The municipality has important shopping centers, named Plaza Patria, Plaza del Sol, Plaza Bonita, Plaza Universidad, Plaza Mexico (one part), Plaza Antares, La Gran Plaza, SAM'S, Price Club, Wall- Mart, Plaza San Isidro. Financial, professional, technical, administrative, communal, social, personal, tourist and maintenance are provided.

The number of insured workers also increased this year, where IMSS reported a total of 327,641 workers newly registered, representing in 55,025 more insured workers compared to the same month in 2012 (IIEG, 2016). Also, by 2015 life expectancy in Jalisco where of 75 years old; 73 for men and 78 for women (IIEG, 2015). The Economically Active Population (EAP) represents 45.20% of the total population, that constitute 562,233 habitants, of whom, (96.49%) are employed and the rest (3.51%) are unemployed. 6,293 inhabitants are employed in the primary sector of the economy (Agriculture, Livestock, Forestry, hunting and fishing), 141,375 inhabitants in the secondary sector (Mining, oil and gas extraction, manufacturing, electricity, water and construction) 388,48 work in the tertiary sector (Government, transportation, commerce and other services). And the remaining 6,781 inhabitants do not specify the sector to which their economic activity belongs (Gobierno de Zapopan, 2016).

Gross Domestic Product in 2015 was 889,703 pesos at 2008 prices. The per capita gross domestic product was 146,746 pesos (INEGI, 2015). The participation of Zapopan in the Gross Domestic Product in 2000 was 10630.2 (adjusted million dollars), which represented 31.9%, placing it in the second municipality in Jalisco, only after Guadalajara with 43.6% (Ayuntamiento de Tlajomulco de Zúñiga, Jalisco, 2015). GDP of Guadalajara and Zapopan as a percentage of the GDP of Jalisco 2000-2009 at current prices were 10.22. From the analysis of these data, it can be observed that there was a reduction in Zapopan for the GDP.

Zapopan is also one with highest index of wealth and income in the GDP of the State of Jalisco. Its urban panorama is made up of modern buildings and luxurious shopping centers, residential housing and green areas, that show the highest level in the metropolitan area (Zona Guadalajara, 2017). For the year 2013 intermediate consumption was 108,762 million pesos. (Gobierno de Zapopan, 2016). The municipality has air transportation, with a military base that receives airplanes DC-9 and the airport "La Cebadilla", which is a particular property able to receive airplanes. Near Zapopan is the International Airport of Guadalajara Miguel Hidalgo y Costilla for the public air service which is located 50 minutes from the municipal center.

The land transportation to the municipality of Zapopan is done through the Mexico-Nogales, Guadalajara-Saltillo and Guadalajara-Barra de Navidad roads. It has a network of dirty and paved roads that communicate to localities. Because of its importance, the highway that connects with the north of the State of Jalisco with the State of Zacatecas stands out. Rail transportation is carried out through the Guadalajara-Nogales line of the "Ferrocarril Del Pacífico" system, only for cargo movement. Through the municipality passes the train called "Tequila Turístico" that goes from Guadalajara to the population of Tequila.

The terrestrial foreign transportation is done in direct buses for passengers concentrated in the terminals located in Zapopan, and other places such as Tlaquepaque and Tonalá in the Metropolitan Area of Guadalajara. Urban and rural transportation is done in rental vehicles, private vehicles and buses. It also has a bus terminal which is next to the roundabout Emiliano Zapata, on the road to Tesistán. The nearest ports are Puerto Vallarta and Manzanillo both located on the Pacific Ocean. The Agro ecological Park has a community garden where the citizens can grow and harvest organic food, a classroom, built with natural materials, a module of dry ecological baths, a nursery area for plant production, a compost area for fertilizer processing and recycling nutrients, an edible forest, a rainwater harvesting and distribution system and an ecological market area.

The surface it's occupied by the project which has 1.8 hectares, a neighborhood with about 40 thousand inhabitants, near the Pedagogical Water Forest in the area of the Colomos III Forest. Both park are connected as part of a network of agro ecological parks in the Guadalajara Metropolitan Area.

What used to be a rubble and rubbish dump, is now the first Agro ecological Park in Zapopan, thanks to the work of the neighbors, the Teocintle Collective and also with government support. It was inaugurated on March 27, 2015 by the Mayor Héctor Robles Peiro. The "Pedagogical Forest of Water" has local and national connection to roads, ports, railways and walking accessibility to markets & customers.

The municipality of Zapopan has important shopping centers, named Plaza Patria, Plaza del Sol, Plaza Bonita, Plaza Universidad, Plaza Mexico, La Gran Plaza, SAM'S, Price Club, Wall- Mart, Plaza San Isidro. Regarding supply, in terms of popular consumption services, this need is covered by 2,571 grocery stores selling food and beverages, 485 butchers and 459 establishments selling prepared foods). In Zapopan there are 15 municipal markets and 77 established markets, which makes this municipality a center of supply of localities and surrounding municipalities. The Market of the Sea stands out for its variety and quality of its products.

ENVIRONMENTAL AND TERRITORIAL CONDITIONS

The Municipal Urban Development Program of Zapopan aims to establish urban and environmental policies based on the determinations of the current programs and plans of the State Planning System, adequate and adjusted to the local needs and considering the established by the applicable environmental instruments in the municipal territory. The nature and characteristics of the Zapopan's ecosystem, within the environmental regionalization of the state is characterized by the environmental impact of new human settlements, agricultural, industrial, and commercial and service works or activities. The presence of more than half of the total population of the State in the Metropolitan Area of Guadalajara, being the municipalities of Guadalajara and Zapopan that shelter the greater part of this, generates a series of environmental and mobility problems.

Air pollution in Zapopan is one of the main pollutants generated in the metropolitan area, this is due to agricultural activities (burning), unpaved roads, diesel vehicles in circulation, combustion emissions in industry, forest fires, and suspension of dust from construction activities including the transport of material and those extractive activities as is the case with material banks, among others. The fraction particles smaller than 10 microns is the one that is most concentrated in the metropolitan area. The highest contribution in tons of pollutants corresponds to mobile sources, accounting for 96% of the emissions generated. Particles suspended in the atmosphere (PM10) are now considered to be the best indicator of air quality. They are constituted by nitrates and sulfates or by organic carbon - due to their conformation which may be of natural origin or also by photochemical reaction (Reyes, Castellanos y Gutierrez, 2009).

Another aspect that is involved in the problem of pollution in the ZMG is the winds and their effects on the concentration and dispersion in the atmosphere of ozone and suspended particles, generally, at higher wind speeds, greater dilution of pollutants. The annual wind regime in the region is divided into two defined periods: One from November to June in which the West winds prevail, and from June to October in which the East winds prevail. (Cohen, 1979). Ozone, which is due to the reaction of hydrocarbons in the atmosphere, is another pollutant that has exceeded one hundred µg / m3. As the easterly winds contribute to the ozone concentrations in the west of the ZMG, mainly due to the frequency of calm periods, and the western winds carry the ozone towards the center. The slightly moderate winds of the southwest and southeast of The ZMG transport this pollution to the north. For the spring period, there is a decrease in the air quality index, since it registers 97 IMECA ozone points as the maximum level. Towards the north and south of Zapopan the season of the year that concentrates higher levels of pollution by particles of ozone is the winter. (Reyes, Castellanos y Curiel, 2009).

In the case of nitrogen dioxide (NO2), whose main source is combustion in industries and vehicles, it turns out to be the other pollutant present in the atmosphere of the municipality of Zapopan. It is observed that 13.0% of NO2 measurements exceed 40 µg / m3 which is the annual average recommended by WHO. Sulfur dioxide (SO2) - a product of the combustion of coal, diesel, fuel oil and gasoline with sulfur, in addition to sulfur-rich metallic veins, industrial processes and volcanic eruptions - has been located within the limits established by both the Mexican standard of 340 µg / m3 and the WHO standard of 40 µg / m3.

This place was all constructed with natural materials. It counts with a main building, a classroom, an office, a small room that has domestic technologies, dry bath module and a community garden fenced with forty-seven beds of cultivation (10m2 each) plotted by Tierra Cruda but excavated in the rubble by Collective Teocintle Agro ecological and volunteers; Bamboo structure for composting and nursery of nurseries. It also has a winery that was built by Farid Morales in collaboration with DIF Zapopan, Collective Teocintle Agro ecological and other volunteers, while the bamboo structures where given and placed by Fernando Partida of BambuXal also with the help of collective.

Due to the altitude and the hydrographic network of the region, it is considered that there are no sufficient water resources in quality and quantity to satisfy the current and future demand. The overexploitation of the aquifers and the presence of heavy metals such as arsenic, requires among other measures, improving the management of existing sources of fresh water and addressing the problems of waste and pollution control. Knowing this, it can be said that it is due to the change of land uses, with the growth of the urban spot, both in residential areas and in areas of industrial use, where the pollutants have been present significantly affecting the environment.

THEORETICAL APPROACH: ENTREPRENEURIAL INCLUSIVE CIVIC CULTURE

Entrepreneurship, inclusiveness, civil and culture are variables that have complex but straightforward linkages and processes among them and much is still unknown. The last few years have witnessed the generation of extensive theoretical and empirical literature on entrepreneurship and its impact at the levels of regional and firm economic performance (Holmes and Schmitz, 1990; Evans and Leighton, 1990). However, when linking entrepreneurship to the variables of inclusiveness and civic culture, the literatures is inexistent. There is a relative void, despite some recent efforts to study the relationship between entrepreneurship in some other related fields beyond economic growth, which may attributable to the lack of theoretical frameworks.

However, studies in economic development have shown reversed causality influencing entrepreneurial activities. Entrepreneurial activities tend to be overestimated in regions where there are start-ups playing a relevant role while entrepreneurship activities tend to be underestimated in regions where there is a new entrepreneurial formation and the startups are relatively few (Baptista, Escária, and Madruga, 2017).

The role of entrepreneurship in economic development has received some attention by researchers that have the intuition that there is an impact of entrepreneurship on employment and social development. Entrepreneurial intentions promote entrepreneurial behaviors (Krueger et al., 2000; Veciana et al., 2005; Souitaris et al., 2007). Entrepreneurship activity can be associated with human necessity providing an opportunity to earn money for living, until better alternative opportunities are found on the labor market (Carree and Thurik, 2010).

The concept of entrepreneurship is multidimensional and related to individual willingness, abilities and activities on their own, in teams and in organizations to make decisions facing obstacles and uncertainty on the use of institutions and resources to create and develop new opportunities (Wennekers and Thurik, 1999). Entrepreneurial opportunities are the result of unemployment the influences start-up activity, the effect of a thriving economy and experience in entrepreneurial activities (Lin, Manser and Picot, 1998; Pfeiffer and Reize, 2000).

Entrepreneurship is the recognition and exploitation of opportunities leading to the creation and development of a firm (Aragon-Sanchez, Baixauli-Soler, Carrasco-Hernandez, 2017). Moreover, entrepreneurial intentions predict entrepreneurial behaviors, according to the theory of planned behavior (Ajzen, 1991). Entrepreneurial activity creates opportunities to influence economic performance (van Stel, Carree and Thurik, 2005) such as entering the markets with new production processes and products (Acs and Audretsch, 2003). Among the entrepreneurial models there is evidence that the entrepreneurial intentional models (Krueger et al., 2000) supports the theory of planned behavior.

The theory of planned behavior has been used in the analysis of entrepreneurial intentions (Shook et al. 2003). The determinants have significant positive relationships with behavior intention (Armitage and Conner 2001). Do Paço et al. (2011) found a positive and significant influence between entrepreneurial intentions, attitudes and perceived behavior control. However, subjective norms have an indirect impact on entrepreneurial intentions.

The determinants of entrepreneurial intentions are linked by the access to financial, natural, human and cultural capital and resources through the influence of attitudes, individual subjective norms, perceived social control and self-efficacy. The attitude is the individual favorable evaluation to start a new opportunity. Individual subjective norms are the perceived social pressure to start a new opportunity and perceived social control and self-efficacy is the perceived ease to start a new opportunity.

Based on the Shapero and Sokol (1982) model, attitudes and subjective norms are linked to desirability and perceived behavioral control or self-efficacy with feasibility (Krueger et al., 2000).

It is suggested in this analysis that these determinants of entrepreneurial intentions may lead to inclusive civic culture behaviors influenced by access to resources.

Inclusiveness is an all-embracing societal ideology embedding the policy and practice of including all individuals who might otherwise be excluded or marginalized due to its personal conditions such as being member of minority groups, having physical and mental disabilities, etc. As a social determinant, social inclusiveness is the improvement of conditions in which the individuals and groups participate in society, communities and organizations improving their dignity, abilities and opportunities of being disadvantaged on their basis of personal and group conditions such as their identity.

An inclusive community project is one that has not restrictions to membership due to age, gender, sex, ethnic origin, race, religion, etc. Therefore, nobody is excluded from the program and enables all the inhabitants for economic, social, political and cultural participation. Participation of all urban inhabitants without any restriction in a community agro ecological project on the basis of relationships of trust and cooperation to create an entrepreneurial inclusive civic culture and social capital as the major achievements, demands economic efficiency, social justice, political democratic participation and cultural dispensations.

Cultural relativism and postmodernism have received critical attention in the literature of inclusion (Villa & Thousand, 2000). The social constructivist model of inclusiveness is advocated by the alternative post-modern paradigm that treat human disabilities as being inclusion (Zaretsky, 2005) beyond the functionalist paradigm that considers the disability to be a pathology.

Civic culture is an issue much discussed in the 1960s and since then has become an important determinant of entrepreneurial intentions and opportunities with the study of Putman (2002, 200, 1993, Putnam et al. 2000) on democracy and social capital. Civic culture is an awareness of political behavior embedding individual attitudes, habits, emotions and sentiments related to the functioning of democratic societies, institutions and organizations that have implications in the democratic rights and decision making processes. Civil culture assumes the attitudes and values related to norms of civility and good citizenship, strengthening relationships of cooperation and trust, increased level of tolerance and good society, supportive behaviors of engagement, commitment and involvement in democratic processes.

Civic culture from the theoretical perspective of Almond and Verba (1965) in civic culture; Almond and Verba (1989) in their classic work, "Civic culture revisited" consider it to be a balanced mix of orientations in which political activity, involvement and rationality are balanced by passivity, tradition and commitment. with parochial values (Almond and Verba, 2001). Civic culture goes beyond the activist rationality model that justifies political participation, information and decision-making guided by reason and not by emotions.

The interest of this study is to identify some of the key intersections among the determinants of the stakeholder's intentions that leads to entrepreneurial in terms of their interests and access to opportunities in an inclusive civic culture in an urban community. Stakeholders are heterogeneous, distributed, and may be dependent, independent and inter dependent, and their interrelationships are complex.

METHODS

The research questions: In seeking to understand the role that the entrepreneurial inclusive civic culture plays in promoting socio-economic transformations in urban communities, some of the questions that this study addresses are:

1) How do actors embedded in different and disparate logics create and develop a new logic that builds an entrepreneurial inclusive civic culture, trust between each other's, shared understandings and governs interactions across different fields of interest interests?
2) What are the main success determinant factors that have contributed to the development of entrepreneurial inclusive civic culture intentions have led to the achievement of socio-economic and environmental transformation of an urban community?
3) What are some of the main obstacles and challenges as determinant factors that hamper the entrepreneurial inclusive civic culture of an urban community?
4) How can this transformative intervention be implemented in other urban communities with more efficiency and effectiveness to ensure economic, social and environmental sustainability?

To address and answer these questions, it was conducted a qualitative analysis of a multi-stakeholder based on a case study. Methodology employed through grounded multi-stakeholder social and community constructions in action.

For data gathering the instruments employed were:

1) Formal and informal interviews, informal and formal conversations, meetings, conferences, and social gaps.
2) Non participant observation of behavioral intentions, attitudes, individual subjective norms, perceived social control and self-efficacy.
3) Archival data: Documental, minute meetings, journaling and media articles, web site data and information, presentations, workshop reports, end note reports, video presentations.

However, some challenges and obstacles have been met and overcame at the beginning of the research, among others, the access to the community because de stigma and fear to estrangers, using the voice, language and terms of the different stakeholders and actors involved and the capture of the contextual determinants and their impacts on the formation of the entrepreneurial inclusive civic culture.

Data analysis: Grounded theory construct coding based on processual analysis: temporal bracketing, visual mapping.

Identifying causal effects is very hard in this type of study based on empirical evidences on the long term results.

It is assumed that determinants of entrepreneurial intentions may lead to inclusive civic culture behaviors influenced by access to resources (Figure 1).

To conduct this study, it was spent eight months attending the Zapopan Agro ecological Park and observing the individual activities of the members of the community and the collective Teocintle organization, social gatherings, training sessions and cultural festivals, learning about their plans and issues. The individual and collective emotions were very strong during the interviews, formal and informal conversations with members of the community. During this period of eight months, it was created and developed some very strong relationships of trust and cooperation.

Also for the general analysis of the study, the methodology principles of RRBM is applied in general terms:

1) Service to community and society at large.
2) Basic and applied emotions, embeddedness, and governance.
3) Pluralistic and multidisciplinary processes.
4) Methodology employed through grounded multi-stakeholder social and community constructions in action.
5) Involvement of stakeholders and actors at every stages.
6) Impact of stakeholders, better understanding of what works and what does not.
7) Broad implementation and dissemination to all internal and external involved stakeholders.

The process model of entrepreneurship fostering social inclusive culture is shown in figure 1 below:

Figure 1.

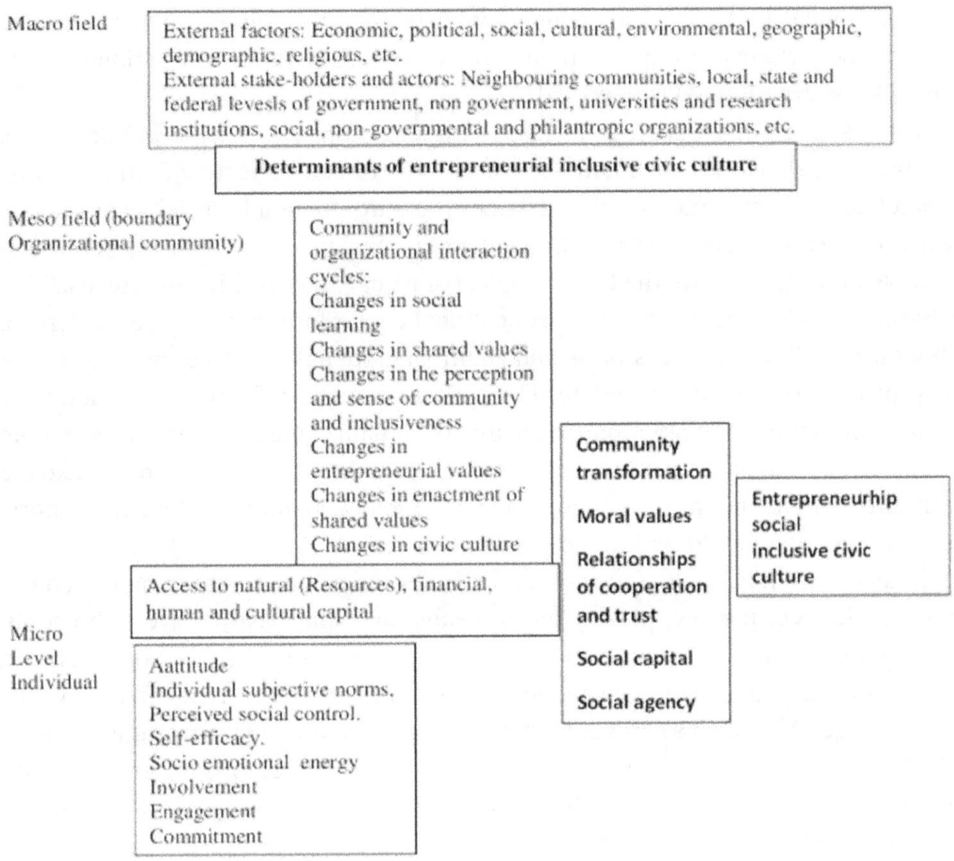

Source: Own development.

PARQUE AGROECOLÓGICO DE ZAPOPAN, A SPACE OF ENTREPRENEURIAL INCLUSIVE CIVIC CULTURE

The Zapopan Agro ecological Park is in the bio-economy field of agro ecology food, health, and energy. It is an innovative public space that combines the direct participation of the community of an urban farm project that practices that support of the sustainability culture (such as the recollection of organic waste for the production of compost) as well as training workshops on different agro ecological themes to generate a unique space in the city open to all citizens. Within the programs of the Public Space Authority of the municipality, Zapopan focused on the needs of the community, to generate job opportunities and entrepreneurship in the agro ecological Park. The kids connect with the eco technicians, which can give them the opportunity to improve their own housing, generate construction projects and self-construction (Martínez, 2016).

The Zapopan Agro ecological Park, is a space open to all the public where, through workshops, practice and coexistence, there is a collective learning on issues related to agro ecology, self-sufficiency, environmental knowledge and social awareness (Traffic ZMG, 2016). This center of inclusion is a space that generate and promote opportunities for the local people. (Martínez, 2016). Citizens are also able to have access to areas such as: An educational center built with natural materials, a boardroom/ library, a classroom, and an urban garden that is an important part of the project so the people can relate. The park has a nursery for the reproduction of plants, a compound area to produce fertilizers, a main square, the first West Edible Forest, ecological baths, a rainwater collection, and distribution system to make the park self-sustainable. In addition, several ecological workshops, cultural and sports activities are being held within the areas (Gobierno de Zapopan, 2015).

In this space it has been found that it had a fertile ground to grow: radish, chard, cabbage, lettuce, parsley, parsley, corn, beans, arugula, basil, chayote, broccoli, chili, potato, chives, sunflower, etc., are some of the more than eighty species of edible consumption, medicinal plants, etc. In the orchard you can find crops of various vegetables such as chard, lettuce, lavender, squash, squash, arugula, onion, cilantro, parsley, pineapple, bean, celery, cabbage, chayote, tomato, green tomato and African cucumber, among others (Rocha, 2016). The main goal of this project is to continue fostering social cohesion and work for a better health through orchards and urban agriculture. Zapopan Government has a agro ecological network of parks in strategic areas of the municipality. An agro ecological park is the perfect project for public space, an environmental sustainability component where people of the community can produce their own food (El Informador, 2017). See figure 2 below.

Figure 2.

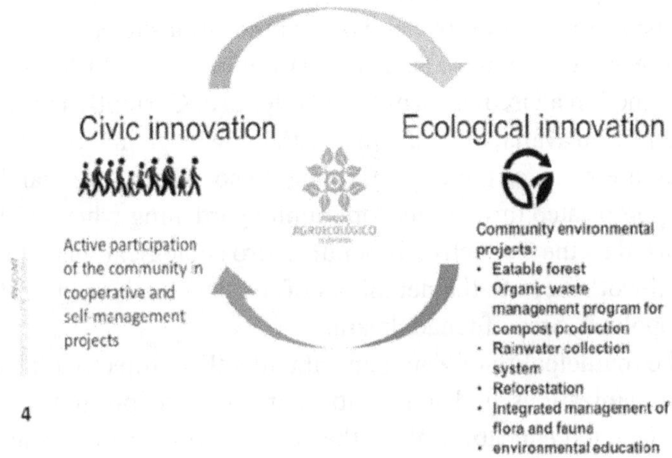

Source: Medina, 2017.

The Zapopan Agro ecological Park it's a space that became a meeting and a development space for the community in an urban environment which is committed to sustainability and to organize events such as the "Teocintle" fest, which is celebrated to raise awareness about the existence of the capacity of the human beings to generate his own resources, this, to allow them to subsist (food, utensils) and to connect the community, land, work and practice their traditions. The events celebrated and organized in the park, offer different activities such as: workshops of urban gardens, rally, craft market, food area, barter, dance, music, conversation and networking, outdoor cinema, among others (Trafico ZMG, 2016). César Medina in collaboration with the Municipal Government of Zapopan and the University Center of Biological and Agricultural Sciences (CUCBA) of Universidad de Guadalajara keep working in this and other projects (Gobierno de Zapopan, 2016).

As the matter of time spend starting with "Tierra Crudas" work, began with the drafting of the project to manage the funds in the month of June 2013. Many people have collaborated in the construction of this park, specifically "Tierra Cruda". The municipal government of Zapopan was in charge of the design and the general master plan of the park, construction of the classroom-office complex, the module of dry baths and the perimeter fence of the orchard. The local authorities also were in charge of design and build the social aspect of the park, which means it generate the social-neighborhood appropriation for the project and train them in agro ecological sowing. From this social process, the Collective Agro ecological Teocintle (CAT) was emerged (Gobierno de Zapopan, 2015).

The people that works and participate in the park always produce their own compost, build beds, seek to improve and make innovations in environmental terms, seek the common good, and make decisions. (El Informador, 2017). The community garden is designed in a circular form for a better use. Currently there are forty-seven beds of cultivation available for anyone with knowledge in bio intensive crops and meets the requirements of the collective. In the social matter it can be said that the park was appropriated through its community gardening where 32 families are working organized by the Collective Teocintle Agro ecological. In addition, this space offers several workshops to the neighbors of the park as the rest of the inhabitants of the Metropolitan Area of Guadalajara.

The municipality of Zapopan catapults this project with collaboration of other civil organizations and universities, in order to promote self-consumption and environmental education. With the collaboration of the Collective Teocintle Agro ecological, Farid Morales, who became the coordinator of the park employed by DIF in Zapopan, officials of the institution, with help of Carlos Bauche and Fernando Partida BambuXal, as well as the consultants for the general design of the park, the orchard and the edible forest by Máshumus and also the Cooperative "Las Cañadas" (Gobierno de Zapopan, 2015). The Teocintle Collective helps those who come and teach them how to grow their own food, which makes citizens feel productive and healthier.

Local Authorities from the municipality of Zapopan want to empower them, increase capacities with projects and workshops that are specialized in urban agriculture and has knowledge in seed production and compost. All this focused on community organization. The municipality oversees coordinating and managing the workshops and activities of the collective and community. Once a month, the local authority of the municipal government and the city Council, organize a tour to different orchards, including this park that is open to the community and is a public space meaning that anyone can be part of it.

Is important to say that the proper authority of this public space is responsible for the Park, which includes the orchard and the edible forest. It is managed by the collective Teocintle and is a project belonging to these local spaces authorities from the municipal administration of Zapopan, Jalisco. This is also impelled through the Direction of Public Spaces. Teocintle Agro ecological Collective is an organization that works in the management of the orchard of the park. The chief of the Public Spaces in Zapopan among César Lepe Medina, coordinator of this project and manager of the Special projects of public spaces office in the city, are now in charge of this park. The collective is divided into commissions involved in gardening activities.

New people can decide if they want to be members. Currently, there are about 40 families from the community, represented by one person, that are part of the park.

STRATEGIC MANAGEMENT OF PARQUE AGROECOLÓGICO DE ZAPOPAN

Speaking of the financial part, the Zapopan Agro ecological Park had an investment of approximately five million pesos and has an important impact in 110 direct beneficiaries, in addition to the communities surrounding the park and people interested in participating in this project (Gobierno de Zapopan, 2015). The budget of the park has an income that comes from several sources of financing and contributions. See table 1 below.

Table 1.

Zapopan Strategic Projects (PEZ) / Metropolitan Fund approximate figure, for a fund for the forest district of ten million pesos out of which are allocated to Zapopan city of all	$ 3, 000, 000.00.
The National Program for the Prevention of Crime (PRONAPRED) contributes with	1, 100, 000.00.
DIF Zapopan- Donations Area with	950, 000.00
and Program Temporary Employment PET / SEMADET with	120, 000.00

The Agro ecological park is in a farm with almost two hectares in the Metropolitan area of Guadalajara (ZMG) that has the highest rate of violence and criminality. This space used to be a ravine and that was filled with rubble. The first intervention took place with the construction of a board and with the installation of urban furniture and public lighting by the Special Projects of Zapopan Office. (Gobierno de Zapopan, 2015). This sustainable project also includes the creation of classrooms made from bamboo, a waste separation and recycling system of plastic, paper, glass, metal, organic waste and PET.

The park has a central classroom that was built with materials such as wood and straw. This building is contemplating its use to be a meeting point, a conference place and a market display, this, to give an opportunity to those who collaborate in the management of the ecological garden, giving them this space to offer their products. The park has a dry bath system that is used to reuse the generated waste as a compost and it also counts rainwater raining dam with capacity of 750-thousand-liter rainwater harvesting board and 20-thousand-liter storage tank that will provide water to the orchard and forest during the dry season which was also constructed by Agro ecological Zapopan Park.

As a result, the Local Authority of the Public Space of Zapopan, through the Zapopan Agro ecological Park, offers a space for community building and collaborative work, where one of its priorities is the orchard where 25 to 35 kilos of food are produced and harvested weekly (Gobierno de Zapopan, 2016). The production has several types of vegetables, fruits, medicinal plants and ornament plants. There are more than 50 species as pumpkin, beet, sesame, strawberry, lettuce, Swiss chard, bean that are gown in this park. Other products are elaborated with this harvests such natural slurries or milks made from seeds such as almond or canary seed. The Solar dehydrators was created to dehydrate foods such as tomatoes, traditional footwear based on pre-Hispanic roots and even the elaboration of biocosmetics made with plants such as lavender and lemon.

The public perception is positive, nowadays, there are a lot of people who finds comfort and relief in this orchards, they like being part of something, connecting with people who feels the same way and are working hard to stay productive, to have a decent income and to live a better and healthier life. The environmental education also has a very important impact in the activities and people working in this park to make a sustainable lifestyle.

CONCLUSION

Parque Agroecologist de Zapopan is a model of entrepreneurial inclusive civil culture. This park marks a milestone in the regeneration of public spaces with a project of social and environmental relevance. It is important to mention that the park was a wasteland and a place of total disuse. A total of 1.8 hectares, on Santa Laura Street, in the colony Santa Margarita (colony with more than 33 thousand inhabitants), now live in peace. This place has now recovered from being abandoned, and today is the reflection of hard work and creativity of citizens and authorities that are a model for this public space with pedagogical purposes and for the constant neighborhood participation.

The entrepreneurial intentions of the stakeholders and actors involved in the project have predicted the entrepreneurial behaviors, confirming the theory of planned behavior and their entrepreneurial activities to create opportunities to influence economic performance. Moreover, the implemented model of entrepreneurial inclusive civic culture has demonstrated that entrepreneurial intentions and activities are beyond the increasing economic growth and efficiency, to have influence in social development, inclusiveness, equality and justice. Moreover, in the field of environmental sustainability, the model clearly has impacts on the improvement of the socio-ecosystem and biodiversity.

The study analyses the determinant factors that successfully have contributed to create and develop an entrepreneurial inclusive culture leading to social transformation of a community based on agro ecology and green practices in an urban space. Changes at the meso level related to community and organizational interaction cycles of the Zapopan Agro ecological Park have been introduced to create and develop an entrepreneurial inclusive civis culture in social learning, shared values, the perception and sense of community and inclusiveness, entrepreneurial values, enactment of shared values and civic culture. All these changes have been possible due to the access to natural resources, financial, human and cultural capital through contributions of the main actors and stakeholders. At the micro level, the participation of these actors and stakeholders are related to their involvement in the individual attitudes, personal subjective norms, perceived social control, self-efficacy, socio emotional energy, involvement, engagement and commitment.

All these determinants at both levels of analysis have led to community transformation, formation of moral values, creation of relationships of cooperation and trust, social capital and social agency. All these determinants have contributed to the creation and development of an entrepreneurial inclusive civic culture model of community development. The results of the implementation of this project have contributed to increase the economic income of families, collectivities and communities participating, while reducing the gaps of social inequality, inclusiveness and justice. Moreover, the results of the analysis clearly show an improvement in biodiversity, socio-eco-ecosystem and environmental sustainability.

Other important contributions derived of the analysis of results, it should be mentioned some important issues such as fair commerce, food security and sovereignty, participative democracy, innovation in urban green areas, and so on. All these topics and issues should be treated in future research.

REFERENCES

Acs, Z. J., & Audretsch, D. B. (2003). Innovation and Technological Change. In Acs, Z. J., & Audretsch, D. B. (Eds.), *Handbook of Entrepreneurship Research* (pp. 55–79). Kluwer Academic Publishers. DOI: 10.1007/0-387-24519-7_4

Ajzen, I. (1991). The theory of planned behavior. *Organizational Behavior and Human Decision Processes*, 50(2), 1–63. DOI: 10.1016/0749-5978(91)90020-T

Almond, G., & Verba, S. (1965) The civic culture. Little, Brown and Company(Inc.), Boston: MASS, 1965.

Almond, G., & Verba, S. (Eds.). (1989), The Civic Culture revisited. Political Attitudes and Democracy in Five Nations, California, sage Publications Inc.

Almond, G., & Verba, S. (2001). La cultura política. In Batlle, A. (Ed.), *Diez textos básicos de ciencia política* (pp. 171–201). Ariel.

Aragon-Sanchez, A., Baixauli-Soler, S., & Carrasco-Hernandez, A. J. (2017). A missing link: The behavioral mediators between resources and entrepreneurial intentions. *International Journal of Entrepreneurial Behaviour & Research*, 23(5), 752–768. Advance online publication. DOI: 10.1108/IJEBR-06-2016-0172

Armitage, C. J., & Conner, M. (2001). Efficacy of the theory of planned behavior: A meta-analytic review. *British Journal of Social Psychology*, 40(4), 471–499. DOI: 10.1348/014466601164939 PMID: 11795063

Ayuntamiento de Tlajomulco de Zúñiga. Jalisco (2015). *Caracterización del subsistema social.* Retrieved from https://tlajomulco.gob.mx/sites/default/files/documentos/poel/poet_tlj_1.3_caracterizacion_subsistema_social.pdf

Baptista, R., Escária, V., & Madruga, P. (2017). *Entrepreneurship, regional development and job creation: The case of Portugal. Discussion papers on entrepreneurship, growth and public policy.* Max Planck Institute for Research in Economic Systems.

Carree, M. A., & Thurik, A. R. (2010). The impact of entrepreneurship on economic growth. In Zoltan, J., & Audretsch, D. (Eds.), *Handbook of entrepreneurship research.* Springer. DOI: 10.1007/978-1-4419-1191-9_20

Cohen, M. (1979). *La Contaminación Atmosférica y la Salud.* IGE. UdeG. México.

CONAPO. (2017). *Estimación de la mortalidad infantil para México, las entidades federativas y los municipios 2005.* Retrieved from http://www.conapo.gob.mx/es/CONAPO/Base_de_datos

Dirección de Estadística. (2013). *Secretaría de Educación de Jalisco, México 2013.* Retrieved from http://www.informador.com.mx/jalisco/2017/699906/6/zapopan-proyecta-red-de-parques-agroecologicos.htm

Do Paço, F., Arminda, M., Ferreira, J. M., Raposo, M., Gouveia, R., & Dinis, A. (2011). Behaviours and entrepreneurial intention: Empirical findings about secondary students. *Journal of International Entrepreneurship*, 9(1), 20–38. DOI: 10.1007/s10843-010-0071-9

Evans, D. S., & Leighton, L. S. (1989). Some empirical aspects of entrepreneurship. *The American Economic Review*, 79, 519–535.

Gobierno de Jalisco (2010). *Desarrollo humano y demografía de grupos vulnerables en Jalisco.*

Gobierno de Jalisco. (2013). *Equidad de oportunidades 16 Educación. Un plan de Todos para un futuro compartido.* Retrieved from https://transparencia.info.jalisco.gob.mx/sites/default/files/PED%20-%20Educaci%C3%B3n.pdf

Gobierno de Zapopan. (2015). *Zapopan estrena parque agroecológico.* Retrieved from: https://www.zapopan.gob.mx/zapopan-estrena-parque-agroecologico/

Gobierno de Zapopan. (2016). *Proyecto de presupuesto 2016. Diagnóstico del municipio para la elaboración del proyecto de presupuesto para el ejercicio fiscal 2016.* Retrieved from https://www.zapopan.gob.mx/wp-content/uploads/2016/01/Anexo4de12_DiagnosticoDelMunicipio.pdf

Gobierno de Zapopan. (2016). *Parque Agroecológico de Zapopan: Un modelo de Agricultura Urbana Sustentable.* Retrieved from: https://www.zapopan.gob.mx/parque-agroecologico-de-zapopan-un-modelo-de-agricultura-urbana-sustentable/

Holmes, T. J., & Schmitz, J. A.Jr. (1990). A theory of entrepreneurship and its application to the study of business transfers. *Journal of Political Economy*, 98(2), 265–294. DOI: 10.1086/261678

IIEG (2015). *Nota Técnica Jalisco registra 7.8 millones de pobladores al inicio de 2015. Instituto de Información Estadística y Geográfica Guadalajara.*

IIEG (2016). *Diagnóstico municipal Septiembre 2016. Instituto de Información Estadíastica y Geografía.*

IIEG (2016a). *Instituto de Información Estadística y Geográfica del Estado de Jalisco con base en INEGI, censos y conteos nacionales, 2010-2015.*

IIEG (2016b). *Instituto de Información Estadística y Geográfica del Estado de Jalisco; con información de INEGI, DENUE.*

INEGI. (2011). Censo General de Población y Vivienda 2010. Retrieved from http://www.inegi.org.mx

Krueger, N. F.Jr, Reilly, M. D., & Carsrud, A. L. (2000). Competing models of entrepreneurial intentions. *Journal of Business Venturing*, 15(5-6), 411–432. DOI: 10.1016/S0883-9026(98)00033-0

Lin, Z., Manser, M. E., & Picot, G. (1998), The Role of Self-Employment in Job Creation In Canada and the U.S., *OECD-CERF-CILN International Conference on Self-Employment*, Burlington, Ontario, Canada.

Martínez, I. (2016). *Zapopan busca ser Ciudad Amiga de la Infancia*. Retrieved from http://www.informador.com.mx/jalisco/2016/693500/6/zapopan-busca-ser-ciudad-amiga-de-la-infancia.htm

Medina, C. (2016). The role of innovation in green areas for the revitalization of German and Mexican Cities.

Pfeiffer, F., & Reize, F. (2000). Business Start-ups by the Unemployed - an Econometric Analysis Based on Firm Data. *Labour Economics*, 7(5), 629–663. DOI: 10.1016/S0927-5371(00)00016-6

Putnam, D., Pharr, S. J., & Dalton, R. J. (2000). Introduction: What's troubling the trilateral democracies. In Pharr, S. J., & Putnam, R. D. (Eds.), *Disaffected democracies* (pp. 3–27). Princeton University Press. DOI: 10.1515/9780691186849-005

Putnam, R. (1993). *Making democracy work*. Princeton University Press.

Putnam, R. (2000). *Bowling alone*. Simon & Schuster.

Putnam, R. (Ed.). (2002). *Democracies in flux*. Oxford University Press. DOI: 10.1093/0195150899.001.0001

Reyes, R., Castellanos, T., & Curiel, F. (2009). *La calidad del aire en Zapopan*. Editorial Páramo.

Rocha, A. (2016). *El Espejo: Parque Agroecológico Zapopan, zona de cultivo en la metrópoli*. Retrieved from http://www.cronicajalisco.com/notas/2016/60254.html

Rojas. H (2012) *Una década de participación del Producto Interno Bruto de Puerto Vallarta al estado de Jalisco, 2000-2009*. Investigación y Ciencia de la Universidad Autónoma de Aguascalientes, *vol* (54), pp. 30-39.

Shapero, A., & Sokol, L. (1982). The social dimensions of entrepreneurship. In Kent, C. A., Sexton, D. L., & Vesper, K. H. (Eds.), *Encyclopedia of Entrepreneurship* (pp. 72–90). Prentice Hall.

Shook, C. L., Priem, R. L., & McGee, J. E. (2003). Venture creation and the enterprising individual: A review and synthesis. *Journal of Management*, 29(3), 379–399. DOI: 10.1016/S0149-2063(03)00016-3

Souitaris, V., Zerbinatib, S., & Al-Lahamc, A. (2007). Do entrepreneurship programmes raise entrepreneurial intention of science and engineering students? The effect of learning, inspiration and resources. *Journal of Business Venturing*, 22(4), 566–591. DOI: 10.1016/j.jbusvent.2006.05.002

Trafico, Z. M. G. (2016). *El Parque Agroecológico de Zapopan celebra la autosustentabilidad*. Retrieved from http://traficozmg.com/parque-agroecologico-zapopan-celebra-la-autosustentabilidad/

Van Stel, A., & Suddle, K. (2007). The Impact of New Firm Formation on Regional Development in the Netherlands. *Small Business Economics*.

Veciana, J. M., Aponte, M., & Urbano, D. (2005). University students' attitudes towards entrepreneurship: A two countries comparison. *The International Entrepreneurship and Management Journal*, 1(2), 165–182. DOI: 10.1007/s11365-005-1127-5

Villa, R. A., & Thousand, J. S. (2000). Collaborative teaming: A powerful tool in school restructuring. In Villa, R. A., & Thousand, J. S. (Eds.), *Restructuring for caring and effective education: Piecing the puzzle together* (2nd ed.). Paul H. Brookes Publishing Co.

Wennekers, A. R. M., & Thurik, A. R. (1999). Linking entrepreneurship and economic growth. *Small Business Economics*, 13(1), 27–55. DOI: 10.1023/A:1008063200484

Wennekers, A. R. M., Thurik, A. R., & Uhlaner, L. (2002). Conditions, entrepreneurship and economic performance: The macro view. *International Journal for Entrepreneurship Education*, 1(2), 157–179.

Zaretsky, L. (2005). From Practice to Theory: Inclusive Models Require Inclusive Theories. American Secondary Education, Summer 2005, Vol. 33, No. 3 (Summer 2005), pp. 65-86

Zona Guadalajara. (2017). *Zapopan*. Retrieved from https://zonaguadalajara.com/zapopan/

Chapter 3
Contemporary Supply Chains Shaped by International Trade Trends

M. Hakan Keskin
http://orcid.org/0000-0002-9345-9501
Association for Research and Diplomacy, Bursa, Turkey

Ercan Kaya
Indepented Researcher, Turkey

Ferhat Kökyay
https://orcid.org/0000-0001-5883-7071
İstanbul Nisantasi University, Turkey

Kürşad Derinkuyu
http://orcid.org/0000-0002-4065-8857
İstanbul Aydin University, Turkey

ABSTRACT

The success of global trade depends on various factors. Supply chains play a crucial role in reshaping international trade dynamics. The scholarly focus expanded to earlier historical periods by examining the evolution of business models after World War II. Business history has been shaped by numerous technological, social and economic factors. These include Just-In-Time philosophy, social policies, ideological theories, and management approaches. This chapter begins by examining the contemporary concept of Supply Chain Management, followed by an examination of contemporary supply chain models of some prominent multinational giant com-

DOI: 10.4018/979-8-3693-9241-6.ch003

panies. These case studies, covering modest logistics practices, are useful tools for understanding the interaction between supply chains and international trade.

INTRODUCTION

Numerous factors contribute to the success of global trade, with Supply Chain Management (SCM) not only occupying a prominent position among these factors but also playing a pivotal role in reshaping all processes of international trade. Although business history and financial history emerged as specialized sub-disciplines primarily concentrating on the industrial era, a significant shift transpired as eminent scholars in the field began to refocus their attention on earlier historical periods (Gelderblom & Trivellato, 2019). The prevailing narrative of the rise of the west centered on the development of various business models, whether it was through tracing Europe's economic rise back to late medieval Italy or examining the colonial expansion of Atlantic economies until the 1970s (Coclanis, 2005). In this section addressing the relevance of this book to 'Impacts of Entrepreneurial Orientation on SCM, the first exploration will delve into the contemporary concept of SCM, followed by an examination of the relationship between supply chains and international trade.

Unlocking the Dynamics: Understanding SCM and Logistics

Logistics dates back to the dawn of human history and can be defined simply as the management of the elements necessary to achieve a specific goal. As the concept of 'goal' varies, numerous distinct areas of logistics come into play. When the goal is to treat patients, the processes fall under 'health/hospital logistics'; when it involves hosting tourists, it becomes 'hotel logistics'; and returning to normalcy after large-scale accidents or natural disasters such as earthquakes and floods is supported by 'disaster logistics.' These examples can be expanded with additional categories such as 'military logistics,' 'green logistics,' 'maritime logistics,' 'cold chain logistics,' 'automotive logistics,' 'railway logistics,' 'energy logistics,' and 'hotel logistics,' among others." In contrast to all of these, when the goal is the production of goods/services, logistics takes on the name of 'business logistics.' As types and structures of businesses evolve over time, business logistics undergoes structural changes in response to emerging needs, ultimately adopting its present form. (Keskin, 2018a, 2018b).

Contemporary business structures receive logistical support through a framework known as 'SCM'. In another expression, the supply chain is a complex and cyclical structure created to support all processes of businesses, starting from the design phase of goods [and/or services] through to the disposal of the product after completing its lifecycle (Lyons et al., 2013; Stadtler 2002). The operation of this interconnected and complementary structure, resembling a network of interlinked chains, is more complex than commonly perceived and requires managerial skills. Therefore, the management of all support processes needed to produce goods/services is referred to as SCM (Kildow, 2011; Stock, 2001). From this perspective, unlike logistics, which has a history as ancient as humanity, SCM is a relatively newer concept (Keskin, 2018b).

The Nexus Between SCM and Trade

It is possible to trace the origins of the supply chain, at least in its primitive forms, back to the earliest existence of businesses (Roberts, 2011). However, the transformation of the supply chains into their present-day structure took place in the aftermath of World War II (Murphy, 2004; Bowersox & Closs, 1996; Waters, 2003; Frazelle, 2002). The intricate nature of the modern business world is underpinned by the complex dynamics of the SCM (Hwarng & Xie, 2008).

Figure 1. Trade Movement between Producer (or Seller) and Consumer (or Customer)

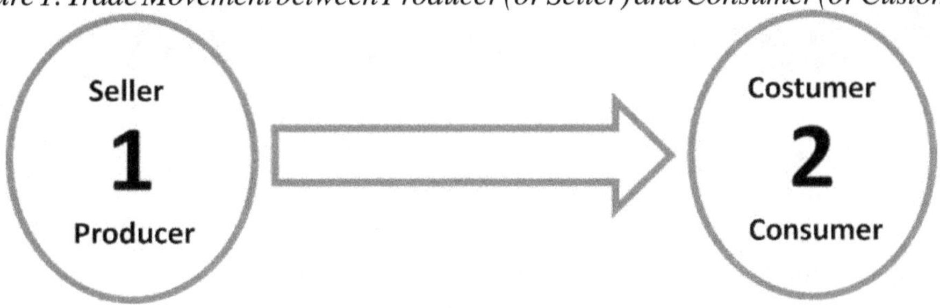

This complexity stems from the commercial relationship between two fundamental actors as depicted in Figure 1. Since the inception of the most primitive form of trade, barter (Xin *et al.,* 2021), commerce has been conducted in its simplest form wherein an individual (or a business) possessing a surplus of a particular good exchanges it with another individual willing to pay a specified amount for that product (Keskin, 2018b). The circular entity marked as 1 represents the producer (or seller), while the one marked as 2 represents the consumer (or customer). For a trade transaction to occur between these two actors, seller (producer) [1 in figure 1] must produce goods and services at a price that consumer (customer) is willing to pay [2 in figure 1]. This exchange, referred to as trade, initially took place among small-scale merchants in local markets established along trade routes that have evolved into modern cities today. However, even on a small scale, successful execution of trade required effective logistical activities, such as the transportation, proper packaging, and delivery of the produced goods to the market where they would meet the customer.

Figure 2. The Historical Silk Road (Shea, 2024).

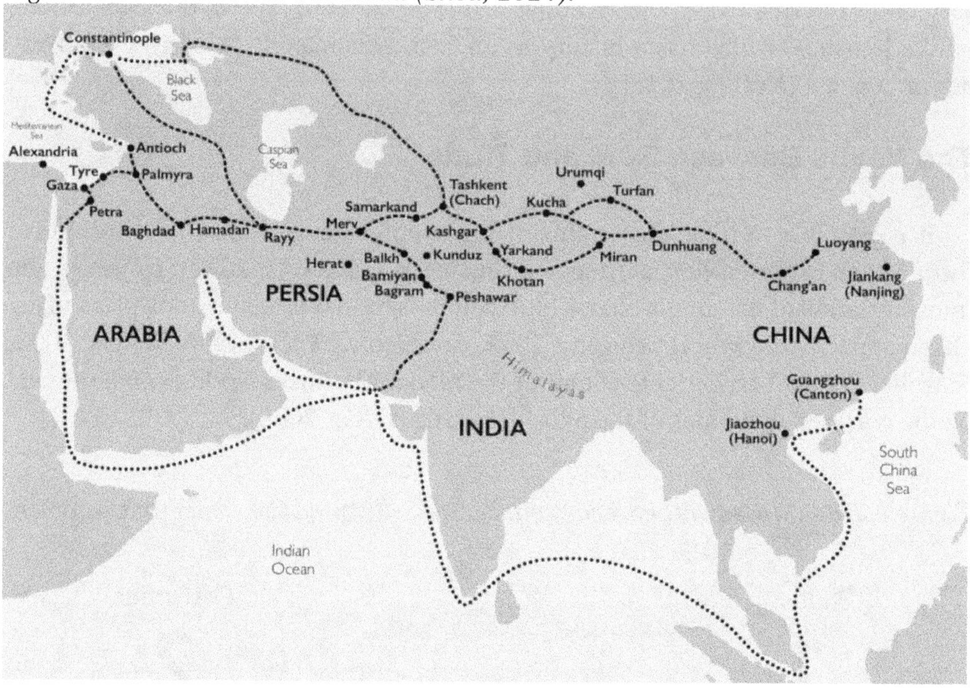

Note. The Silk Road, despite its name, was not a single road but a vast network of routes that facilitated trade and cultural exchange for over 1,500 years. Originating from the Han dynasty's opening of trade in 130 B.C.E. until the Ottoman Empire's closure of Western trade routes in 1453 C.E., this network played a pivotal role in connecting Europe and East Asia. Beyond commerce, the Silk Road facilitated the exchange of ideas, religion, and technology, fostering multicultural cities and catalyzing innovations that reshaped history. The introduction of horses to China bolstered the Mongol Empire's power, while Chinese gunpowder revolutionized warfare in Europe (National Geographic, 2024).

Over time, long-distance trades began to emerge, with the most well-known being the historical Silk Road (Peters, 2021) as illustrated in Figure 2, which has regained prominence in contemporary discussions with the 'One Road One Belt' initiative (Sarker et al., 2018). Transporting various riches, primarily silk and spices, over thousands of kilometers to the West required significant logistical operations. The first professional logisticians were generally acknowledged to be the traders who, with ancient caravans (Abir, 1968) consisting of 40-50 camels, successfully transported goods under challenging weather conditions and without technological resources. However, political, social, and administrative challenges over time led to the exploration of alternatives to trade along the Silk Road. With technological advancements allowing for compass navigation (Beazley, 1913) and the construction of sailing ships capable of carrying cargo far from the coast, international trade shifted to the seas.

Today, approximately 80% of global trade is conducted by sea. However, this was not the case in the 14th century when the first international company, the East India Company, was established with the aim of selling Asian wealth to the West. The journey of the first ship from England in the 14th century took about 14 months to reach its destination (Wilde, 2000). Today, thanks to technology, this duration has decreased by a factor of almost 20. One of the most significant factors contributing to the substantial increase in trade volume is the evolving and changing SC structures driven by technological advancements.

In addition to technological developments, there are other factors contributing to the transformation of supply chains into their present-day structures (Keskin, 2018b):

- *The development of technology:* Thanks to advancements in technology (Magistretti et al., 2020), it has become possible to significantly enhance the processing capacities of computers. This has led to the compression of vast amounts of data to sizes manageable on mobile phones, facilitating instant access to information. Furthermore, these technological developments have enabled swift fund transfers, measured in seconds, and have empowered systems to handle substantial burdens, as shown in Figure 3.

Figure 3. Evolution of Containerships (Geography of Transport Systems, n.d.)

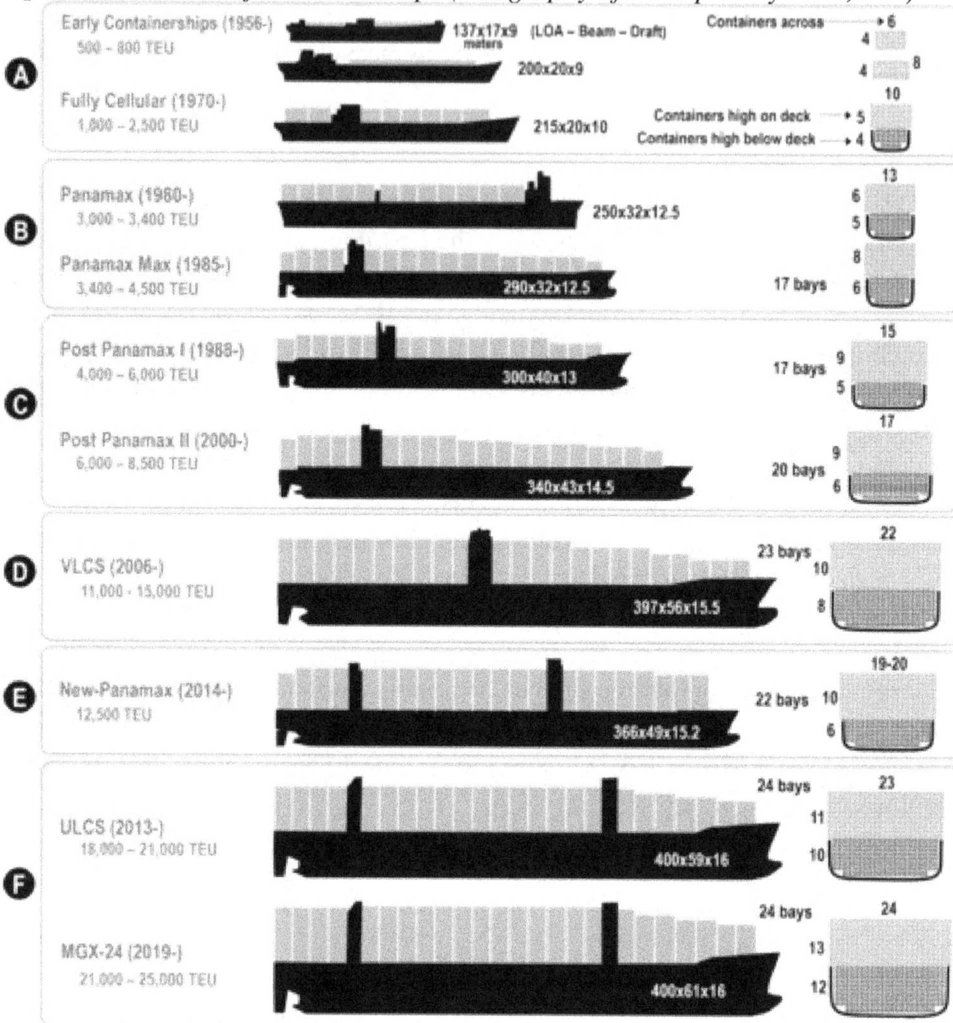

- *The fall of the Berlin Wall in 1989*: Symbolizing the end of the Cold War, this development brought about the demise of the bipolar political system, declaring the victory of the right over the left in political terms, along with the dominance of Western capitalist thought over the entire global economic system (Grosser, 2010).

- *Political and economic collaborations*: The growth of target markets in terms of volume through international collaborations such as NAFTA, EU, and APEC (Spalding, 1997).

- *Global economic system*: The implementation of free trade doctrines initiated by Adam Smith in the late 18th century (Smith, 2018) became possible after the 1950s, leading to the loss of national borders' hindrance to trade.

- *Multinational corporations*: The increase in the number, functions, and business volumes of multinational corporations (Piekkari *et al.,* 2022; Kendall & Tatiana, 2003), along with their need for logistic support systems transcending oceans and national borders, resulted in the shift from amateur logistics support systems to the requirement for professional supply chain solutions.

- *Global competitive pressure*: As a consequence of the aforementioned factors, manufacturers gained the ability to reach markets worldwide (Boone, 2000). However, this also compelled businesses to develop professional logistics support systems to produce more cost-effectively, with higher quality and faster than competitors producing remotely Doz *et al.,* 1981).

The contemporary structure of supply chains (Soonhong *et al.,* 2019) is far more complex than the direct sales from producer to consumer, From the beginning of the industrial revolution, which initiated mechanization, until the post-World War II period, the focus was on 'production' rather than 'consumption' (Ivanov et al., 2010; Frazelle, 2002; Kuglin, 1998).

During this period, efforts were concentrated on achieving more efficient and cost-effective production. One influential figure of this era was Frederick Taylor. Henry Ford, who first applied Taylor's principles of lean production (Selimović, 2022) at the Highland Park automobile factory in 1913, became one of the prominent names associated with this approach.

According to Ford, the principle was more important than technology. In 1906, Ford managed to gain a significant advantage over his competitors by selling a four-cylinder car, priced at $1000 elsewhere, for $600. In 1908, he introduced the legendary Model T for $850. Implementing continuous production on a single model and applying mass production techniques, Ford reduced labor time from 12.5 hours to 1.5 hours and successfully lowered the car's price from $850 to $360.

As depicted in Figure 4, in just 1916 and 1917, he sold 730,041 vehicles, constituting one-third of the entire U.S. automobile market at that time (Alizon et al., 2009). The period that is commonly accepted to have begun with the transition to mass production is referred to as the Fordist era (Taylor, 2006).

Note. One of the earliest pictures of the Ford Motor Company factory in Dagenham, Essex (now in Greater London), England, which opened in 1931. (Encyclopædia Britannica, Inc., n.d.)

Figure 4. Fordist and post Fordist Era

During the Fordist era, production was supply-oriented, and producers had ready-made customers. Customer demands could not be met with the existing production volume. In other words, the quantity supplied was less than the quantity demanded. Naturally, producers did not feel the need to consider customer demands. In the Fordist era, the first actor, the producer, was dominant over the consumer. In other words, supply was more powerful than demand. However, over time, the situation changed. Thanks to lean production, the production volume rapidly increased, ultimately surpassing the quantity demanded. Industrialized countries struggled to find customers for their products, leading to the global crisis known as the Great Depression in 1929 (Samuelson, 2012). Without finding a solution to the economic hardships, the problems caused by the Second World War had to be addressed. The bitter experiences gained from global economic crises and world wars made transnational cooperation imperative in all areas (Keskin, 2018b).

After the 1950s, a new structure emerged. In this new framework, where demand prevailed over supply, referred to as the 'post-Fordist era' denoting the period after the 'Fordist era,' customer demand was at the center of the economic system (Petit, 1999). One of the most significant differences that gradually separated the post-Fordist structure from the Fordist one was the competition phenomenon shaped by the gradual liberalization of trade globally. As competition made its presence felt, all businesses engaged in local or regional production found themselves compelled to compete not only within their regions but also with overseas rival enterprises. Enterprises unable to withstand the pressure of global competition began to face bankruptcy. To sustain their existence, it became imperative for businesses to produce similar products in the market more qualitatively, affordably, and quickly. After the 1950s, the dominance of the post-Fordist structure in markets, which, in contrast to the Fordist structure that was supply-oriented, was based on the customer or demand-oriented approach, led to the increasing importance of the supply chain (Keskin, 2018b).

In simpler terms, global competition required businesses to be superior to their competitors. Creating more efficient supply chains and managing them effectively emerged as crucial steps to outperform competitors. Being superior meant producing faster and more affordably than competitors with a similar range of products. Achieving speed and cost-effectiveness was now only possible through an effective SCM.'

- In the Fordist era, a customer wanting to buy a car (in the early 1900s) had virtually one option: the Model T Ford.
- The customer had no other alternative but to purchase the specific vehicle.
- Hence, the producer could manufacture the car as desired and sell it at a price they determined.
- In the post-Fordist era, a customer desiring to buy a car had numerous options from various brands.
- Customers gained the ability to choose from among these brands.
- As a result, producers had to manufacture the car in a way that aligned with the customer's demands and sell it at a more competitive price compared to their rivals.

A structure has evolved, emphasizing that focusing solely on production is no longer sufficient under the pressure of global competition (Figure 5).

Figure 5. Overview of a Contemporary Supply Chain

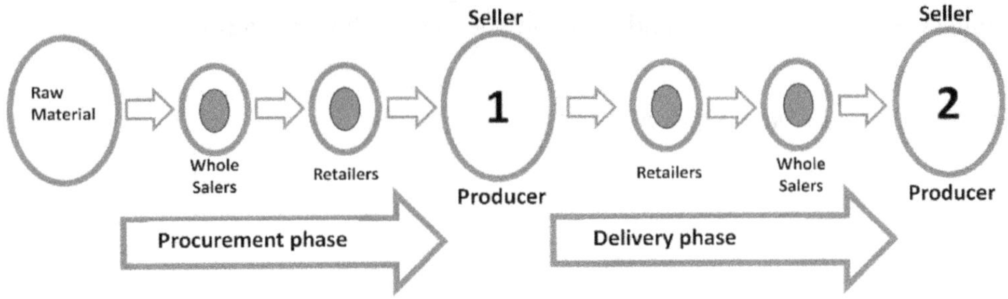

The intricate nature of the business world has given rise to various processes and actors in the journey from production to delivering the product to the customer (Chopra & Meindl, 2004; Ballou, 2004; Shapiro, 2001).

Local companies with small budgets have found themself compelled to compete with global competitors within its target market. With the support of huge global supply chains, brands in global market competition have gained an asymmetric advantage over small businesses in local markets. Many local brands could not compete. This had not only economic but also political and social consequences. As shown in Figure 6, many furniture stores could not compete with IKEA's arrival in the market. A similar situation was valid for local stationery stores and ironmongers' electronics stores.

Figure 6. Global Competitors of Local Businesses

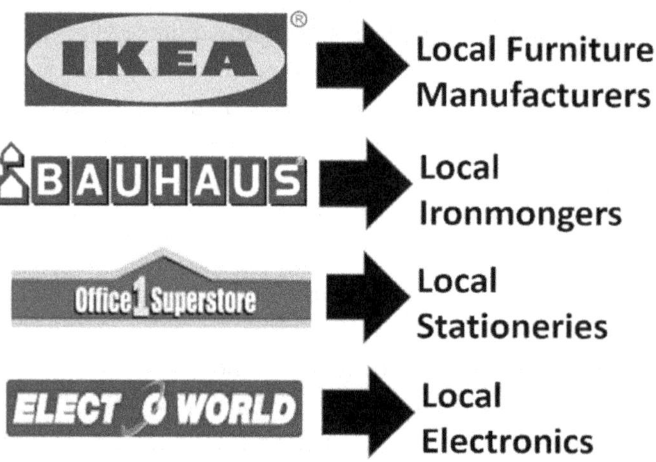

Therefore, to survive, businesses had to be efficient and cost-effective not only in their production processes but also in delivering products to customers and sourcing the necessary raw materials and semi-finished goods for production.

Figure 7. Procurement Processes

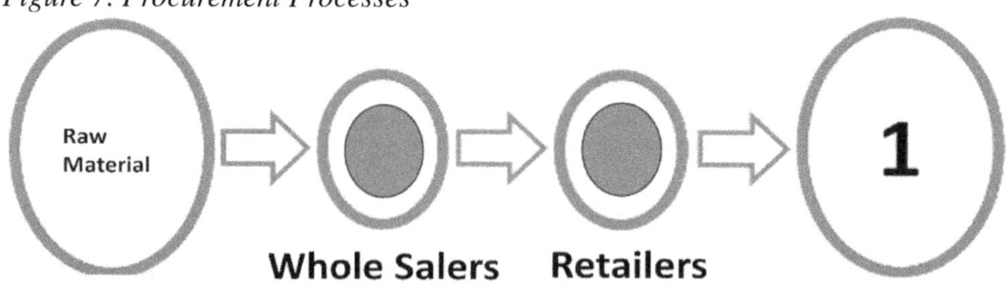

In the first stage illustrated in Figure 7, a business strives to be efficient in the procurement processes of the necessary raw materials and/or semi-finished goods for production. At this stage, raw materials and/or semi-finished goods are sourced from various centers around the world. The process of international trade begins before the production of any product. This is because producers are in search of lower-cost raw materials in all global markets. Low-cost logistics processes are among the prerequisites for procuring low-cost raw materials.

Figure 8. Distribution Processes

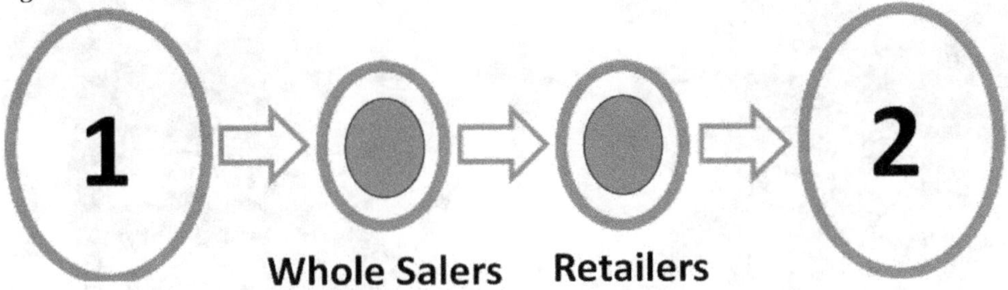

After the completion of the production processes, effective logistics support is required to deliver the final product to the customer. In the business world, where the Just-In-Time (JIT) philosophy (Figure 9) is increasingly prominent (Kee-hung 2009), delivering the product the customer desires under the conditions they specify (Figure 8) is achievable through an efficient supply chain.

Note. In literature, the abbreviation JIT, derived from the first letters of the English phrase 'just-in-time, was developed by the Japanese in the late 1960s. JIT is an approach that focuses on delivering the product the customer wants, in the required quantity, using the least amount of materials, equipment, labor, and space at the needed time. The reason for the contemporary form of production processes today is the pressure created by customer-oriented markets and global competition. Modern supply chains that support the production processes of businesses have transformed to adapt to this pressure, aligning with the JIT philosophy.

Figure 9. SCM and JIT Philosophy (uniformwares)

Because SC spans various disciplines and is highly sophisticated, illustrating every detail in a simple figure is challenging. However, as a final step, the reverse flow of cash and data can be incorporated. With the inclusion of the disposal stage, reverse logistics (Ait-Kadi 2012), and cash/data flow, the SC figure should be redesigned as shown in Figure 10.

Figure 10. A conventional supply chain (Keskin, 2020).

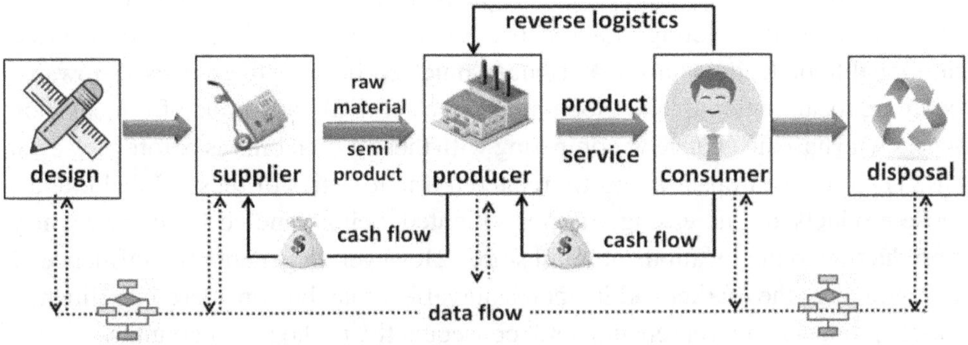

Brands belonging to multinational corporations in today's business world can transform their myriad product varieties, along with tens of thousands of different raw materials and semi-finished goods, through global and highly intricate production and distribution processes to meet the customer. Consequently, the supply chain created for each product contributes to the formation of international trade under the pressure of global competition.

When the supply chain designed for any product is successful, the impact of the brand in the target market can have various political, social, and economic effects. As global brands increase their successful implementations in supply chains, the market shares of local brands are gradually diminishing. The success of global chains, negatively affects the foreign trade potential in the target countries. Local or regional businesses struggle to survive, let alone become global brands (Coyle et al., 2003).

The opening of an IKEA store in Ankara led to the withdrawal of many furniture manufacturers located in Siteler, who were exporting to limited markets. One of the reasons for IKEA's success as a brand and reaching such revenue figures is its ability to keep logistics costs significantly lower than its competitors in the same sector. IKEA markets and releases its products in a disassembled state, providing assembly services to customers for a fee.

As chains in different sectors open more stores, significant disruptions occur in the target country or region for that sector. With the opening of Bauhaus or similar chain stores in Ankara, local shop owners selling the same products in Rüzgârlı Çarşı started vacating their shops and withdrew from the sector. Similar effects have been observed in Office Super Store and similar chains affecting local small-scale stationery stores, as well as Elektro World and similar chains affecting local small-scale electronic product shops.

The impact of this phenomenon on foreign trade has occurred in two dimensions, both positive and negative. The negative aspect is observed in the evaluation of the target country's foreign trade with a focus on exports. The incubation period that global trade leaders have experienced much earlier and the processes towards becoming local, regional, and global businesses have already ended for local shop owners who have no chance of competing with these global brands before they even start. The positive impact is mostly related to the logistics of these global brands, whose products are increasingly import-oriented, being handled from the country of production to the locations of retail stores. However, in general, the influence of these brands in the market and its increasing effect may be considered detrimental to local producers, entrepreneurs, and, consequently, to the target country.

Navigating Supply Chains for the Strategies amidst COVID-19 and International Trade Dynamics

COVID-19 has had significant effects on supply chains across various industries. Manufacturing plants had to shut down or reduce production, leading to shortages of raw materials and finished products. Delays in transportation, especially for international shipments, led to longer lead times. This affected inventory management systems severely. With fluctuating demand and supply constraints, many businesses faced stockouts or excess inventory issues. Many supply chain workers were affected by COVID-19, either falling ill themselves or facing restrictions due to quarantine measures. This led to labor shortages in warehouses, distribution centers, and transportation networks, further impacting operations. Ketchen Jr. and Craighead (2020) highlights opportunities arising from the crisis. As organizations grapple with disruptions, they are compelled to innovate and adapt their SCM strategies to ensure resilience and agility. Micheli et al. (2021) emphasized the acceleration of existing trends in SCM. The pandemic acted as a catalyst for digital transformation, sustainability initiatives, and the reevaluation of supply chain strategies. Moreover, the crisis underscored the importance of building resilience into supply chains, prompting firms to diversify sourcing, invest in automation, and foster closer relationships with suppliers. Raj et al. (2022) delve into the mitigation strategies to address SCM challenges during the pandemic.

These strategies include enhancing supply chain visibility, collaboration, diversifying supplier networks, and embracing digital technologies. Shi et al. (2023) provide insights into future trends of SCM amidst COVID-19. The review outlines the impact and emerging trends. As a conclusion, organizations must anticipate future disruptions, foster collaboration, and leverage technology to build agile, sustainable, and resilient supply chains.

Supply chain disruptions highlighted the importance of building resilience into supply chain design and management practices. These are the highlighted areas:

- Resilience and Agility: The pandemic has emphasized the importance of resilience and agility in supply chains and business operations. Organizations adapted to disruptions, implemented agile strategies, and developed new business models to navigate the crisis. This could include diversifying sourcing locations and implementing risk management practices.
- Digital Transformation: Given the accelerated pace of digitalization during the pandemic, companies have leveraged digital technologies such as IoT, blockchain, and AI to improve supply chain efficiency, transparency and improve supply chain visibility.
- Collaboration and Partnerships: The pandemic highlighted the importance of collaboration and partnerships across organizations, industries, and sectors. Organizations formed partnerships with suppliers, customers, and other stakeholders to share information, resources, and best practices. These collaborations helped improve supply chain coordination and responsiveness.
- Sustainability and Ethical Considerations: Supply chain disruptions shows the growing importance of sustainability and ethical considerations in SCM, particularly in light of the pandemics impact on global trade, regulations, labor conditions and environmental sustainability.

Here are a few case examples of how companies faced challenges in supply chain management during the COVID-19 pandemic:

- Energy Sector Problems: At the onset of the pandemic, the oil market experienced unprecedented volatility, with prices decreasing to historic lows. Companies in the oil and gas industry, such as ExxonMobil and Chevron, had to grapple with reduced demand, excess inventory, and logistical challenges in storing and transporting crude oil. Similarly in electricity market, electricity generation units encountered supply chain disruptions that affected their ability to meet demand. For example, renewable energy projects faced delays in construction and equipment procurement due to supply chain disruptions and labor shortages. Additionally, maintenance and repair activities were impacted by travel restrictions and safety protocols, leading to downtime for power plants.
- Automotive Industry Disruptions: Automotive manufacturers such as, Ford Motor Company had to temporarily shut down several manufacturing plants worldwide due to shortages of critical components, logistics bottlenecks, and workforce issues.
- Food and Beverage Sector Challenges: In this sector, for instance, Nestlé faced disruptions in sourcing raw materials, manufacturing, and distribution. The company adjusted production schedules and found alternative suppliers.

- Retail Supply Chain Struggles: Another problem appeared in retail. For example, Walmart experienced inventory shortages as panic-buying. The company had to implement inventory management strategies, collaborate with suppliers, and ramp up e-commerce operations to meet customer demand.

- Pharmaceutical Supply Chain Pressures: Manufacturing drugs and distributing medical supplies during the pandemic was also difficult. For instance, Pfizer faced supply chain constraints in producing and distributing COVID-19 vaccines globally. The company had to scale up production, optimize distribution networks, and address regulatory hurdles to meet the demand for vaccines.

- Electronics Industry Disruptions: Even the biggest companies such as, Apple experienced delays in the launch of its new iPhone models due to disruptions in the supply of components from suppliers in Asia. The company had to diversify sourcing and implement contingency plans.

These case examples illustrate the diverse challenges that companies faced in managing their supply chains during the COVID-19 pandemic. From disruptions in sourcing raw materials to logistics bottlenecks and changes in consumer demand, organizations had to adapt quickly and implement strategies to ensure the resilience and continuity of their supply chain operations.

Exemplary Cases Illustrating International Trade and SCM

Some cases illustrating international trade and SCM could refer to various real-world scenarios or case studies showcasing successful or notable examples within the realm of international trade and SCM. These ones include innovation, efficiency, responsiveness, and sustainability. Analyzing these cases can provide valuable insights and best practices for businesses seeking to optimize their own supply chain operations on a global scale.

The most renowned companies known for their exemplary supply chain practices include Apple Inc., Zara, Toyota, Amazon, Nike, Adidas, Samsung and Starbucks. However, for the sake of manageable scope within your study, three of these companies, Samsung, Starbucks, and Adidas, is preferred for in-depth analysis to better convey the effects of supply chains on international trade.

Samsung Electronics Case; Arçelik, the dominant brand in the Turkish white goods market until the last 15 years, has lost a significant portion of its market share to Samsung, which manufactures in South Korea. One of the reasons for this shift is cost-effective supply chains.

Figure 11. Samsung Refrigerator from South Korea to Türkiye

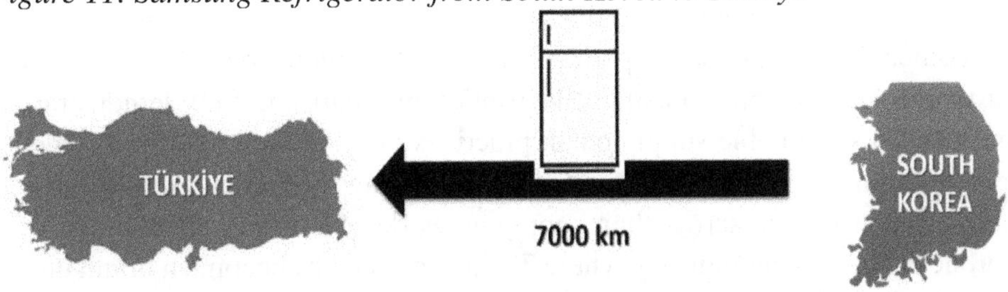

The successful management of the supply chain is evident in the ability to deliver a refrigerator from approximately 7,000 km away (Figure 11) to a consumer's kitchen in Istanbul at a lower cost than a refrigerator located 350 km away in Eskişehir (Keskin, 2018a).

Samsung boasts an extensive supply chain comprising approximately 2,500 suppliers worldwide, each playing a crucial role in the company's operations. Recognizing the potential for broader positive impacts if all suppliers embraced Green Management practices, Samsung actively supports and guides its suppliers toward sustainability. Technical and economic assistance, along with dedicated consultants, are provided to encourage suppliers to adopt Green Management practices, fostering a sustainable supply chain. In the selection of new suppliers, Samsung Electronics implements an environmental management assessment through its in-house Eco-Partner scheme. This assessment evaluates a candidate's environmental commitment, eco-friendly production willingness, and practical implementation of environmental values before making a final decision. Similarly, Samsung SDI, a key component of Samsung's supply chain, collaborates with partner companies supplying raw materials for products, emphasizing mutual growth and cooperation. Through mutual growth agreements with 250 1st/2nd tier suppliers, Samsung SDI offers support in finance, education, technology, market expansion, and performance sharing, guided by the shared value of "we can go farther when we go together." Conducting assessments for 91 partner companies across various regions, Samsung SDI ensures compliance with mandatory requirements, including the prohibition of child labor. Feedback from assessments informs the creation of education programs covering labor contracts, environmental law compliance, ethics, and waste management. Moreover, Samsung SDI dispatches specialists in environment, safety, health, and utilities to assist partner companies, with plans to evaluate an additional 100 domestic and international partners. Strengthening partner companies' compliance systems, Samsung SDI provides support through environment management and CSR training, and the standardization of inspection methods. To enhance transparency and effectiveness, Samsung SDI introduces the Win-Win payment system, allowing secondary and tertiary partner companies to convert Samsung SDI-issued bonds into cash at commercial banks with the same fee level as large companies. With 26 partner companies already participating, Samsung SDI plans to expand this initiative further. In conclusion, Samsung Electronics and Samsung SDI demonstrate a commitment to sustainable supply chain practices through proactive engagement, support programs, and transparent partnerships, aiming for mutual growth and environmental stewardship across their supply networks (Samsung, 2024).

Starbucks Case; In an industry where Turkish coffee has become a brand under the name 'Turkish Coffee,' the presence of multiple global brands in Türkiye creates one of the finest examples of a successful supply chain. One of the most well-known among them is Starbucks, with a revenue of almost 150 million dollars per year. Starbucks, a globally recognized coffee retailer and chain, has built its reputation on premium coffee and innovative customer service. Central to its continued success is a robust supply chain strategy, continually invested in to maintain competitiveness.

At first glance, this figure may not convey much. However, this revenue figure exceeds the total of the top 100 Turkish brands (Figure12). The success of supply chains in specific fields, such as coffee, is achieved by superior international trade, allowing the delivery of the same quality of service to customers worldwide.

Figure 12. Supply Chain Structure of Starbucks

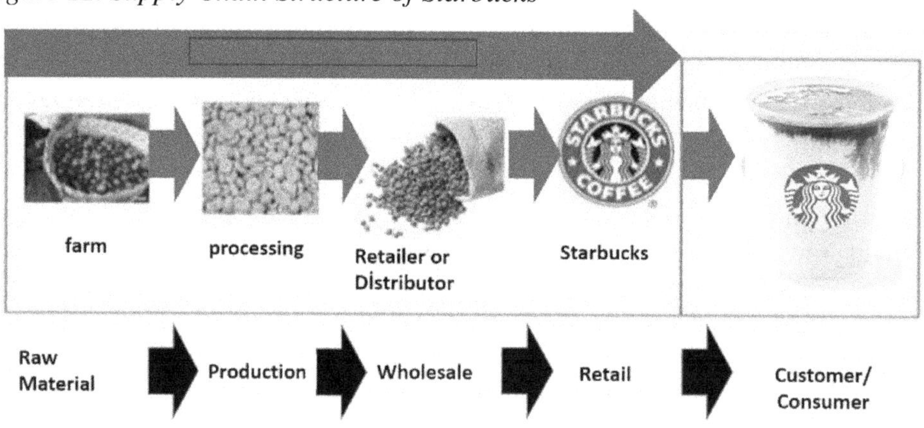

Starbucks' supply chain strategy is to ensure that its customers receive the freshest, highest-quality coffee and other beverages while providing a positive experience through its supply chain. This includes sourcing the best beans, investing in technology and processes, and building relationships with suppliers and customers. At the core of Starbucks' supply chain strategy lies efficient sourcing of coffee beans, meticulous manufacturing, seamless logistics, and swift distribution. This strategy ensures customers receive the freshest products while keeping costs in check, a crucial factor in Starbucks' success. Utilizing technology and automation, Starbucks streamlines operations, optimizing inventory management to swiftly respond to fluctuating customer demands. Strong supplier relationships contribute to securing top-quality coffee beans and ingredients at competitive prices. Moreover, Starbucks prioritizes sustainability and waste reduction throughout its supply chain. By implementing various eco-friendly practices, the company minimizes environmental impact while maximizing efficiency. In essence, Starbucks' supply chain strategy is centered on delivering top-notch quality while balancing cost-effectiveness and environmental responsibility. Through ongoing innovation and investment, Starbucks remains a formidable presence in the dynamic retail landscape.

When dissecting Starbucks' SC Strategy, it's imperative to delve into its various components;

- Efficient Sourcing Process: Starbucks meticulously sources the finest coffee beans globally, prioritizing freshness and flavor. Close collaboration with suppliers and farmers ensures adherence to ethical and sustainable practices.
- Robust Manufacturing Process: Leveraging technology and automation, Starbucks ensures maximum efficiency in its manufacturing operations, enabling timely and cost-effective production of high-quality products.
- Efficient Logistic System: Starbucks boasts an extensive network of warehouses, distribution centers, and retail stores, facilitating swift product delivery to customers. Advanced technology aids in inventory management and shipment tracking, enhancing overall efficiency.
- Effective Distribution Strategy: With a diverse range of physical and online retail outlets, Starbucks efficiently reaches customers while employing targeted marketing campaigns to enhance customer awareness and engagement.

The role of information technology in Starbucks' SC Strategy is crucial. Information technology is integral to Starbucks' supply chain strategy, enabling streamlined operations, cost reduction, and enhanced customer satisfaction. Utilizing enterprise resource planning (ERP) systems and advanced analytics tools, Starbucks efficiently manages inventory levels and monitors performance. Digital logistics management tools, such as GPS tracking systems and automated robots, further optimize operations.

There are some challenges and opportunities facing Starbucks' SC Strategies. While Starbucks must continually invest in technology to remain competitive and ensure supplier compliance with ethical and sustainable practices, opportunities exist to enhance efficiency and cost-effectiveness through data analytics and supplier collaboration. Starbucks' successful SC strategy, driven by technology, efficiency, and quality, has cemented its position in the retail landscape. By prioritizing these elements and fostering strong supplier partnerships, Starbucks ensures cost-effective and reliable product delivery. Starbucks is committed to providing full transparency across its SC. The company regularly publishes reports and updates on its progress toward sustainability goals and has a dedicated transparency website with detailed information on its suppliers, practices, and progress (Dffreight, 2024).

Adidas Case; Adidas essentially documented its supply chain success during the 2014 FIFA World Cup. The final match featured the national teams of Germany and Argentina, and not only the teams but also the trio of referees were wearing Adidas tracksuits during the ceremony. For viewers watching the final live on television, Germany's supply chain championship was confirmed (Keskin, 2018a). Adidas operates production centers across a global network spanning 100 locations in 50 countries worldwide. In Asia, including China, Vietnam, South Korea, Indonesia, and India, as well as in the Americas with presence in the USA, Brazil, Argentina, Canada, and El Salvador, and in the EMEA region encompassing Germany, Türkiye, Italy, the United Kingdom, and Spain.

The company's global supply chain (Adidas, 2024) extends through various tiers, from strategic manufacturing partners to componentry and materials suppliers, and down to raw material sources such as cotton, leather, and natural rubber. Collaborating closely with key strategic partners, the majority of Adidas products are manufactured in around 110 facilities worldwide. Adidas values long-term relationships, with 65% of its independent manufacturing partners having worked with the company for at least a decade, and 35% for over 20 years. Supplier relationships are evaluated based on specific performance criteria that are regularly measured and reviewed. Suppliers are incentivized to maintain high performance levels through the awarding of higher orders.

Adidas predominantly outsources its production, working with over 400 independent factories worldwide across approximately 45 countries. Its supply chain is global and multi-layered, involving various types of business partners, including directly contracted factories.

In terms of social and environmental compliance, the strength of partnerships is linked to the scale and stability of orders. Adidas utilizes three sourcing models: direct, indirect, and local market production. The direct sourcing model involves contractual relationships with core suppliers centrally supervised by the Global Operations function. These suppliers, managed by Global Operations, produce the majority of Adidas products. The indirect sourcing model accounts for a minor part of the product volume, sourced through agents or under license. Agents place orders with preferred suppliers, while licensees may directly place orders or use agents as intermediaries. The indirect supply chain complements direct sourcing by meeting specific requirements not serviced through Global Operations. Local market production is utilized to quickly seize short-term opportunities in local markets, satisfy niche market requirements, or adhere to specific trade regulations. Adidas subsidiaries may source from local suppliers in specific countries, requiring authorization from the Social and Environmental Affairs team for production. This extensive chain operates successfully due to the smooth execution of international trade.

Adidas' supplier network encompasses five primary categories:

- Manufacturing Partners: These entities maintain a direct contractual relationship with Adidas, supplying products for both export and domestic markets.
- Subcontractors: Factories subcontracted by Adidas' primary suppliers to handle manufacturing operations beyond their own capabilities.
- Material and Service Providers: While not directly affiliated with Adidas, these entities supply goods and services to the company's primary suppliers.
- Licensees: Independent companies licensed by Adidas to oversee the design, production, and distribution of specific products.
- Agents: Independent firms acting as intermediaries, sourcing manufacturing, managing production processes, and selling finished products to Adidas.

Within this framework, Adidas also identifies strategic suppliers, comprising both manufacturing partners and materials suppliers. These strategic partners are selected for their engagement in social and environmental initiatives that exceed standard compliance measures. They are viewed as long-term collaborators, providing top-tier facilities, significant business share with Adidas (as Tier 1 manufacturers), or serving as key material sources for Tier 1 manufacturers. Strategic suppliers demonstrate strong management in development and manufacturing, possess economies of scale, and exhibit advanced supply chain capabilities.

Adidas employs a comprehensive approach to mapping supply chain risks, ensuring that its suppliers adhere to socially and environmentally responsible practices. This involves a combination of processes for systematic monitoring and support for improvement, along with tools for swift response to critical situations. By doing so, Adidas aims to mitigate adverse impacts on workers and the environment. Key sources of information for risk-mapping exercises include government-provided databases, as well as ongoing engagement with civil society organizations, unions, employer federations, and direct interactions with workers.

CONCLUSION

In the foreseeable future, several indicators may aid in predicting upcoming developments. The impending future is expected to witness a widespread shift toward digitization in nearly every aspect of planning and execution. Certain tools incorporating fuzzy logic (Moraga, 2005) are poised to enhance the optimization efficiency of SC. The Internet of Things (IoT) encompasses the network of physical objects, commonly referred to as "things," which are equipped with sensors, software, and various technologies. The primary objective is to enable these objects to connect and exchange data with other devices and systems via the internet (Kumar et al., 2019; Sandro et al., 2020). This extensive array of devices spans from everyday household items to advanced industrial tools. Presently, there are over 7 billion connected IoT devices, and industry experts anticipate this number to escalate to 22 billion by the year 2025. In the near future, the potential of IoT applications to acquire real-time data on items, encompassing factors such as size, density, and identification numbers, is anticipated to reach unprecedented levels in terms of volume and speed. The integration of IoT technology is expected to elevate the accuracy of SC operations, simultaneously mitigating common errors. The utilization of sensors for monitoring the flow and movement of items and personnel will contribute to a safer operational environment by preventing accidents. Modern cloud based systems provide many benefits to the small business which needs a solution without remarkable problems. Dark warehouses (Hwang & Kim 2023) are characterized by the automation of warehouse operations, eliminating the need for human labor. They represent a component of 'Logistics 4.0,' which envisions a supply chain devoid of human involvement. The integration of automation in warehouses has already begun to some extent, with industrial handle robotics, autonomous picking vehicles, and similar technologies being deployed for tasks such as picking, handling, and storage. However, their widespread adoption has been limited to companies with substantial budgets due to the high costs involved. Predictions suggest that these systems will become more affordable and commonplace in the near future. Blockchain technology extends beyond the realm of logistics. In essence, it is a chain of blocks, but not in the sense of a physical structure composed of blocks Saha et al. (2019). Here, 'block' signifies digital pieces of information, such as item features, times, and dates, while 'chain' refers to their method of storage. Blockchain utilizes specific and unique codes, rather than names, for data storage. In the near future, it is anticipated that nearly all SC will adopt blockchain technology. Many vehicles and equipment, which have been introduced recently, ease to cope with the problems of SC due to the technology. Drones are supposed to be a problem solver in the coming years for the retail logistics which faces so many delays and hitches while delivering to the populated city centers with heavy traffic congestions (Srinivas & Sanjeev, 2023). Drones and autonomous vehicles will be an efficient tool for SC with huge size for different goals as well. SC which are are supposed to provide services nonstop 7/24 will be tailored by these factors in the coming years.

In addition to these, a myriad of challenges confronted companies in orchestrating their supply chains amidst the COVID-19 pandemic. Ranging from disruptions in raw material sourcing to logistical constraints and fluctuations in consumer demand, organizations were compelled to swiftly adapt and enact strategies to fortify the resilience and seamless operation of their supply chain networks.

These technological developments with other factors including COVID -19 are expected to make a significant contribution to overcoming various challenges in the logistics support of products, such as administrative constraints, political barriers, and technical obstacles encountered at national borders. Additionally, substantial cost savings in logistics are anticipated. In today's supply chains, distribution centers (DC) at specific hub points, created based on logistics dynamics, may gradually become positions where manufacturing machines are located.

Figure 13. A prediction for the future of supply chains (Keskin, 2020)

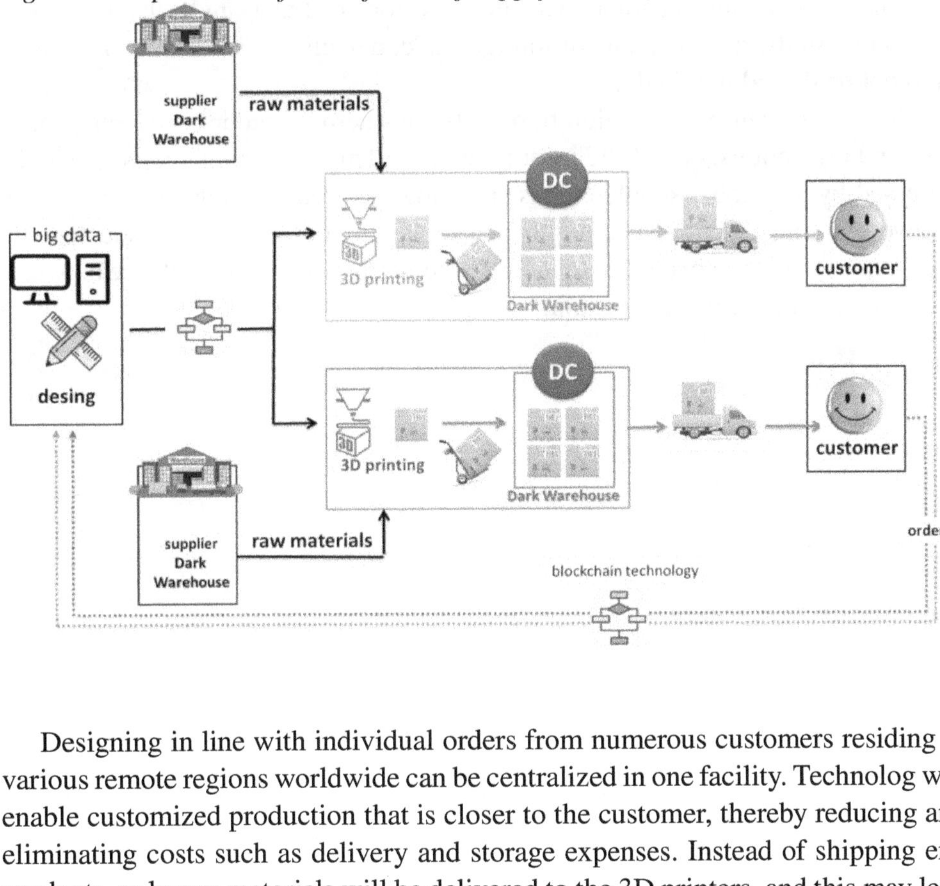

Designing in line with individual orders from numerous customers residing in various remote regions worldwide can be centralized in one facility. Technolog will enable customized production that is closer to the customer, thereby reducing and eliminating costs such as delivery and storage expenses. Instead of shipping end products, only raw materials will be delivered to the 3D printers, and this may lead to some products not being purchased by customers. A prediction for the future of supply chains is illustrated in Figure 13. Nevertheless, there will still be a need for Distribution Centers (DCs) to supply raw materials located at an optimal distance from the 3D printer locations. Despite the transformative nature of contemporary supply chains, warehousing will remain crucial to support the dispersed supply chain network across the globe (Keskin 2020).

So, in today's world, the cycles symbolized by circles, demonstrating all the processes from raw material turning into a product to reaching the customer, are, in practice, executed as highly intricate and multidimensional activities. For these complex structures to function seamlessly, they require nearly flawless logistical support. Hence, the success of businesses in becoming global brands and dominating worldwide markets is achieved through the creation of their globally dispersed supply chains. The success of global chains is directly proportional to the success of cross-border commercial activities.

All types of international trade are integrated into SCM. The relationship between SCM and foreign trade is a topic that cannot be confined to a single chapter. However, in this study, the backbone of foreign trade, namely maritime transportation, could not be delved into in detail.

While the execution of foreign trade activities across borders, customs procedures and regulations, one of the most crucial challenges encountered, and widely addressed by the global supply chains spanning hundreds of countries, could not be covered in this section. The number of topics not covered here is substantial; however, the study has been able to identify the extensive interdependence between international trade and supply chains.

REFERENCES

Abir, M. (1968). Caravan Trade and History in the Northern Parts of East Africa. *Paideuma*, 14, 103–120. https://www.jstor.org/stable/40341453

Adidas. (2024). Sustainability Supply Chain. https://www.adidas-group.com/en/sustainability/social-impacts/supply-chain/#/training-and-empowering-suppliers/

Ait-Kadi, D., Chouinard, M., Marcotte, S., Riopel, D. (2012). "Sustainable Reverse Logistics Network: Engineering and Management" Wiley-ISTE: 35-87.

Alizon, F., Shooter, S., & Simpson, T. (2009). Henry Ford and the Model T: Lessons for Product Platforming and Mass Customization. *Design Studies*, 30(5), 588–605. DOI: 10.1016/j.destud.2009.03.003

Ballou, R. H. (2004). *Business Lojistik / Supply Chain Management* (5th ed.). Pearson Education.

Beazley, R. (1913). The Early History of the Compass and the First Scientific Maps. *History (London)*, 2(1), 46–52. https://www.jstor.org/stable/44991448

Boone, J. (2000). Competitive Pressure: The Effects on Investments in Product and Process Innovation. *The RAND Journal of Economics*, 31(3), 549–569. DOI: 10.2307/2601000

Bowersox, D. J. & Closs, D.J. (1996). *Lojistical Management: The Integrated Supply Chain Process.* McGraw-Hill Companies. 88-100.

Chopra, S., & Meindl, P. (2004). *Supply Chain Management Strategy, Planning, and Operation* (2nd ed.). Pearson Education International.

Coclanis, P. A. (Ed.). (2005). *The Atlantic Economy during the Seventeenth and Eighteenth Centuries: Organization, Operation, Practice, and Personnel.* University of South Carolina Press., DOI: 10.2307/j.ctv1169bdh

Coyle, J. J., Bardi, E. J., Langley, C. J. (2003). *The Management of Business Logistics, A Supply Chain Perspective.* South-Western, Thomson Learning. 13-174.

Dffreight. (2024). An Insight into Starbucks Supply Chain Strategy, https://dfreight.org/blog/an-insight-into-starbucks-supply-chain-strategy/

Doz, Y. L., Bartlett, C. A., & Prahalad, C. K. (1981). Global Competitive Pressures and Host Country Demands Managing Tensions in MNCs. *California Management Review*, 23(3), 63–74. DOI: 10.2307/41172603

Encyclopædia Britannica, Inc. n.d. https://www.britannica.com/money/Fordism

Frazelle, E. (2002). *Supply Chain Strategy, the Logistics of Supply Chain Management.* McGraw-Hill; 145-166.

Gelderblom, O., & Trivellato, F. (2019). The business history of the preindustrial world: Towards a comparative historical analysis. *Business History*, 61(2), 225–259. DOI: 10.1080/00076791.2018.1426750

Geography of Transport Systems. n.d. https://transportgeography.org/contents/chapter5/maritime-transportation/evolution-containerships-classes/

Grosser, P. (2010). The Fall of the Berlin Wall: The Revolutionary Legacy of 1989. *Cold War History*, 10(4), 578–579. DOI: 10.1080/14682745.2010.513513

Hwang, J., & Kim, Y. J. (2023). Challenges of Dark Stores and Urban Planning: A Case Study of B-Mart, *Seoul.* DOI:DOI: 10.20944/preprints202305.0084.v1

Hwarng, H. B., & Xie, N. (2008). Understanding supply chain dynamics: A chaos perspective. *European Journal of Operational Research*, 184(3), 1163–1178. DOI: 10.1016/j.ejor.2006.12.014

Ivanov, D. & Sokolov, B. (2010). *Adaptive Supply Chain Management.* Springer.

James, R. (2001). *Stock, Douglas M. Lambert, "Strategic Logistics Management"* (4th ed.). McGraw Hill.

Kee-hung Lai and T.C.E. Cheng, "Just-in-Time, Logistics", Gower: 47-108, 2009.

Kendall, R., & Tatiana, K. (2003). The Use of the Multinational Corporation as a Research Context. *Journal of Management*, 29(6), 883–902. DOI: 10.1016/S0149-2063(03)00083-7

Keskin, M. H. (2018a). *Tedarik Zinciri Yönetimi* (Vol. II). Baskı, Nobel Yayın Dağıtım.

Keskin, M. H. (2018b). *Lojistik El Kitabı* (Vol. III). Baskı, Nobel Yayın Dağıtım.

Keskin, M. H. (2020). *Warehousing, Explained for Making Money, Principles, Policies and Practices.* Sharp and Sharp Publishing.

Ketchen, D. J.Jr, & Craighead, C. W. (2020). Research at the intersection of entrepreneurship, supply chain management, and strategic management: Opportunities highlighted by COVID-19. *Journal of Management*, 46(8), 1330–1341. DOI: 10.1177/0149206320945028

Kildow, B. A. (2011). *A Supply Chain Management Guide to Business Continuity.* AMACOM Division of American Management Association International. https://www.jstor.org/stable/j.ctt1d2qzhb

Kuglin, F.A. (1998). *Customer-Centered Supply Chain Management (A link-by-link guide)*. American Management Assosication. 226-247.

Kumar, S., Tiwari, P., & Zymbler, M. (2019). Internet of Things is a Revolutionary Approach for Future Technology Enhancement: A Review. *Journal of Big Data*, 6(111), 111. Advance online publication. DOI: 10.1186/s40537-019-0268-2

Lyons, A. C., Mondragon, A. E. C., Piller, F., Poler, R. (2012). *Customer-Driven Supply Chains from Glass Pipelines to Open Innovation Networks*. Springer, 113-130.

Magistretti, S., Dell'Era, C., & Verganti, R. (2020). Searching for the Right Application: A Technology Development Review and Research Agenda. *Technological Forecasting and Social Change*, 151(119879), 119879. Advance online publication. DOI: 10.1016/j.techfore.2019.119879

Micheli, P., Johnson, M., & Godsell, J. (2021). Editorial How the Covid-19 pandemic has affected, and will affect, operations and supply chain management research and practice. International Journal of Operations &amp. *International Journal of Operations & Production Management*, 41(6), 773–780. DOI: 10.1108/IJOPM-06-2021-902

Moraga, C. (2005). Introduction to Fuzzy Logic. *Facta universitatis - series. Electronics and Energetics*, 18(2), 319–328. DOI: 10.2298/FUEE0502319M

Murphy, P. R., Jr., & Wood, D. F. (2004). "Contemporary Logistics", Eight Edition, Pearson Education International, Prentice Hall: 35-49.

National Geographic. (2024). Encyclopedic Entry: The Silk Road. https://education.nationalgeographic.org/resource/silk-road/

Peters, M. A. (2021). The ancient Silk Road and the birth of merchant capitalism. *Educational Philosophy and Theory*, 53(10), 955–961. DOI: 10.1080/00131857.2019.1691481

Petit, P. (1999). Structural Forms and Growth Regimes of the Post-Fordist Era. *Review of Social Economy*, 57(2), 220–243. DOI: 10.1080/00346769900000037

Piekkari, R., Welch, C., & Westney, D. E. (2022). The Challenge of the Multinational Corporation to Organization Theory: Contextualizing Theory. *Organization Theory*, 3(2). Advance online publication. DOI: 10.1177/26317877221098766

Raj, A., Mukherjee, A. A., de Sousa Jabbour, A. B. L., & Srivastava, S. K. (2022). Supply chain management during and post-COVID-19 pandemic: Mitigation strategies and practical lessons learned. *Journal of Business Research*, 142, 1125–1139. DOI: 10.1016/j.jbusres.2022.01.037 PMID: 35079190

Roberts, K. (2011). *The Origins of Business, Money, and Markets*. Columbia University Press., DOI: 10.7312/robe15326

Saha, S., Jana, B., & Poray, J. (2019). A Study on Blockchain Technology, *SSRN*, DOI: 10.2139/ssrn.3477373

Samsung. (2024). Shaping the Future Together: We Aim for a Sustainable Supply Chain, https://www.samsung.com/us/aboutsamsung/sustainability/environment/sustainable-supply-chain/

Samuelson, R. J. (2012). Revisiting the Great Depression. *The Wilson Quarterly*, 36(1), 36–43. https://www.jstor.org/stable/41484425

Sandro, N., Petar, Š., Diego, L. I. G. A., & Luigi, P. (2020). Internet of Things (IoT): Opportunities, Issues and Challenges towards a Smart and Sustainable Future. *Journal of Cleaner Production*, 274(22877), 122877. Advance online publication. DOI: 10.1016/j.jclepro.2020.122877 PMID: 32834567

Sarker, M. N. I., Hossin, M., Yin, X., & Sarkar, M. (2018). One Belt One Road Initiative of China: Implication for Future of Global Development. *Modern Economy*, 09(4), 623–638. DOI: 10.4236/me.2018.94040

Selimović, I. (2022). Advantages and Disadvantages of Principles of Scientific Management and Lean Organisation. *Izzivi prihodnost*, 7. DOI: DOI: 10.37886/ip.2022.001

Shapiro, J. F. (2001). *Modeling the Supply Chain*. Thomson Learning. 3-23.

Shea, E. (2024). The Silk Roads. https://smarthistory.org/reframing-art-history/the-silk-roads/

Shi, X., Liu, W., & Zhang, J. (2023). Present and future trends of supply chain management in the presence of COVID-19: A structured literature review. *International Journal of Logistics*, 26(7), 813–842. DOI: 10.1080/13675567.2021.1988909

Smith, A. (2018). *The Wealth of Nations*. CreateSpace Independent Publishing Platform.

Soonhong, M., Zach, G. Z., & Carlo, D. S. (2019). Defining Supply Chain Management: In the Past, Present, and Future. *Journal of Business Logistics*, 40(1), 44–55. Advance online publication. DOI: 10.1111/jbl.12201

Spalding, M. J. (1997). Lessons of NAFTA for APEC. *Journal of Environment & Development*, 6(3), 252–275. https://www.jstor.org/stable/44319277. DOI: 10.1177/107049659700600303

Srinivas, R. E., & Sanjeev, G. (2023). Review article: The Emerging Drone Technology and the Advancement of the Indian Drone Business Industry. *The Journal of High Technology Management Research*, 34(2), 100464. Advance online publication. DOI: 10.1016/j.hitech.2023.100464

Stadtler, H. (2002). *Christoph Kilger, "Supply Chain Management and Advance Planning, Concepts, models Software and Case Studies"* (2nd ed.). Springer.

Taylor, F. (2006). *The Principles of Scientific Management.* Cosimo Classics.

Waters, D. (2003). *Logistics: An Introduction to Supply Chain Management.* Palgrave MacMillan, 27-54.

Wilde, A. (2000). *The East India Company: Trade and Conquest.* The Lyons Press.

Xin, B., Zhang, F., Hu, Z., Yang, Y., & Ma, X. (2021). Complex Dynamics Analysis of Closed-Loop Supply Chain considering CSR and Fairness Concerns. *Discrete Dynamics in Nature and Society*, 2021, 1–23. Advance online publication. DOI: 10.1155/2021/7787420

KEY TERMS AND DEFINITIONS

Global Competition: Global competition refers to the intense rivalry among companies operating on an international scale to sell their goods and services. This competition has escalated significantly due to advancements in technology, transportation, and communication systems, which have facilitated easier access to global markets and streamlined supply chains. In essence, global competition has transformed traditional business landscapes, requiring companies to continuously strive for excellence and differentiation to succeed in an increasingly interconnected and competitive global marketplace.

International Trade: International trade encompasses the exchange of goods and services between companies located in different countries. This exchange includes a wide range of products, from consumer goods and raw materials to food and machinery, all traded within the global marketplace. By engaging in international trade, countries can diversify their sources of supply and expand their customer base, fostering economic growth and development. Furthermore, the competitive nature of international trade encourages efficiency and innovation among businesses, leading to improved product quality and competitive pricing. Additionally, some countries adopt policies of national treatment towards imported goods, treating them equally to domestically produced products. This practice promotes fair competition and facilitates the integration of foreign goods into domestic markets, benefiting consumers with a wider array of choices and potentially lower prices.

Logistics: Logistics, tracing its origins to the earliest human endeavors, can be defined as the systematic management of resources to accomplish specific objectives. The notion of "goal" varies widely, leading to the emergence of diverse logistical domains. For instance, healthcare logistics pertains to patient care, hotel logistics focuses on hospitality services, and disaster logistics aids in recovery efforts post-catastrophe events like earthquakes or floods. These categories expand to encompass various specialized fields such as military logistics, green logistics, maritime logistics, cold chain logistics, automotive logistics, railway logistics, and energy logistics, among others. This ongoing evolution has shaped the contemporary framework of business logistics, reflecting the dynamic nature of business operations in today's globalized economy.

Multinational Corporations: A multinational corporation is characterized by having business offices and operations in two or more countries across the globe. These companies typically maintain a central headquarters in their home country, from which they manage their international operations. It's important to note that merely exporting goods for sale abroad does not qualify a business as a multinational corporation. Instead, they engage in various activities beyond exporting, such as establishing subsidiaries, joint ventures, or wholly-owned operations in foreign markets. These companies often adapt their business strategies and operations to suit the diverse cultural, regulatory, and economic environments of the countries in which they operate. Moreover, MNCs may engage in global sourcing, production, marketing, and distribution activities to leverage advantages in different regions and enhance their competitive position in the global marketplace.

Post Fordist Era: Post-Fordism refers to a shift in production methods and labor relations that emerged following the decline of Fordist production practices. This transition is characterized by several key features, including flexible production techniques, the individualization of labor relations, and the fragmentation of markets into distinct segments. Post-Fordism emphasizes adaptability and responsiveness in production processes. Unlike the standardized and rigid assembly line methods of Fordism, flexible production allows for customization, rapid adjustment to changing demand, and the incorporation of new technologies. Post-Fordism sees a departure from the mass production model of Fordism towards more personalized and flexible labor arrangements. This may include the use of temporary or contract workers, as well as increased autonomy and responsibility for individual workers within the production process. Instead of mass-producing standardized goods for a homogeneous market, Post-Fordism recognizes the diversity of consumer preferences and seeks to target niche markets with specialized products. This fragmentation of markets into distinct segments allows for more targeted marketing strategies and product differentiation.

Silk Road: The Silk Road, despite its name, was not a single road but an extensive network of trade routes that spanned thousands of miles, connecting East and West for over 1,500 years. Originating from the Han dynasty's initiation of trade in 130 B.C.E. until the Ottoman Empire's closure of Western trade routes in 1453 C.E., this network played a crucial role in facilitating commerce and cultural exchange between Europe and East Asia. Beyond its economic significance, the silk road served as a conduit for the exchange of ideas, religions, and technologies, contributing to the enrichment of civilizations along its path. Multicultural cities flourished, serving as hubs of innovation and learning where diverse peoples interacted and exchanged knowledge. Its legacy continues to resonate in the interconnected world of today, underscoring the enduring power of exchange and collaboration across borders.

Supply Chain Management: SWCM is commonly defined as the orchestration of business logistics activities encompassing the design, planning, execution, control, and monitoring. The overarching goal is to generate net value, establish competitive infrastructure, harness global logistics, synchronize supply with demand, and evaluate performance on a global scale. This involves overseeing the movement and storage of raw materials, work-in-process inventory, finished goods, and end-to-end order fulfillment from origin to consumption. Supply chains consist of interconnected, interrelated, or interlinked networks, channels, and node businesses collaborating to deliver products and services to end customers efficiently and effectively.

Chapter 4
Global Supply Chain in Japan's IT Service Sector

Tetsuro Saisho
https://orcid.org/0000-0002-1470-8558
Kokushikan University, Japan

ABSTRACT

In today's global economy, global supply chains are being built in every business process from a perspective that transcends national and regional boundaries. In the past, efforts in building a global supply chain were initially focused on "visible products" of manufacturing and other industrial sectors. In recent years, however, the use of global supply chains in business strategies has spread beyond the manufacturing industry into such areas as the IT service sector, which target "invisible products." Many developing and emerging countries in Asia have excellent IT companies and engineers as the IT service sector is one of the most suitable industries for starting a new business because there is no need to collect large capital investments or hold inventories of materials and components. For this reason, there is a high entrepreneurial spirit in the IT service fields in developing and emerging countries. This paper discusses the current state and challenges of global supply chains in Japan's IT service sector, in which Japanese and overseas IT companies are involved.

INTRODUCTION

Supply chain is a means of business management which aims to improve efficiency, optimize operations, and reduce costs by comprehensively reviewing and upgrading all manufacturing and supply procedures of products or goods in the manufacturing

DOI: 10.4018/979-8-3693-9241-6.ch004

industry and various other industries. Supply chains cover the flow of goods from suppliers to final consumers, which can either be organizations or individuals.

In the manufacturing industry, the supply chain is generally characterized by the "flow of products," consisting of development, procurement of raw materials and parts, manufacturing (assembly and processing), logistics (transportation, storage, cargo handling, packaging, distribution, and information processing), intermediaries (wholesalers and middlemen), retail and sales (indirect and direct), and final consumption (by organizations and individuals). It can also be characterized by the "flow of money" based on purchases made by organizations and individuals and the "flow of information" that is generated in each process.

In the manufacturing industry, each process is analyzed and evaluated based on the status of these three flows. The results of the analysis and assessment are then shared, coordinated, and controlled to bolster efficiency, optimize operations, and cut costs of all processes, ranging from the procurement of raw materials and parts to the supply of finished products.

In recent years, most manufacturers have adopted the concept of management in their supply chains, from development to production and sales, and have achieved significant improvements. In addition, large manufacturers have established a global supply chain, which is a supply chain that encompasses multiple countries and regions, not just a single country or region.

Initially, the global supply chain was a concept and approach that focused on "tangible products," particularly in the manufacturing industry. However, in recent years, business strategies utilizing global supply chains have been developed in the IT service and other sectors as well, targeting "intangible assets."

In this paper[1], we discuss the actual state and challenges of global supply chains in Japan's IT service sector.

BACKGROUND

Manufacturing Industry and Global Supply Chain

During the period of significant yen appreciation beginning in the late 1980s, the Japanese manufacturing industry started accelerating the relocation of its production bases to overseas bases. Amid the rise of mass production and mass consumption of virtually all kinds of products in Japan, manufacturers, with major Japanese companies taking the lead, extended their reach to Asian countries and regions such as

China, Thailand, and Indonesia, where labor costs were low. There, they established factories one after another to significantly reduce production costs.

As manufacturers expanded their operations overseas, a new intra-Asian division of labor network was established, with companies in certain countries specializing in raw materials and parts, and those in other countries in intermediate production, final manufacturing and assembly, wholesale, or sales. Establishing a global supply chain covering numerous manufacturing bases became a focus in major companies' business management and planning.

Subsequently, due to the region's reputation for producing cost reduction effects, not only Japanese companies but also foreign companies in various industries and business sectors started expanding into developing countries and emerging economies in Asia. Furthermore, these countries are now attracting attention not only as locations for factories in the initial stages of the supply chain but also as markets for selling consumer goods.

A manufacturer is a company that produces its own or other party's (consignor's) brand product (OEM: Original Equipment Manufacturing) by assembling and processing raw materials and parts procured from suppliers, including subsidiaries and affiliated companies, and providing products to final consumers (end users) through direct sales or distributors (retailers).

Therefore, a manufacturer is not limited to a specific industry or type of business. Many of Japan's leading companies in the automotive, petrochemical, food, daily necessity, and apparel industries fall under the category of manufacturer. The automotive industry is a typical industry in which a global supply chain is constructed (SGAGSC, 2023). As shown in Figure 1, the automotive industry consists of tier 1 or primary contractors, tier 2 or secondary contractors, and tier 3 or tertiary contractors, with finished-product manufacturers at the top of the global supply chain structure (Saisho, 2024a) (Figure 1).

In the global supply chain, tier 1 manufacturers supply electrical components, car bodies, braking systems, and transmission parts to finished product manufacturers. tier 2 manufacturers supply components such as electronic parts, metal stamping, forging, casting, and car body parts to tier 1 manufacturers. Manufacturers in tier 3 and beyond supply tier 2 manufacturers with metal heat treatment, molds, plating, cutting, plastic products, springs, screws, and other components.

In terms of land transportation of raw materials, parts, and products in the global supply chain, there is also a hierarchical structure of subcontractors, including large, medium, small, and micro carriers in Japan and overseas. In some cases, railroad companies are also used.

In the global supply chain, the transport of raw materials, parts, and products is not limited to land transportation using trucks or railroads. For example, in the case of transportation across countries and regions, air transportation with airplanes is used. In this case, speed is prioritized over costs. Also, ships are used for mass transportation by sea. The optimal means must be considered based on the needs of each company.

One issue in truck transportation is that, depending on the destination, season, and other factors, trucks may be fully loaded on the way to the destination but not (or almost not) on the way back (one-load problem). This could lead to a decline in the truck utilization rate, which is the ratio of the distance actually traveled with the cargo loaded to the total distance. A low utilization comprises a cost issue for the business. In the manufacturing industry, supply chain management (SCM) between the location of suppliers and the actual manufacturing base is important. Thus, manufacturers must carefully consider where to set up their factories and production bases when they expand overseas.

Case of Global Supply Chains in Asia

Traditionally, SCM for the entire manufacturing process only covered a single country or region. This includes the procurement of raw materials and parts, manufacturing, inventory control, delivery, sales, and consumption. However, in the modern world, the logistics strategy by major manufacturers is to establish a global supply chain to procure raw materials and parts from business partners not only in one's own country but also in neighboring countries and regions. Such decisions are made based on a comprehensive judgment on how to achieve procurement in an optimal, timely and appropriate manner,

considering such aspects as quality, cost, and speed.

To ensure the timely and appropriate procurement of goods and components from other countries and regions, supernational organizations, in which nations are incorporated into a single regional unit, have been established. Representative examples are the European Union (EU) and the Association of South-East Asian Nations (ASEAN). In such supernational organizations, tariffs on trades within the region are exempted.

ASEAN was established in August 1967 by the original five member states of Indonesia, Malaysia, the Philippines, Singapore, and Thailand, which are located on the Indochina Peninsula and the South China Sea, under the "ASEAN Declaration" also known as the "Bangkok Declaration." Its purpose was to promote good neighborly relations and friendship. Subsequently, ASEAN was joined by Brunei in 1984, Vietnam in 1995, Laos and Myanmar in 1997, and Cambodia in 1999, bringing the total number of member countries to 10.

Figure 1. Global supply chain structure in the manufacturing (automotive) industry

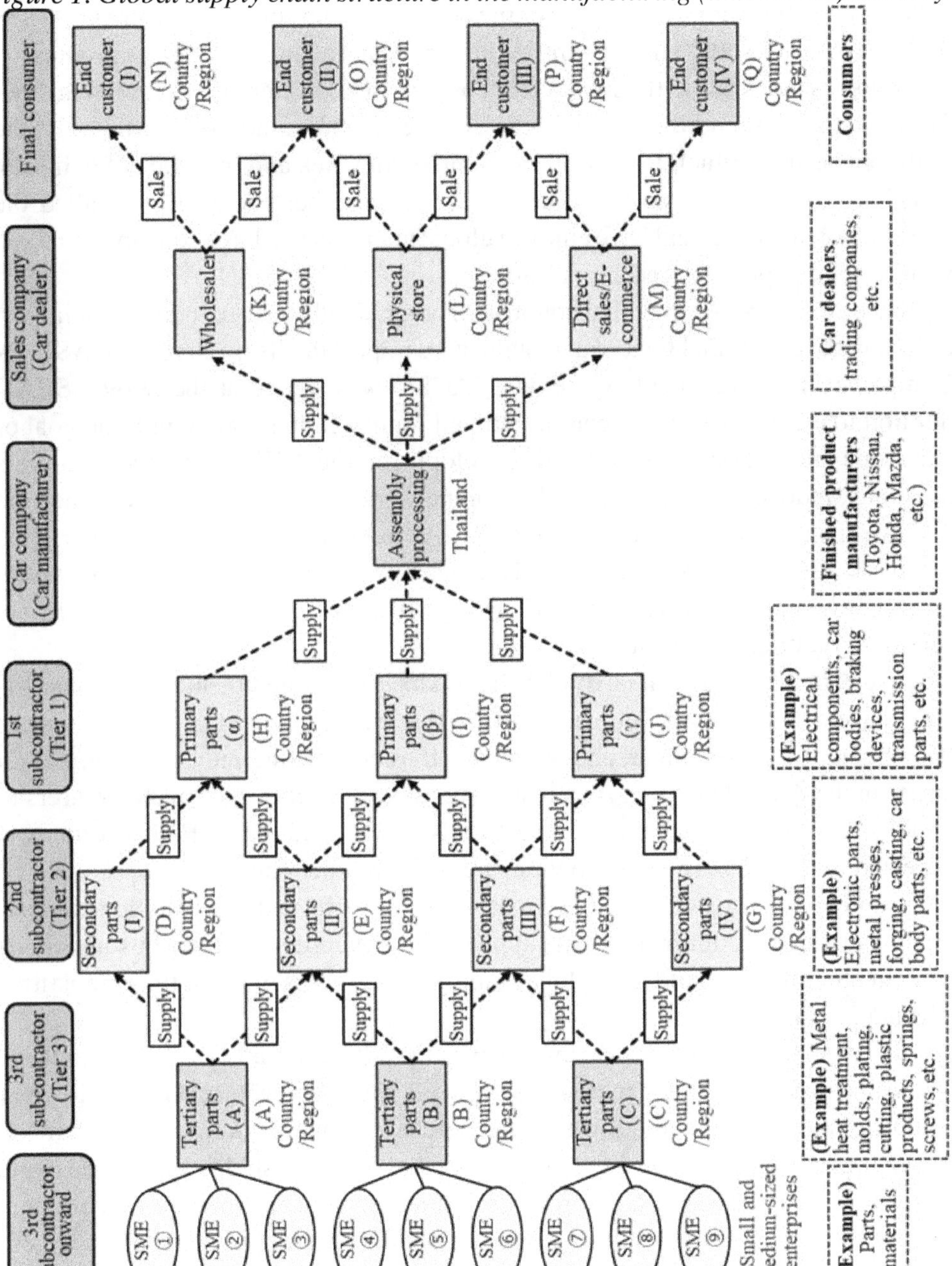

Source: Created by the author from Saisho T. (2024a). A Study on the Actual Situation of Global Supply Chains in ASEAN: Focusing on the Case of Japanese Auto Parts Company A. Kokushikan University bulletin of the Research Institute of Business.

The ASEAN members of Thailand, Vietnam, Cambodia, Laos, and Myanmar, located in the Indochina Peninsula, or the continental part of ASEAN, are known as the "ASEAN of Land." These countries have been attracting attention as production and logistics bases due to their low labor costs, with a constant rise in capital inflows from countries around the world. Meanwhile, Singapore, Indonesia, Malaysia, the Philippines, and Brunei, located in the South China Sea and the Malay Peninsula, constitute the maritime part of ASEAN. These member countries are called the "ASEAN of the Seas," and have enjoyed global attention as a huge consumer market, with its total population reaching 2 billion.

Since 2007, ASEAN member countries have gradually been reducing their import tariffs, with the original goal of achieving zero import tariffs by 2016. The ASEAN Comprehensive Investment Agreement (ACIA) was signed at the 2009 ASEAN Summit to create a free and open investment regime in the region with the goal of economic integration. Alongside this development, the ASEAN member countries of Brunei, Indonesia, Malaysia, the Philippines, Singapore, and Thailand signed the ASEAN Trade in Goods Agreement (ATIGA) in February of the same year. This is a basic agreement on trade in goods to achieve free movement of goods within the ASEAN region. Subsequently in January 2010, the elimination of tariffs by six ASEAN countries was achieved.

Furthermore, additional tariff elimination measures implemented on January 1, 2018 have resulted in zero import tariffs in the least developed ASEAN countries (Cambodia, Laos, Myanmar, and Vietnam), thus completing the elimination of all tariffs in the ASEAN region. As a result, it has become easier for manufacturers to establish global supply chains in the ASEAN region, and the ASEAN economy is expected to grow due to the inflow of capital from other countries.

Manufacturers are able to differentiate themselves from their rivals and competitors by creating an optimal global supply chain structure with their business partners. In other words, building a global supply chain serves to boost the competitive advantage of manufacturers.

In Japan, there was once a time of mass production and mass consumption, when all companies needed to do to earn profits was manufacture products in great volumes, and those products would be purchased by consumers without much marketing effort. In such an era, consumers were not interested in the efforts made by manufacturers toward planning or designing the concepts behind new product development or toward building a global supply chain for the efficient procurement of raw materials and parts.

Particularly, mass production and consumption expanded further as the country entered the bubble economy in the late 1980s. During this time, it became increasingly important to find the best way to mass produce goods. In other words, manufacturers concentrated their efforts in building a highly efficient global supply chain, including from the perspective of costs. In this way, global supply chain strategies were devised based solely on the manufacturers' perspective.

However, more recently, consumers and end users have also paying attention to the planning and development behind products. Since the 1980s, the environment surrounding the consumer has changed dramatically with the rapid progress in IT and acceleration of globalization. On the consumer side, preferences in products have diversified as their daily and social lives became more affluent. More specifically, consumers have come to value the quality, social context, and impact of products over quantity.

This has led to a rise in demand for the transition from a low-mix high-volume production model, in which a limited variety of products are produced in large quantities through mass production, to a high-mix low-volume production model, in which a wide range of products are produced in small quantities. Against this backdrop, manufacturers have inevitably been required to review not only their product lines but also their global supply chains utilizing state-of-the-art technologies.

Information Society and Global Supply Chains

Global supply chains that straddle countries and regions have been built riding on the arrival of the information society, with businesses utilizing cutting-edge technologies and innovative concepts such as IT, digital transformation (DX)[2], artificial intelligence (AI)[3], internet of things (IoT)[4], robotics (RPA: Robotic Process Automation)[5], 5th generation mobile communication method (5G)[6], big data[7], cloud computing[8], and extended reality (XR)[9].

Today's information society has brought an end to the era of mass production and consumption and with that, an end to the traditional global supply chains that supported the growth of Japanese manufacturers. At the same time, the business environment has changed dramatically in terms of not only manufacturing site (production) but also distribution site (logistics).

In today's society, manufacturers are required to quickly plan, develop, and produce products that meet the diversifying needs of end users and deliver them to the market in a timely and appropriate manner. This means that manufacturers have had to shift from a small-mix high-volume production model based on mass production and consumption to a high-mix low-volume production model. In addition, the demand for prompt deliveries has also risen.

Some manufacturers have introduced build-to-order (BTO)[10] production, in which they receive orders (including direct sales) from end users (organizations or individuals), procure raw materials and parts, manufacture and ship the products on a case-by-case basis. In such cases, the global supply chain is largely oriented toward the perspective of end users. The process has become more complex accompanying the active incorporation of the end user's perspective.

In recent years, research on global supply chains has focused on the relationship with the global value chain, ASEAN, socioeconomic system selling (benefits), the Sustainable Development Goals (SDGs)[11], small and medium-sized enterprises (SMEs), new models of manufacturing and sales, resilience (recovery, resilience, and endurance), and the digital age.

GLOBAL SUPPLY CHAIN OF IT SERVICE SECTOR

Global Supply Chain of Animation Industry

As mentioned above, the global supply chain has been a mechanism to optimize the entire flow of products in the manufacturing industry, from the procurement of raw materials, through manufacturing, inventory management, logistics, and sales to the end user. It is a mechanism to achieve the timely and appropriate delivery of products, not only domestically but also internationally.

Today, industries other than the manufacturing sector are also working to optimize their supply chain both in and outside of Japan. For example, Japan's animation industry is increasingly employing an international division of labor. It initially started off with a supply chain based on a domestic division of labor and then moved on to a global supply chain system that involves companies across national and regional borders (Saisho, 2010).

The animation industry is labor-intensive, and thus labor costs are directly reflected in animation production costs. The reality is that many of these operations are outsourced to companies in overseas countries and regions.

Based on this background of the animation industry, the production work of the modern animation industry can be roughly divided into the processes shown in Figure 2: scriptwriting, direction, original picture, animation (drawing), coloring, background, and filming, release, and promotion at each stage (Hanzawa, 2013; Akima et al., 2015) (Figure 2). Among these processes, the more labor-intensive elements of drawing and coloring images tend to be outsourced to contractors in overseas countries and regions.

In animation production, it is assumed that the work of a certain process can only begin after receiving the deliverables of the previous process. This makes it easy to separate each process and facilitate progress management, quality control, and project management (Ichifuji, 2022).

Thus, a global supply chain system has been established in the animation industry with an international division of labor, where each operation is handled separately in a certain country or region.

In addition, the animation industry has experienced a fundamental reform in its business operations and processes accompanying the shift in the format of its deliverables, from analog handwritten paper-based media to digital file media. This has also helped promote the establishment of global supply chains, as digital deliverables can be checked and sent or received via the internet.

Figure 2.

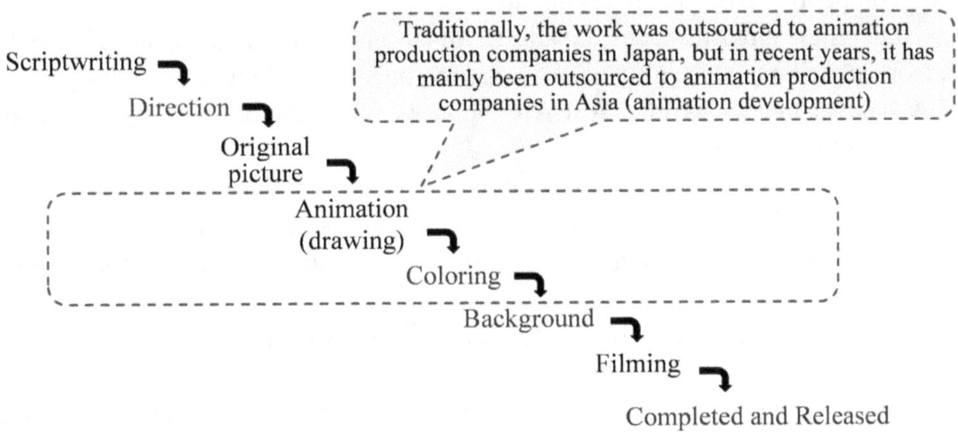

Source: Created by the author Saisho, T. (2024c). Ajia ni okeru guroobaru sapurai cheen ni kansuru kousatu [A study on global supply chains in Asia: A case study of global supply chains in the IT service Sector]. Globalization Research.

In Japan, the animation industry in the 1960s underwent a major transformation with the advent of the TV animation era. In response to the need for mass production, the business model transformed from in-house animation production by a single company to production by multiple companies utilizing a supply chain (outsourced production).

In the 1970s, the animation industry faced a management challenge in its operations. Namely, the cost of labor became a heavy burden in animation production. Personnel expenses had traditionally been a major weight when outsourcing animation production to domestic Japanese companies. Therefore, Japanese animation production companies went through a second major transformation to introduce a global supply chain system, outsourcing certain processes to companies in overseas countries and regions such as China, Korea, and Taiwan, in order to reduce labor costs in animation production.

The reason why East Asia was the main focus when outsourcing parts of the production process to overseas companies was because the time difference between Japan and these countries and regions is generally 2 to 3 hours. Thus, companies in each country and region can respond in real time (confirmation, questions, failure response, etc.).

For a long while, processes outsourced to overseas companies were mostly those at the downstream. The dependency on overseas outsourcing by Japanese animation production firms in animation and coloring was said to have reached approximately 40% in 2004, which is about two decades ago (Yamaguchi. Eds., 2004).

In the late 1980s and 1990s, companies in China, South Korea, and Taiwan enhanced their capabilities in downstream processes. However, they gradually lost their competitive edge due to rising labor costs.

Under these circumstances, Japanese animation production companies began to outsource their more labor-intensive work to companies in Thailand, the Philippines, Malaysia, Vietnam, and other ASEAN countries, where the benefits of lower labor costs could be expected.

To the present day, the Japanese animation industry has been utilizing overseas contractors for animation production. In particular, for the animation process, which is labor-intensive work, more than 80% of the task is dependent on overseas contractors.

System Development Industry and Global Supply Chain

The IT service industry does not involve the physical movement of tangible goods but instead, exchanges digitized files and data via the internet. As such, it is an industry in which transactions across countries and regions is easy. System development falls under the IT service industry.

In the case of the animation production in the contents industry described in the previous section, processes and procedures can be divided into separate clusters by reviewing the overall operation. Each process is carried out utilizing the deliverables of the preceding process. Over the years, labor-intensive processes in animation production have been outsourced to overseas subcontractors in certain regions. In this way, the animation industry has built a track record in international division of labor over its long history. This has led to the establishment of a global supply chain system centered on overseas countries and regions. A major factor that has made this global supply chain possible is the transformation in the industry's business practice. More specifically, deliverables in animation production shifted from physical objects such as paper to digital media such as files.

The same can be said for system development in the IT service sector. By reviewing and analyzing all processes involved in system development, it is possible to divide such processes into individual tasks and allocate such tasks to specialists of each field, thereby designing an adequate division of labor.

Each process in system development can only commence after the goal of the previous process has been achieved. In other words, each process depends entirely on receiving high-quality deliverables of the immediately preceding process.

Among those processes, mainly labor-intensive tasks are outsourced to overseas companies. Thus, establishing a global supply chain translates to making a shift toward offshore development primarily in labor-intensive work.

Therefore, it can be said that the system development industry resembles the animation industry in that it is possible to construct a global supply chain by separating tasks and assigning them to different companies in different countries or region.

In Japan, as shown in Table 1, the real annual GDP (% of the previous year) of the domestic economy has stagnated, but the number of system development projects and sales have increased (METI, 2019; METI, 2024; Cabinet Office, 2024) (Table 1). However, there is a chronic shortage of IT engineers related to system development, as well as the problem of a noticeable aging of domestic human resources. Therefore, as a measure to supplement IT human resources in Japan, systems are increasingly being developed offshore (IPA-SIC. Eds., 2020; MIAC, 2021).

IT engineers include system engineers who design and develop systems and software, web engineers who design and develop websites and web applications, infrastructure engineers who build the infrastructure that runs the systems, and bridge engineers who negotiate with management, manage projects, and facilitate offshore development projects.

Offshore development mainly consists of the downstream operations in system development.

Table 1. Trends in Japan's real annual GDP (% change from previous year) and sales of the information service industry (past 10 years)

Year	Real GDP (% change from previous year)	Information services sales	Number of IT human resources supplied	Number of IT human resources shortage	Average age of IT human resources
	(%)	(million yen)	(people)	(people)	(years old)
2014	-0.4	10,632,784	915,052		38.7
2015	1.7	10,796,754	918,921	170,700	39
2016	0.8	10,993,032	921,082	194,608	39.2
2017	1.8	11,321,617	922,491	218,976	39.5
2018	0.2	11,583,822	923,094	243,805	39.7
2019	-0.8	12,064,266	923,273	268,655	39.9
2020	-3.9	12,910,208	923,002	293,499	40.2
2021	2.8	15,296,981	919,924	320,638	40.3
2022	1.6	15,998,202	916,447	347,611	40.5
2023	1.2	16,989,262	912,370	374,564	40.6

Source: Created by the author based on Ministry of Economy, Trade and Industry (METI). (2019). IT jinzai jyukyuu ni kansuru chousa (gaiyo) [Survey on IT human resources supply and demand (summary)]. Dejitaru jinzai no ikusei [Developing Digital Human Resources]; Ministry of Economy, Trade and Industry (METI). (2024). Jouhou saabisu gyoukai [Information services industry]. Tokutei saabisu sangyou doutai toukei chousa [Statistical Survey of Specific Service Industries]; and Cabinet Office. (2024). Nenji GDP seichouritsu [Annual GDP growth rate]. Kokumin keizai keisan (GDP toukei) [National Economic Accounts (GDP Statistics)].

The waterfall model, shown in Figure 3, is a traditional and common system development model that often involves a global division of labor. In this model, system development is divided into tasks and organized into a sequential order, with one following the other. This can be likened to water falling down and not going back. Each process kicks off after the output of the previous process is handed over. The model is especially fit for large-scale system developments, with different specialized companies being responsible for each process.

Meanwhile, the current mainstream in the development of web systems is the agile software development (ASD) model[12]. It is a more flexible method in which processes are divided into smaller units but are not necessary lined up in sequence. Feedback, requirement changes, and corrections can be integrated into every process even as the project progresses, and as such, coding and testing can be repeated as necessary with the aim of maximizing the value of the final deliverable.

The waterfall model is used in more large-scale system developments, for which agile development is said to be unsuitable. In the waterfall model, processes and steps are separated, and each independent process becomes subject to progress, quality, issue, change, and risk management. This makes it an ideal development method for large-scale system developments. As shown in Figure 3, in the waterfall model, the system development process is roughly divided into the following: requirement analysis, functional design (high-level design), technical design (low-level design), coding and implementation, unit testing, integration testing, functional testing (user acceptance testing), and deployment, migration, and release. A global supply chain system has been established in line with the international division of labor, with each of these operations being handled separately or in the same country or region.

Figure 3. Main business processes and global supply chain in the system development industry

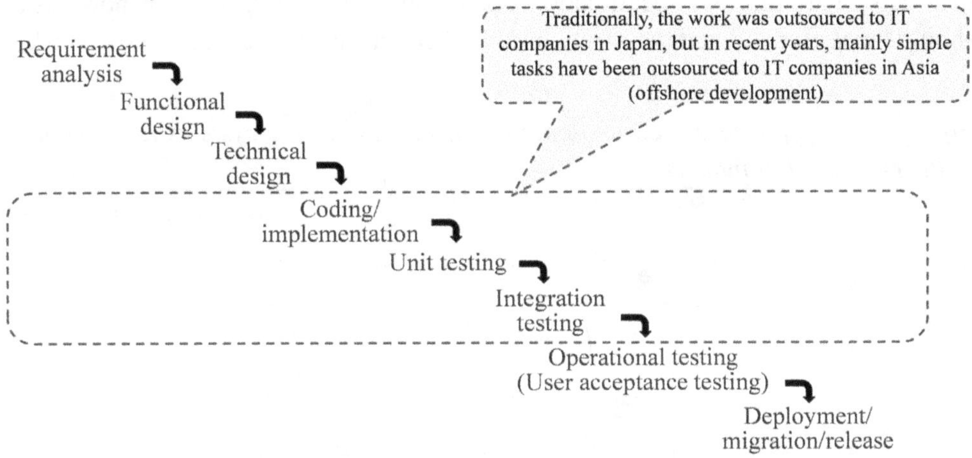

Source: Created by the author Saisho, T. (2024c). Ajia ni okeru guroobaru sapurai cheen ni kansuru kousatu [A study on global supply chains in Asia: A case study of global supply chains in the IT service Sector]. Globalization Research.

This paper will take a deep dive into the waterfall model in system development and consider the current state and issues in the global supply chain in this industry.

In the case of the system development industry, the global supply chain consists of offshore developments. In a global supply chain based on the waterfall model, processes/projects flow in sequence from upstream to downstream, with each phase cascading into the next like a waterfall. As mentioned earlier, each process can only be initiated after receiving the deliverables of the process in the previous phase. System development based on the waterfall model can generally be illustrated as shown in Figure 4, with a broad classification between two categories: product development and quality management (Saisho, 2024b) (Figure 4). Product development, shown on the left half of Figure 4, can consist of requirements analysis and definition, functional and technical design (external and internal design), program design, and programming and coding. Meanwhile, quality management, shown on the right half, can consist of unit testing, acceptance testing, link testing, system testing, user testing, operational testing, and production release. By broadly dividing the phases into development and management, the progress and scope can be visualized, which is an advantage especially in large-scale projects.

Currently, offshore development mostly takes place in the downstream processes of the waterfall model, such as programming and coding.

As a characteristic of the Japanese business style, there is the concept of tacit knowledge, which is a way of moving business forward based on a consensus or shared knowledge among all relevant parties that is not clearly written in business contracts or design and specification documents. This could include how tasks should be carried out and what outcomes and effects are expected from such tasks.

Figure 4. Example of a global supply chain process in the systems development industry (waterfall model)

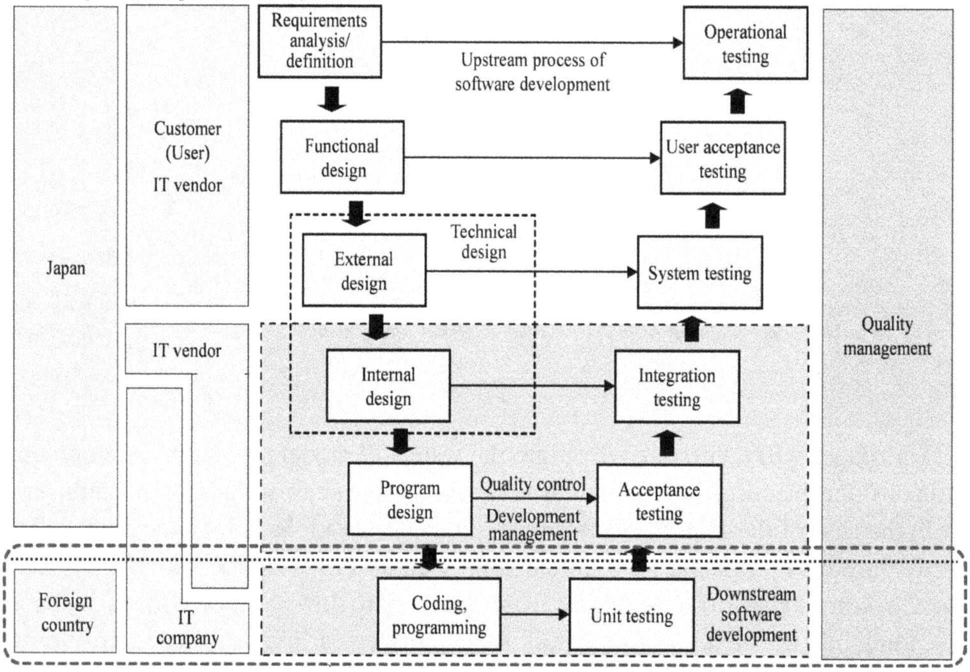

Source: Created by the author Saisho T. (2024b). Saisho, T. (2024b). Shikisha ni kiku: Shikisha ga shimesu sofuto kaihatsu no "guroobaru sapurai cheen" gijutsu busoku to guroobaruka, futatsu no keieikadai wo kaiketsu suru hinto towa [Ask the experts: Experts' hints for solving two management issues, shortage of engineers in the global supply chain for software development and globalization]. Global Vision 2024 Handout. FPT Japan Holdings.

On the other hand, companies in many other countries and regions operate based on the concept of formal knowledge. This means that tasks and expected outcomes and effects are explicitly and objectively specified in business contracts or design and specification documents to avoid misunderstandings.

Therefore, when Japanese companies outsource development to offshore counterparts, they must be aware of this difference and make an effort to value the business styles and values of overseas companies rather than imposing their own customary practices and business practices.

It should be noted that the shortage of engineers is a problem not only in Japan but across the globe, especially among developed countries. Companies in many other developed countries are also seeking talented engineers from countries and regions with low labor costs. Thus, the labor market for Asian engineers is extremely tight. Under the rapid depreciation of the yen that began around mid-March 2022, the Japanese market is not as attractive as it used to be for overseas IT subcontractors in Asian countries. Such subcontractors might not be willing to take project orders from Japanese companies any longer if they are forced to collaborate based on tacit knowledge.

Business-Specific System Development and Global Supply Chain

It is expected that a change will occur in the dynamics of the global supply chain going forward as overseas subcontractors become more adept in upstream processes by accumulating system development experience and skills, while becoming more proficient in Japanese and fostering an understanding toward the difference between tacit and formal knowledge.

Offshore development can take two forms: (1) outsourced contract development and (2) laboratory-based development. (1) In outsourced contract development, the offshore IT company develops the system based on the specifications and requirements prepared by the client and delivers the deliverables by the deadline set at the time of the contract. (2) In laboratory-based development, the offshore personnel (engineers) of overseas IT companies are dispatched to the client and develop the system under the clients' instructions. A dispatch contract is concluded for a fixed period of time.

In recent years, Japanese IT companies have been outsourcing not only simple labor-intensive task within the entire development process but also the development of entire subsystems. Subsystems are independent modules focused on a certain function within a client's internal system, as shown in Figure 5 (Saisho, 2024c) (Figure 5). For example, the entire development process of an individual module, such as the HR or accounting system, can be outsourced separately to offshore subcontractors.

Figure 5. Internal system and individual modules

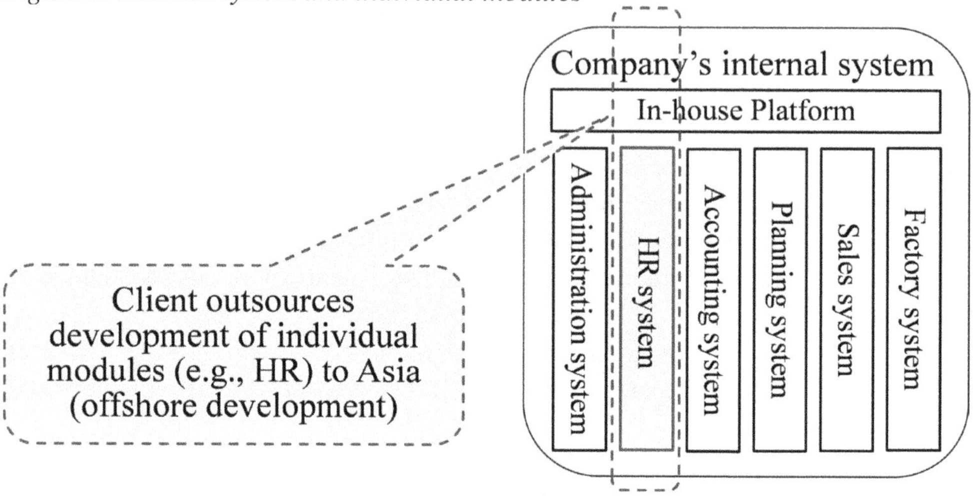

Source: Created by the author Saisho, T. (2024c). Ajia ni okeru guroobaru sapurai cheen ni kansuru kousatu [A study on global supply chains in Asia: A case study of global supply chains in the IT service Sector]. Globalization Research.

When outsourcing the development of individual modules to offshore subcontractors, it is possible to classify the modules further into individual tasks, as shown in Figure 6. This is similar to the division of labor seen in the automobile industry (Saisho, 2024c) (Figure 6). The development of each individual task can then be outsourced to different companies in overseas countries and regions.

In the system development industry, global supply chains that span countries and regions can be built because it is possible to develop systems for each individual task. In this case, each individual task is basically independent and not affected by the data or processes of other tasks.

Figure 6. Individual Human Resource Tasks

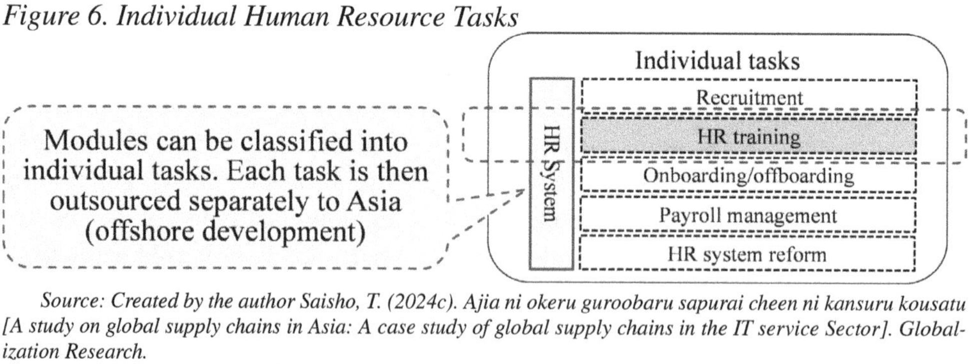

Source: Created by the author Saisho, T. (2024c). Ajia ni okeru guroobaru sapurai cheen ni kansuru kousatu [A study on global supply chains in Asia: A case study of global supply chains in the IT service Sector]. Globalization Research.

TYPES OF GLOBAL SUPPLY CHAINS IN THE SYSTEM DEVELOPMENT INDUSTRY

Outsourced Development and Global Supply Chain

As shown in Table 2, system development types can be illustrated as a matrix, placing outsourcing (external system development using the resources of other companies) and in-house (internal system development using the resources of the company itself or its group companies) on the vertical axis, and onshore or near-shore (domestic system development) and offshore (overseas system development) on the horizontal axis. (Saisho, 2014) (Table 2).

Table 2. Types of system development

	Onshore (domestic)	Offshore (overseas)
Outsourcing/ external resources <resources of other companies>	Domestic (onshore) outsourced development <resources of domestic IT company>	Overseas (offshore) outsourced development <resources of overseas IT company>
In-house/ internal resources <resources of own company>	Domestic (onshore) in-house development <regular and temporary employees>	Overseas (offshore) in-house development <employees of overseas subsidiaries, group companies, or branches>

Source: Created by the author Saisho, T. (2014). Chuugoku to betonamu no inobeeshon shisutemu [Dai 2 han] [Innovation systems in China and Vietnam [2nd edition]]. Hakuto-Shobo.

Based on this matrix, the types of software development can be described as follows. In the upper left box is onshore or near-shore (domestic) outsourcing, in which system development is outsourced to contractors or IT vendors in Japan.

In the upper right box is offshore (overseas) outsourcing, in which system development is outsourced to contractors or IT vendors in other countries and regions.

In the lower left box is onshore (domestic) in-house development, in which the company's own regular and temporary workers develop the system in Japan.

In the lower right box is offshore (overseas) in-house development, in which regular and temporary workers of the company's overseas subsidiaries, group companies, or branches are responsible for developing the system.

Thus, there are four different forms of system development depending on whether tasks are carried out within or outside of Japan and whether an external vendor is used or not.

In today's business environment, it is virtually impossible for major companies to build their own systems using only the resources and environment of their own company or group (excluding temporary employees). Therefore, system development is dependent on a domestic or global supply chain, utilizing not only the company's own resources but also those of other more specialized companies.

System Development and Global Supply Chain

In the global supply chain for system development, the main constituents are the client, the IT vendor, and overseas subcontractors (offshore IT companies).

Clients request the development of a new system, software or network, the addition of new functions to existing products, or the customization of package software (e.g., data linkage[12]) to the IT vendor. Clients can include companies, government agencies, independent administrative agencies, and various other organizations. They request IT vendors to develop systems for them as they normally do not have their own system development team, environment, or sufficient know-how.

IT vendors are IT companies that develop and sell new systems and software to a client, add new functions to a client's existing systems, or customize packaged software at the request of the client. IT vendors can broadly be classified into system vendors, who specialize in selling systems including packaged software, and system integrator vendors (SI vendors)[13], also called system integrators (Sier)[14], who plan, develop, operate, and maintain systems at the request of a third party.

In Japan, the IT industry related to system development has a pyramid-shaped multi-tiered subcontracting structure. At the top are first-tier contractors. This includes major Japanese IT companies represented by Fujitsu, NEC, and Hitachi. This is followed by second-tier contractors that receive orders from the major IT companies, third-tier contractors that receive orders from the second-tier contractors, and then fourth-tier, fifth-tier, and other lower-tier IT companies, forming a pyramid structure.

In the pyramid structure of Japan's IT industry, the number of companies and talents (IT human resources) is smaller in the upper tiers and larger in the lower tiers.

The IT companies at the lower levels of the pyramid are very often small and medium-sized or micro companies that do not have any interactions with the client of the project. It is not uncommon for them to only be responsible for the coding part of the entire development, or the development of a certain module or component within the entire system being developed.

In contrast, the IT industry of other Asian countries and regions can be characterized by the absence of the multi-tier pyramid structure that is common in Japan.

For example, in Vietnam, there are many small and medium-sized and micro companies in the IT industry. However. FPT, which is the country's leading IT company, does not form a subcontracting hierarchical structure with micro- to medium-sized IT companies. This is because in Vietnam's IT industry, business is basically conducted on the basis of a flat relationship rather than a hierarchal one between IT companies.

Participants of the global supply chains in the IT industry include clients (end users), contractors such as IT vendors, and overseas subcontractors to which development is outsourced. The types of global supply chains in the IT industry can be broadly divided into five: (1) simple global supply chain (simple bridge offshore development), (2) modified global supply chain (modified bridge offshore development), (3) direct global supply chain (direct offshore development), (4) modified direct global supply chain (modified direct offshore development), and (5) indirect global supply chain (indirect global offshore development) (Saisho, 2014).

(1) Simple global supply chain (simple bridge offshore development)

This is an offshore development model commonly practiced in Japan.

In this type of global supply chain, a Japanese client (e.g., a company or governmental organization) places an order for system development with Japanese IT vendor Company A. Company A then outsources some labor-intensive functions to an overseas IT firm Company B. The IT industry, like the animation industry, is labor-intensive in many respects, and as such, all labor costs are directly reflected in system development costs. In a simple global supply chain, the Japanese IT vendor is responsible for the high value-added aspects of the system development project, such as requirement analysis/definition and functional design, while overseas subcontractors with lower labor costs are responsible for the labor-intensive tasks, such as programming and coding.

In a simple global supply chain, no communication takes place between the client and the offshore subcontractors. In other words, only the Japanese IT vendor communicates to the offshore subcontractor regarding development tasks. Such communication does not involve the movement of goods and is conducted using the internet or a virtual private network (VPN)[15], which is a virtual private line using the internet that can eliminate security concerns.

(2) Modified global supply chain (modified bridge offshore development)

This is a form of global supply chain in which the client outsources system development directly to an overseas IT company rather than an IT vendor in Japan. The client might outsource development to its own overseas base, or an overseas base of a Japanese IT vendor. In this type of global supply chain, two communication methods exist.

In the first method, the Japanese client uses shared services (intra-group outsourcing) with their own overseas subsidiary Company A. Company A then outsources labor-intensive operations of some functions to local IT firm Company B.

In the second method, the Japanese client orders system development to a Japanese IT vendor's local subsidiary Company C. Company C then outsources labor-intensive processes of certain functions to local IT firm Company B.

In both communication methods, the client does not interact directly with Company B but communicates directly with Company A, its overseas base, or Company C, the local subsidiary of a Japanese IT vendor.

(3) Direct global supply chain (direct offshore development)

This is a form of global supply chain in which clients directly outsource offshore development to overseas IT companies (not including their own overseas offices) without going through an IT vendor in Japan.

Japanese clients use this model when they do not have their own overseas base. The Japanese client outsources some labor-intensive functions to Company A, a local IT company. As the client does not go through a domestic IT vendor or its own overseas bases, significant cost reduction effects can be expected.

The client communicates directly with Company A. Thus, the client will need to have a high level of IT-related knowledge as well as high language skills in English or the local language to be able to communicate closely with Company A.

(4) Modified direct global supply chain (modified direct offshore development)

This is a form of global supply chain system in which the client outsources offshore development directly to an overseas IT company without going through an IT vendor in Japan and then dispatches its own engineers to the development site.

The Japanese client outsources some labor-intensive functions to Company A, an overseas IT company. In addition, the client dispatches its own engineers to Company A to facilitate operations in cases where there is still some uncertainty about communication.

This type of system development is not intermediated by a domestic IT vendor or the company's own overseas offices and can thus lead to large cost reductions. However, costs will incur to dispatch engineers to the offshore site.

The client communicates with the overseas IT firm Company A through the dispatched engineers. Such engineers will need to have a high level of IT expertise and language skills in either English or the local language to be dispatched and carry out their duties.

(5) Indirect global supply chain (indirect global offshore development)

This is a form of global supply chain in which overseas subsidiaries of Japanese companies or overseas companies are the client. Development is outsourced directly to overseas IT companies.

The foreign client Company A (such as an overseas subsidiary of a Japanese company) places an order for system development with a Japanese IT vendor. The Japanese IT vendor then outsources some of the labor-intensive functions to overseas IT company B. Since the client is an overseas company (including overseas subsidiaries of a Japanese company), revenue is based on US dollars and is thus affected by the exchange rate.

Communication is required between the Japanese IT vendor and the overseas client Company A as well as overseas IT company B.

ESTABLISHMENT AND ISSUES OF GLOBAL SUPPLY CHAIN

Establishment of Global Supply Chain

(1) Manufacturing industry

In the manufacturing industry, the main purpose of establishing a global supply chain is to reduce the costs of labor, materials, and logistics through local procurement, distribution, and production, while expanding overseas operations.

In ASEAN, Thailand and Vietnam have been setting up mother factories in their own countries and labor-intensive factories in neighboring Cambodia and Laos. Both Thailand and Vietnam are establishing global supply chains with neighboring countries because there is less risk in terms of logistics, including transportation time and costs.

One of the reasons that global supply chains have become more popular in ASEAN is because all tariffs were eliminated in principle on January 1, 2018 within the region. Back in 2010, tariffs in several of the member countries were eliminated under the ASEAN Trade in Goods Agreement (ATIGA). Subsequently, in 2018, the least developed ASEAN of Cambodia, Laos, Myanmar, and Vietnam (CLMV) abolished tariffs in principle.

Companies outside of the ASEAN region can also take measures against tariffs by building a global supply chain that incorporates ASEAN countries.

Meanwhile, tariffs of many products were either removed or lowered in 15 countries including Japan and ASEAN, which account for 30% of the world's population and gross domestic product (GDP), under the Regional Comprehensive Economic Partnership (RCEP) Agreement, signed in 2020.

The establishment of global supply chains has also been driven by the introduction of an integrated trade data platform, which digitalizes and consolidates the trade operations and data of domestic and foreign importers and exporters, transportation and logistics companies, port facilities, customs and import/export supervisory authorities, banks, insurance companies, and other relevant players.

Until now, the IT integration of trade operations had been considered unfeasible due to the complexity in information exchange among the participants scattered across different countries and regions.

However, the introduction of the trade information platform has made it possible to smoothly conduct operations among trade participants in various countries and regions. This has helped reduce complicated procedures, thereby leading to the active establishment of global supply chains.

(2) System development industry

In the past, the only choice of destination for offshore system development by Japanese IT companies was China from the perspective of requiring proficiency in Japanese when collaborating. However, since then, Japanese language education has been spreading throughout ASEAN. In addition, driven by active trades and a closer economic relationship, the use of Japanese has been increasing in business scenes as well.

For example, in the case of Vietnam, Japanese language education from the third grade of elementary school was introduced on a trial basis in a total of five schools in Hanoi and Ho Chi Minh City from 2016 under the National Foreign Language Project. Japanese language education has since been officially introduced in two elementary schools, 81 junior high schools, and 36 high schools in 10 of the 63 provinces and cities in Vietnam (as of February 2021) (JF, 2023). Accompanying this, the number of students studying in Japan has increased, as has the number of such students staying in the country after graduation and finding employment. Many have even started their own IT business upon returning to Vietnam. To top it off the young people of Vietnam tend to have a very high entrepreneurial spirit and to be extremely self-motivated.

Such movements are also reflected in the rising number of foreign students in Japan, standing at 231,146 in 2022. Among this, figure, 103,882 (44.9%) were from China, 37,405 (16.2%) from Vietnam, and 24,257 (10.5%) from Nepal (as of May 2022) (JASSO, 2023).

In general, offshore development relies on the use of bridge SEs[16] to bridge the language barrier between the outsourcer (company in Japan) and the outsourcee (local system engineers in country to which operations are outsourced). Since there are currently many local engineers in Vietnam who are fluent in Japanese, including those who have studied in Japan, some IT companies can now directly communicate with the outsourcer in Japanese.

In the past, large-scale system developments used to only be outsourced to Chinese IT companies, which tended to have employees who were fluent in Japanese. Today, however, there are many IT companies in ASEAN countries and regions that can provide Japanese support. In addition, ASEAN IT firms are currently capable of developing systems at the same quality level and using the same technology as companies in China and India. Therefore, it is expected that the shortage in Japanese system engineers can be resolved on a wider scale. In addition, development expenses can be reduced as ASEAN countries tend to have lower labor costs than China.

Issues of Global Supply Chain

(1) Manufacturing industry

As global supply chains straddle countries and regions, it could be difficult to grasp the accurate situation of each company or base involved.

In addition, laws, business practices, tax system, culture, currency, and settlement methods differ from country to country and region to region. Thus, the logistics involved in a global supply chain can be very complex and prone to a variety of risks.

In terms of currency and settlement, there are exchange rate risks as well accompanying the growing trend toward US dollarization and Chinese yuanization. Such internationalization of the US and Chinese currencies are beyond the control of the monetary policy of each country.

Also, in recent years, there is a rise in the security risk of supply chains being cyberattacked. Malicious organizations or even individuals can infiltrate the target company's network for example, by eavesdropping on e-mail communications between the target company and its trading partner and sending a forged e-mail to the target company while pretending to be the trading partner. Supply chain attacks can be classified into two categories. One attacks the target company's business partners or affiliates that have inadequate security measures, as seen in the example with the fraudulent email above. The other type involves installing malicious programs or products updates to the target company's IT devices, software, or network. Such security risks tend to become higher when overseas counterparts are involved in the supply chain. This is because communication networks tend to be more difficult to monitor, leading to security weaknesses.

(2) System development industry

In offshore system development, it is sometimes impossible to fully understand the political and geological risks of the country or region to which operations are outsourced. It is thus necessary to understand the differences in laws and regulations, culture, and business styles. For example, when outsourcing system development, it is essential to acknowledge the gap between tacit and formal knowledge, clearly define the scope of tasks and division of roles, and secure an adequate means of communication (e.g., in Japanese or English).

It is also necessary to ensure the quality of deliverables (e.g., systems, software, documents) since there may be a gap in the expectations for quality level between different countries and cultures.

In addition, there is always a risk of information leakage, including of programs, software, documents, or data. Deliverables could also be copied and provided to third parties due to the lack of awareness of intellectual property rights and compliance specific to each country. It is therefore vital to consider security measures with great care.

Furthermore, in the case that the offshore subcontractor has a policy of "bring your own device (BYOD)"[17] (the use of a personal terminal for work), it is highly possible that an engineer's personal device might not have a high-quality security software installed. As such, care must be taken to avoid the allowance of such business styles in offshore development projects.

Lastly, outside of Japan, system engineers frequently engage in job-hopping, following the Western style of designing one's career. This is where talents repeatedly change jobs in a relatively short period of time in search of better compensation and to enhance their skills, or because they are not fully satisfied with the human relations or work assignments in their current workplace. Thus, it is necessary to keep in mind that the assignment of offshore engineers should not be considered permanent, as would be the case in a traditional Japanese work environment.

CONCLUSION

The benefits that companies can gain from adopting a global supply chain are not limited to achieving cost-competitiveness, in which the reduction in costs of materials and labor enable the company to provide more inexpensive but high-quality products to consumers or clients compared to their competitors. In the manufacturing industry, companies can benefit from the stabilization of product supplies, optimization of inventories and transactions, as well as expansion of sales channels and enhancement of international competitiveness. As for Japan's system development industry, companies can not only keep development costs low but also overcome the shortage of IT human resources by utilizing a global supply chain.

Japan is projected to face a shortage of up to 800,000 IT personnel by 2030, which makes the outlook for the country's IT service industry extremely grim, particularly in system development (METI, 2019).

Meanwhile, ASEAN countries are seeing a rapid rise in their population and IT workforce. Taking Vietnam as an example, the country's population in 2023 was projected to increase by about 834,800 or 0.84% from the previous year to about 130 million, according to the General Statistics Office. This would make Vietnam the third largest country in ASEAN (after Indonesia and the Philippines) in terms of capability to supply human resource to developed countries and regions that are facing a shortage in their labor force (MFA, 2024).

In addition to its expanding population, Vietnam embraces a national policy of fostering IT personnel who are proficient in English and Japanese. Driven by such initiatives, the number of excellent IT talents in the country has been increasing.

By establishing a global supply chain system and making good use of talented human resources in a particular country or region, a win-win relationship can be built between the country that outsources operations and the country to which operations are outsourced. However, in all industries, sectors and business lines, it is necessary to consider not only the benefits, or advantages, of building a global supply chain but also the risks, or disadvantages, that come with it, including geopolitical risks, quality control issues, and confidentiality breaches. It is thus vital to carefully deliberate how to hedge such risks and avoid or minimize any adverse effects.

REFERENCES

Akima, H., Goto, H., & Yamamura, T. (2015). Toukyou seibu ni okeru animeshon sangyou no ricchi senkou to sono hensen: Dejitaruka ni tomonau sagyou koutei no henka ni tsuite [Location preferences and changes of the animation industry in Western Tokyo: Changes in work processes due to digitalization]. *Urban Planning Papers*, 50(3), 644–649.

Cabinet Office. (2024). Nenji GDP seichouritsu [Annual GDP growth rate]. *Kokumin keizai keisan* (GDP toukei) [National Economic Accounts (GDP Statistics)]. https://www.esri.cao.go.jp/jp/sna/menu.html

Hanzawa, S. (2013). Animeshon sangyou ni okeru bungyou taisei no henyou [Transformation of the division of labor in the animation industry]. *Cultural Economics*, 10(1), 20–33.

Ichifuji, H. (2022). *(Gakui ronbun youyaku) Seizougyouteki kanten kara mita animeshon seisaku: Seisaku genba no bunka ni chuumoku shite* [(Thesis summary) Animation production from a manufacturing perspective: Focusing on the culture of the production site], Graduate School of Education, Hiroshima University. https://ir.lib.hiroshima-u.ac.jp/54233/files/46207

Information-technology Promotion Agency, Social Infrastructure Center (IPA-SIC) (Ed.). (2020). IT jinzai doukou chousa [IT Human Resources Trends Survey]. *IT Jinzai Hakusho 2020* [IT Human Resources White Paper 2020]. https://www.ipa.go.jp/archive/publish/hjuojm0000007e6n-att/000085255.pdf

Japan Student Services Organization (JASSO). (2023). "2022 (Reiwa 4) nendo gaikokujin ryuugakusei zaisekijoukyou chousa" nado kekka no kouhyou [Publication of the results of the 2022 (Reiwa 4) survey on the enrollment status of international students]. *Press release*. https://www.jasso.go.jp/about/press/__icsFiles/afieldfile/2023/03/01/jp2023030701.pdf

Ministry of Economy, Trade and Industry (METI). (2019). IT jinzai jyukyuu ni kansuru chousa (gaiyo) [Survey on IT human resources supply and demand (summary)]. *Dejitaru jinzai no ikusei* [Developing Digital Human Resources]. https://www.meti.go.jp/policy/it_policy/jinzai/gaiyou.pdf

Ministry of Economy, Trade and Industry (METI). (2024). Jouhou saabisu gyoukai [Information services industry]. *Tokutei saabisu sangyou doutai toukei chousa* [Statistical Survey of Specific Service Industries]. https://www.meti.go.jp/statistics/tyo/tokusabido/result-2.html

Ministry of Foreign Affairs (MOFA). (2024). Betonamu kiso deeta [Basic data on Vietnam]. *Socialist Republic of Viet Nam*. https://www.mofa.go.jp/mofaj/area/vietnam/data.html

Ministry of Internal Affairs and Communications (MIC). (2021). (3) ICT jinzai no fusoku, henzai [(3) Shortage and uneven distribution of ICT human resources]. *Jouhou tsuushin hakusho 2021* [Information and Communications White Paper 2021]. https://www.soumu.go.jp/johotsusintokei/whitepaper/ja/r03/html/nd104300.html

Saisho, T. (2010). Chuugoku no dejitaru kontentsu bunya ni okeru sangyou kurasutaa senryaku [Industrial cluster strategy in China's digital content sector]. *Kanto Gakuin University Research Institute for Economics and Business Management Annual Report*, 32, 162–178.

Saisho, T. (2014). *Chuugoku to betonamu no inobeeshon shisutemu [Dai 2 han]* [Innovation systems in China and Vietnam [2nd edition]]. Hakuto-Shobo.

Saisho, T. (2024a), A study on the actual situation of global supply chains in ASEAN: Focusing on the case of Japanese auto parts Company A. *Kokushikan University bulletin of the Research Institute of Business*, March 2024, 1-21.

Saisho, T. (2024b). Shikisha ni kiku: Shikisha ga shimesu sofuto kaihatsu no "guroobaru sapurai cheen" gijutsu busoku to guroobaruka, futatsu no keieikadai wo kaiketsu suru hinto towa [Ask the experts: Experts' hints for solving two management issues, shortage of engineers in the global supply chain for software development and globalization]. *Global Vision 2024 Handout*. FPT Japan Holdings.

Saisho, T. (2024c). Ajia ni okeru guroobaru sapurai cheen ni kansuru kousatu [A study on global supply chains in Asia: A case study of global supply chains in the IT service Sector]. *Globalization Research*, 21(1), 61–80.

Saisho, T. (2024d). Waga kuni no jouhouka shakai no shinten ni okeru jouhourenkei to jouhoutougou ni kansuru kousatsu [A study on the progress of Japan's information society and information collaboration: Focusing on the current status and possibilities of information collaboration]. *Kokushikan Business Review*, 14(1), 1–22.

Study Group on Advanced Global Supply Chains in the Digital Era (SGAGSC). (2023). *Dejitaru jidai ni okeru guroobaru sapurai cheen koudoka kenkyukai* [Report of study group on advanced global supply chains in the digital era, Asia and Oceania division]. https://www.meti.go.jp/shingikai/external_economy/global_supply_chain/pdf/20230331_1.pdf

The Japan Foundation (JF). (2023). *Betonamu (2022): Nihongo kyouiku kuni chiiki betsu jouhou* [Vietnam (2022): Japanese language education country/region information]. https://www.jpf.go.jp/j/project/japanese/survey/area/country/2022/vietnam.html

Yamaguchi, Y. (Ed.). (2004). *Nihon no anime zenshi: Sekai wo seishita nihon anime no kiseki* [The complete history of Japanese anime: The miracle of Japanese anime that conquered the world]. Ten Books.

KEY TERMS AND DEFINITIONS

Contents Industry: The contents industry is where companies produce and provide music, movies, animations, cartoons, game software, and other creative works, which are mainly fiction, to users.

Developing and Emerging Countries: A developing country is a country whose level of economic development and industrial capacity is lower than that of developed countries and whose economy is still growing. Of the 196 countries in the world, about 150, or 70%, are developing countries. Emerging countries are countries with high growth potential, although their current economic level is still low compared to developed countries such as Japan, those in Europe, and the United States. Specifically, they include countries in Latin America, Southeast Asia, the Middle East, Eastern Europe, etc. Countries that are seen as having potential for future growth are represented by groups such as BRICs (Brazil, Russia, India, China, South Africa), VISTA (Vietnam, Indonesia, South Africa, Turkey, Argentina), and Next 11 (Iran, Indonesia, Egypt, South Korea, Turkey, Nigeria, Pakistan, Bangladesh, Philippines, Vietnam, Mexico).

Global Supply Chain: A global supply chain generally refers to a large international inter-network involving a large number of suppliers and partners across different countries and regions in the manufacturing and other industries. Taking the manufacturing industry as an example, from the perspective of international logistics management, a global supply chain involves a series of processes, including the production, transportation, delivery, and inventory management of goods, among many countries and regions.

Internet Environment: Internet environment refers to the state of the connection to the internet. In many places where people gather, such as train stations, airports, restaurants, hotels, cafes, and retail stores in developing and emerging countries, WiFi (Wireless Fidelit), which is a service that provides internet connections to users within a certain area, is provided free of charge to users.

IT Service Sector: The IT service sector provides services that use IT to support people's daily lives and corporate activities. For example, IT service companies develop and provide online shopping sites, credit card payment systems, reservation systems for bullet trains and airplanes, business systems used by companies, accounting systems, and so on.

Labor-Intensive Operations: Labor-intensive operations are those that rely on human labor for a major part of their business activities, have low capital investment per worker, and have high labor costs as a percentage of sales. Labor-intensive operations are most common in primary and tertiary industries. Primary industries include operations that act on the natural world, such as crop cultivation and harvesting. On the other hand, the tertiary industry includes the distribution and hospitality industries, as well as the animation and other content industries.

ENDNOTE

1 This paper is based on the materials distributed at the time of the presentation at "Global Vision 2024: Challenges for Japan's Revival and Enhancing Resilience for Sustainable Growth" (FPT Japan Holdings) held on Friday, March 15, 2024, at Toranomon Hills (Saisho, 2024b).

2 Digital transformation (DX) is the use of digital technology to fundamentally change the way business and society work. The purpose of DX is for companies to respond quickly to changes in the market and maintain and strengthen their competitiveness. For example, it goes beyond simply digitizing paper documents to creating new and high added value by making full use of digital technology.

3 Artificial intelligence (AI) is a technology that gives computers and robots the ability to learn, solve problems, and make decisions like humans. Using methods such as machine learning and deep learning, AI learns patterns from large amounts of data to recognize, predict, judge, infer, and make suggestions like humans do.

4 Internet of Things (IoT) is a technology that equips various objects in the world with communication functions, connects them to the internet, and communicates with each other, enabling automatic recognition, automatic control, remote measurement, etc. For example, by connecting "things" such as home appliances and automobiles to the internet, it becomes possible to operate, measure, and control the objects from remote locations.

5 Robotic Process Automation (RPA) is a technology that uses robots to automate operations performed on PCs. RPA can automate a wide range of tasks, including Office applications and web browsers. RPA also makes it possible to automate a variety of tasks without large-scale capital investments such as system development.

6 The 5th generation mobile communication method (5G) is the latest communication standard that has the characteristics of high speed, large capacity, low latency, and simultaneous multiple connections. For example, by using 5G communication, you can get the information you want at an order of magnitude faster than before (high speed, large capacity), send commands quickly (low latency), and connect to the things around you through the nternet (simultaneous multiple connections).

7 Big data refers to data of various shapes, types, quantities, speeds, veracity, and value, and is a huge collection of data that is difficult for humans to grasp in its entirety. Big data is used in a variety of fields, including predictive analysis, real-time decision-making, new product development, autonomous driving technology, and smart factory construction.

8 Cloud computing refers to the use of computing services (servers, storage, networks, databases, software, etc.) in a cloud environment (internet environment), and cloud computing technology allows companies to enjoy a variety of benefits. Cloud computing is generally classified into three categories: (1) SaaS, (2) PaaS, and (3) IaaS. (1) SaaS (Software as a Service) uses software and application functions as a service in an internet environment. (2) PaaS (Platform as a Service) uses an execution environment for the functions required for application development as a service. (3) IaaS (Infrastructure as a Service) uses an infrastructure environment for the functions of compute resources such as CPU (Central Processing Units), memory, storage, and networks as services.

9 Extended Reality (XR) is an image processing technology that combines the real world with the virtual world to make various tasks in daily life, work, etc. more efficient and faster. XR is a general term for the cutting-edge technologies "VR (Virtual Reality)," "AR (Augmented Reality)," "MR (Mixed Reality)," and "SR (Substitutional Reality)," and is also known as "cross reality,"

10 Build To Order (BTO) is a made-to-order production method in which products are manufactured after receiving an order from a customer. For BTO to be successful, it is necessary to respond to orders from an unspecified number of customers and deliver them quickly. The background to the introduction of

BTO is that the development of the information society has made it possible to share information closely with suppliers and delivery companies.

11 Sustainable Development Goals (SDGs) are international goals set out in the 2030 Agenda for Sustainable Development, which was unanimously adopted by member states at the United Nations Summit in September 2015 as the successor to the Millennium Development Goals (MDGs) formulated in 2001. The SDGs consist of 17 goals and 169 targets, and pledge to "leave no one behind" on Earth, aiming for a sustainable and better world by 2030.

12 Agile Software Development (ASD) is one of the most popular system and software development methods today. The most distinctive feature of ASD is that the development process of "Plan → Design → Implement → Test" is repeated in small cycles of functional units. For example, development proceeds in order of priority, and each function developed forms a large system as an aggregate. And since ASD development proceeds on the assumption that "project changes are possible," it can respond to sudden specification changes and focuses on maximizing the value of the product.

12 Details about data sharing and information sharing are described in detail in the following paper "Saisho T. (2024d). A Study on the Progress of Japan's Information Society and Information Collaboration: Focusing on the Current Status and Possibilities of Information Collaboration. KOKUSHIKAN BUSINESS REVIEW" (Saisho, 2024d).

13 Originally, vendor meant a sales company or seller that delivers products to users, and vendors are also used outside the IT industry. Therefore, vendors in the IT industry refer to companies that sell IT products and services. Although manufacturers and vendors are often confused, a manufacturer is a company that produces products sold by a vendor. However, there are many companies in the IT industry that serve as both vendors and manufacturers, so the boundary between the two is blurred.

14 SIer is a coined word shortened from "System Integrator," and refers to a company that develops systems at the request of customers. Therefore, in a broad sense, SIers are also included in IT vendors, but they are distinguished from IT vendors in the sense that they are "companies that conduct tailor-made development in accordance with customer requests.

15 A virtual private network (VPN) is a private network built within a public network in order to take advantage of the economies of scale and management facilities of a larger network. A VPN connection uses various technologies to treat a shared line as if it were a virtually independent dedicated line.

16 A bridge SE (System Engineer) is an engineer who plays a bridging role to facilitate "offshore development" projects, in which part of the system development is done overseas to reduce costs. The bridge SE may be a local engineer overseas, or an engineer in Japan may take on the bridge SE role. The Bridge SEs, who combine overseas engineering and business operations, are required to have a variety of business skills in addition to system development skills.

17 Bring Your Own Device (BYOD) refers to the use of devices such as PCs, smartphones, and tablets that are owned privately by individuals for work. By introducing BYOD, employees can use their personal devices for work, which has the advantage of allowing them to work with devices that they are familiar with on a daily basis. The company also benefits by reducing the cost of purchasing those devices. On the other hand, if the device model and OS used for work differs from employee to employee, various problems may occur for each device. In addition, there is a risk of personal information such as passwords leaking from BYOD devices or virus infection, so adequate security measures are necessary.

Chapter 5
Attitudes of Hungarian Enterprises Towards the Establishment of Partnerships in the 21st Century

Tamás Faludi
https://orcid.org/0000-0001-6102-8152
University of Miskolc, Hungary

ABSTRACT

The 21st century has brought many challenges for supply chains and their actors. Ever-changing customer demands, changes in the economic sphere, events that are shaking the world economy to its core, all force businesses to be as secure as possible. One of the best "weapons" that businesses have against unforeseen risks is to cooperate with each other at some level. The higher the level of cooperation, the greater the chances of jointly averting a threat or minimising potential damage. The aim of this study is to examine the extent to which companies prefer forms of cooperation. It illustrates how attitudes towards cooperation have changed over the past decades by using real-life examples. The study also examines the views of Hungarian companies: a group of experts has been formed to identify the most important factors influencing the choice of partners, in order to draw conclusions about the demand for partnerships among Hungarian companies in the 21st century.

DOI: 10.4018/979-8-3693-9241-6.ch005

INTRODUCTION

Supply chains have undergone and are undergoing major changes and developments in the 21st century. Chains have become wider, with more and more members joining global supply chains, making supply chains much more like supply networks. It is no coincidence that they are often referred to in the literature as supply networks (Demirel, 2022; Li et al., 2024). At the same time, the behaviour of supply chain members has changed. In the past, even when companies worked within a chain, they very often treated each other as adversaries. This is still a difficult issue today, as companies' fundamental aim is to make profits and operate cost-effectively. But then they were supply chains with very few members. Today, it is unthinkable that supply chains and networks should not cooperate with each other. But the level of cooperation is far from equal.

The aim of the study is to show how cooperation between supply chain actors has changed in the 21st century and how it has become a more important factor than in previous periods. In the era of co-opetition, it is particularly important that chain members know each other's needs, know the needs of the final consumer, so that they can identify more accurate needs based on more accurate forecasts, which can help reduce uncertainty within the supply chain. Co-opetition, or cooperation in a competitive environment, is now more relevant to supply chain competition (Manzhynksi & Biedenbach, 2023). Within supply chains, it is more likely to be characterised by increasingly higher levels of cooperation. This is the hypothesis that the study aims to test with the help of Hungarian companies. I asked a group of experts from companies in Hungary how important they think cooperation is. I measured this by using different joint activities, i.e. I examined how important the members of the expert group of company decision-makers considered the use of each activity to influence the level of cooperation to be. I compare this with the results of previous research that also examined the need for and importance of collaboration. In order to understand the importance of collaboration within the supply chain, it is first necessary to understand the concept of supply chain management and then the current situation of supply chains. The paper will then describe in detail the possible forms of cooperation and the tools that can be used to support cooperation. The aim of the paper is to present the reader with the trend that supply chain management and within it supply chain coordination has become a very important topic in the 21st century, with one of the most important segments being the management of cooperation between members. The right level of cooperation is a prerequisite for the efficient and effective functioning of the individual members and thus of the entire supply chain. For this reason, it is necessary to support and manage cooperation that is tailored to the attitudes and characteristics of the members and that meets their expectations, which is handled by relationship management within management science and supply chain management.

RESEARCH QUESTIONS AND METHODS

The relatively stable demand trends of the mid-21st century have gradually changed, with the emergence of mass production and the ever-changing individual consumer needs that have evolved with the emergence and spread of consumer society, making it increasingly important to have real-time information flows to respond to changes as quickly and efficiently as possible. This requires the accuracy and speed of information flows, which in turn requires companies to be willing to share information with each other.

Thus, the question of what factors can be identified as influencing an organisation's choice of partner is a research question. I identify these factors through empirical research based on the opinions of a group of experts. With the help of the decision-makers participating in the study, it will be possible to examine what kind of partnerships are generally preferred by Hungarian companies and what factors are used to select partners.

It is also necessary to understand what partnerships can be established. So, a further research question is what types of cooperation can be distinguished. A literature search will help to identify these types.

Another basis for comparison is the previous experience of researchers on the subject. Through a literature search, I will examine articles, and case studies that identify the need for, and the extent of, partnerships. This will allow a comparison to be made of the extent to which the findings of older research and the views of the current expert group differ. During the research, I will compose the expert group from decision-makers and managers of Hungarian firms, and thus, during the literature search, I will mainly look for articles that have a Hungarian relevance and that have drawn conclusions for Hungarian firms, as this will provide a relevant basis for the comparative study.

CONCEPTUAL FRAMEWORK FOR SUPPLY CHAIN MANAGEMENT

Supply chains started to evolve rapidly in the 21st century. Initially, supply chains, together with logistics, provided only a framework for the flow of materials, but later supply chains began to be understood in a much broader sense (Malik et al, 2010; Sluis & De Giovanni, 2016; Nagy-Bota & Moldovan, 2022). It has been identified as a network of organisations that encompasses the entire production, distribution and delivery process to the consumer, where the back and forth flow of information and the integration of value creation processes have become very important factors (Mentzer et al., 2001; Zouaghi & Laghouag, 2021). Thus, the entire value creation process is one big process that needs to be managed, directed, organised and controlled. This is essentially the task of supply chain management (Larson & Rogers, 1998; Mentzet et al., 2001).

To help companies understand that they are part of a large system, and that their processes influence those upstream and downstream, the concept of the supply chain had to be implemented. This provides the systems and process approach that will allow the focus on individual goals to be increasingly pushed into the background (Giannoccaro, 2018; Tliche et al., 2018). This will provide the basis for establishing collaborations and relationships. The members will realise that they cannot operate effectively without each other's value-creating processes, and will therefore establish some level of cooperative relationship with each other, depending on the strategic importance. Indeed, the integration of value-creating processes is a primary aspect of maximising customer satisfaction, as these are the activities that contribute directly (as production, marketing, etc.) and indirectly (as human resources, organisational processes) to satisfying customer needs (Porter, 1991).

SUPPLY CHAINS IN THE 21ST CENTURY

The current situation of supply chains is quite specific. On the one hand, with the dynamic and rapid development of IT, more and more tools are available to facilitate and speed up processes within and between companies. The tools created by Industry 4.0 and 5.0 already require the digitalisation of companies (Tjahjono et al., 2017; Huang et al., 2023; Jamil et al., 2024; Garrido et al., 2024). These are tools that facilitate collaboration between supply chain members by virtually connecting and integrating value-creating activities. Cloud-based systems, enterprise management systems that integrate firms and enable various real-time data and information flows, also enable adaptation to dynamic changes in consumer demands (Ali et al., 2021; Ivanov et al., 2022; Taj et al., 2023). They also help to optimise supply chain costs and support and assist controlling tasks (Galka & Wappler, 2023; Cai et al., 2024; Liu et al., 2024).

On the other hand, there are many externalities that make supply chains vulnerable. The pandemic situation caused by COVID-19 has had a very strong negative impact on the transport market, on the manufacturing and service sectors. The drastic drop in demand due to quarantine and curfews forced producers and service providers to produce fewer goods and services. This has naturally affected the partners of the companies producing these products and services - suppliers, distributors, manufacturers (Aday & Aday, 2020; Chowdhury et al., 2021; Ye et al, 2024). The main challenge for companies in this situation is to manage supply disruptions as quickly as possible and at the lowest possible cost (Bonadio et al, 2021; Chowdhury et al, 2021). In addition, the issue of supply chain resilience has become increasingly important, which has been exacerbated by the Russian-Ukrainian war conflict. Both events caused supply disruptions for companies using trade routes to or from the region (Ginn, 2024; Nikookar et al, 2024; Wu et al, 2024). Resilience refers to the flexibility of supply chains to adapt, i.e. how quickly and efficiently the organisation can adapt to a given negative impact event, a new situation, and how quickly it can return to the original organisational operating system (Bianco et al, 2023; Pellegrino & Gaudenzi, 2023). The purpose of supply chains has become not only to react to the current new situation, but also to achieve a preventive approach, which in this case means that chains need to be better prepared for any crisis and thus a great deal of supply disruptions can be prevented or at least their impact can be greatly reduced (Ho et al, 2015; Qi et al., 2024). These potential risks need to be managed, and therefore the management of supply chain risks has become a very important topic in the 21st century (Sodhi & Tang, 2021; Jagtap et al., 2022).

Uncertainty is therefore the biggest threat to the functioning of supply chains. Addressing this by addressing supply chain resilience, a preventive, risk-managed approach can go a long way to avoiding cost increases and efficiency losses. One of the most basic solutions is to establish the right partnerships. Of course, the right partnerships cannot, solve these kinds of problems completely, but they have a much better chance of finding a solution than if they had to do it alone.

PARTNERSHIPS WITHIN THE SUPPLY CHAIN

The increased importance of partnerships dates back to the time when more and more members joined supply chains. The primary objective is to vertically integrate the entire supply chain, i.e. to create an arrangement that unifies the entire supply chain and treats it as one large entity (Giannoccaro, 2018). However, it is very difficult to fully integrate a larger scale supply network, which is typical today. Therefore, often only chain segments or the links of adjacent members in the chain are treated as a single entity and attempts are made to coordinate the links of these members (Coltman, 2009; Sluis & De Giovanni, 2016).

This paper narrows the research to the issue of pairwise integration and the partnering of adjacent members.

The study considers the forms of cooperation defined by Cohen and Roussel (2005) and Besanko et al. (2004) as the etalon. Based on the authors' research, five main forms of cooperation between firms can be identified, which also define the cooperation between supply chain members (Figure 1).

Figure 1. Types of cooperation between supply chain actors

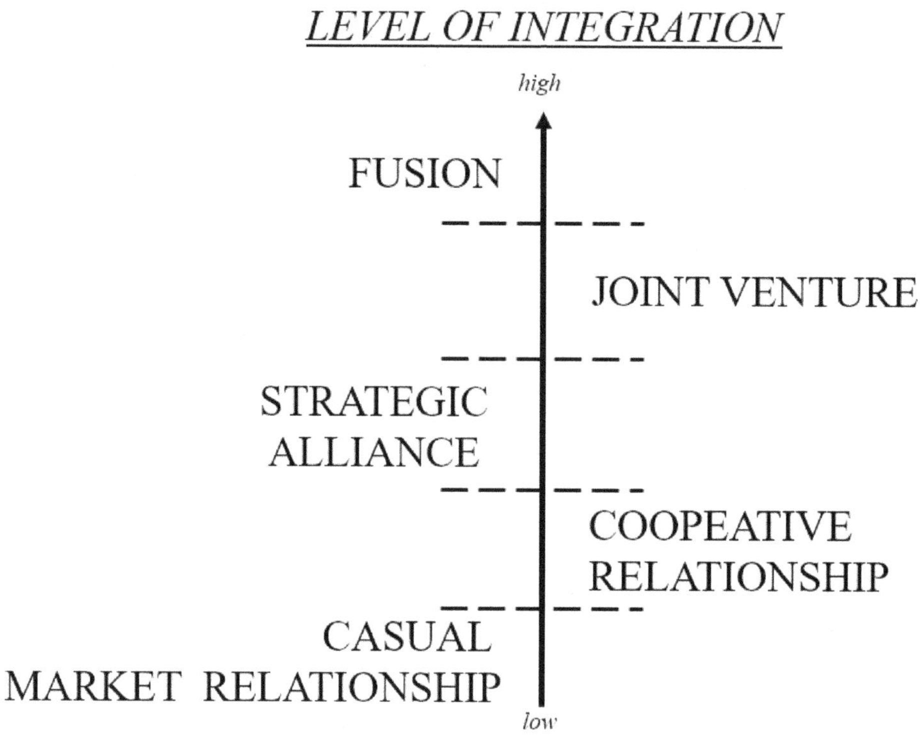

Source: own construction based on Cohen and Roussel (2005) and Besanko et al. (2004)

The first and least cooperative form of cooperation is the casual market relationship. It is a short-term transaction form, less likely to be called cooperation. It is often limited to one or a few transactions and thus creates almost no dependency between the business parties involved in the transaction. The relationship between the partners can be seen as distant.

A cooperative relationship can be defined as a form of cooperation that promotes the development of short-term cooperation. Minimal cooperation and dependency is already established between the parties, but there is no major integration yet. It explicitly supports the development of a higher level of cooperation, and can be seen as a first step on the way to this.

The strategic alliance has grown in popularity since the 1990s. It has been defined as a new level of strategic management based on the development of corporate values, leadership capabilities, organisational responsibility and administrative systems that link strategic and operational - i.e. long- and short-term - decision making at all levels of management, not only within companies but also between companies (Sambasivan et al, Strategic alliance itself is a mutually beneficial, longer-term corporate collaboration and integration in which the partners maintain their strategic autonomy but create a closer integration of activities with the partner company by providing each other with the resources necessary to achieve the objectives of the strategic alliance. In other words, the resources needed to achieve the goal are shared between the partners so that they can work together more effectively to achieve the goal of the alliance (Sammut-Bonnici & McGee, 2015). Based on these considerations, the strategic alliance is a higher form of cooperation that already creates interdependence between the cooperating parties.

A joint venture is a special form of cooperation. Companies build their scope of activities on their joint economic activities. In this case, the activities of the founding companies do not necessarily have to be the same, but a new company with legal personality is created following the integration. The degree of integration is high, so the level of cooperation must also be high, as not only are the value-creating processes merged between the cooperating partners, but in fact all processes become common.

The fusion is a merger of two or more separate companies, in which case at least one of the companies ceases to exist. This complete fusion represents the highest degree of integration. The maximum level of cooperation is reached in this case, but the disadvantage of cooperation is that at least one of the companies ceases to exist in the event of a merger. On these grounds, it can be considered as a case of extreme cooperation.

The establishment of partnerships is therefore a very important issue. As the relationships have a time horizon, the choice of the form of cooperation and the establishment of partnerships can be considered as strategic decisions. The question of with whom and to what extent a company establishes cooperation is not negligible. In the latter case, there is also the question of the degree of integration that the organisation requires or undertakes. The issue of establishing partnerships is therefore an important and strategic one.

THE BASICS OF PARTNERSHIPS

There is no doubt that any cooperation requires that you know and trust your partner, and that he or she meets a set of criteria set by your own preference system.

This is where relationship management helps. One of the most important segments of supply chain management, and within it supply chain coordination, is the management of relationships between members. It aims to select the collaborating members according to the company's preference system, to design the appropriate forms of collaboration also adapted to the nature of the relationship, and to make the chosen form of collaboration sustainable (Vandchali et al., 2021; Carissimi et al., 2023).

The main aim of partnerships is to reduce the cycle time of the supply chain. This is important because in the fast-paced world of the 21st century, meeting demand on time has become a key competitive advantage. Responding to dynamic and rapidly changing customer needs has become a key issue in supply chain management. It also puts the flexibility of supply chains to the test. Flexibility to adapt to change has also become an important factor. This of course requires the identification of needs as accurately as possible. This requires information. Another objective is therefore to increase the efficiency of information flows. This in turn requires information, which must be obtained from the market and from partners. Thus, it is essential to increase the willingness to share information between the members of the supply chain. This can best be achieved through a properly negotiated cooperation agreement that reflects company attitudes, characteristics and expectations. Thus, the fundamental objective of partnerships is to build trust between the members in order to establish the highest possible level of partnership (Figure 2).

Figure 2. The target-hierarch system of partnerships

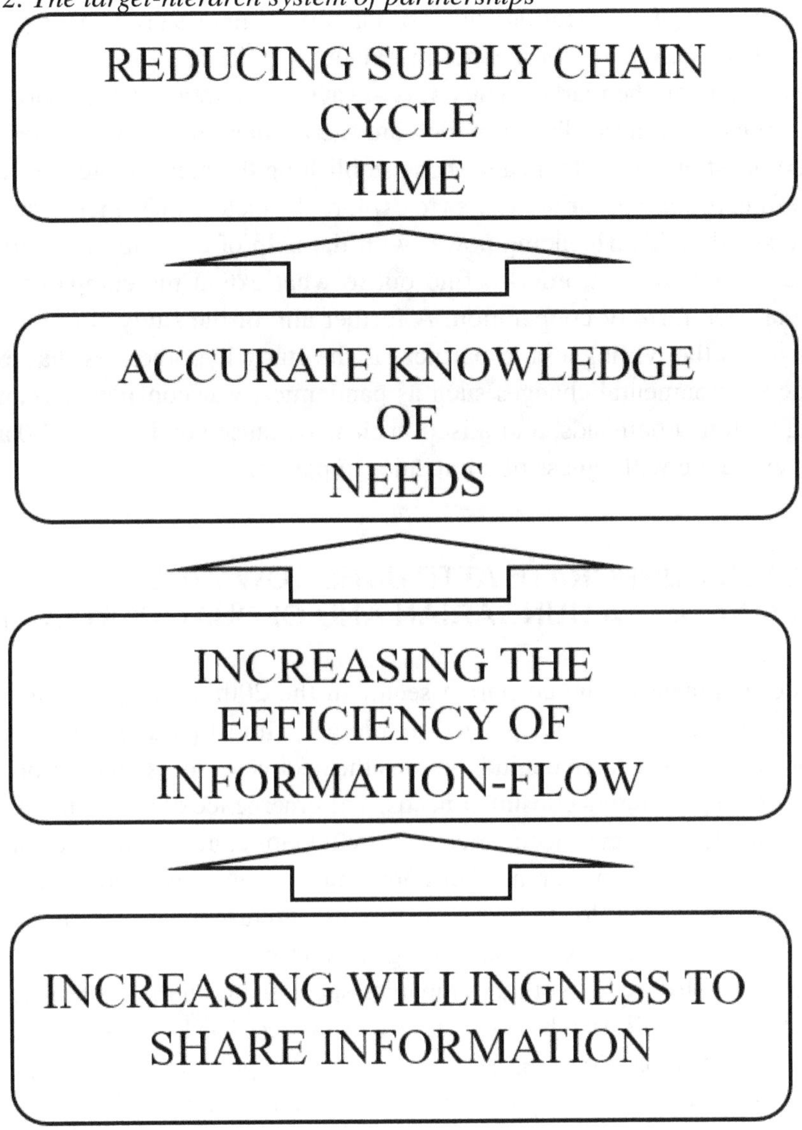

Source: own construction

However, this is not an universal solution to the problems mentioned above. It is not recommended to establish partnerships without a concept. Careful consideration should be given to the level of partners the company has. For example, a supplier of raw materials to a manufacturing company, which supplies the company with strategically important raw materials without which the final product would not be produced, it is strongly recommended to establish a higher level of cooperation (strategic alliance or even a joint venture). However, it may not be worth entering into a higher level of cooperation with a supplier that imports products (e.g. screws for assembly or only parts for a certain product specification) for which there are several suppliers on the market. Thus, it is always worth treating each partner separately, typing them according to which are the partners used for cost reduction, which are the strategic partners and then establishing the appropriate partnership.

Therefore, the aim of the study was to explore the factors influencing the choice of partners and their influencing power with the help of a group of experts from Hungarian companies, in order to find out to what extent the companies of our time prefer each form of cooperation. A further aim of the study is to investigate the changes in the willingness to partner, as the study hypothesises that external economic environmental changes such as pandemics, war conflicts, dynamically changing customer demands, digitalisation changes caused by Industry 4.0 and 5.0 have increased the willingness of companies to partner.

CHANGING CORPORATE ATTITUDES TOWARDS COOPERATION – A HUNGARIAN AND GLOBAL PERPECTIVE

The development of the corporate sector in the 20th century was shaped by many factors. Many small changes led to a larger, almost paradigm-shifting phenomenon. The driving force behind this was the decline of mass production, which was generated by changing consumer needs. The emergence of a consumer society, which has made consumer needs increasingly dynamic, and companies have had to adapt. The external environment of companies has also evolved. Flexibility in meeting consumer needs led to higher costs, which in turn led to outsourcing. This has meant that many processes such as logistics, transport, warehousing, finance, etc. have been outsourced to other companies specialising in these services.

In addition, globalisation has occurred. This process has led companies to enter the international arena. From the 1990s onwards, this process accelerated as more and more international trade agreements were concluded and, as borders between countries opened up, more and more companies moved outside their own borders.

In fact, the Upsalla-model identified these two factors as the main incentives for firms to internationalise (Johanson-Vahlne, 1977). The increase in consumer demand, the saturation of domestic markets, made it a necessary step to enter foreign markets. The model suggests that this was achieved primarily through export activity, followed by the establishment of distribution depots or sales centres abroad. This was followed by the setting up of subsidiaries as the final step in globalisation, i.e. production subsidiaries were set up in foreign countries in order to meet customer needs there more flexibly and quickly. Of course, the fact that certain countries have better economic conditions, better infrastructure and cheaper labour is also a very important factor. So cost reduction is also a factor when setting up foreign subsidiaries. This attitude was also characteristic of Hungarian companies and the process of internationalisation was based on this model (Pásztor, 2022).

In parallel with the emergence of multinational companies, the issue of cooperation has become increasingly important. As early as the 1970s, the issue of vertical integration was raised among Hungarian firms. The high production figures made it possible to sell abroad, i.e. export activity boomed. Thus, firms looked for foreign partners with whom they could establish long-term cooperation. This was still almost exclusively a seller-buyer relationship, but this later broadened (Szentes, 1976). The need for higher levels of integration emerged in Hungary in the 1990s, whereas internationally this process was already prevalent in the decade or two before, as many national companies became multinationals, following the trend of the 1970s and 1980s (Cantwell & Sanna Randaccio, 1990). Expanding the scope of activities and achieving economies of scale are the main objectives of multinationalisation. While the latter is clearly aimed at reducing costs, the former is generated by the need to adapt to dynamically changing customer needs (Kiechel, 1988; Artner, 1995). In addition, the need for growth of firms is also a factor in the increase in the demand for cooperation among firms.

From the 1990s onwards, the demand for cooperation has been growing. In the post-communist period, the automotive industry became one of the leading industries in Hungary. Cooperation within the automotive sector became of strategic importance in this period (Bakos, 1996; Czakó, 2014; HIPA, 2018; Natsuda et al., 2022). Thus, it is not enough to conclude a cooperation, so in the 2000s the question was how to manage, lead and coordinate these cooperations, as more and more cooperative relationships and strategic alliances were established. Several studies on the management and characterisation of collaborations have been carried out both in Hungary and internationally (Dobos & Pintér, 2010; Gelei, 2014; Gelei & Dobos, 2016; Piricz, 2017; Kacz, 2019; Ibsen et al., 2022; Li et al, By the 2010s and 2020s), the focus has shifted to the management of established global chains, one of the most important aspects of which is the development and management of collaborations, as the alignment and coordination of value-creating processes of companies operating across countries and even on other continents is the key to the efficient and effective operation of the chain, which ultimately aims to satisfy the final consumer needs (Lőrincz, 2017; Gáspár et al., 2023).

It can therefore be concluded that the willingness to cooperate has shown an increasing trend both in Hungary and globally. At the global level, the willingness to cooperate has been growing dynamically since the 1970s, while in Hungary it exploded mainly in the 1990s, mainly due to the end of the socialist era and the liberalisation of trade borders. In the late 1990s, the development of the IT sector made it even easier to manage collaborations, as integrated business management systems, which also connected companies, provided virtual connectivity for companies, which now offer even greater opportunities for digital solutions for the 21st century and especially for the 2010s and 2020s.

EMPIRICAL RESEARCH TO IDENTIFY THE COOPERATION ATTITUDES OF HUNGARIAN COMPANIES

The aim of the empirical research conducted in this study is to identify the factors influencing the choice of partners through the opinions of managers of Hungarian companies. By setting up a group of experts and using a smaller number of focus group interviews, I investigate the cooperation attitudes of Hungarian companies.

Research Design

I sought the views of the expert group through a focus group interview. The interview outline included the main interview outline and the main questions to identify the main factors influencing partner choice (Figure 3).

Figure 3. Structure of the interviews

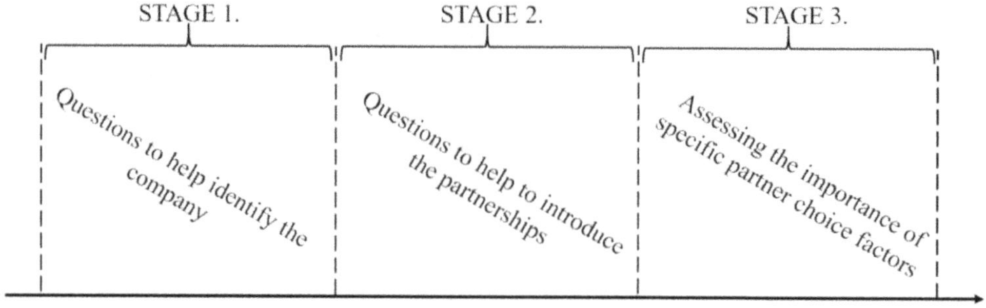

Source: own construction

The questions were firstly concerned with the identification of firms, i.e. they included questions on the size of the firm, its ownership, its scope of activity and its position in the supply chain. This was followed by questions on cooperation: what kind of partners the company currently has, how it selected its current partners, what factors influenced its choice of partners. The extent to which the use of certain collaboration tools (such as the use of a cross-company integrated management system, joint sales planning, etc.) is considered, was also asked, which also helped to understand and identify collaborative attitudes.

Thus, the most important objective of empirical research is to identify the factors that emerge as influencing factors in a partner choosing situation. Once the factors have been identified, their influencing power can be assessed to determine the time span and depth of the relationship preferred by the members of the research group. Thus, based on the experience, information and literature gathered so far, the research hypothesis that there is an increasing demand for cooperation in the corporate sector due to the changing environment can be tested.

Characteristics of the Research Sample

To conduct the empirical research, I contacted decision-makers at managerial level in Hungarian companies and formed a group of experts.

The companies participating in the research requested anonymity, so the members of the expert group are not named in the study. The following data on composition are available and in the public domain.

The expert group consisted of 34 people. These managers are representatives of 12 companies, which means that 2 or 3 managers from each company were interviewed. The interviews were conducted on a company by company basis, so there were 12 interviews with 2-3 people. These companies are mostly Hungarian owned or majority Hungarian owned. Only managers of small and medium-sized enterprises participated in the research. All of the companies are involved in international trade and are mainly active in the supply chain as producers and manufacturers. In terms of industry, the companies interviewed are active in the manufacturing sector.

Results

Figure 4 summarises the results of the research.

Figure 4. Partner-choosing factors indentified by the expert group

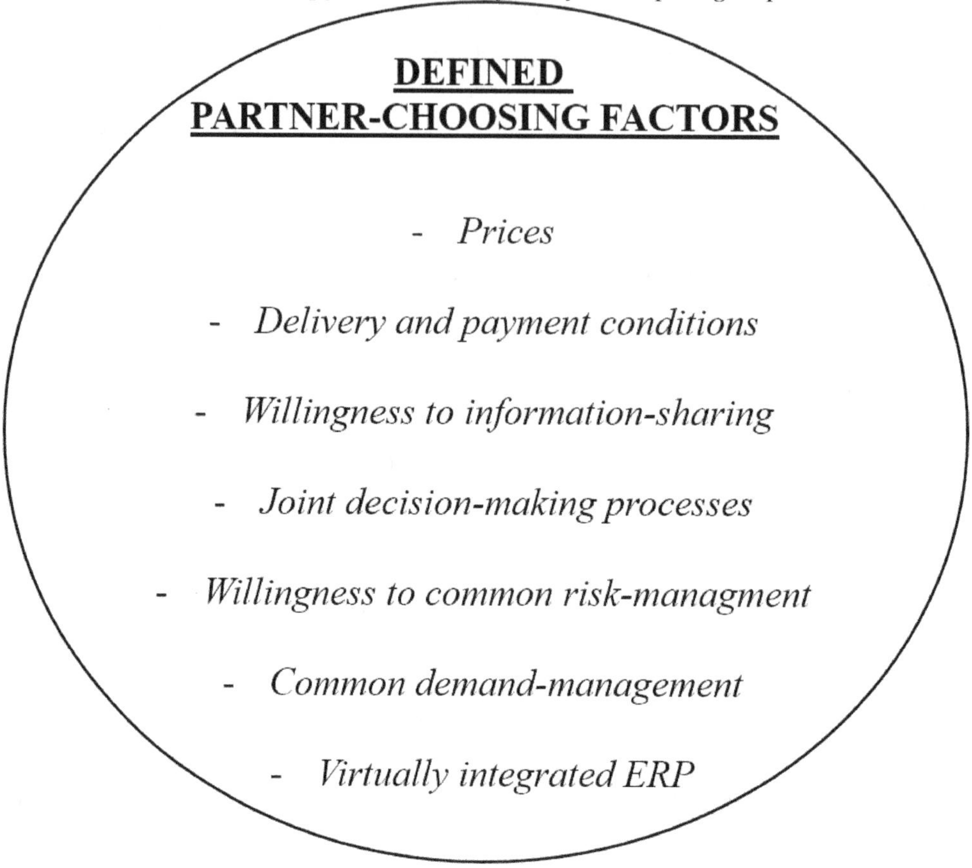

Source: own construction

As can be seen in the figure, factors that can be considered as standard for partner choice were also present in the responses of the expert group. Prices, delivery and payment conditions are factors that have a major influence on the agreement with a partner. This is not a surprising result, as these factors are limited by the economic situation of the company. With a more expensive partner that the firm cannot afford, it is likely that it will not be able to conclude a cooperation agreement. The same is true for payment and delivery terms. Specific requirements of their own may be based on the characteristics of the goods produced and distributed by the company, which, if a potential partner cannot meet, will again result in a situation where they cannot enter into a partnership.

The other factors identified need to be examined from a different perspective, because they are more interpretable in terms of the decision-makers and the attitudes of the company. The previous group (price, payment and delivery conditions) were more constraints based on the financial and the nature of the goods, but the other factors are considered important depending on the nature, depth and duration of the cooperation. It is precisely for this reason that the members of the expert group were asked to prioritise the factors from the less important to the most important. In this way, the type of cooperation preferred by the members of the expert group could be identified, taking into account the importance of the factor in question.

The factors that respondents considered important in their choice of partner were as follows (Figure 5).

Figure 5. The influence of each partner choosing factor

NAME	*PERCENTAGE OF IMPORTANCE*
Prices	91%
Delivery and payment conditions	56%
Willingness of information-sharing	91%
Joint decision-making processes	94%
Willingness to common risk-management	79%
Common demand-management	74%
Virtually integrated ERP	82%

Source: own construction

Figure 6 summarises the importance of the different partner selection factors and common tools, which are summarised in the figure. In determining importance, I asked the respondent managers to rate the identified partner choosing factors on a five-point scale. This scale was used to assign percentages to the values. I considered those values that scored a 4 or higher, as a score of 4 or 5 represents a very strong level of importance. In order of importance, this is as follows (Figure 6).

Figure 6. The order of importance of partner-choosing factors

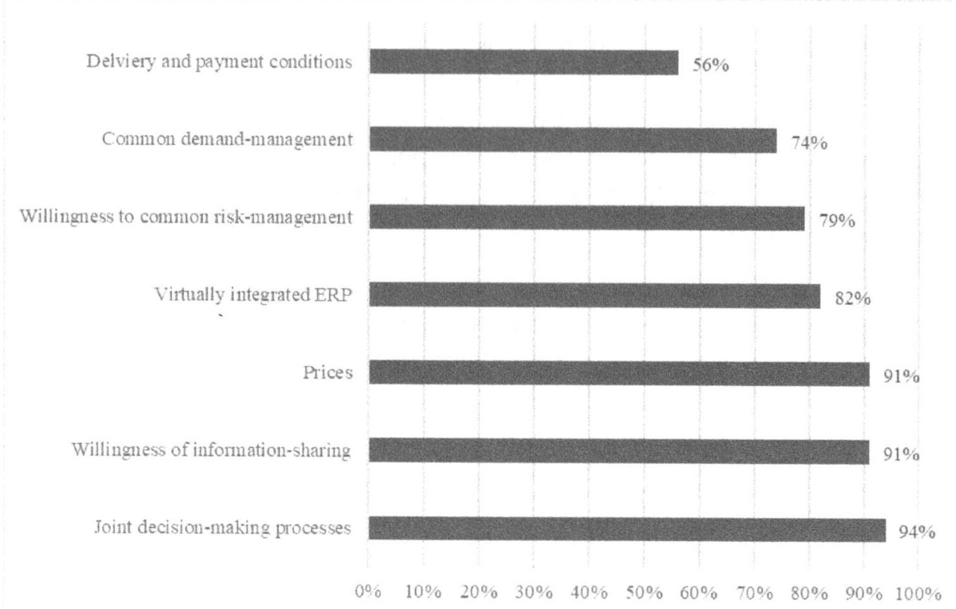

Source: own construction

Based on the overall prioritisation order in Figure 6, the strongest factor is the use of joint decision-making processes. These are processes that require a higher level of cooperation, since without a higher level of cooperation, specific joint decision-making processes between companies could not be developed. This is confirmed by the fact that decision-makers expect a higher level of information sharing from their partners. Improving the efficiency of information flows also has a positive impact on the quality of decisions. Price is also an important influencing factor, according to respondents. It is worth looking at this from a different angle, as it is a factor that is not necessarily linked to the attitudes of decision-makers, but rather to their financial and infrastructural characteristics. Delivery and payment conditions can also be included in this group of factors. These are also characteristics that can be set by the framework within which the company operates. Yet an interesting result is that the expert group considers this to be a much less important factor than price developments. This implies that the flexibility of the companies interviewed in terms of delivery and payment conditions may have a low influence. The use of integrated management systems or ERPs are also emerged as a relatively important factor among the managers surveyed. Today's integrated ERP systems no longer just connect individual departments within a company. Industry 4.0 and 5.0 have also led to huge advances in IT tools, resulting in the development of internet-based, cloud-based collaboration platforms. These platforms enable companies to virtually connect their value-creating processes. Thus, real-time information flow can be given, response times can be significantly reduced, and thus there are many benefits that can be derived from the use of an integrated ERP system to support and facilitate collaboration (Nwankpa, 2015; Hietala & Päivärinta, 2021). Therefore, as with price, the use of an ERP system can be seen as a factor constrained by the corporate infrastructure, as it is closely linked to the existing IT background. However, the need for virtual integration puts the issue into a different perspective, as the attitude of decision makers has a major influence on whether they want integration and, if so, to what extent. Joint risk management or joint sales management is the least important factor according to the expert group. The latter, i.e. joint sales management, could be placed in one of the last places due to the composition of the expert group. As the companies involved in the research are producers and manufacturers, they are located at the beginning of the distribution channel, i.e. relatively far away from the final consumer. Thus, sales to the consumer market are not necessarily relevant for them. This is why this factor was placed at the bottom of the priority order. Of course, it is also important for a manufacturing company to sell the components, semi-finished products and possibly finished products that it produces, but in the present case, even depending on the industrial mix, there is not much need or demand for this. Nor is there a need for joint risk management. The research shows that companies prefer to manage risks independently, i.e. they are less likely to consider it important to manage risks jointly with a partner.

The higher level of demand for joint processes and the relatively high level of influence these factors have, according to the expert group members, suggests that the demand for cooperation is high. The high level of demand for joint decision-making mechanisms, as well as the expected high level of willingness to share information, suggests that a cooperative relationship is preferred by decision-makers. When comparing the characteristics of the forms of cooperation typified in the literature with the responses of the expert group, it can be concluded that the firms participating in the expert group prefer at least a cooperative relationship, but also the establishment of a strategic alliance.

CONCLUSIONS DRAWN FROM THE RESULTS OF THE RESEARCH

The empirical research explored, with the help of a group of experts from Hungarian companies, the partner selection factors that determine with whom they decide to enter into a cooperation relationship. The interview also revealed the strength of each partner selection factor in a partner selection situation. The interviews were conducted in groups of a few people, with only one company representative being interviewed at a time. Here it was found that managers' partner selection factors can be grouped into two main categories. Some factors are influenced by the company infrastructure and others by the financial situation of the company. These can be considered as hard tools or factors, as they are not something that the company can simply change, they are given factors that can only be changed through a larger scale change process. Furthermore, these factors are not linked to the competences of decision makers. The other group of factors, which include the company's attitude to cooperation, i.e. the company's attitudes, already require the existence of decision-making and management competences, as these will have the greatest influence on the decisions taken. So this is the group that is greatly influenced by the soft skills of corporate decision-makers. That is the reason why, it is called soft factors of soft tools (Figure 7).

Figure 7. Typification of partner choosing factors identified in the research

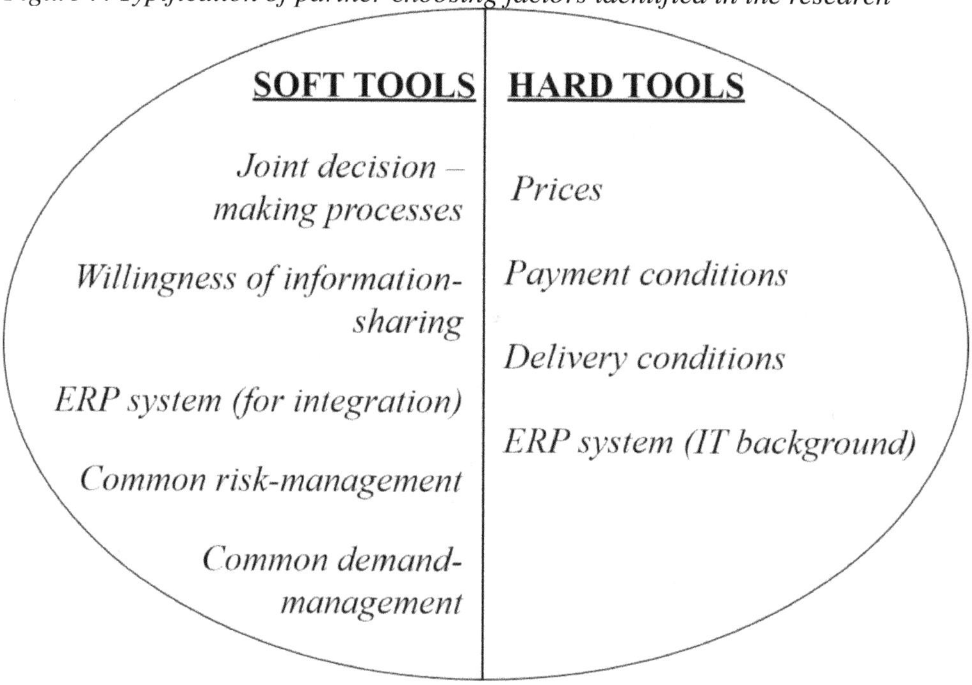

Source: own construction

Of the first group of factors, the hard factors, price became the most important factor influencing the choice of partner. This is self-evident, so this result was not a big surprise. Delivery and payment terms are also included. These factors depend on the financial situation of the company, its invoicing and payment system, where the decision-maker has no influence on the choice of factors, and these factors are given. The use of ERP systems is reflected in both sets of factors. The reason for this is that we can look at it from two and a half perspectives: the aspect belonging to this group of factors is the IT background that ensures the functioning of the ERP system. If this is not in place, it is not possible to talk about the functioning of an ERP system. This is also part of the corporate infrastructure, which is why it is included in the hard factors. The second group of factors comprises those factors which mainly relate to the attitudes of decision-makers at management level towards corporate objectives. In other words, factors can be classified in this group which, based on the decision-makers' own competences, skills and knowledge, will have different influencing power in a partner selection situation, in line with the company's objectives, and will thus have different importance. Of these factors, the need for joint decision making processes had the strongest influencing power, i.e. the factor with the highest weight according to the expert group responses. It also includes the willingness to share information, which has a similar weight. I interpreted the use of ERP in this group in terms of the need for integration. The need for joint risk management and joint sales management also emerged as a partner selection factor.

The basic premise of the research was that the demand for cooperation has been strong and growing since the middle and end of the 20th century. Case studies, articles and studies in the literature confirmed this. The main question of my research was to what extent this is true for Hungarian companies. The results showed that soft factors are more important in a partner selection situation, as the two strongest influencing factors were found in this group: joint decision-making processes and high information sharing. Of the partner selection factors defined by the research as hard factors, price is the more important factor, with delivery and payment terms appearing to be almost negligible factors in the order of priority.

Based on the responses of the established expert group, one of the factors that best supports cooperation - and one of the most demanding - is joint decision-making processes, which are the most important of the factors for choosing a partner. In addition, the willingness to share information, which is also one of the most important foundations for cooperation, is also a very important factor. The importance of these two factors confirms that cooperation is also an important aspect for Hungarian companies. The changing economic environment, events with global impact such as pandemics or war, dynamic and changing customer needs require supply chain members to cooperate with a high level of integration and cooperation, also with a high level of trust. This can also be seen as a safety factor, as economic operators can overcome the trends and events of recent years much more effectively by joining forces. This is perhaps the reason why the question of the willingness of companies to cooperate in the 21st century has become even more important.

Limitations of the Research

The empirical analysis presented in this study is limited to Hungary and reflects the opinion of a specific group of experts. During the research I took care to select companies in the expert group that have a strong background and are involved in international trade, so I wanted to create a group from which relevant information could be obtained. Still, a higher level of opinion research, a questionnaire survey with a larger sample, would give a more accurate picture of the perception of Hungarian companies on cooperation. Thus, the results detailed in this study, which are part of the empirical research, reflect only the opinion of the expert group. The information provided by the group was complemented by the results of the literature research, which helped to formulate the conclusions.

Future research directions will be to extend this research. My aim is to interview many more companies through a more extensive questionnaire survey in order to obtain more accurate and detailed results. I would replace interviews with online questionnaire surveys so that I can reach more companies. The expected outcome is similar to the research results of this study, but I assume that there may be more partner selection factors than those identified here, or their order of importance may vary.

Finally, I would like to thank the companies and managers who took the time to participate in our focus interviews and who helped me to achieve relevant results in my research.

REFERENCES

Aday, S., & Aday, M. S. (2020). Impact of COVID-19 on the food supply chain. *Food Quality and Safety*, 4(4), 167–180. DOI: 10.1093/fqsafe/fyaa024

Ali, S. I., Ali, A., AlKilabi, M., & Christie, M. (2021). Optimal supply chain design with product family: A cloud-based framework with real-time data consideration. *Computers & Operations Research*, 126, 105112. Advance online publication. DOI: 10.1016/j.cor.2020.105112

Angwin, D., & Sammut-Bonnici, T. (2015): *Strategic Alliances*, in: Cooper (ed): Wiley Encyclopedia of Management, John Wiley & Sons, Ltd. DOI: 10.1002/9781118785317.weom120047

Artner, A. (1995). Vállalati együttműködés a mai világgazdaságban (Corporate cooperation in today's global economy). *Közgazdasági Szemle*, XLLII(1), 104–115.

Bakos, G. (1996). Magyar Suzuki and the Emergence of Japanese Direct Investmen in Central Europe. In Darby, J. (Ed.), *Japan and the European Periphery* (pp. 244–253). Palgrave Macmillian. DOI: 10.1007/978-1-349-25196-4_15

Besanko, D., Dranove, D., Shanley, M., & Schaefer, S. (2004). *Economics of strategy*. John Wiley & Sons Inc.

Bianco, D., Bueno, A., Filho, M. G., Lata, H., Ganga, G. M. D., Frank, A. G., & Jabbour, C. J. C. (2023). The role of Industry 4.0 in feveloping resilience for manufacturing companies during COVID-19. *International Journal of Production Economics*, 256, 108728. Advance online publication. DOI: 10.1016/j.ijpe.2022.108728

Bonadio, B., Huo, Z., Levchenko, A. A., & Pandalai-Nayar, N. (2021). Global supply chains in the pandemic. *Journal of International Economics*, 133, 103534. Advance online publication. DOI: 10.1016/j.jinteco.2021.103534 PMID: 34866652

Cai, J., Sharkawi, I., & Taasim, S. I. (2024). How does digital transformation promote supply chain deversification? From the perspective of supply chain transaction costs. *Finance Research Letters*, 63, 105399. Advance online publication. DOI: 10.1016/j.frl.2024.105399

Cantwell, J., & Sanna Randaccio, F. (1990). The Growth of Multinationals and the Cathing up Effect. *Economic Notes*, (1), 1–23.

Carissimi, M. C., Creazza, A., & Colicchia, C. (2023). Crossing the chasm: Investigating the relationship between sustainability and resilience in supply chain management. *Cleaner Logistics and Suppyl Chain*, 7, 100098. Advance online publication. DOI: 10.1016/j.clscn.2023.100098

Chowdhury, P., Paul, S. K., Kaisar, S., & Moktadir, Md. A. (2021). COVID-19 pandemic relatd supply chain studies: A systematic review. *Transportation Research Part E, Logistics and Transportation Review*, 148(April). Advance online publication. 102271 PMID: 33613082

Cohen, S., & Roussel, J. (2005). *Strategic supply chain management: the five disciplines for top performance*. McGraw-Hill.

Coltman, T., Bru, K., Perm-Ajchariyawong, N., Devinney, T. M., & Benito, G. R. (2009). Supply Chain Contract Evolution. *European Management Journal*, 27(6), 388–401. DOI: 10.1016/j.emj.2008.11.005

Czakó, K. (2014): Az Audi Hungaria Motor Kft. hatása a helyi gazdasági és társadalmi folyamatokra (The Impact of Audi Hungaria Motor Ltd on Local Economic and Social Processes), *Tér és Társadalom, 28(2)*, pp. 188–198.

Demirel, G. (2022): Network science for the supply chain: theory, methods, and empirical results, *The Digital Supply Chain*, pp. 343-359.

Dobos, I., Pintér, M. (2010): *Cooperation in supply chains: A cooperative game theoretic analysis*, working paper in: Corvinus University of Budapest

Galka, S., & Wappler, M. (2023). Integration of cash flow management and further aspects of the supply chain management in production system design. *IFAC-PapersOnLine*, 56(2), 947–952. DOI: 10.1016/j.ifacol.2023.10.1687

Garrido, S., Muniz, J.Jr, & Ribeiro, V. B. (2024). Operations Management, Sustainability & Industry 5.0: A critical analysis and future agenda. *Cleaner Logistics and Supply Chain*, 10, 100141. Advance online publication. DOI: 10.1016/j.clscn.2024.100141

Gáspár, T., Sass, M., Koppány, K., & Bi, S. (2023). Foreign trade relations of Hungary with China: A global value chain perspective. *Society and Economy*, 45(3), 229–249. DOI: 10.1556/204.2023.00018

Gelei, A. (2014). Az üzleti kapcsolatok irányítása – fókuszban a bizalom (Managing business relationships – focus on trust). *Köz-gazdaság*, 9(2), 85–99.

Gelei, A., & Dobos, I. (2016). Bizalom az üzleti kapcsolatokban (Trust in business relationships). *Közgazdasági Szemle*, 63(3), 330–349. DOI: 10.18414/KSZ.2016.3.330

Giannoccaro, I. (2018). Centralized vs. decentralized supply chains: The improtance of decision maker's cognitive ability and resistance to change. *Industrial Marketing Management*, 73, 59–69. DOI: 10.1016/j.indmarman.2018.01.034

Ginn, W. (2024). Global supply chain disruptions and financial conditions. *Economics Letters*, 239, 111739. Advance online publication. DOI: 10.1016/j.econlet.2024.111739

Hietala, H., & Päivärinta, T. (2021). Benefits Realisation in Post-Implementation Development of ERP Systems: A Case Study. *Procedia Computer Science*, 181, 419–426. DOI: 10.1016/j.procs.2021.01.186

HIPA. (2018). *Automotive Industry in Hungary*. Hungarian Investment Promotion Agency.

Ho, W., Zheng, T., Yildiz, H., & Talluri, S. (2015). Supply chain risk management: A literature review. *International Journal of Production Research*, 53(16), 5031–5069. DOI: 10.1080/00207543.2015.1030467

Huang, K., Wang, K., Lee, P. K. C., & Yeung, A. C. L. (2023). The impact of industry 4.0 on supply chain capability and supply chain resilience: A dynamic resource-based view. *International Journal of Production Economics*, 262, 108913. Advance online publication. DOI: 10.1016/j.ijpe.2023.108913

Ibsen, C. L., Sezer, L., & Doellgast, V. (2022). Coordination versus organization: Diverging logics of firm cooperation in Denmark and Sweden. *British Journal of Industrial Relations*, 61(3), 526–549. DOI: 10.1111/bjir.12704

Ivanov, D., Dolgui, A., & Sokolov, B. (2022). Cloud supply chain: Integrating Industry 4.0 and digital platforms in the „Supply Chain-as-a-Service. *Transportation Research Part E, Logistics and Transportation Review*, 160, 102676. Advance online publication. DOI: 10.1016/j.tre.2022.102676

Jagtap, S., Trollman, H., Trollman, F., Garcia-Garcia, G., Parra-López, C., Duong, L., Martindale, W., Munekata, P. E. S., Lorenzo, J. M., Hdaifeh, A., Hassoun, A., Salonitis, K. (2022): The Russia-Ukraine Conflict: Its Implications for the Global Food Chains, *Foods, 11(14)*, doi: 2098

Jamil, M., Mustofa, R., Hossain, N. U. I., Rahman, S. M. A., & Chowdhury, S. (2024). A structural equation modeling framework for exploring the industry 5.0 and sustainable supply chain determinants. *Supply Chain Analytcs*, 6, 100060. Advance online publication. DOI: 10.1016/j.sca.2024.100060

Johanson, J., Vahlne, JE. (1977): The Internationalization Process of the Firm – A Model of Knowledge Development and Increasing Foreign Market Commitments

Kacz, K. (2019). Local Product Within Short Food Supply Chains in Hungary. *Annals PAAAE*, XXI(4), 172–181. DOI: 10.5604/01.3001.0013.5952

Kiechel, W.III. (1988). Corporate Strategy for the 1990s. *Fortune*, 117(5), 34–42.

Larson, P. D., & Rogers, D. S. (1998). Supply Chain Management: Definition, Growth, and Approaches. *Journal of Marketing Theory and Practice*, 6(4), 1–5. DOI: 10.1080/10696679.1998.11501805

Li, H., Chai, J., Qian, Z.-F., & Chen, H. (2022). Cooperation strategies when leading firms compete with small and medium-sized enterprises in a potentially competitive market. *Journal of Management Science and Engineering*, 7(3), 489–509. DOI: 10.1016/j.jmse.2022.02.003

Li, J., Wang, H., Qu, Q., Zhu, J., & Wang, J. (2024). Actors' interactions in the evolution of service supply networks of manufacturing firms. *International Journal of Production Economics*, 272, 109224. Advance online publication. DOI: 10.1016/j.ijpe.2024.109224

Liu, S., Han, W., Zhang, Z., & Chan, F. T. S. (2024). An analysis of performance, pricing, and coordination in a supply chain with cloud services: The impact of data security. *Computers & Industrial Engineering*, 192, 110237. Advance online publication. DOI: 10.1016/j.cie.2024.110237

Lőrincz, N. (2017). Main Characteristics of Nowadays' Global Value Chains and their Relevance to the Hungarian Automotive Manufacturing Industry, *Vezetéstudomány – Budapest. Management Review*, 48(5), 35–48.

Malik, A. K., Singh, A., Jit, S., & Garg, C. P. (2010). Supply Chain Management: An Overview. *International Journal of Logistics and Supply Chain Management*, 2(2), 97–101.

Manzhynski, S., & Biedenbach, G. (2023). The knotted paradox of coopetition for sustainability: Investigating the interplay between core paradox properties. *Industrial Marketing Management*, 110, 31–45. DOI: 10.1016/j.indmarman.2023.02.013

Mentzer, J. T., DeWitt, W., Keebler, J. S., Min, S., Nix, N. W., Smith, C. D., & Zacharia, Z. G. (2001). Defining Supply Chain Management. *Journal of Business Logistics*, 22(2), 1–25. DOI: 10.1002/j.2158-1592.2001.tb00001.x

Nagy-Bota, S., & Moldovan, L. (2022). Key Differences and Common Aspects of Logistics and Supply Chain Management. *Acta Marisiensis Seria Technologica*, 19(1), 42–46. DOI: 10.2478/amset-2022-0008

Natsuda, K., Sass, M., & Csonka, L. (2022). Developing a local supply chain network: The case of Magyar Suzuku in Hungary. *Acta Oeconomica*, 72(4), 531–552. DOI: 10.1556/032.2022.00034

Nikookar, E., Gligor, D., & Russo, I. (2024). Supply chain resilience: When the recipe is more important than the ingredients for managing supply chain disruptions. *International Journal of Production Economics*, 272, 109236. Advance online publication. DOI: 10.1016/j.ijpe.2024.109236

Nwankpa, J. K. (2015). ERP system usage and benefit: A model of antecedents and outcomes. *Computers in Human Behavior*, 45, 335–344. DOI: 10.1016/j.chb.2014.12.019

Pásztor, Sz. (2022): A külpiacra lépés kezdetei néhány hazai vállalat szemszögéből (The beginnings of foreign market entry from the perspective of some domestic companies), Oecaonomus Gazdaságkutató Alapítvány, online: https://www.oeconomus.hu/irasok/a-kulpiacra-lepes-kezdetei-nehany-hazai-vallalat-szemszogebol/ (download: 03. 01. 2024.)

Pellegrino, R., & Gaudenzi, B. (2023). Impacts and Supply Chain Resilience Strategies to Cope with COVID-19 Pandemic: A Literature Review. *Springer Series in Supply Chain Management*, 21, 5–18. DOI: 10.1007/978-3-031-16489-7_1

Piricz, N. (2017): The Role and Impact of Fairness on Cooperation in Hungarian Metal and Machinery Supply Chains, *Management, Enterprise and Benchmarking in the 21st Century, pp. 312-322.*

Porter, M. E. (1991). *Strategy: Seeking and Securing Competitive Advantage*. HBR Book Series.

Qi, R., Ma, G., Liu, C., Zhang, Q., & Wang, Q. (2024). Enterprise digital transformation and supply chain resilience. *Finance Research Letters*, 66, 105564. Advance online publication. DOI: 10.1016/j.frl.2024.105564

Sambasivan, M., Siew-Phaik, L., Mohamed, Z. A., & Leong, Y. C. (2013). Factors influencing strategic alliance outcomes in a manufacturing supply chain: Role of alliance motives, interdependence, asset specificity and relational capital. *International Journal of Production Economics*, 141(1), 339–351. DOI: 10.1016/j.ijpe.2012.08.016

Sammut-Bonnici, T., & McGee, J. (2002). Network Strategies for the New Economy. *European Business Journal*, 14(4), 174–185.

Sluis, S., & De Giovanni, P. (2016). The selection of contracts in supply chains: An empirical analysis. *Journal of Operations Management*, 41(1), 1–11. DOI: 10.1016/j.jom.2015.10.002

Sodhi, M. S., & Tang, C. S. (2021). Supply Chain Management for Extreme Conditions: Research Opportunities. *The Journal of Supply Chain Management*, 57(1), 7–16. DOI: 10.1111/jscm.12255

Szentes, T. (1976). A Few Thoughts on the Problem of Hungarian Cooperation With Developing Countries. *Acta Oeconomica*, 17(2), 145–158.

Taj, S., Imran, A. S., Kastrati, Z., Daudpota, S. M., Memon, R. A., & Ahmed, J. (2023). IoT-based supply chain management: A systematic literature review. *Internet of Things : Engineering Cyber Physical Human Systems*, 24, 100982. Advance online publication. DOI: 10.1016/j.iot.2023.100982

Tjahjono, B., Esplugues, C., Ares, E., & Pelaez, G. (2017). What does Industry 4.0 mean to Supply Chain? *Procedia Manufacturing*, 13, 1175–1182. DOI: 10.1016/j.promfg.2017.09.191

Tliche, Y., Taghipour, A., & Canel-Depitre, B. (2018). Downstream Demand Inference in decentralized supply chains. *European Journal of Operational Research*, 274(1), 65–77. DOI: 10.1016/j.ejor.2018.09.034

Vandchali, H. R., Cahoon, S., & Chen, S.-L. (2021). The impact of supply chain network structure on relationship management strategies: An empirical investigation of sustainability practices in retailers. *Sustainable Production and Consumption*, 28, 281–299. DOI: 10.1016/j.spc.2021.04.016

Wu, M., Fu, C., Holguin-veras, J., Enz, M. G., & Mondy, C. (2024). The impact of digital technology deployment on mitigating supply chain disruptions: Evidence from Chinese automotive manufacturers during the COVID-19 crisis. *Journal of Purchasing and Supply Management*, 30(3), 100936. Advance online publication. DOI: 10.1016/j.pursup.2024.100936

Ye, Y., Wang, H., Tian, K., Li, M. (2024): Supply chain risks and the cost of debt: Evidence from the COVID-19 pandemic, *Research in International Business and Finance, 70(B)*, DOI: 10.1016/j.ribaf.2024.102399

Zouaghi, I., & Laghouag, A. (2021). A Research Note on Defining the Concept of Supply Chain. *International Journal of Scientific Engineering and Science*, 5(9), 6–10.

Chapter 6

A Comprehensive Entrepreneurship Model for the Internationalization of Green Innovation Business

José G. Vargas-Hernandez
https://orcid.org/0000-0003-0938-4197
Tecnológico Nacional de México, ITS Fresnillo, Mexico

Omar C. Vargas-González
https://orcid.org/0000-0002-6089-956X
Tecnológico Nacional de México, Ciudad Guzman, Mexico

Francisco J. González-Ávila
Tecnológico Nacional de México, ITS Fresnillo, Mexico

ABSTRACT

The objective of this paper is to analyze the functioning of an integral model of entrepreneurship in green innovation business (GIB) that is currently emerging and in the process of internationalization. Therefore, this work aims to study the central perspectives of technology that are based on the phenomenon of entrepreneurship and thus develop a strategy that adapts to companies with an ecological basis to achieve internationalization. This article analyzes a particular company, which specializes in ecological biomineral organic fertilizer, where no chemical product

DOI: 10.4018/979-8-3693-9241-6.ch006

is used to produce the composition, everything that is marketed is made up of a base of organic minerals and other organic compounds.

INTRODUCTION

Currently, there is a new business model which has as the objective to be eco-efficient. Eco-efficiency is defined as the production of products and services at competitive prices that meet human needs and provide quality of life, while the ecological consequences and the use of numerous resources during the life cycle are progressively reduced. level equivalent, at least, to the estimated capacity of the planet (World Business Council for Sustainable Development, 1991).

On the other hand, it is mentioned that eco-efficiency has the purpose of establishing production of manufactured products of high durability, reducing the intensity in the application of energy for the production of goods and services, maximizing the use of raw materials, managing and disposing of hazardous materials and waste in an efficient and environmentally acceptable manner, have management systems and environmental quality, as well as procedures in occupational safety and health, among other provisions, that will bring them financial benefits and competitiveness (Cantú, 2008, p. 78).

In both definitions, the authors agree that eco-efficient companies should have as their main objective, to develop quality products at competitive prices, as well as to reduce the environmental impact of producing or offering their products and services. Castro (1998) mentions that eco-efficiency aims to address three relevant aspects that correspond to 1) the total quality, which involves productivity and quality in the company, 2) the preservation of the environment, which is related to sustainable development; 3) occupational health and safety (Castro, 1998).

A Comprehensive Entrepreneurship Model of Green Business Innovation (GBI)

Entrepreneurship, inclusiveness, civil and culture are variables that have complex but straightforward linkages and processes among them and much is still unknown. The last few years have witnessed the generation of extensive theoretical and empirical literature on entrepreneurship and its impact at the levels of regional and firm economic performance (Holmes and Schmitz, 1990; Evans and Leighton, 1989). However, when linking entrepreneurship to the variables of inclusiveness and civil culture, literature is inexistent. There is a relative void, despite some recent efforts to study the relationship between entrepreneurship in some other related fields beyond economic growth, which may be attributable to the lack of theoretical frameworks.

However, some studies conducted in economic development have shown reversed causality influencing entrepreneurial activities (Ortega-Anderezand, and Lai, 2017). Entrepreneurial activities tend to be overestimated in regions where there are start-ups playing a relevant role while entrepreneurship activities tend to be underestimated in regions where there is a new entrepreneurial formation and the startups are few (Baptista, Escária, and Madruga, 2017).

The role of entrepreneurship in economic development has received attention from researchers showing the impact of entrepreneurship on employment and social development. Entrepreneurial intentions promote entrepreneurial behaviors (Krueger et al., 2000; Veciana et al., 2005; Souitaris et al., 2007). Entrepreneurship activity can be associated with human necessity providing an opportunity to earn money for living, until better alternative opportunities are found on the labor market (Carree and Thurik, 2010).

The concept of entrepreneurship is multidimensional and related to individual willingness, abilities, and activities on their own, in teams and in organizations to make decisions facing obstacles and uncertainty on the use of institutions and resources to create and develop new opportunities (Wennekers and Thurik, 1999). Entrepreneurial opportunities are the result of unemployment the influences start-up activity, the effect of a thriving economy and experience in entrepreneurial activities (Lin, Manser and Picot, 1998; Pfeiffer and Reize, 2000).

Entrepreneurship is the recognition and exploitation of opportunities leading to the creation and development of a firm (Aragon-Sanchez, Baixauli-Soler, Carrasco-Hernandez, 2017). Moreover, entrepreneurial intentions predict entrepreneurial behaviors, according to the theory of planned behavior (Ajzen, 1991). Entrepreneurial activity creates opportunities to influence economic performance (van Stel, Carree and Thurik, 2005) such as entering the markets with new production processes and products (Acs and Audretsch, 2003). Among the entrepreneurial models there is evidence that the entrepreneurial intentional models (Krueger et al., 2000) supports the theory of planned behavior.

The theory of planned behavior has been used in the analysis of entrepreneurial intentions (Shook et al. 2003). The determinants have significant positive relationships with behavior intention (Armitage and Conner 2001). Do Paço et al. (2011) found a positive and considerable influence between entrepreneurial intentions, attitudes, and perceived behavior control. However, subjective norms have an indirect impact on entrepreneurial intentions.

The determinants of entrepreneurial intentions are linked with access to financial, natural, human, and cultural capital and resources through the influence of attitudes, individual subjective norms, perceived social control, and self-efficacy.

The attitude is the individual favorable evaluation to start a new opportunity. Individual subjective norms are the perceived social pressure to start a new opportunity and perceived social control and self-efficacy is the perceived ease to start a new opportunity. Based on the Shapero and Sokol 1982) model, attitudes and subjective norms are linked to desirability and perceived behavioral control or self-efficacy with feasibility (Krueger et al., 2000).

METHODOLOGY OF RESEARCH

Background of the Problem and Assumption

Green innovation in urban areas is a neglected issue in terms of urban planning and policing. Still, more neglected is a concern for changes in urban green areas toward the implementation of green innovation initiatives to revitalize the cities, increase the economic growth, improve the social justice and inclusiveness, as well as the improvement of environmentally sustainable development, strengthen the biodiversity and socio-ecosystems. To achieve these goals, it is necessary to implement some actions following the design and implementation of a comprehensive entrepreneurship model.

This new eco-efficient business entrepreneurship model will be analyzed in the context of the integral model, analyzing in this way the tripod of the strategy, which integrates considerations based on industry, resources, and institutions. This paper begins with the assumption that the companies of ecological base present major difficulty at the time of wanting to internationalize, in comparison to the companies of the industrial base.

Instrument and Procedures

This analysis is based on the specific case study of an eco-efficient company using the methodological tools proposed for each one of the theoretical approaches.

For the analysis industry-based considerations are employed in the model of the five forces, also called the diamond model proposed by Porter (1980). The resource and capabilities analysis of the eco-efficient company is employed the model proposed by barney (2001) complemented with the SWOT analysis. Finally, the eco-efficient company is also analyzed in terms of the institutional considerations considered as the "rules of the game," formal and informal, that frame the entrepreneurial activities and the creation and development of companies according to the territorial environment.

Data Analysis: Use of Fertilizers in Mexico

The National Development Plan 2019-2024 establishes among the priority actions for food self-sufficiency and the rescue of the field the Fertilizer Program for the benefit of agricultural producers.

The Mexican Government's National Fertilizer Program aims to address the problem of low availability of national fertilizers at competitive prices for small producers. Includes chemical fertilizers and biofertilizers._This National Fertilizer Plan aims to reduce dependence on the import of these fertilizers. To achieve this, the Cosoleacaque Petrochemical Complex plants and the Pajaritos plant are reactivated to produce ammonia, an input to produce urea, which Mexico imports from Ukraine. In the case of phosphates, in the Pacific, the Lázaro Cárdenas plant is operational and is the largest in Latin America.

The National Bio Fertilizer Program shows incipient progress. The fertilizer production in Mexico estimated for 2019 was 1.85 million tons, reflecting an annual reduction of 2%; while demand continues to rise, with a record estimate of around 5.5 million mt. However, by July 2020, the production volume of nitrogen fertilizers in Mexico almost reaches 48,800 metric tons, which represents a decrease of 32.7% compared to that reported during the same month in 2019. The production volume of phosphate fertilizers in Mexico exceeded 75,600 metric tons, which represents a decrease of 29.1% compared to that reported during the same month in 2019 ((Burgueño Salas, 2020).

Fertilizer Demand in Mexico

A recent analysis of the fertilizer market in Mexico pointed out that the consumption of fertilizers has changed the structure in favor of consumers with the highest concentration and diversification (UACH). This situation has contributed to a consumption drop of fertilizers since the farmer's real income has fallen.

On the change in the consumption pattern (sources), I have no accurate information about it. From experience in the field, there has been a growth in the use of physical fertilizer mixtures where the distributor makes certain formulations, mixing fertilizers, and thus the producer only buys one product. Regarding those of high concentration, it is precise because there has been significant growth in the protected agriculture area. As the strawberries and high-value vegetable area, where the drip irrigation system is used and through it, fertilizers are applied, as a result, highly soluble sources with minimal impurities are usually used, but these are not traditional sources.

However, with more recent data reported by Instituted Trusts concerning Agriculture (FIRA 2020), in the agricultural year, 2019, 71.8% of the sown area was fertilized, representing the seventh consecutive year with increases in the percentage of fertilized area. According to this report, the consumption of fertilizers in Mexico grew 5.8%.

In an interview with a FIRA fertilizer specialist analyst; Gallegos Cedillo (2021), asking about the trend in fertilizer consumption and asked about the demand and supply of fertilizers in Mexico, he warned that the lack of information with hard data does not always support trends in which the market moves. Regarding the consumption of fertilizers, the production information indicates that production has fallen: 15.4% from 2013 (2.06 million tons) to 2020 (1.75 million tons) from January-September. Even though, in 2014 and 2019, it increased compared to the previous year and the same period.

Now, if we consider that fertilized area has increased, as a percentage of the sown area. This proportion has increased from 2013 to 2019, the last reported year, going from 65.3% in 2012 to 71.8% in 2019. However, if we look at the apparent consumption, it increased from five million tons in 2013 to 6.7 in 2018, in 2019 (January-December), it does drop to 5.8, and in September 2020, it is 5.2 (Graph in the quarterly report). There are no elements to attribute the drop in consumption from 2018 to 2019 to the decrease in producers' income. But if someone affirms this, it is difficult to prove otherwise (See figure 1).

Figure 1. Production and consumption of fertilizer in Mexico (Millions of tons)

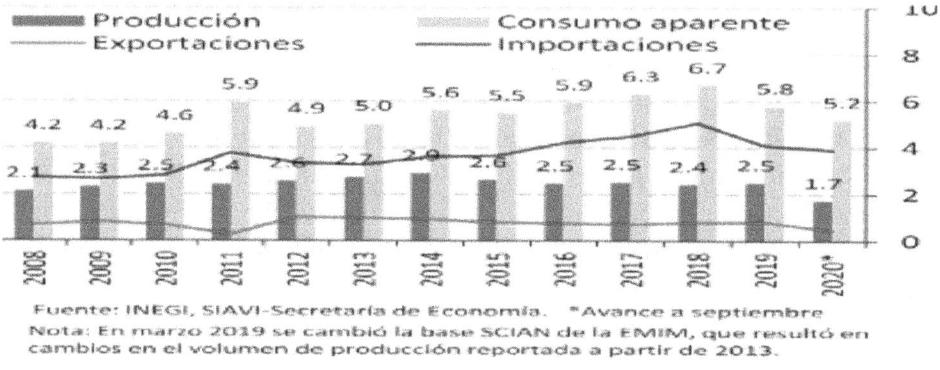

Fertilizer Production in Mexico

The increase in Mexican fertilizer production during the last years is attributed, in part, to the reforms made to the Pemex Law since 2008. These had the objective of promoting the production and productivity of the Mexican fertilizer industry, through the supply of raw materials, such as ammonia, at competitive prices for national manufacturers. In 2018, national production contributed 30.7% of apparent national consumption, which is estimated at 6.2 million dollars and represents an annual increase of 7.9%. The preceding shows the country's high dependence on fertilizer imports.

With data from 2019 the national production of fertilizers is composed of Phosphate fertilizers (diammonium and others) with 55.7%. Nitrogen fertilizers (ammonium sulfate and nitrate and others) with 32.2% Acidic fertilizers (phosphoric, sulfuric, and nitric) with 10.9%. The estimated value of the fertilizer industry in Mexico in 2019 is 13,616.4 million pesos, 2% lower than that registered in 2018.

Fertilizer production processes in Mexico are not integrated, a situation that has an impact on domestic producers, especially urea and nitrate, being at a disadvantage compared to producers of international competition (UACH). According to data from the latest Quarterly Report on Fertilizers from the Directorate of Research and Economic Evaluation of the Instituted Trusts concerning Agriculture (FIRA, 2020), the production of fertilizers in Mexico decreased at an annual rate of 8.4% in the first nine months of the year compared to the same period in 2019.

Regarding the fact that the national producers of urea and ammonium nitrate are at a disadvantage with international competition, as a consequence of the lack of integration of their production processes, if the statement is well understood, especially the reason that is manifested by the lack of integration of their production processes, in general, it would be expected that greater integration greater profitability, but this is not considered to be the main reason for the disadvantage of domestic producers. It can affect but is not the main reason.

More weight would be given to the characteristics of the Mexican farmer, small areas and little specialized, farmer grow various products, as well as the dependence to a large extent on the import of fertilizers that expose him to have fertilizers without due quality control, lack of weight in the containers (49 kg bags instead of 50 for example), exchange rate, etc. Gallegos Cedillo, 2021) (See figures 2 and 3).

Figure 2. Acid fertilizer production in Mexico, 2013-2020 (Thousands of tons)

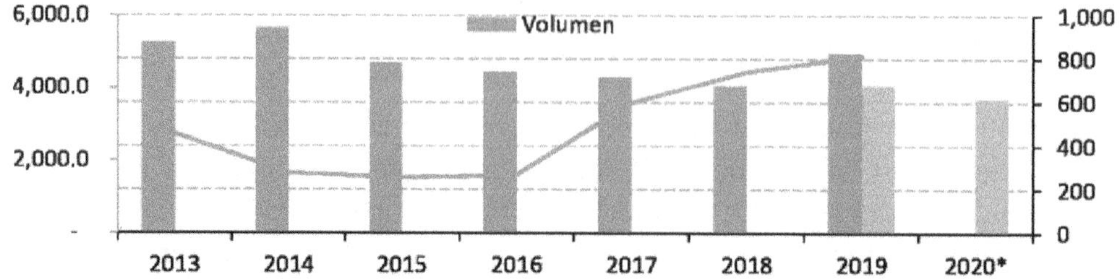

Figure 3. Fertilizer production in Mexico, 2013-2020 (Millions of tons)

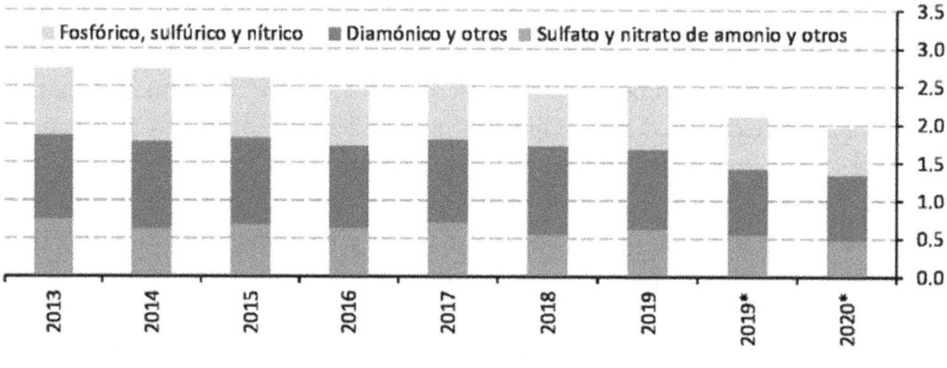

Fertilizer Exports and Imports in Mexico

In this regard, with information from the Ministry of Economy, imports of fertilizers in Mexico, during 2018, registered a volume of 5.06 million dollars and represented an annual increase of 12.6 percent. In said year, imports came from Russia (30.9%), the United States (14.3%), Norway (12.1%), and China (11.1%). In the last five years, these countries participated with 69.5% of the national fertilizer imports. In the case of exports, these stood at 0.79 million pesos and registered an annual growth of 10.5%. Between 2008 and 2018, consumption and imports grew on average at an annual rate of 6.3 percent.

Imports in 2019 are estimated at around 2.9 million tons, of which an advance of 92% was recorded as of November. Of the total imported, 67.2% corresponded to nitrogenous, 15.5% to phosphate, 12.5% to potash, and others with 4.8%. The commercial value of these imports was 807.8 million dollars, reflecting a reduction of 14.3% to the record of 943.1 million dollars registered in 2018. The main supplying countries were Russia 30.6%, China 16.9%, United States 11.3%, Algeria 7.9%, Malaysia 3.8%, Chile 2.9%, Canada 2.1%, Egypt 1.4%, and others 23.1%.

Between January and September 2020, Mexican fertilizer imports grew 9.9%, while exports decreased 16.6% at an annual rate, totaling 3.9 and 0.46 million dollars, respectively (See figures 4, 5, 6 and 7).

Figure 4. Mexican Fertilizer Exports, (Millions of dollars)

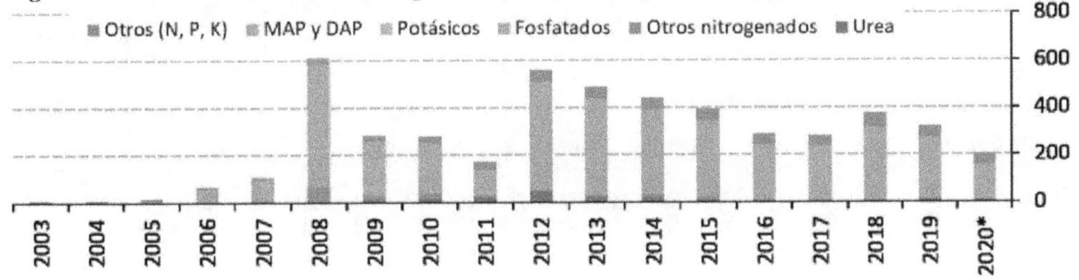

Figure 5. Mexican fertilizer imports, 2003 -2020 (Millions or dollars)

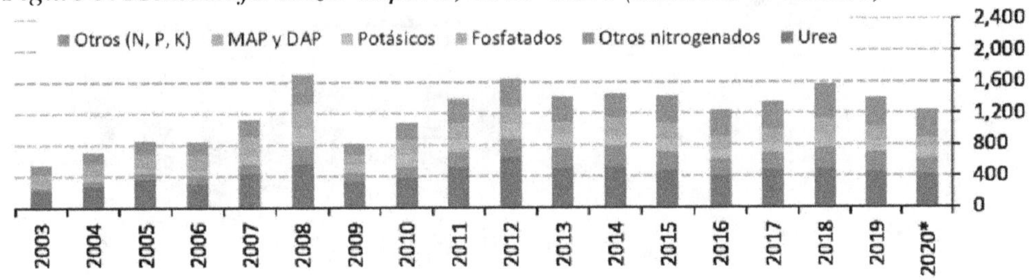

Figure 6. Balance of the fertilizer trade balance, 2003-2020 (Millions of tons)

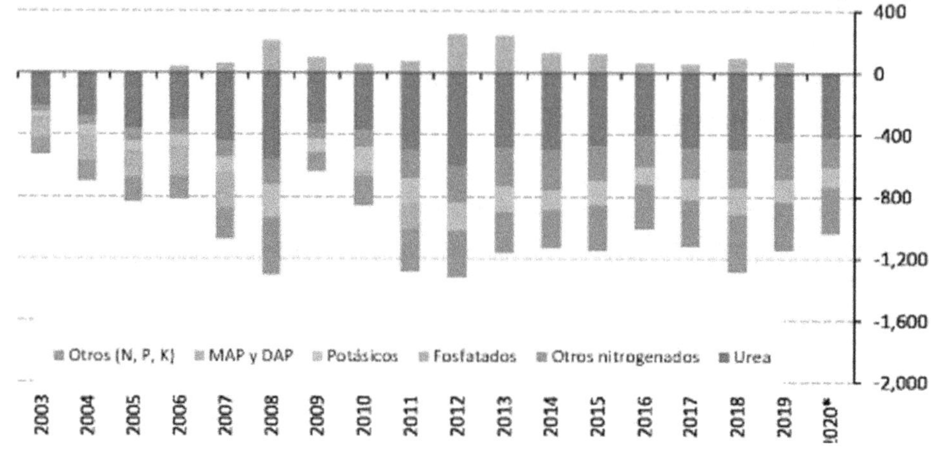

Figure 7. Trade balance (Millions of tons)

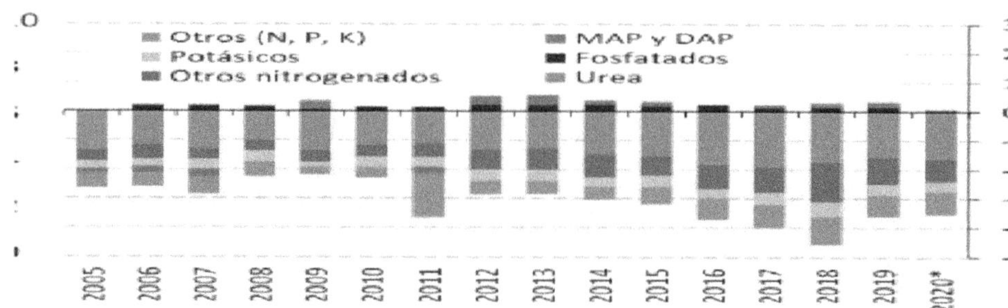

Fuente: SIAVI-Secretaría de Economía. *Avance a septiembre de 2020.

The Fertilizer Markets

The implicit price of fertilizer imports in Mexico in 2018 was $ 322.3 per ton and represented an annual increase of 6.7%. The implied fee of imports from Russia was 283.4 dollars per ton; 387.2 from China and 416.1 for those from the United States, and showed an annual growth of 10.8, 24.2, and 9.7%, respectively. Regarding the average price level of fertilizers in Mexico, since 2014, the behavior has been on the rise. In 2018, a ton of fertilizer in distribution centers was quoted on average, at 10,254 pesos, which represents an increase of 3.5% compared to 2017.

The fertilizers with the highest annual increases in prices were: diammonium phosphate (DAP) (10.4%), Triple 17 (10%), and potassium nitrate (9.4 percent). During January and February 2019, the average price was reduced by 2.0 and 1.3% compared to December 2018, so it would be expected that the average price in 2019 will be at similar levels to those registered during 2018. In the domestic market, urea prices increased 7.3% from 2018 to 2019; while those of diammonium phosphate rose 4.8%.

The average price of fertilizers in the country maintains an upward trend. In November 2020, it registered a growth of 2.7% at an annual rate and 3.3% from December 2019 to date. As of November, the price increases of triple 17 (12.2% annually), ammonia (9.9%), ammonium sulfate (8.3%), and ammonium nitrate (7.9%) stand out. The prices of simple superphosphate and potassium chloride were the ones that showed the highest annual decrease, at rates of 7.1 and 4.6%, respectively.

Bio Organic Fertilizers in México

The use of organic fertilizers in Mexico is not quite common, this is because industrial-based companies need chemical products that make plants grow at a faster rate due to market demand. But these fertilizers damage the soil causing it to become unusable after a time for the harvest, as a result, the food absorbs these fertilizers that are harmful to the human being overall. (Please see figures 8, and 9).

Figure 8. Prices in the international market (In Mexican pesos per ton)

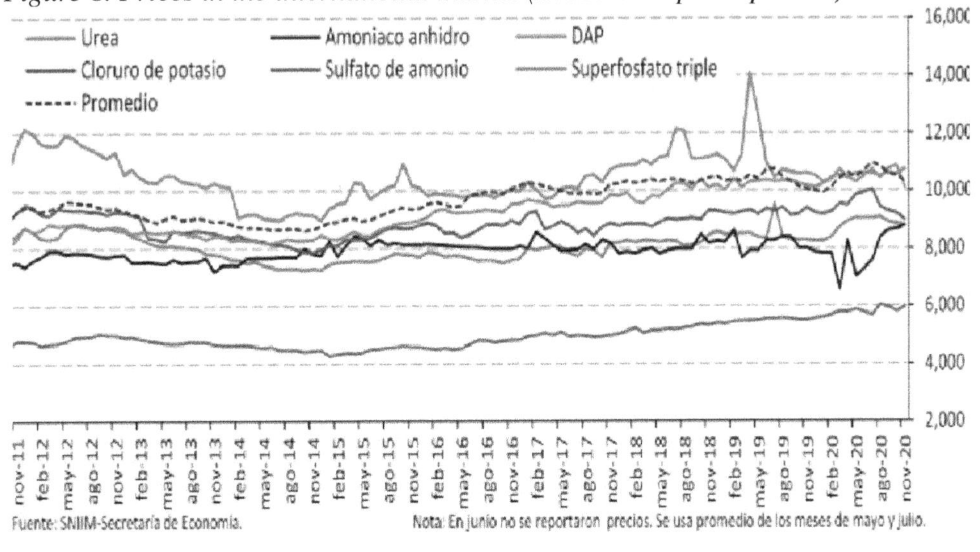

Figure 9. Production, foreign trade, and apparent consumption of fertilizers in Mexico, 2013-2020 (Millions of tons)

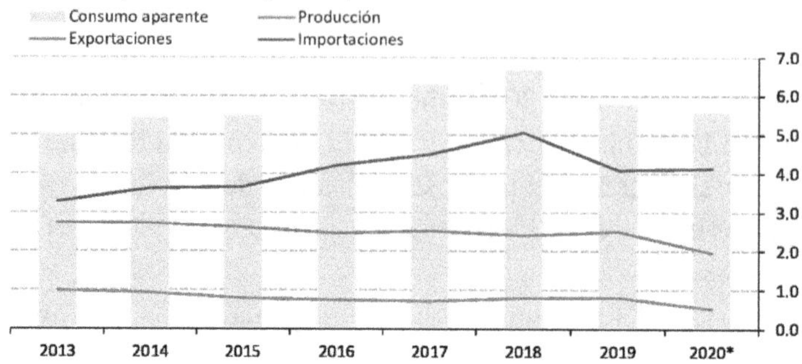

On the other hand, organic fertilizers bring many benefits to the soil along with plants and food. According to a study conducted by SAGARPA, organic fertilizers favorably influence the physical characteristics of the soil (physical fertility); These characteristics are structure porosity, air action, water retention capacity, infiltration, hydraulic conductivity, and stability of aggregates. The following table 1 shows a comparison made by the National Agricultural Survey (ENA) in which there is an increase in the use of chemical fertilizers in Mexico and a decrease in organic fertilizers. (See table 1).

Table 1. Comparison of the use of chemical and organic fertilizers in Mexico National

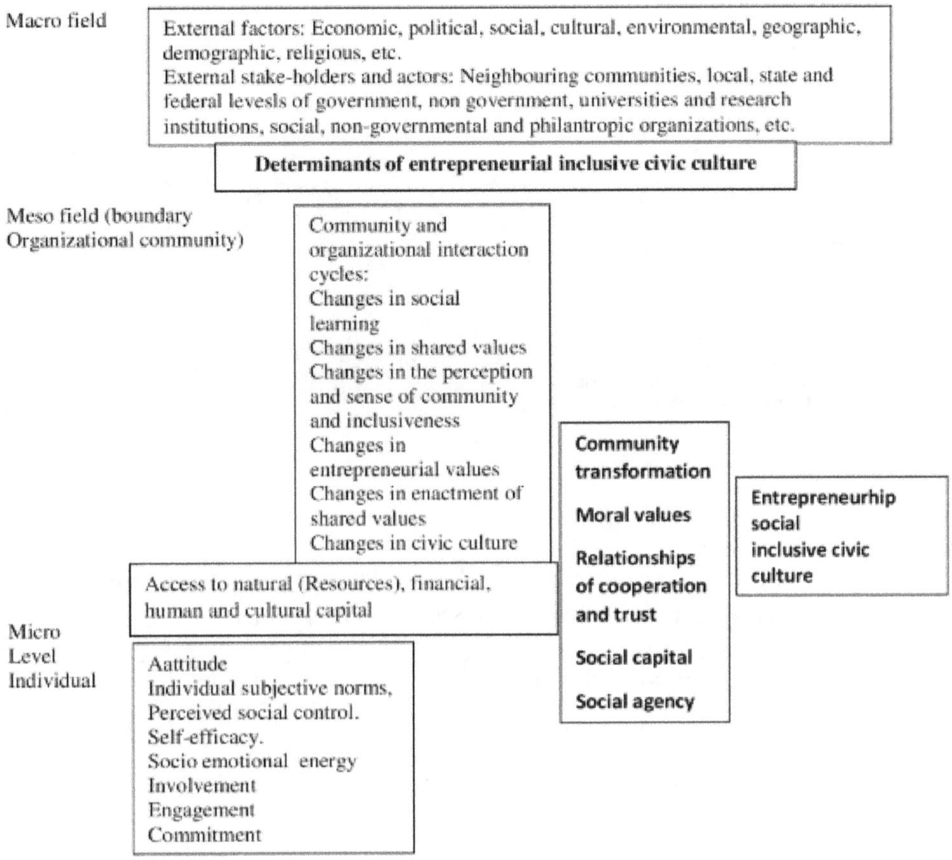

Source: Own development.

THEORETICAL-CONCEPTUAL FRAMEWORK

The theoretical framework applied in this study is based on the analysis of the coefficient company using the main three theories of strategic design and implementation: The industry-based considerations, the resource and capabilities considerations, and the institutions-based considerations, as shown below in figures 10 and 11.

Figure 10. Model of strategic analysis

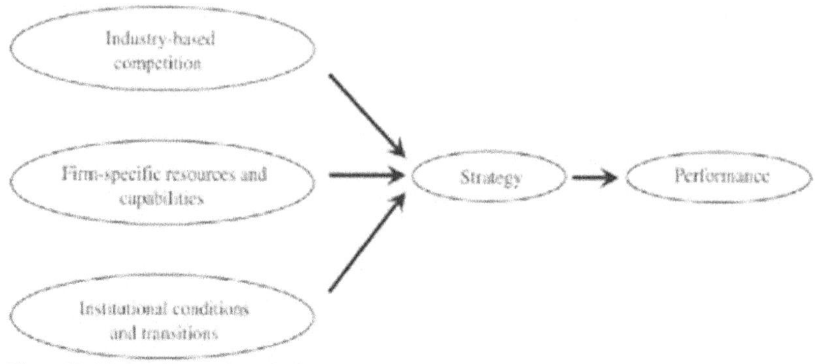

Figure 10. Model of strategic analysis
Source. Own elaboration based on Peng (2012).

Figure 11. A comprehensive entrepreneurship model for the internationalization of green innovation business (GIB) and eco- efficient companies

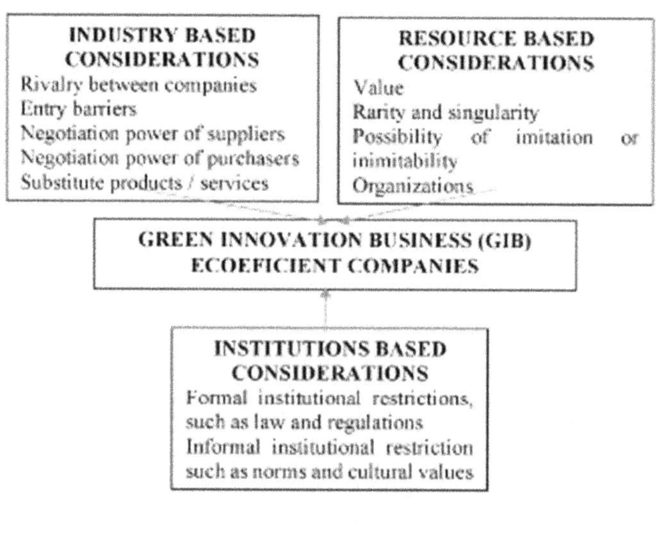

THE GREEN INNOVATION BUSINESS (GIB): BIO-FOM

BIO-FOM is a green innovation business (GIB) also characterized as an eco-efficient company to promote sustainable, profitable, and inclusive development through highly competitive Mexican seeds with fair prices. Using organic mineral bio-fertilizers healthily increased the profitability of the producers. It is in the metropolitan area of Guadalajara (Figure 12).

Figure 12. Localization of BIO-FOM a green innovation business (GIB).

Source: Web page of the company

BIO-FOM is the most complete Organic Mineral Bio-fertilizer available on the market, which is made from the interaction of elements: biological, organic, and mineral. It is a mineral organic bio-fertilizer for plant nutrition. The interaction of the BIO-FOM elements forms a Functional Plant Nutrition System; its results reflect: improving seed germination and initiation, healthy and adequate growth, larger roots, greater flowering, and tie, increase in the quality of the fruits, and provide resistance to pests and diseases. BIO-FOM increases soil fertility and contributes to the decontamination and regeneration of the soil.

BIO-FOM bases its functionality on the interaction of the biological, organic, and mineral elements that compose it: A Poly-Functional Consortium of Micro-organisms, among them: antagonists to pests and diseases, nitrogen fixers, and mycorrhizal fungi; that help release the nutrients provided by the BIO-FOM blend itself. The 17 Basic Mineral Elements of plant nutrition (nitrogen, phosphorus, potassium, calcium, magnesium, sulfur, iron, boron, copper, manganese, silicon, zinc, iodine, sodium, cobalt, molybdenum, selenium) Organic Matter, Amino Acids, Acids Humic, and Fulvi.

BIO-FOM contains live microorganisms: 8 bacteria and mycorrhizal fungi that help unblock the chemical components that exist in the soil allowing their absorption, in addition to an important contribution of organic matter, amino acids, humic and fulvic acids, this, together with its content of 16 mineral elements (nitrogen, phosphorus, potassium, magnesium, calcium, iron, boron, copper, manganese, silica, zinc, iodine, sulfur, sodium, cobalt and chlorine) together give rise to a molecular dialogue that results in a functional plant nutrition system, fertile soil, larger root size and helps improve pH, which is essential for proper and healthy plant growth.

Among other benefits, it potentiates the chemical fertilizers that complement the application of BIO FOM as:

a) It recovers the soil fertility, unlocking mineral nutrients present but not available, favoring their absorption due to their bio-organic profile.
b) Increases the specific weight of grains, resulting in higher production.
c) Increases the Br ix degrees of the fruit, having better sales possibilities.
d) Stimulates the immune system, so healthy, vigorous, and productive plants are achieved. Strengthens the root system of the plant, thereby improving the use of water and mineral nutrients available in the soil.
e) Respect the ecosystem, avoiding the contamination of the water table.
f) 100% assimilable, achieving a greater expression of the genetic potential of plants.
g) Retains and conserves moisture in soils.

EMPIRICAL RESULTS AND CONCLUSIONS

Industry-Based Considerations

When analyzing industry-based considerations, the framework of Porter's five forces is used, which considers factors such as rivalry between firms, barriers to entry, the power to negotiate with suppliers and buyers, as well as substitute products.

The Rivalry Between Companies

When talking about the rivalry of companies, it refers to the struggle that companies face every day to obtain a position before consumers. These battles can be for prices, quality in products, advertising battles, etc. On the other hand, the author

Huyghebaert mentions that the rivalry between firms generates a direct impact on the likelihood that a business will be successfully undertaken, as well as having an impact on the existence of barriers to entry since fewer firms exist in one industry more complicated will be the entry of new firms (Huyghebaert, 2004).

The company to analyze is dedicated to organic fertilizers made from organic minerals. As it is an innovative product, it does not have much competition, nonetheless, there is competition with the substitute products that would be all chemical fertilizers, due to a vast variety of substitute products that are available in the market. It is difficult to compete for price in the same way as being a medium-sized company is not even positioned in the consumer's mind when thinking of organic fertilizer.

Nowadays fertilizers and other chemical products for the treatment of the soil represent 15.7% of the income of the Nurseries and gardens industry in 2019. The industry has experienced a rapid growth in recent years, thanks to the constant increase in disposable income per capita and the consumer segment strengthened.

A decent part of the US market has been occupied by large companies such as Scotts Miracle-Gro Company, Walmart, and Lowe's. Because economies of scale, as well as large corporations can maintain a low cost while offering affordable prices. Price competition among large companies has led to slow growth throughout the sector and low profit margins. Some less profitable companies have been forced to leave the industry. Successful companies are those able to compensate the highest prices by offering a deeper knowledge of the product and superior customer service.

Over the next five years, the nursery and garden store industry are expected to continue to grow, as economic conditions are expected to remain stable. As the disposable income per capita increases, the consumer will be able to invest more time and money in the appearance and operation of their gardens. It is also expected that the industry will benefit from a growing demographic interest in small plants, gardening, and organic horticulture.

Below is a list of companies with which Mary's Poop competes in the United States.

Scotts Miracle-Gro Company (OH, USA)

Founded in 1868, Scotts Miracle-Gro Company is a multinational corporation and industry leader in the lawn and garden market. Its products include the infamous Miracle-Gro and a complete line of plant foods. The most popular Miracle-Gro fertilizers are inorganic, which are much less expensive than organic fertilizers.

PacaProGro (CA, USA)

The PacaProGro farm is in Somis, California, with an estimated 180 alpacas producing alpaca fiber and alpaca manure. Not only sell alpaca fertilizers, but also merchandise made of alpaca fiber, such as hats, gloves, scarves, and stuffed animals.

Alpaca Grow (VT, USA)

Alpaca Grow is a small family business operated in Vermont that began in 2014. Like Mary's Poop, Alpaca Grow sells only alpaca fertilizers.

Isolated Wood Farm (British Columbia, Canada)

Secluded Wood Farm is headquartered in British Columbia, Canada. They sell alpaca fiber and manure products.

Alpaca Island Company of Martha's Vineyard (MA, USA)

Island Alpaca Company has more than fifteen acres and around fifty alpacas. They sell alpaca fiber and manure products, and they are charging higher prices.

Camelot Haven Alpacas (British Columbia, Canada)

Founded in 2002, Camelot Haven Alpacas produces and sells alpaca clothing, accessories, gifts, and alpaca fertilizers.

Entry Barriers

As already mentioned before, BIO-FOM faces competition from large chemical and organic fertilizer companies. Due to this, there are difficulties when it comes to wanting to enter the foreign markets, as the big brands are doing well positioned in the market, and it would be complicated to unseat them or compete for prices so that the company, in this case, could compete for product quality as well as innovation and for the benefits that its product provides.

It is also important to consider the transaction cost and the transportation cost if working with foreign currencies. If the costs become too high, BIO-FOM products would be less competitive in the foreign market. An alternative to export is the franchise, which allows local business units to produce BIO-FOM products for a fee.

One of the competing companies of Mary's poop is already positioned in 10 states of North America, and has large sales volumes, being this way, the products of Mary's poop and other small alpaca farms cannot compete by prices and volume, as already mentioned previously, which makes it be managed as an oligopoly market among large companies. These in turn set entry barriers when playing with prices since, if they see that a new product wants to enter the market, they lower their prices to continue to have an advantage over others or use promotions which makes them more attractive. the purchase of their products to the final consumer.

It is also important to consider the transaction cost and the transportation cost if working with foreign currencies. If the costs become too high, Mary's Poop products would be less competitive in the foreign market. An alternative to export is the franchise, which allows local alpaca farms to produce Mary's Poop products for a fee.

Substitute Products or Services

In the global marketplace and more specifically, North America, large, medium-sized, and small competitors produce related products. Geographically, most of the production plants are in rural areas and seem to serve only local markets. The competitive advantage of BIO-FOM is that it is the company with the highest social awareness among all its competitors. And although its product is easy to imitate, it gives it a plus by mixing it with some other ingredients that make the compost a better quality. It is also easy to use as they pack the product inside disposable pod-made biodegradable materials that only must be deposited in a container with water waiting for it to dissolve and starts to water in a normal way.

But there is a high range of substitute products that, although they are not organic, the final use is the same (serve as fertilizer to the plants), sharing with substitute products is complicated since the raw material they are made with are very economical and this it makes the prices of the products accessible to all types of publics. On the other hand, the organic products that Mary's poop handles are of a slightly higher price, this is due to the handmade process with which they are manufactured.

Bargaining Power With Buyers

According to Porter, at this point, it is defined as the ability of customers to impose prices and conditions of sale (Porter, 1980). This force can be established by customers directly, whether negotiating a discount or financing model, demanding delivery forms, or indirectly which is summarized with competitive purchases.

The bargaining power of buyers may depend on some variables such as a high supply of products and/or services and low demand for them. Another may be that the products offered have no differentiation among themselves, etc. At this point, the customer has the option to choose any product or service that is presented to them and that they consider to be the best and meet their expectations. As well as defining what is the maximum price customers are willing to pay for a product or service, as well as some other requirements that could be delivery times, product quality, etc. All this has an impact on the company's profits.

Mary Forte, the owner of Mary's Poop, manages and operates the company and interacts with customers and other interested parties through social networks. Nowadays, online / digital marketing is the most important marketing tool, especially in social networks. For example, use "Pinterest" to communicate with the company's audience. This social networking platform is popular with many users who share images that can be easily shared. Therefore, she can approach her audience, attract their attention, and thus know what customers need and adapt to the needs of the market.

Bargaining Power With Buyers

In one of his writing papers, Peng mentions that when the bargaining power of suppliers becomes too great, business solutions must be found that can reduce it (Peng, 2012, page 127); this is since many options must be available to purchase inputs at reasonable prices.

The organic fertilizer based on organic minerals requires many inputs because of a lot of raw materials are used for its elaboration, so it is necessary to have many suppliers. But if it is necessary that with few suppliers that have contact make and establish the negotiation agreements and delivery times among many other things, in this way can reduce and to a certain extent eliminate transaction costs.

Considerations Based on Resources and Capabilities

The resources are any input in a productive system in which an output is generated. These can be classified as financial, physical, human, technological, organizational, knowledge, management team experience, and customer service, among others. The consideration based on resources groups some indispensable factors for entrepreneurship, some of them are creating value, being unique through the rarity factor among other aspects. For example, in an analysis Peng mentions that it is important to consider the resources of the company, they must be oriented to create value, they must have rarity, they must be difficult to imitate and finally business resources must be immersed in the organization (Peng, 2012).

On the other hand, Barney dogmatizes that the heterogeneity of organizations is due to the possession of resources: i) valuable, which must respond to environmental threats and take advantage of their opportunities; ii) rare or scarce, those that cannot allow obtaining competitive advantages with competitors; iii) difficult resources to imitate, without substitutes and organizational, which means that the company has aspects of order (Barney, 2001, page 41).

The company BIO-FOM offers the market an innovative product because it is taking the greatest benefit to a product that people see as a waste and transformed it into a product with added value; the strengths which this product provides are that they are organic, have a higher performance compared to other fertilizers, are favorable to the environment, are not expensive to produce. Something that gives a higher value is that the packaging is biodegradable by which makes the whole product itself is ecological and there is no waste of plastic or any other material that is difficult to decompose, the product is safe for children and pets so anyone can use it.

Therefore, for the considerations based on resources, a SWOT analysis was conducted to analyze both: the internal and external factors that provide added value to the firm, as the positive and negative factors that can cause the company not to grow as rapidly as expected (See table 2).

Table 2. SWOT Analysis

Strengths	**Opportunities**
Organic products / products without chemicals Excellent performance compared to other inorganic fertilizers environment friendly It is not expensive to produce The packaging is biodegradable No toxic, safe for children and pets It is not easy to imitate	Growing trend in organic products Market development Product development Product differentiation
Weaknesses	**Threats**
Lack of advertising + visibility Small production capacity-challenge for the company at scale The products have limited functions The products are not standardized Hard to forecast production Limited capital and strategic partners Do not go alone Expensive compared to inorganic fertilizers	Regulations that exist for exports Animal diseases Environmental factors may affect production Breach of demand levels Low market level

Source: Prepared by the Authors

In this table, it is shown that the firm has many strengths that make its product different but also has many threats. This is due to the same rarity of the product that makes it complicated for sale, likewise, the product is easy to imitate, so at any time it could have a lot of competition, which can quickly get to the market firm. In his essay, Porter states that the competitive advantage comes from the value that a company manages to create for its customers, by offering special benefits that compensate a higher price of the product (Porter, 1980).

Considerations Based on Institutions

When talking about considerations based on institutions, we are talking about the rules of the game of these, in which the behavior of the company is determined and how they are developed around the world. Peng points out five strategies for an entrepreneurial company to be successful, which can be applied together, and they are growth, innovation, networks, financing/government, and harvest/output (Peng, 2012).

The BIO-FOM company integrates some of these strategies such as innovation in their products, as well as networks since they try to have a wide network to get known as well as to obtain advice and keep growing as the company participates in a program called X-culture where companies are assigned a group of people from different parts of the world, advising companies so they can expand or internationalize at the time the company uses all the networks that are possible for be able to expand. Peng mentions that there is evidence that networks, personal and organizational, represent significant resources and opportunities and that the successful creation of networks can lead to the efficient performance of firms (Peng, 2012, page 13).

Instead, McDougall notes that network analysis builds a very solid foundation and helps identify international opportunities, as well as establish credibility, provide access to critical resources, as well as knowledge, and lead strategic and cooperative partnerships (McDougall, 2000).

CHALLENGES AND OPPORTUNITIES

Green innovation business (GIB) is in the field of organic fertilizers are contributing with an input of fundamental importance in primary agricultural activity. The rehabilitation of organic fertilizer-producing plants in the country is not economically viable in the short term, because the reactivation of activities in the plants takes time. Besides, it is not common to find these kinds of producer units in urban areas.

It is necessary to invest more resources in the qualification and to reduce the import of organic inputs and other ingredients necessary in the production of fertilizers. The importation of chemicals as well as organic fertilizers will continue, since the national production of 2020 only covers 33.7% of the total demand, and the remaining 66.3% is brought from the foreign market.

CONCLUSIONS

When analyzing the green innovation business (GIB) and eco-efficient company through the comprehensive method of entrepreneurship, it is observed that just as the company has some advantages in the product also with many threats that are the large companies that are already positioned and that also compete with competitive prices. It is also determined that although the green innovation business (GIB) has a wide network that is using the best way possible, it is necessary to increase the international network of contacts so that the business can grow quickly.

Although BIO-FOM has been positioned in the local, regional, and national markets for a brief time and has grown steadily, it has the challenge to enter the international markets in an extremely competitive position. The company Mary's poop has a competitive advantage that differentiates it from other firms, and that is that its product is innovative and ecological, as well as its processes are conducted in an ecological way which makes it an eco-efficient company.

Likewise, due to the culture of planting in Mexico, this company faces problems to become highly competitive in the country, since most farmers prefer chemical fertilizers and thus produce more in less time than caring for the land and having a product of a higher quality with organic fertilizers.

It is necessary to implement a culture of conscience in Mexico when we talk about caring for the land since the use of organic fertilizers would not only help the environment but also people, this is because the foods that are consumed will have better nutrients and they would not be contaminated with pesticides. Today some people started to make their gardens at home, so they grow their food, this is a good technique because they can be sure that the consumption of food is one hundred percent organic. Here is the importance of the topic for green innovation in urban areas.

REFERENCES

Acs, Z. J., & Audretsch, D. B. (2003). Innovation and Technological Change. In Acs, Z. J., & Audretsch, D. B. (Eds.), *Handbook of Entrepreneurship Research* (pp. 55–79). Kluwer Academic Publishers. DOI: 10.1007/0-387-24519-7_4

Ajzen, I. (1991). The theory of planned behavior. *Organizational Behavior and Human Decision Processes*, 50(2), 1–63. DOI: 10.1016/0749-5978(91)90020-T

Aragon-Sanchez, A., Baixauli-Soler, S., & Carrasco-Hernandez, A. J. (2017). A missing link: The behavioral mediators between resources and entrepreneurial intentions. *International Journal of Entrepreneurial Behaviour & Research*, 23(5), 752–768. Advance online publication. DOI: 10.1108/IJEBR-06-2016-0172

Armitage, C. J., & Conner, M. (2001). Efficacy of the theory of planned behavior: A meta-analytic review. *British Journal of Social Psychology*, 40(4), 471–499. DOI: 10.1348/014466601164939 PMID: 11795063

Barney, J. (2001). Is the resource-based “view” a useful perspective for strategic management research? *Academy of Management Review*, 26(1), •••.

Burgueño Salas, E. (25 Sept. 2020). *Volumen de producción mensual de fertilizantes fosfatados en México de enero de 2019 a julio de 2020 (en toneladas métricas).* Statista. Retrieve on the 2 of July 2021 from https://es.statista.com/estadisticas/594554/volumen-de-produccion-de-fertilizantes-superfosfatados-en-mexico/

Cantú, P. (2008). Desarrollo sustentable: conceptos y reflexiones. *Universidad Autónoma de Nuevo León*. Colección: *Tendencias Científicas. ISBN: 978-607- 433-117-2*

Carree, M. A., & Thurik, A. R. (2010). The impact of entrepreneurship on economic growth. In Zoltan, J., & Audretsch, D. (Eds.), *Handbook of entrepreneurship research*. Springer. DOI: 10.1007/978-1-4419-1191-9_20

Castro, A. (Julio de 1998). *Hacia el desarrollo sostenible y la ecoeficiencia: integración de las normas ISO 9000, ISO 14000 e ISO 18000 diseño de un sistema de gestión ambiental certificable. (Tesis de maestría inédita).* Obtenido de Facultad Regional de Buenos Aires: http://posgrado.frba.utn.edu.ar/investigacion/tesis/MIA-1998-Castro.pdf

Consejo Mundial Empresarial para el Desarrollo Sostenible. (1991). Ecoeficiencia y sustentabilidad. *Ciencia* UANL, 35.

Do Paço, F., Arminda, M., Ferreira, J. M., Raposo, M., Gouveia, R., & Dinis, A. (2011). Behaviours and entrepreneurial intention: Empirical findings about secondary students. *Journal of International Entrepreneurship*, 9(1), 20–38. DOI: 10.1007/s10843-010-0071-9

Evans, D. S., & Leighton, L. S. (1989). Some empirical aspects of entrepreneurship. *The American Economic Review*, 79, 519–535.

FIRA (2020). Reporte trimestral de fertilizantes, Dirección de Investigación y Evaluación Económica del Fideicomisos Instituidos en relación con la Agricultura. Diciembre 2020.

Gallegos Cedillo, G. (2021). Interview to a specialist of FIRA conducted on January 13th, 2021.

Gallegos Cedillo, G. (2021). Working paper Agronegocios FIRA.

Holmes, T. J., & Schmitz, J. A.Jr. (1990). A theory of entrepreneurship and its application to the study of business transfers. *Journal of Political Economy*, 98(2), 265–294. DOI: 10.1086/261678

Huyghebaert, N. (2004). *Comportamiento estratégico de los titulares en los mercados financieros y la salida de los arranques empresariales.*

Krueger, N. F.Jr, Reilly, M. D., & Carsrud, A. L. (2000). Competing models of entrepreneurial intentions. *Journal of Business Venturing*, 15(5-6), 411–432. DOI: 10.1016/S0883-9026(98)00033-0

Lin, Z., Manser, M. E., & Picot, G. (1998), The Role of Self-Employment in Job Creation in Canada and the U.S., *OECD-CERF-CILN International Conference on Self-Employment*, Burlington, Ontario, Canada.

McDougall, P. (2000). *International entrepreneurship*. AMJ.

Ortega-Anderezand, D., & Lai, E. (2017, February). The Main Factors Influencing Entrepreneurial Activities and Intentions within a Country—A Case Study of Spain. *International Journal of Innovation, Management and Technology*, 8(1), •••.

Peng, M. (2012). *Global Strategy*. Thomsom South-Western.

Pfeiffer, F., & Reize, F. (2000). Business Start-ups by the Unemployed - an Econometric Analysis Based on Firm Data. *Labour Economics*, 7(5), 629–663. DOI: 10.1016/S0927-5371(00)00016-6

Porter, M. (1980). *Competitive Strategy*. Free Press.

Shapero, A., & Sokol, L. (1982). The social dimensions of entrepreneurship. In Kent, C. A., Sexton, D. L., & Vesper, K. H. (Eds.), *Encyclopedia of Entrepreneurship* (pp. 72–90). Prentice Hall.

Shook, C. L., Priem, R. L., & McGee, J. E. (2003). Venture creation and the enterprising individual: A review and synthesis. *Journal of Management*, 29(3), 379–399. DOI: 10.1016/S0149-2063(03)00016-3

Souitaris, V., Zerbinatib, S., & Al-Lahamc, A. (2007). Do entrepreneurship programmes raise entrepreneurial intention of science and engineering students? The effect of learning, inspiration and resources. *Journal of Business Venturing*, 22(4), 566–591. DOI: 10.1016/j.jbusvent.2006.05.002

Van Stel, A., & Suddle, K. (2007). The Impact of New Firm Formation on Regional Development in the Netherlands. *Small Business Economics.*

Veciana, J. M., Aponte, M., & Urbano, D. (2005). University students' attitudes towards entrepreneurship: A two countries comparison. *The International Entrepreneurship and Management Journal*, 1(2), 165–182. DOI: 10.1007/s11365-005-1127-5

Wennekers, A. R. M., & Thurik, A. R. (1999). Linking entrepreneurship and economic growth. *Small Business Economics*, 13(1), 27–55. DOI: 10.1023/A:1008063200484

Chapter 7
Towards the Application of fsQCA Method in Operations Management: A Conceptual Framework

Molk Oukili Garti
Sidi Mohamed Ben Abdellah University, Fez, Morocco

Jabir Arif
https://orcid.org/0000-0002-5285-7976
Sidi Mohamed Ben Abdellah University, Fez, Morocco

Fouad Jawab
https://orcid.org/0000-0002-0508-7278
Sidi Mohamed Ben Abdellah University, Fez, Morocco

ABSTRACT

This chapter highlights the role of fsQCA in supply chain management operations, building on previous research. It develops a conceptual framework for sustainable supply chain management using fsQCA, analyzed through content and Pareto analysis. The study examines 75 publications from 19 leading journals (2015-2024). Results, presented as clusters, indicate fsQCA's frequent application in production strategies, sourcing, risk management, and sustainability within logistics operations. The analysis also offers new perspectives on fsQCA's applicability in other research areas and provides recommendations for future studies. The chapter identifies significant research challenges and factors for improvement. It advocates for developing new models for better global adaptation and execution of fsQCA within predefined frameworks, urging business managers and academics to consider these insights. Additionally, it calls for an in-depth analysis of how fsQCA can be applied

DOI: 10.4018/979-8-3693-9241-6.ch007

to existing logistics structures.

INTRODUCTION

Supply chain management is a central area of scientific research (Arif et al., 2023), particularly highlighted by the post-COVID-19 crises that disrupted supply chains and caused temporary production halts (Farooq et al., 2021). According to (McKinsey, 2022), the pandemic affected all business operations, with a 60% decline in airline revenues in 2020, and a return to 2019 levels expected by 2024. (McKinsey, 2022) also noted that "the COVID-19 pandemic created short-term disruptions and provoked long-term changes in how the world lives and does business".

In response to these challenges, a transition towards Industry 5.0 is emerging, emphasizing sustainability, resilience, and human-centricity (Garrido et al., 2024). This necessitates rigorous supply chain management, utilizing robust technologies to strengthen logistics systems, as demonstrated by Deloitte's recent commitments to sustainability and achieving carbon neutrality by 2030 (Deloitte, 2021).

In research, traditional methods are being questioned in the face of increasing complexity, leading to the adoption of approaches like Fuzzy Qualitative Comparative Analysis (fsQCA) (Kumar et al., 2022). FsQCA, based on Boolean algebra and configurational relationships, allows for identifying causal and asymmetric configurations as well as complex alternatives (Prentice, 2019), making this method particularly valuable for exploring supply chain sustainability and resilience (Farooq et al., 2021). However, its application in supply chain management remains limited, presenting a promising field of research.

In this context, a comprehensive literature review was conducted in a previous chapter on the application of this method in logistics operations management, based on a systematic literature review (SLR) followed by bibliometric analysis. The existing literature was thoroughly explored, and the most impactful contributions were identified. The results showed a continuous increase in the number of published articles in recent years, with the majority coming from China and India. These findings suggest that an increasing number of researchers from these regions are inclined to use the fsQCA method in studies related to logistics operations management, aiming to find solutions for sustainable supply chain management.

To complement this study, the present chapter aims to build upon the results of the SLR, which targeted 75 publications focusing on the application of the fsQCA method in logistics operations management. The main goal is to identify key components following the use of the fsQCA method in supply chain management and to provide new and holistic perspectives on future studies. Moreover, this study aims to delve deeper into the correlation between the utility of the fsQCA method and sustainability, in order to examine to what extent, the application of this method can contribute to achieving sustainable supply chain management, while outlining a conceptual framework that envisions the key elements of this study. This is well explored by addressing the following three research questions, which will be at the core of this study:

RQ1: What are the different research clusters that have emerged from related studies?

RQ2: What are the recommendations for advancing research in sustainable supply chain management by applying the fsQCA method?

RQ3: What are the theoretical and practical implications of this study?

To effectively address the research questions, the article is structured into five main sections. After introducing the research topic, it begins with a literature review on the elements that describe logistics management operations, followed by the methodology in the form of a content analysis based on Pareto analysis to present and interpret the results in clusters and provide new perspectives. Subsequently, it transitions to the discussion, where it presents the research framework, including theoretical and practical implications, concluding with a conclusion.

LITERATURE REVIEW

Review of Supply Chain Operations Management Elements

It is absolutely confirmed that supply chain management involves the management of a set of processes where input elements are transformed with added value into output elements (El Jaouhari et al., 2023), while the operations describing these processes differ in terms of perspective from one sense to another. However, several researchers have described these supply chain management processes through a set of operations primarily encompassing procurement, planning, and transportation management (Ahi & Searcy, 2013), while others have focused solely on the purchasing and procurement aspect in their description of supply chain operations. Ilya Jackson, however, in his article elaborating on "Generative artificial intelligence in supply chain and operations management: a capability-based framework for analysis and implementation," has provided a more comprehensive and detailed description of all operations that describe supply chain management, naming it with the term "SCOM" (Supply Chain Operations Management). In his article, he has identified these operations into 13 SCOM elements:

- **Demand forecasting** is one of the essential processes in supply chain and operations management that guides decisions regarding inventory, production, and distribution (Liang et al., 2024).
- **Distribution and transportation strategy:** The main objective of this operation is to maximize the length of the shortest path a follower can traverse, considering a limited interdiction budget (Jackson et al., 2024).
- **Inventory management and warehousing** is an operation that enables the management of future stock needs based on production quantity with the aim of eliminating any risk of inventory distortion as well as avoiding stock-level issues and increasing sales (Jackson et al., 2024).
- **Process design** is the study of manufacturing processes with the objective of detecting anomalies and pattern recognition to contribute to process efficiency and quality control (Jackson et al., 2024).
- **Production planning and control** is an operation that allows for the management and scheduling of production orders based on the execution of a production schedule with the objective of ensuring timely delivery of orders (Jackson et al., 2024).
- **Production strategy** encompasses all action plans aimed at understanding production constraints, planning solutions, and making decisions (Jackson et al., 2024).
- **Quality management:** These are all operations that ensure control in terms of resources, time, and also the detection of defective products before they are passed to shipping operations with the ultimate goal of ensuring customer satisfaction (Jackson et al., 2024).
- **Revenue management** involves maximizing the revenues of multiple products with limited inventory over a finite selling season (Jackson et al., 2024).
- **Sales and Operations Planning** is the process that ensures effective coordination of the supply chain with the aim of minimizing the overall costs of these operations (Jackson et al., 2024).
- **Scheduling and routing** is the operation aimed at managing and resolving all difficulties related to routing problems (Jackson et al., 2024).
- **Sourcing strategy** is the set of operations that involve negotiating with suppliers, making decisions beneficial for both parties involved, with the aim of achieving strategic procurement planning (Jackson et al., 2024).
- **Supply chain design** is the operation of creating optimal configurations by taking into account multiple intervening factors and their complex interactions, such as establishing the most suitable replenishment policies while adeptly adapting to environmental changes (Jackson et al., 2024).

- **Supply chain risk management** involves strategies aimed at identifying, assessing, mitigating, and monitoring unexpected events that could negatively impact any part of a supply chain (Jackson et al., 2024).

Figure 1. Supply chain operations management (SCOM)

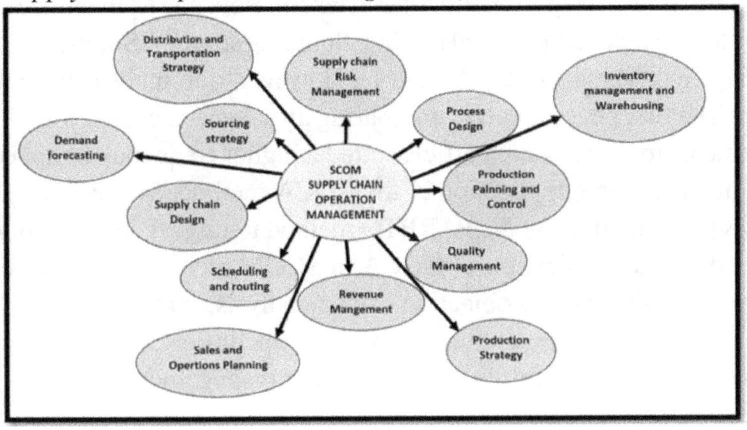

Content Analysis

Content analysis is a systematic coding and classification method for analyzing large amounts of data. It combines qualitative methods that retain rich meaning and perform robust quantitative analysis, complementing bibliometric analysis (Zhang et al., 2023). As bibliometric analysis of the fsQCA method in supply chain management only shows research trends (by year, by journals, by authors), however, the internal relationships and influencing mechanisms of related variables could not be obtained (Zhang et al., 2023). Therefore, we used literature content analysis to provide a comprehensive examination of the relationships and correlations between variables in research on the application of fsQCA in supply chain operations management. To complement bibliometrics with content analysis, the method is oriented towards analyzing the words and terms used by studies addressing a certain subject to identify patterns and trends.

The objective of this analysis is to highlight the application of the fsQCA method in operations that describe supply chain management in order to extract the various clusters that encapsulate this study, and subsequently develop a framework in which a new sustainable supply chain management strategy can be distinguished. To establish this analysis, an exploitation of the results of an analysis conducted by Ilya Jackson in his article "Generative artificial intelligence in supply chain and operations management: a capability-based framework for analysis and implementation" regarding the identification of the 13 distinct decision-making domains in supply chain operations management (SCOM) was undertaken. These domains include respectively: Demand forecasting, Distribution and Transportation Strategy, Inventory management and Warehousing, Process Design, Production Palnning and Control, Production Strategy, Quality Management, Revenue Mangement, Sales and Opertions Planning, Scheduling and routing, Sourcing strategy, Supply chain Design, Supply chain Risk Management (Figure 1). However, our analysis is conducted in two phases. The first phase involves comparing all selected articles with the distinct SCOM elements to detect which articles cited a higher frequency of appearance of SCOM elements in their application of the fsQCA method. Subsequently, a classification was performed using the PARETO method to target Class A articles, those most focused on the application of fsQCA in SCOM elements. The second phase aims to highlight the second objective of our analysis, which is to distinguish if there is sustainable management in supply chain operations through the extraction of distinct levers of sustainability in supply chain management.

Pareto Analysis

After determining the necessary SCOM elements to detect in each of the 75 selected articles, it was necessary to apply an analysis that classifies and prioritizes the critical elements, which in our case are the set of 13 supply chain management operations in existing studies. To do this, a Pareto analysis was conducted to identify the most common SCOM elements in each article. Pareto analysis is a quality control tool that ranks data classifications, in descending order, from the highest to the lowest frequency of occurrences (Wuni, 2022). The Pareto principle posits that for many events, roughly 80% of the effects come from 20% of the causes, resulting in the heuristic rule of Pareto's "80/20" principle (Wuni, 2022). Pareto analysis was used in the study because the main data consisted of keyword frequencies or citations, which limited the scope of applicable analytical methods (Wuni, 2022). The Pareto analysis method was appropriate for the study's objective because it was necessary to prioritize the SCOM elements in each of the 75 selected articles to extract the most impactful SCOM operations when applying the fsQCA method in a supply chain. This made the technical approach appropriate as it was used to classify and prioritize critical "SCOM" elements in existing studies. The total (cumulative) frequency is equivalent to 100%, so that the "essential" SCOM elements occupy a substantial portion (80%) of the cumulative percentage of citation and keyword frequencies, while the "useful" SCOM elements represent only the remaining 20% of occurrences. This study used a Pareto chart (i.e., histograms and a curve) to identify the SCOM elements present in each article. The set of SCOM elements in each article generating cumulative citation and keyword frequencies of 80% are considered the most critical.

The result, sometimes detected, indirectly depends on the focus of the article being studied. Subsequently, the results were classified into a table 1, in order to calculate the percentage of occurrence of each operation across all the articles studied. After obtaining the Pareto chart, it was necessary to calculate how many SCOM elements are contained in class A, which will subsequently determine the key SCOM elements and the objective of this analysis. Additionally, the number of SCOM elements contained in each of classes B and C was calculated to observe the decreasing distribution of SCOM elements in each of these three classes. However, to determine the elements of class A, the calculation was performed by multiplying the percentage 20% by the total of 13 SCOM elements, which represents 80% for all SCOM elements. The result yielded 3 SCOM elements, which are: "Production strategy, Sourcing strategy, and Supply chain risk management". Next, to calculate class B, the calculation was performed by multiplying the percentage 30% by the total of 13 SCOM elements, representing 15% for all SCOM elements. The result yielded 4 SCOM elements, which are: "Revenue Management, Process Design, Demand forecasting, and Production Planning and Control". Finally, class C was determined by multiplying the percentage 50% by the total of 13 SCOM elements, representing 5% for all SCOM elements. The result yielded 6 SCOM elements, which are: "Quality Management, Sales and Operations Planning, Distribution and Transportation Strategy, Supply Chain Design, Inventory Management and Warehousing, and Scheduling and Routing".

•Class A comprises the top 20% of SCOM area representing 80% of all SCOM elements. This implies:

A = (20x13)/100 = 3 SCOM elements.

•Class B is the category of the next 30% of SCOM area representing 15% of all SCOM elements. This implies:

B = (13x30)/100 = 4 SCOM elements.

•Class C is the bulk category, consisting of 50% of SCOM area with low occurrences of criteria, representing 5% of all SCOM elements:

C = (50x13)/100 = 6 SCOM elements.

The representation of these results on the graph is described in (Figure 2).

The analysis is subsequently developed by focusing on Class A, which precisely determines the three clusters distinguished in this research, consisting of: the application of fsQCA in production strategy, the application of fsQCA in sourcing strategy, and the application of fsQCA in supply chain risk management.

The second phase of the research involves assessing the presence of sustainability management in the three selected SCOM elements. To better elaborate on this, a filter was applied to target all articles that focused on the application of fsQCA in the three targeted fields: production strategy, sourcing strategy, and supply chain risk management. The filtering process identified 39 articles that address these three elements (after removing duplicates). A comparison was made based on the three fundamental pillars of sustainable management, which also reflect the sustainable development goals within a supply chain: environmental, economic, and social aspects (Weihua et al., 2017). To further refine the research, a selection was made of articles that mentioned environmental, economic, and social criteria in their titles, abstracts, keywords, or throughout the article, as well as articles that referenced "sustainable development goals" (Weihua et al., 2017).

The comparison was conducted to extract the presence rate of sustainable management in articles elaborating on the fsQCA method in the three identified clusters: production strategy, sourcing strategy, and risk management in the supply chain (Figure 3). The results showed that 74% of the 39 analyzed articles reflect sustainability management while applying fsQCA. On the other hand, 23% of the selected articles are based on two pillars that fall within sustainability management (economic and social, economic and environmental, or environmental and social aspects), indicating that the majority of studies related to the application of fsQCA in supply chain operations are focused on sustainability in management. However, a fourth cluster is extracted and can also be added to the scope of our study, which is the application of fsQCA and sustainability management.

Figure 2. Classification ABC

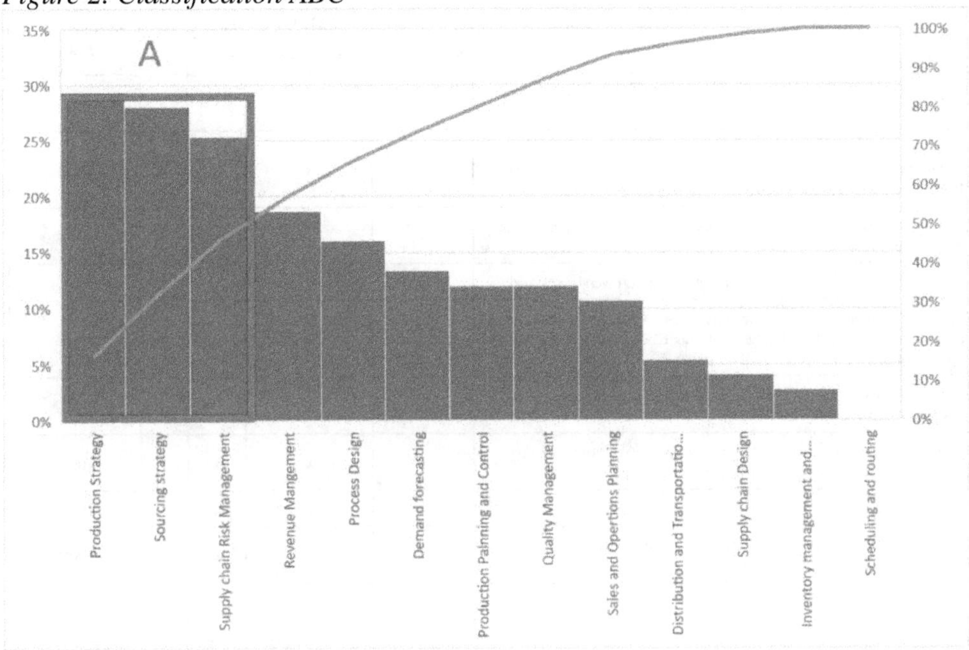

Figure 3. The dispersion of sustainability rates in management

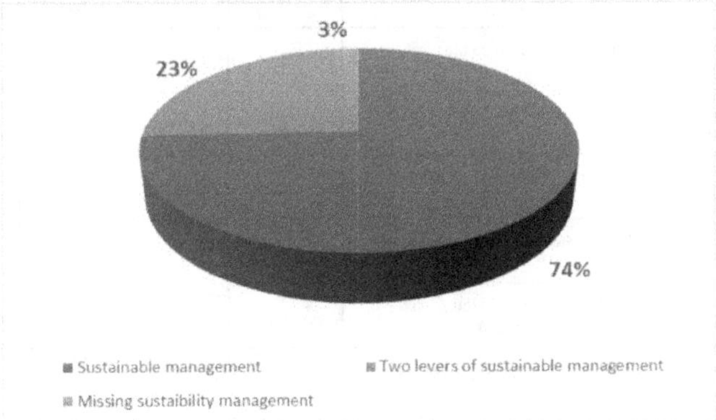

Table 1. Evaluation of sustainable management in the 39 studied articles

Articles Title	Sustainability management			Sum	Sustainability Rates
	Economical	Environmental	Social		
Pathways to sustainability: A fuzzy-set qualitative comparative analysis of rural water supply programs	x	x	x	3	100%
Mechanism of governance pressures, green production and collaboration on the performance of maritime supply chain: Evidence from the moderating effect of government subsidies	x	x	x	3	100%
Water and waste management strategies as drivers of the financial performance of food companies	x	x	x	3	100%
Dynamic capabilities that matter for business failure versus survival	x	x	x	3	100%
Pathways to improve energy efficiency under carbon emission constraints in iron and steel industry: Using EBM, NCA and QCA approaches	x	x	x	3	100%
Exploring the relationship between quality ambidexterity and sustainable production	x	x	x	3	100%
A contingency perspective on manufacturing configurations for the circular economy: Insights from successful start-ups	x	x	x	3	100%
Impact of digital transformation on the automotive industry,	x	x	x	3	100%
A framework for determining the impacts of a multiple relationship network on green innovation	x	x	x	3	100%
Natural resource dependence theory: Impacts of extreme weather events on organizations	x	x	x	3	100%
What factors determine the survival of green innovative enterprises in China? -- A method based on fsQCA	x	x	x	3	100%
Under which conditions do manufacturing companies choose FDI for service provision in foreign markets? An investigation using fsQCA	x	x	x	3	100%
From offshore-provider to brand creator: fsQCA of footwear industry	x	x	x	3	100%
COVID-19-related innovations: A study on underlying motivations and inter-organizational collaboration	x	x	x	3	100%
Untying the knot: Drivers of the intention to downgrade the relationship in B2B service contexts	x	x	x	3	100%
From zero-sum to win-win - Organisational conditions for successful shared value strategy implementation	x	x	x	3	100%
Mapping out the sharing economy: A configurational approach to sharing business modeling	x	x	x	3	100%
Tackling the complexity of guests' food waste reduction behaviour in the hospitality industry	x	x	x	3	100%
Extending social responsibility to small and medium-sized suppliers in supply chains: A fuzzy-set qualitative comparative analysis	x	x	x	3	100%
When supplier development initiatives fail: Identifying the causes of opportunism and unexpected outcomes	x	x	x	3	100%
B2B digital platform adoption by SMEs and large firms: Pathways and pitfalls	x	x	x	3	100%
Supplier selection, control mechanisms, and firm innovation: Configuration analysis based on fsQCA	x	x	x	3	100%
Organizational intention to adopt big data in the B2B context: An integrated view	x	x	x	3	100%
Treat me well and I may leave you kindly: A configurational approach to a buyer's relationship exit strategy	x	x	x	3	100%

continued on following page

Table 1. Continued

Articles Title	Sustainability management			Sum	Sustainability Rates
	Economical	Environmental	Social		
Relation between managerial cognition and industrial performance: An assessment with strategic cognitive maps using fuzzy-set qualitative comparative analysis	x	x	x	3	100%
Factors influencing proactiveness in supply chain risk identification: A fuzzy-set qualitative comparative analysis,	x	x	x	3	100%
The impact of supply chain social responsibility on sustainable performance	x	x	x	3	100%
A novel decision support system for the appraisal and selection of green warehouses	x	x	x	3	100%
Modelling firms' interventions in ISO 9001 certification: A configurational approach	x	x	x	3	100%
Path selection of lean digitalization for traditional manufacturing industry under heterogeneous competitive position	x	x		2	67%
Decoding digital transformational outsourcing: The role of service providers' capabilities		x	x	2	67%
Unpacking value creation and capture in B2B relationships	x		x	2	67%
Financial performance of servitized manufacturing firms: A configuration issue between servitization strategies and customer-oriented organizational design	x	x		2	67%
Green supply chain management practices and third-party logistics providers' performances: A fuzzy-set approach		x	x	2	67%
Customizing governance mechanisms to reduce opportunism in buyer–supplier relationships in the digital economy	x		x	2	67%
A decision support system for demand forecasting with artificial neural networks and neuro-fuzzy models: A comparative analysis	x	x		2	67%
Co-alignment of supplier quality management practices and cognitive maps – A neo-configurational perspective	x	x		2	67%
Supply chain collaboration in the petroleum sector of an emerging economy: Comparing results from symmetrical and asymmetrical approaches	x	x		2	67%
To be or not to be (loyal): Is there a recipe for customer loyalty in the B2B context?				0	0%
An environmental-based perspective framework: integrating IoT technology into a sustainable automotive supply chain	x	x	x	3	100%

Representation of the Extracted Clusters

The clustering extraction step involves consolidating and grouping all the findings into clusters or categories. In our case, the extraction was carried out in the first part, based on the results of the Pareto analysis performed, which represents all the SCOM elements found in class A and which represent the major part impacted by the application of the fsQCA method in supply chain management operations across all the analyzed articles. However, the three clusters that were able to encompass the highest number of occurrences in the various selected article studies are respectively:

the application of fsQCA in production strategy with an occurrence percentage of 29%, the application of fsQCA in sourcing strategy with a percentage of 28%, and the application of fsQCA in risk management in logistics chains with a percentage of 25%. The second part of the cluster extraction was carried out based on the results of the initial analysis, which involved conducting a second search focusing on articles containing the 3 SCOM elements captured in cluster A, representing the top 3 clusters. The filter yielded 39 articles. The phase that followed these results was to also evaluate the articles highlighted in the first set of results to determine if there is sustainable management in the studies applying fsQCA in supply chain operations. The results showed that 74% of the articles confirmed in their studies that there is a strong correlation between the application of the fsQCA method and the presence of sustainability aspects in supply chain operations management. The study in this case is focused on considering four clusters upon which the framework of our study is based.

Cluster 1: The Application of fsQCA in Production Strategy

The first cluster was chosen based on its occurrence in various topics of the studied articles, with a level of 22 occurrences out of the 75 articles, which represents the highest level found compared to other SCOM elements analyzed. This indicates that most analyses conducted on fsQCA primarily focus on the application of this method to highlight its effects on production strategy in various logistics chains. This is best described firstly by the diversity of types of logistics chains studied in the 22 articles that addressed the application of fsQCA in water management and treatment, such as the article "Pathways to sustainability: A fuzzy-set qualitative comparative analysis of rural water supply programs", in the maritime sector, such as the article "Mechanism of governance pressures, green production and collaboration on the performance of maritime supply chain: Evidence from the moderating effect of government subsidies", and in the agri-food sector, such as the article "Water and waste management strategies as drivers of the financial performance of food companies". Secondly, in the management strategies proposed in each of these selected articles. For example, among the articles selected in this regard, there are those that relied on the strategy of green production and collaboration for supply chain performance, such as the article "Mechanism of governance pressures, green production and collaboration on the performance of maritime supply chain: Evidence from the moderating effect of government subsidies." Others were based on production strategy concerning interorganizational collaboration, such as the article: "COVID-19-related innovations: A study on underlying motivations and inter-organizational collaboration." Still, others were also based on waste reduction strategy, like the article "Tackling the complexity of guests' food waste reduction behavior in the hospitality industry."

Furthermore, we have included a summary of the overall research direction, as well as the challenges for this cluster, along with a suggestion of research questions that could be addressed in subsequent research in Table 2.

Table 2. Research questions for future studies emanate from the challenges in cluster 1

Research direction of cluster 1	**Challenges in cluster 1**	**Proposed research questions**
Improving production strategies in supply chains using the fsQCA method.	The complexity of applying the fsQCA method in production processes, for example: manufacturing processes, raw materials, equipment. The processing and analysis of these data using the fsQCA method may not be straightforward enough.	**PRQ1:** What is the degree of applicability of the fsQCA method in production processes?
	Challenges associated with collecting, cleaning, and validating production data, especially if they originate from diverse and potentially unreliable sources.	**PRQ2**: How to obtain a validated and reliable data source to ensure the necessary input elements for the application of fsQCA analysis?
	Methodological limitations that may restrict its relevance or applicability in certain specific production contexts. These limitations should be considered during the design and interpretation of the study.	**PRQ3:** How can the fsQCA method contribute to achieving performance in production processes?
		PRQ4: How can the fsQCA method assist in decision-making within production strategies?

Cluster 2: The Application of fsQCA in Sourcing Strategy

The second cluster was chosen based on its appearance in 21 articles that conducted an analysis using the fsQCA method in various supply chains to address strategies related to supplier selection and correlations between customer-supplier or supplier-supplier relationships. The results of this analysis show that the sourcing strategy ranks second in appearance compared to other SCOM elements studied when applying fsQCA to topics related to supply chain management. This is well described in the diversity of studies covered in the 21 articles, demonstrating the impact of the applicability of fsQCA in sourcing strategy within supply chains. This is exemplified, for instance, in the article "Customizing governance mechanisms to reduce opportunism in buyer–supplier relationships in the digital economy," which utilizes fsQCA analysis to delineate the strategy between supplier-customer relationships in a digital economy framework. In other cases, fsQCA study has been leveraged to outline a framework for adopting a B2B digital platform in managing a sourcing strategy in a supply chain, as seen in the article "B2B digital platform adoption by SMEs and large firms: Pathways and pitfalls." Apart from this, fsQCA has also been utilized to succeed in supplier selection, as addressed in the article "Supplier selection, control mechanisms, and firm innovation: Configuration analysis based on fsQCA," which also falls within the context of the sourcing strategy. And finally, we have included a summary regarding the overall research direction, as well as the challenges related to this cluster and research questions that could be addressed in future research (Table3).

Table 3. Research questions for future studies emanate from the challenges in cluster 2

Research direction of cluster 2	Challenges in cluster 2	Proposed research questions
Improving sourcing strategies in supply chains using the fsQCA method.	Identification of key success factors to enhance sourcing strategies	**PRQ1:** How organizations can determine the prioritized factors to consider for enhancing sourcing strategies by applying the fsQCA method?
	Optimal and efficient utilization of resources	**PRQ2**: How can we apply the fsQCA method to identify the most performing suppliers, procurement processes, and cost optimization?
	Challenges related to achieving sourcing performance in making more informed decisions	**PRQ3:** How can the fsQCA method contribute to identifying potential risks in different sourcing strategies?
		PRQ4: What will be the impact of applying fsQCA in decision-making related to supplier selection, location of sourcing resources, and definition of procurement contracts?

Cluster 3: The Application of fsQCA in Supply Chain Risk Management

The application of fsQCA in supply chain risk management is considered the third cluster, as it ranks third in appearance among all articles that addressed fsQCA in SCOM elements, with a score of 19 appearances in the articles. Supply chain risk management is also considered one of the most discussed topics when applying fsQCA in supply chain management. This is particularly notable in subjects that used fsQCA in determining factors influencing proactiveness in supply chain risk identification, as seen in the article "Factors influencing proactiveness in supply chain risk identification: A fuzzy-set qualitative comparative analysis." Additionally, it is evident in topics that focused on green management of supply chains, addressing environmental risks in supply chain management, as discussed in the article "Green supply chain management practices and third-party logistics providers' performances: A fuzzy-set approach," as well as in the article "Pathways to sustainability: A fuzzy-set qualitative comparative analysis of rural water supply programs." Risk management in supply chain management is also utilized to better demonstrate that supply chain managers take all necessary measures to ensure sustainable and effective management of supply chains, by mastering economic, social, and especially environmental factors (Weihua et al., 2017). Additionally, Table 4 represents certain research directions of this cluster, as well as research challenges and emerging future research questions.

Table 4. Research questions for future studies emanate from the challenges in cluster 3

Research direction of cluster 3	Challenges in cluster 3	Proposed research questions
The applicability of fsQCA in supply chain risk management	Challenges related to identifying variables associated with risk management in supplier relations, inventory management, and shipping processes.	**PRQ1:** How to identify the most influential variables on supply chain risks by applying the fsQCA method?
	Challenges related to Implementing fsQCA analysis software for data processing and risk identification in supply chains.	**PRQ2**: Is it feasible to implement software designed for fsQCA analysis to process data and identify configurations of variables associated with high or low levels of risk in the supply chain?
	Ensure regular and effective monitoring of action plans implemented using the fsQCA method and adjust them based on the evolution of risks in the supply chain.	**PRQ3:** How can we develop regular monitoring of action plans implemented following fsQCA analysis and adjust them based on the evolution of risks in the supply chain?

Cluster 4: The Application of fsQCA in Sustainability Management

The fourth cluster was the focus of the second phase of our research, which aimed to examine the presence of sustainable management during the application of the fsQCA method in supply chain management. This was best examined by comparing the 39 articles found within the scope of the three clusters identified previously with the three key objectives of sustainable development: Economic, Social, and Environmental aspects (Weihua et al., 2017; Garrido et al., 2024). The results showed that among the 39 articles, 29 confirmed sustainable management by elaborating on the fsQCA study in the selected supply chain operations within the three clusters. Additionally, the remaining 9 articles were also based on two aspects out of the 3 key objectives of sustainable management. This indicates that the majority of articles addressing fsQCA in supply chain operations still focus their studies on examining and evaluating sustainability aspects in their research. This implies that the fsQCA methodology is among the methodologies that assess the degree of presence of a sustainable aspect in each management. And in our case, it contributes to examining the rate of sustainable management presence within the operations describing supply chain management. Additionally, Table 5 provides the concise research direction and challenges of this cluster, along with some proposed research questions for future scholars.

Table 5. Research questions for future studies emanate from the challenges in cluster 4

Research direction of cluster 4	Challenges in cluster 4	Proposed research questions
Improving the contribution of fsQCA to sustainable management of supply chains.	Limitations of applying fsQCA in comprehensively addressing qualitative factors such as social responsibility, which is one of the sustainability approaches.	**PRQ1:** How can we enhance the applicability of the fsQCA method in addressing qualitative aspects?
	The fsQCA method may require adaptations to meet the specific needs of different industries or sustainability contexts. This may involve challenges in identifying and selecting appropriate variables for each particular case.	**PRQ2**: How to optimize the identification and selection of appropriate variables for each particular case in the sustainability context within supply chains?
	Determining how to measure sustainability meaningfully and holistically can be a challenge in itself. Selecting relevant variables to assess sustainability and defining appropriate success criteria can be critical aspects for the application of the fsQCA method.	**PRQ3:** How to overcome sustainability-related challenges through the application of the fsQCA method?
		PRQ4: Can we combine the fsQCA method with other analytical methods to achieve sustainable management within logistics chains?

Avenues for Future Research

In the results of this analysis, the applicability of the fsQCA method in previous research has been well-focused, especially on the four clusters extracted in the preceding section. However, it was deemed necessary to draw attention and consideration in future research towards other axes that may also be important for enriching the body of knowledge using fsQCA in sustainable management (Marks et al.,2018) of supply chain operations. Firstly, fsQCA is a method that can be better utilized in integrating and globalizing all operations describing supply chain management.

This implies that for future research, the application of this method may hold more value in operations related to procurement demands, distribution and transportation strategy, warehouse management, product design, and other specifically determined operations within the SCOM elements (Jackson et al., 2024). Secondly, within the framework of sustainable supply chain management, which draws inspiration from key factors of Industry 5.0 (Leng et al., 2022), a sharp focus can be considered in future research. This involves linking research findings from the fsQCA method to achieve supply chain management that values sustainability with its three factors - economic, social, and environmental aspects (Weihua et al., 2017; Garrido et al., 2024), emphasizing resilience while highlighting the robustness of actions taken against any uncertain or unstable factors and through the centralization of the human factor in all supply chain management operations.

Strategic Perspective for the Future

The objective of our study is to establish an applicable theoretical framework within sustainable logistics management while employing a method that has been rarely utilized in this field of research. This aims to leverage our study to foster collaboration between academics and industry practitioners (Kumar et al., 2022) in utilizing fsQCA in supply chain operations management and to overcome all constraints related to achieving sustainability in their supply chain processes. However, the goal for academics in such a collaboration is not only to address academic research questions but also to solve real-world problems in pursuit of impactful research (Kumar et al., 2022). This implies that academics are encouraged to chart new research opportunities considered as extensions of the research outlined in the present review (Kumar et al., 2022), thereby enabling the resolution of complex problems related to the constraints of an unstable market towards sustainable logistics management. On the other hand, industry practitioners' collaboration involves leveraging academics' expertise in fsQCA and considering it as a valuable resource (Kumar et al., 2022) they can apply to solve all problems related to supply chain management, thus fostering complementarity between theory and practice. This can have a significant impact on enhancing capabilities related to research and development (R&D) activities, which can also contribute to the development of new sustainable strategies in supply chain management.

DISCUSSION

The present research began with the three research questions, and then we proposed, using systematic literature review, a bibliometric analysis that helped us address the first question, which involves examining and evaluating the impact of contributors by authors, sources, publication period, and also by region. Next, we proposed a content analysis in which we conducted a PARETO analysis, drawing on previous literature findings regarding supply chain management operations. We were able to identify key clusters from the results of our analyses conducted on selected articles, which was the objective of the second research question. The analysis results allowed us to select the four most impactful clusters: The application of fsQCA in production strategy, the application of fsQCA in sourcing strategy, the application of fsQCA in Supply Chain Risk Management, and the application of fsQCA in Sustainability Management. Lastly, to address the final question, we carefully targeted various future perspectives that could guide further research. Additionally, to offer a more comprehensive view, we proposed an integrative framework primarily based on the findings of our research and also on the results provided by the study of Ilya Jackson regarding supply chain management operations. The framework (see Figure 4) was developed based on previous literature.

Description of the Study Framework

The framework of our study is situated within the context of sustainable management of supply chains in the era of Industry 5.0 (Masoomi et al. 2023), which is primarily based on sustainability aspect, through the application of the fsQCA method with the objective of tracing its ability to extract sustainability aspects in operations describing supply chain management. Despite this method being rarely used by researchers and research studies addressing cases related to direct management of supply chain operations, the existing study has outlined this new framework through the establishment of a systematic and bibliometric research on all previous research provided in this direction. After processing and analyzing data regarding the application of the fsQCA method, extraction of clusters was performed to trace the key elements around which the utility of the fsQCA method is shown, firstly, in managing supply chain operations such as production strategy management, sourcing strategy management, and risk management in the SC. Secondly, the utility of fsQCA in enhancing sustainability aspect in any application of the method in logistic management was highlighted. Research has shown that there is a strong correlation between the application of this method fsQCA and achieving sustainable development goals (Marks et al.,2018) within SCOM elements (Jackson et al., 2024).

Figure 4. Description of the study framework

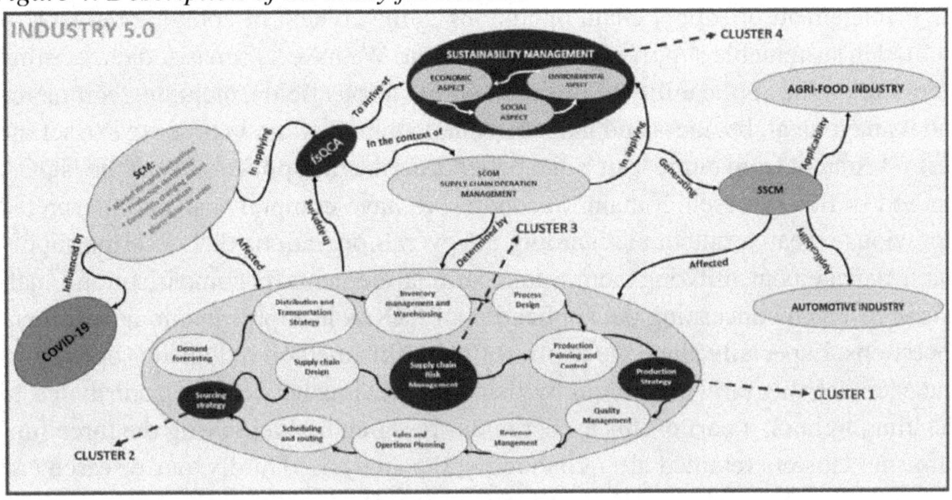

The utility of our present research is to demonstrate a portion of a framework that could be broader in the sense of enabling future research to leverage the fsQCA method in demonstrating and extracting sustainability aspect in a deeper manner within other logistic management operations beyond the three clusters extracted from our present research. This article serves as an invitation both for researchers to draw inspiration from the fsQCA method in their future research (Kumar et al., 2022) to showcase its utility in studies related to sustainable management of supply chains and as an invitation for industries to apply theoretical research findings in various sectors (Kumar et al., 2022) such as the automotive industry or the agri-food industry.

Theoretical Implications

According to previous research findings, which have provided several models and configurations using the fsQCA method to achieve supply chain performance through improved procurement practices (Innocent, 2024), other studies have also utilized the fsQCA method to achieve a good management in business models as an example (Kumar et al., 2022) or in improvement practices in green supply chain management (Stekelorum et al., 2021). fsQCA remains a useful configurational method for tracing various contributions in research areas related to supply chain management, particularly in operations covering these supply chains, which are rarely explored as specific cases in the application of the fsQCA method by previous research. Hence, the specificity of our research sheds light on this aspect. However, the contribution of the research results of this article to theory is mainly divided into three parts. First, our research has enriched the content of research related to the management of supply chain operations in the context of applying the fsQCA method in sustainable supply chain management. We have summarized the existing literature on the applicability of this method in various fields, including commerce and management, business and management, and marketing, in order to extract the desired content from our research and better describe the applicability of the fsQCA method in this research domain. Secondly, we have comprehensively interpreted a previous research outcome regarding the overall operations that describe supply chain management, utilizing them as foundational elements for comparison and analysis in research concerning the application of fsQCA in supply chain management operations. Especially since the applicability of this method in logistics operations management was rarely explored by theorists previously, we have contributed to shedding light on a part of this aspect in our research by identifying the three fundamental clusters retained after conducting the analysis. Thirdly, our research can be applied in the context of Industry 5.0 as it reflects a fundamental aspect and pillar of Industry 5.0, which is achieving sustainable management of supply chain operations. This is well demonstrated in the results of our analysis as the fourth distinguished cluster has proven a comprehensive correlation between the applicability of fsQCA in SCOM operations and the achievement of sustainability in this management, subsequently describing a comprehensive framework of this study. However, the use of this causal asymmetry method can inspire more researchers to complete research on other possible aspects, thus encouraging a more in-depth study on the applicability of this method within logistics operations by achieving sustainable management of supply chains.

Practical Implications

The practical implications of this study are described in the context where companies do not have sufficient resource-based capacity, thus they need to be more open in their internal R&D investments in a way that directs their research strategies towards collaborations with universities and research institutes to obtain optimal and more sustainable solutions for their production systems based on the results and implementation of new methods that ensure the performance of these systems. In a recent report by (Deloitte, 2022), it is stated that the main drivers motivating companies to invest more in R&D are the availability of skilled and experienced researchers (38%) and the potential to utilize a larger volume of grants/tax incentives (26%) to gain an economic advantage over other countries. Additionally, it confirmed that the majority of companies (65%) are collaborating with third parties, such as universities and research institutes, which proves beneficial for all parties involved. Faced with complex constraints related to supply chain management and the various disruptions encountered by companies, as well as the difficulties encountered regarding research and development activities in this regard, it also became important for the government, on its part, to encourage and support the establishment of partnerships and collaborations between business managers and academics to provide strong R&D support so that these companies can overcome the major challenges related to environmental, social, and economic constraints by leveraging the various outcomes provided through the implementation of new practices and frameworks that can have significant results in terms of the sustainable development of these companies.

CONCLUSION

The study uses content analysis to leverage existing findings based on an SLR methodology to analyze the research domain related to the application of the fsQCA method in supply chain management operations. To address the three research questions (RQ1, RQ2, and RQ3) of this study, it presented a perspective of 75 articles targeting the studied domain using Pareto analysis. To the best of our knowledge, this review is the first of its kind to report on the evolution of research related to the application of fsQCA in supply chain operations management.

The results of the Pareto analysis also showed that among the logistics operations most adopting the fsQCA method are production strategy, sourcing strategy, and risk management in supply chain management. Furthermore, the presence of sustainability aspects through the three sustainable development goals has been consistently significant in all studies addressing the fsQCA method in logistics management. This has revealed the correlation between the application of fsQCA and sustainability aspects in any study involving supply chain management.

However, the first three clusters extracted from this research only represent a part of a broader decomposition that encompasses all supply chain management operations, which, according to Ilya Jackson, consist of 13 SCOM elements. This does not contradict the research findings that have shown that through the application of fsQCA in each supply chain operation, there is certainly a convergence towards focusing on sustainable development goals while emphasizing the economic, social, and environmental aspects. The ultimate goal is to achieve sustainable management in every operation that describes supply chain management.

This review serves as an invitation to encourage aspiring researchers to adopt the fsQCA method to study various case scenarios related to sustainable management within supply chains. The aim is to shed more light on all aspects of supply chain management operations, thereby advancing sustainability practices in logistics management. On the other hand, a globalized framework has been outlined based on the findings of this research, aiming to be adopted in practice by industries across various sectors. Its impact in addressing constraints related to different global crises is to be measured, as we are all challenged to find sustainability in our production systems.

Limitations

There are still some shortcomings in this paper. First, previous research related to the application of the fsQCA method in supply chain operations management has been quite limited, resulting in the complexity of finding the necessary data and selecting a research sample size that does not exceed 75 articles. This can also be explained by the limited scope and quantity of research data in the Web of Science database. Secondly, it is also necessary to state that there are still limitations in the bibliometric methods and the knowledge mapping function of the tool utilized. Based on this paper, subsequent research can obtain more extensive research data in the field of fsQCA and logistics operations management and use a variety of qualitative and quantitative analysis methods and software to conduct a more in-depth and objective analysis and comparative study of its development. Furthermore, this paper contains a large amount of data, and although it can present a comprehensive framework of research related to sustainable supply chain management through the application of the fsQCA method, the analysis of variables related to all supply chain operations is still not encompassed enough.

Future Perspectives

This article presents an initial research path that can be exploited in future studies to complement the proposed research framework regarding the application of the fsQCA method in sustainable supply chain management operations. This can also be considered as a new opportunity and research perspective applicable to other studies that can deepen their analyses to measure and evaluate this hybrid approach in enhancing the robustness of results and provide a more comprehensive view of the factors influencing sustainable supply chain management. However, they can introduce in other case studies all the operations that describe supply chain management. Moreover, this work represents an invitation to apply this method in potential real-world scenarios, as input data from the fieldwork. While exploring new configurations using variables derived from the results of this research to design sustainable supply chain management models. This can also inspire us to use new suggestions for analysis tools and configurations, specifically the fsQCA software (Ragin & Davey, 2014, version 2.5).

REFERENCES

Acquah, I. S. K., Naude, M. J., & Sendra-García, J. (2021). Supply chain collaboration in the petroleum sector of an emerging economy: Comparing results from symmetrical and asymmetrical approaches. *Technological Forecasting and Social Change*, 166, 120568. DOI: 10.1016/j.techfore.2020.120568

Ahi, P., & Searcy, C. (2013). A comparative literature analysis of definitions for green and sustainable supply chain management. *Journal of Cleaner Production*, 52, 329–341. DOI: 10.1016/j.jclepro.2013.02.018

Alsuwaidi, M., Eid, R., & Agag, G. (2022). Tackling the complexity of guests' food waste reduction behaviour in the hospitality industry. *Tourism Management Perspectives*, 42, 100963. DOI: 10.1016/j.tmp.2022.100963

Ambroise, L., Prim-Allaz, I., & Teyssier, C. (2018). Financial performance of servitized manufacturing firms: A configuration issue between servitization strategies and customer-oriented organizational design. *Industrial Marketing Management*, 71, 54–68. DOI: 10.1016/j.indmarman.2017.11.007

Bai, Y., Wang, J., & Jiao, J. (2021). A framework for determining the impacts of a multiple relationship network on green innovation. *Sustainable Production and Consumption*, 27, 471–484. DOI: 10.1016/j.spc.2021.01.014

Bergmann, A., Stechemesser, K., & Guenther, E. (2016). Natural resource dependence theory: Impacts of extreme weather events on organizations. *Journal of Business Research*, 69(4), 1361–1366. DOI: 10.1016/j.jbusres.2015.10.108

Castka, P. (2018). Modelling firms' interventions in ISO 9001 certification: A configurational approach. *International Journal of Production Economics*, 201, 163–172. DOI: 10.1016/j.ijpe.2018.05.005

Deloitte. (2021). A year of connection, action and impact, 2021 GLOBAL IMPACT REPORT. 98. gx-about-deloitte-global-report-full-version-2021.pdf

Deloitte 2022. Save & Close Corporate Research & Development Report 2022 (deloitte.com)

Efendigil, T., Önüt, S., & Kahraman, C. (2009). A decision support system for demand forecasting with artificial neural networks and neuro-fuzzy models: A comparative analysis. *Expert Systems with Applications*, 36(3), 6697–6707. DOI: 10.1016/j.eswa.2008.08.058

El Jaouhari, A., Arif, J., Samadhiya, A., & Kumar, A. (2023). Net zero supply chain performance and industry 4.0 technologies: Past review and present introspective analysis for future research directions. *Heliyon*, 9(11), e21525. DOI: 10.1016/j.heliyon.2023.e21525 PMID: 38027864

El Jaouhari, A., Arif, J., Samadhiya, A., Kumar, A., & Garza-Reyes, J. A. (2023). An environmental-based perspective framework: Integrating IoT technology into a sustainable automotive supply chain. *Benchmarking*. Advance online publication. DOI: 10.1108/BIJ-05-2023-0322

El Jaouhari, A., Arif, J., Samadhiya, A., Kumar, A., Jain, V., & Agrawal, R. (2023). Are metaverse applications in quality 4.0 enablers of manufacturing resiliency? An exploratory review under disruption impressions and future research. *The TQM Journal*.

El Jaouhari, A., Fellaki, S., Amejwal, M., & Arif, J. (2023). Industry 4.0 Implementation in Lean Supply Chain Management: A Systematic Literature Review. *Statistics, Optimization & Information Computing*, 11(1), 178–185. DOI: 10.19139/soic-2310-5070-1539

Farooq, M. U., Hussain, A., Masood, T., & Habib, M. S. (2021). Supply Chain Operations Management in Pandemics: A State-of-the-Art Review Inspired by COVID-19. *Sustainability (Basel)*, 13(5), 2504. DOI: 10.3390/su13052504

Garrido, S., Muniz, J.Jr, & Batista Ribeiro, V. (2024). Operations Management, Sustainability & Industry 5.0: A critical analysis and future agenda. *Cleaner Logistics and Supply Chain*, 10, 100141. DOI: 10.1016/j.clscn.2024.100141

Gomes, P. J., Silva, G. M., & Sarkis, J. (2020). Exploring the relationship between quality ambidexterity and sustainable production. *International Journal of Production Economics*, 224, 107560. DOI: 10.1016/j.ijpe.2019.107560

Greco, M., Campagna, M., Cricelli, L., Grimaldi, M., & Strazzullo, S. (2022). COVID-19-related innovations: A study on underlying motivations and inter-organizational collaboration. *Industrial Marketing Management*, 106, 58–70. DOI: 10.1016/j.indmarman.2022.07.014

Gupta, N., Sardana, D., & Lee, R. (2024). Dynamic capabilities that matter for business failure versus survival. *Industrial Marketing Management*, 116, 40–50. DOI: 10.1016/j.indmarman.2023.11.004

Habib, F., Bastl, M., Karatzas, A., & Mena, C. (2020). Treat me well and I may leave you kindly: A configurational approach to a buyer's relationship exit strategy. *Industrial Marketing Management*, 84, 237–250. DOI: 10.1016/j.indmarman.2019.07.008

Han, B., Zheng, M., Fan, L., & Shi, W. (2022). Mechanism of governance pressures, green production and collaboration on the performance of maritime supply chain: Evidence from the moderating effect of government subsidies. *Research in Transportation Business & Management*, 43, 100820. DOI: 10.1016/j.rtbm.2022.100820

Huang, G., Tong, Y., Ye, F., & Li, J. (2020). Extending social responsibility to small and medium-sized suppliers in supply chains: A fuzzy-set qualitative comparative analysis. *Applied Soft Computing*, 88, 105899. DOI: 10.1016/j.asoc.2019.105899

Jackson, I., Ivanov, D., Dolgui, A., & Namdar, J. (2024). Generative artificial intelligence in supply chain and operations management: A capability-based framework for analysis and implementation. *International Journal of Production Research*, •••, 1–26. DOI: 10.1080/00207543.2024.2398583

Jiao, J., Zhang, X., & Tang, Y. (2020). What factors determine the survival of green innovative enterprises in China? — A method based on fsQCA. *Technology in Society*, 62, 101314. DOI: 10.1016/j.techsoc.2020.101314 PMID: 32834233

Jing, S., Feng, Y., & Yan, J. (2021). Path selection of lean digitalization for traditional manufacturing industry under heterogeneous competitive position. *Computers & Industrial Engineering*, 161, 107631. DOI: 10.1016/j.cie.2021.107631

Jovanovic, J., & Morschett, D. (2022). Under which conditions do manufacturing companies choose FDI for service provision in foreign markets? An investigation using fsQCA. *Industrial Marketing Management*, 104, 38–50. DOI: 10.1016/j.indmarman.2022.03.018

Kalpana, P. (2023). Factors influencing proactiveness in supply chain risk identification: A fuzzy-set qualitative comparative analysis. *International Journal of Disaster Risk Reduction*, 88, 103614.

Kosmol, T., Reimann, F., & Kaufmann, L. (2018). Co-alignment of supplier quality management practices and cognitive maps – A neo-configurational perspective. *Journal of Purchasing and Supply Management*, 24(1), 1–20. DOI: 10.1016/j.pursup.2017.11.002

Kumar, S., Sahoo, S., Lim, W. M., Kraus, S., & Bamel, U. (2022). Fuzzy-set qualitative comparative analysis (fsQCA) in business and management research: A contemporary overview. *Technological Forecasting and Social Change*, 178, 121599. DOI: 10.1016/j.techfore.2022.121599

Kumbure, M. M., Tarkiainen, A., Luukka, P., Stoklasa, J., & Jantunen, A. (2020). Relation between managerial cognition and industrial performance: An assessment with strategic cognitive maps using fuzzy-set qualitative comparative analysis. *Journal of Business Research*, 114, 160–172. DOI: 10.1016/j.jbusres.2020.04.001

Leng, J., Sha, W., Wang, B., Zheng, P., Zhuang, C., Liu, Q., Wuest, T., Mourtzis, D., & Wang, L. (2022). Industry 5.0: Prospect and retrospect. *Journal of Manufacturing Systems*, 65, 279–295. DOI: 10.1016/j.jmsy.2022.09.017

Liang, M., Yang, L., Li, K., & Zhai, H. (2024). Improved collaborative filtering for cross-store demand forecasting. *Computers & Industrial Engineering*, 190, 110067. DOI: 10.1016/j.cie.2024.110067

Liu, W., Bai, E., Liu, L., & Wei, W. (2017). A Framework of Sustainable Service Supply Chain Management: A Literature Review and Research Agenda. *Sustainability (Basel)*, 9(3), 421. DOI: 10.3390/su9030421

Llopis-Albert, C., Rubio, F., & Valero, F. (2021). Impact of digital transformation on the automotive industry. *Technological Forecasting and Social Change*, 162, 120343. DOI: 10.1016/j.techfore.2020.120343 PMID: 33052150

López-Cabarcos, M. Á., Piñeiro-Chousa, J., Quiñoá-Piñeiro, L., & López-Pérez, M. L. (2024). Water and waste management strategies as drivers of the financial performance of food companies. *Technological Forecasting and Social Change*, 200, 123138. DOI: 10.1016/j.techfore.2023.123138

Lou, Z., Ye, A., Mao, J., & Zhang, C. (2022). Supplier selection, control mechanisms, and firm innovation: Configuration analysis based on fsQCA. *Journal of Business Research*, 139, 81–89. DOI: 10.1016/j.jbusres.2021.09.045

Marks, S. J., Kumpel, E., Guo, J., Bartram, J., & Davis, J. (2018). Pathways to sustainability: A fuzzy-set qualitative comparative analysis of rural water supply programs. *Journal of Cleaner Production*, 205, 789–798. DOI: 10.1016/j.jclepro.2018.09.029

Marzi, G., Marrucci, A., Vianelli, D., & Ciappei, C. (2023). B2B digital platform adoption by SMEs and large firms: Pathways and pitfalls. *Industrial Marketing Management*, 114, 80–93. DOI: 10.1016/j.indmarman.2023.08.002

Masoomi, B., Sahebi, I. G., Ghobakhloo, M., & Mosayebi, A. (2023). Do industry 5.0 advantages address the sustainable development challenges of the renewable energy supply chain? *Sustainable Production and Consumption*, 43, 94–112. DOI: 10.1016/j.spc.2023.10.018

Mazumder, S., & Garg, S. (2021). Decoding digital transformational outsourcing: The role of service providers' capabilities. *International Journal of Information Management*, 58, 102295. DOI: 10.1016/j.ijinfomgt.2020.102295

McKinsey. (2022). Coronavirus' business impact: Evolving perspective | McKinsey

Meneses, R., Quelhas Brito, P., & Coelho Gomes, P. (2016). From offshore-provider to brand creator: fsQCA of footwear industry. *Journal of Business Research*, 69(11), 5540–5546. DOI: 10.1016/j.jbusres.2016.04.168

Minerbo, C., Kleinaltenkamp, M., & Brito, L. A. L. (2021). Unpacking value creation and capture in B2B relationships. *Industrial Marketing Management*, 92, 163–177. DOI: 10.1016/j.indmarman.2020.11.011

Mühlbacher, H., & Böbel, I. (2019). From zero-sum to win-win—Organisational conditions for successful shared value strategy implementation. *European Management Journal*, 37(3), 313–324. DOI: 10.1016/j.emj.2018.10.007

Muñoz, P., & Cohen, B. (2017). Mapping out the sharing economy: A configurational approach to sharing business modeling. *Technological Forecasting and Social Change*, 125, 21–37. DOI: 10.1016/j.techfore.2017.03.035

Prentice, C. (2019). Testing complexity theory in service research. *Journal of Services Marketing*, 34(2), 149–162. DOI: 10.1108/JSM-09-2019-0353

Prosman, E. J., & Cagliano, R. (2022). A contingency perspective on manufacturing configurations for the circular economy: Insights from successful start-ups. *International Journal of Production Economics*, 249, 108519. DOI: 10.1016/j.ijpe.2022.108519

Ragin, C., & Davey, S. (2014). fsQCA (Version 2.5) [Computer software]. University of California.

Russo, I., Confente, I., Gligor, D. M., & Autry, C. W. (2016). To be or not to be (loyal): Is there a recipe for customer loyalty in the B2B context? *Journal of Business Research*, 69(2), 888–896. DOI: 10.1016/j.jbusres.2015.07.002

Sandra, M., Narayanamoorthy, S., Ferrara, M., Innab, N., Ahmadian, A., & Kang, D. (2024). A novel decision support system for the appraisal and selection of green warehouses. *Socio-Economic Planning Sciences*, 91, 101782. DOI: 10.1016/j.seps.2023.101782

Scarpi, D., Raggiotto, F., & Visentin, M. (2022). Untying the knot: Drivers of the intention to downgrade the relationship in B2B service contexts. *Industrial Marketing Management*, 105, 200–210. DOI: 10.1016/j.indmarman.2022.06.005

Stekelorum, R., Laguir, I., Gupta, S., & Kumar, S. (2021). Green supply chain management practices and third-party logistics providers' performances: A fuzzy-set approach. *International Journal of Production Economics*, 235, 108093. DOI: 10.1016/j.ijpe.2021.108093

Sun, S., Hall, D. J., & Cegielski, C. G. (2020). Organizational intention to adopt big data in the B2B context: An integrated view. *Industrial Marketing Management*, 86, 109–121. DOI: 10.1016/j.indmarman.2019.09.003

Tran, P. N. T., Gorton, M., & Lemke, F. (2021). When supplier development initiatives fail: Identifying the causes of opportunism and unexpected outcomes. *Journal of Business Research*, 127, 277–289. DOI: 10.1016/j.jbusres.2021.01.009

Wang, X., Zhang, T., Luo, S., & Abedin, M. Z. (2023). Pathways to improve energy efficiency under carbon emission constraints in iron and steel industry: Using EBM, NCA and QCA approaches. *Journal of Environmental Management*, 348, 119206. DOI: 10.1016/j.jenvman.2023.119206 PMID: 37898049

Wuni, I. Y. (2022). Mapping the barriers to circular economy adoption in the construction industry: A systematic review, Pareto analysis, and mitigation strategy map. *Building and Environment*, 223, 109453. DOI: 10.1016/j.buildenv.2022.109453

Yin, Q., Song, D., Lai, F., Collins, B. J., & Dogru, A. K. (2023). Customizing governance mechanisms to reduce opportunism in buyer–supplier relationships in the digital economy. *Technological Forecasting and Social Change*, 190, 122411. DOI: 10.1016/j.techfore.2023.122411

Yu, Y., Xu, J., Huo, B., Zhang, J. Z., & Cao, Y. (2023). The impact of supply chain social responsibility on sustainable performance. *Journal of Cleaner Production*, 385, 135666. DOI: 10.1016/j.jclepro.2022.135666

Zhang, N., Guo, M., Bu, X., & Jin, C. (2023). Understanding green loyalty: A literature review based on bibliometric-content analysis. *Heliyon*, 9(7), e18029. DOI: 10.1016/j.heliyon.2023.e18029 PMID: 37483765

Chapter 8
Circular Business Models With Resource Sharing and Product-as-a-Service

Amit Kumar Yadav
https://orcid.org/0000-0002-4565-5284
O.P. Jindal Global University, India

Preet Kanwal
https://orcid.org/0009-0006-5114-8381
Lovely Professional University, India

Narayanage Jayantha Dewasiri
https://orcid.org/0000-0002-5908-8890
Sabaragamuwa University of Sri Lanka, Sri Lanka

ABSTRACT

This chapter explores the transformative potential of circular business models, focusing on Resource Sharing and Product-as-a-Service (PaaS). These models represent a shift from traditional linear approaches to a more sustainable, resource-efficient economy. The chapter examines key enablers such as technological advancements, regulatory frameworks, and evolving consumer behavior, while also addressing the challenges and risks associated with implementing circular practices. Strategic recommendations are provided to help businesses navigate operational complexities, financial barriers, and market dynamics. The future outlook highlights opportunities for innovation and growth within circular ecosystems, emphasizing the need for collaboration and adaptability. By embracing circular business models, companies can contribute to sustainability goals, enhance resource efficiency, and build a competitive edge in the evolving market landscape.

DOI: 10.4018/979-8-3693-9241-6.ch008

INTRODUCTION TO CIRCULAR BUSINESS MODELS

The model adopted for business in the global economy so far has been nearly linear: make, take and dispose. That is, resources are harvested or extracted, converted into products, and at the end of their useful life become waste. This model has been the base for economic growth and industrialization but also created huge environmental degradation, basic resource depletion, and waste generation. With the world slowly but surely inching its way toward a realization of the primal need to change the current method of producing and consuming goods, the dilemmas on climate change, resource scarcity, and the path to environmental sustainability intensify.

The term coined to effect this change is now the circular economy—a way, or rather, an economy aimed to bring social benefits through redesigning the way life is produced and consumed. Unlike the linear model, the circular economy is regenerative by design and gradually decouples growth from the consumption of finite resources. In a nutshell, a circular economy builds on the idea of continuous resources used; hence, waste is minimized, and with systems enabling it, recycling, reusing, and remanufacturing of materials and products should be done.

In the light of circular economy, circular business models have recently appeared as innovative means of ensuring sustainability without economic unviability. The models are meant to create value in the long lifetime of products, which capitalizes on resources while minimizing the negative environmental effect. There could either be the selling and repurchasing, reverse logistics, or PSS under circular business models (Sehnem et al., 2019).

Particularly important among the developing circular business models in the last couple of years are those with regard to resource-sharing and PaaS. Resource-sharing refers to the collaborative use of assets, such as tools, vehicles, or spaces, among many users. This model allows for the maximum usage of any resource and minimizes the production of new resources by decreasing the demand that, in turn, will reduce the generation of waste by conserving natural resources. Examples of resource-sharing models include car-sharing services, tool libraries, and co-working spaces.

While Product-as-a-Service shifts from ownership to access, it's unlike conventional leasing, which requires payments to be made on a regular basis regardless of actual use. Instead of selling a product, companies will sell what the product does. That is, instead of the customer acquiring the product in itself, they pay for the service the product provides. It resonates interests of the businesses and consumers in sustainability, in that very solid, high-quality products are at stake, which are valid and valuable to keep, upgrade, and to resell with time. Common examples of

PaaS include subscription services for electronics, pay-as-you-wear clothes, and pay-per-use machinery.

The growing rate of circular business models represents rising awareness for sustainability needs in production and consumption. Businesses and consumers are fast realizing the environmental and economic benefits associated with circularity, making such models a front-runner in the change towards a more sustainable, consequently more resilient, economy. In this chapter, we further explore resource sharing and product-as-a-service concepts and assess their potential to transform industry, support decoupling and act as a driver for sustainable growth (Bocken et al., 2019; Bocken & Ritala, 2021).

Resource Sharing Models

Resource sharing models are one of the key elements of the Circular Economy and break with the established idea of ownership, with a heavy focus placed on demarcation of access rather than on possession. These models exploit underutilized capacity, allowing the resources that would otherwise sit idle to be shared across many numbers of users. By making better use of goods, crude resource sharing meets not only lessened demand for new production but better, more efficient, and sustainable use of the already-existing resources. This section discusses the conceptual framework behind resource sharing in a circular economy, models used in resource sharing, shares case studies of the same that have been explored successfully, and further discusses its challenges and opportunities.

Conceptual Framework: Resource Sharing in a Circular Economy

Theoretically, resource sharing fundamentally seeks to maximize available resources for longer lifecycle products in a manner that reduces waste. The linear model, in terms of resource extraction, use, and disposal, is superseded by a consideration of how resources can circulate within the economy for as long as possible under the principles of a circular economy. A sharing model in regard to resources can promote this kind of circularity: Multiple people can have access and find a use for the same piece, thereby making a reduction in the requirement for new materials to be extracted and processed.

Such business models can be adopted in almost every sector, from transportation and housing to consumer goods and industrial equipment. The central insight is that through the sharing of resources, both businesses and individuals are afforded important opportunities to reduce their environmental footprint collectively, drive down costs, and also create new economic opportunities. The sharing of resources, under this new way of thinking, aligns economic activity with sustainability imperatives and presents a concrete pathway to a much more circular and regenerative economy. Figure 1 shows the model representing circular business models with resource sharing and product-as-a-service.

Figure 1. Model representing circular business models with resource sharing and product-as-a-service

Types of Resource Sharing Models

Resource sharing models are quite diversified and can be characterized based on the nature of the assets themselves and the systems involved in facilitating the sharing. Some of the most common types include:

P2P Sharing: In this form of sharing, the peers directly share their assets with others. Examples such platforms include Airbnb, Turo, etc., which hook up owners of underused resources like houses and cars with users who need temporary access. P2P Sharing democratizes access to resources and allows one to monetize his own resources.

Direct Consumer Sharing: This process involves a business deliberately providing shared resource access to consumers. Examples include Zipcar's car-sharing business offering rental access to an automobile on an hourly basis or bike sharing, which many cities around the world offer. In both these models, consumers can experience the convenience of access rather than ownership, along with its responsibilities and challenges, such as storage and maintenance.

3. Business-to-Business (B2B) Sharing: B2B sharing can be defined as business sharing the resources with one another for the optimal use of the resources. For instance, industrial symbiosis is a situation whereby firms located in close proxim-

ity share materials, energy, or by-products, cutting across the production process. That is the waste from an organization becomes a resource for the other company. An example of shared warehousing or logistic services is working together to use warehousing and distribution facilities.

4. Community Sharing: Community sharing models are based on the concept of pooling the resources within a community for common use. Examples include tool libraries that allow for borrowing tools rather than each person buying one and community gardens in which land is shared to grow one's food. This type of community sharing serves to reinforce the sense of togetherness and social cohesion while at the same time minimizing the environmental impact of individual consumption.

Case Studies of Resource Sharing, Business Models that Work

1. Airbnb: Arguably the best instance of a P2P resource-sharing model, it was designed to revolutionize the hospitality industry by allowing people to give rent of their homes or spare rooms to travelers. The organization has developed a global marketplace for shared accommodations. This model offers a variety of affordable alternatives besides traditional hotels and guesthouses, and allows those homeowners to earn an extra income source by monetizing the space that stays unutilized.

2. Zipcar: This is a car-sharing service, which is a classic paradigm of a B2C resource-sharing model, in order to eliminate the over-position of cars. Cars can only be paid for at the time they are used, thereby avoiding the costs and risks that come with ownership. In this sense, it brings relief from urban tightness with minimal air discharge and transportation resource storage.

3. Kalundborg Symbiosis: Located in Denmark, Kalundborg Symbiosis is one of the pioneering examples of B2B resource sharing amongst industrial firms working under the tenet of industrial symbiosis. In this symbiotic network, water, energy, and by-products are shared as resources amongst its participants, where what is thought to be a remnant turns into a valuable resource. The major expost advantage of such a symbiotic relationship is waste reduction and resource efficiency respectively for the production process of the participating firms, and it results in lower operating costs.

Challenges and Opportunities

While sharing models bring about enormous environmental and economic benefits, a number of challenges must be addressed before they can be widely adopted:

1. Trust and Security: Trust is an essential ingredient of resource sharing. In particular, the P2P models require that people share their personal assets with strangers. It is important to ensure security, privacy, and protection for shared resources to facilitate trust among users (Özdemir et al., 2018).

2. Regulatory and Legal Barriers: Resource sharing models often present a challenge, as current laws often do not support these new forms of economic activity. Issues like zoning regulations, insurance requirements, and liability issues present hurdles in sharing models' implementation and scaling.

3. Cultural and Behavioural Shifts: Adopting Resource sharing denotes a cultural as well as a behavioural shift of the consumer. And from a position of owning to accessing resources. This is a change that could not be very easy to be achieved in a society where ownership is a matter of status and security.

4. Scalability: Up-scaling sharing models in resources to larger populations for more diversified markets is very challenging. Infrastructure, technology, or network effects are some major driving factors for the success of these models at scale.

But, the possibilities opened up by models of sharing resources are huge. It leads by itself to the principles of a circular economy—less call on new resources, lesser waste, and a more efficient way of using assets. Moreover, these models can create new business opportunities, foster innovation, and enhance social equity by making resources more accessible to a broader range of people.

In summary, resource-sharing models are a powerful driver for the circular economy. As businesses, communities, and people move more to this kind of economy, it is going to have a significant role in sustainable growth, lessening impact, and creating resiliency in society.

Products-as-a-Service (PaaS) Models

Product-as-a-Service, on the other hand, involves a transition in the way products will be offered and consumed, from traditional ownership towards a model wherein what is paid for is a utility or results created by said product. This would also align business interest with sustainability interest because then companies will be driven to make products robust, maintainable, and reusable. PaaS models, with applicability even in markets as wide apart as consumer electronics and transport, potentially provide a far more sustainable and customer-centric evolution of the conventional buy-and-throw economy. This section discusses the ideas underlying PaaS, key exemplary features, and case studies—the important economic and environmental touchpoints linked to these models.

Understanding PaaS: From Ownership to Access

The core of PaaS is the idea that the client is actually interested in service or functionality, rather than the product per se. Instead of selling a product, companies put it together and deliver it as part of an ongoing service; at every stage of the product life cycle, ownership and responsibility are maintained. What this model does is shift the focus; instead of concentrating on selling more products, it presents the better, long-lasting service, making less of a need to have a continuous production and consumption of new goods (Han et al., 2020).

In a PaaS model, companies have an incentive to design products that are durable, easy to repair, and recyclable since they must bear related maintenance and replacement costs for the same over time. This leads to more sustainable use of resources by keeping products in circulation for a longer time and refurbishing or repurposing them at the end of their initial use. Due to PaaS, companies can have more frequent and closer relationships with customers and can provide them continuous improvement, updating their service along with personalization.

Distinct Features of PaaS Models

PaaS models encompass a peculiar set of features, which distinguish them from traditional product offering.

1. Subscription-Based Access: Customers usually pay a recurring fee to access some type of product or service, either on a monthly, yearly, or usage basis. This type of model provides flexibility and savings for consumers who need access to a product for a short period of time or for those who prefer not to be burdened by the up-front costs of ownership.

2. Maintenance and Upgrades: This goes without saying since it is totally the provider's responsibility; it is their product. This ensures that the product remains in proper and updated working condition, giving the customer a hassle-free experience whenever there are technical glitches. This gives a business a nudge to develop a product that would be easy to maintain and upgrade, thus keeping long-term costs low (Swaroop & Gade, 2023).

3. Lifecycle Management: The company retains ownership of products and manages them across their lifecycles. This includes collecting products, refurbishment, and finally recycling at the end of use. By integrating control across a product's whole lifecycle, a business can make sure that its goods are used effectively and disposed of in an environmentally friendly way.

4. Customization and Flexibility: The best part about PaaS is that it provides a lot of customization either in choosing service levels, feature sets, or product configuration personalized to meet the customer's best interest, thus achieving customer satisfaction through increased bonding and retention.

5. Data-driven insight: The majority of PaaS models are delivered with connected products digitizing usage patterns, customer preferences, and performance. This data can be leveraged to use services effectively, optimize them, help in better product design, and offer a customized experience to add incremental value at both ends—customer and business (Giessmann & Legner, 2016).

Case Studies: PaaS Proving to Be a Success

Rolls-Royce: Power by the Hour: The first model of the PaaS business to be presented in the aviation industry was by the Rolls-Royce company with their "Power by the Hour" service. Rolls-Royce makes airlines pay for engine use and maintenance services on a unit of cost per hour of the engine's operation rather than selling them. In that light, it makes all the sense because on one end it would incentivize Rolls-Royce to produce reliable, long-lasting engines, as well as make sure that airlines are receiving the highest level of service without the fuss of engine ownership.

2. *Philips Lighting: Light as a Service:* Philips offers a "Light as a Service" scheme in a PaaS model, where the customers only pay for the use of the lighting. The end users do not have to have any idea to know which manufacturer produces their light bulbs or individual fixtures. The ownership, maintenance, and constant improvement of the lighting systems in terms of energy consumption and efficiency stay with Philips. This model guarantees them a return on investment and thus guarantees the provision of strong and long-lasting solutions that are energy-saving, thus ultimately reducing energy consumption and waste.

3. *Clothing Rental Platforms:* PaaS in the fashion industry is championed by the likes of Rent the Runway, which rents, rather than sells, clothing. Customers can rent designer clothes for special occasions or everyday wear, returning them or swapping items as often as they please. This system lowers the demand for producing new clothes, creates low to no waste, and offers access to more fashion at cheaper costs to consumers.

Economic and Environmental Impact

The PaaS model is immensely beneficial to the economy and the environment in several ways:

1. Reduced Resource Consumption: Through the projected increase in the useful life of products and the reduction in recycling through reuse, the PaaS models contribute to the reduction of raw material extraction and the production of new products. This leads to a decreased environmental burden and safeguards nonrenewable resources.

2. Waste Minimization: PaaS encourages designing products that are essentially robust, repairable, and recyclable, thus minimizing the quantity of waste through discarded products. By introducing a closed-loop lifecycle for the products, no opportunity is lost to either refurbish or recycle, thereby further reducing waste.

3. Cost Efficiency: For consumers, Paas models offer a better, cheaper, and more affordable way of receiving quality in their goods without incurring the costs of owning them. For a business, Paas offers perpetual streams of repeatable revenues and a long list of chances to build long-term customer relationships.

4. Innovation and Competitiveness: The data-driven nature of the PaaS model allows a company to innovate consistently and come up with superior offerings in a consistent manner based on real-time customer feedback, hence being able to beat the market., hence instilling competitiveness in the creation of more sustainable and customer-centered products.

5. Circular Economy Integration: Through PaaS, business practices will be harmonized with the circular principle; PaaS ensures that whatever product reaches the customer is used for the maximum required span and then disposed of safely. In this way, PaaS models can similarly contribute to the formation of closed-loop systems that minimize environmental impacts.

In conclusion, Product-as-a-Service models indicate a powerful shift to fairer and more sustainable business practices. Focusing on access over ownership, the PaaS model drives value for businesses and consumers, supporting, in turn, the goals of the circular economy. The more industrial sectors that adopt PaaS, it experiences a real potential for reduction of its resource consumption, waste minimization, and product/service delivery model innovation.

Integration of Resource Sharing and PaaS

This stands as the inbuilt junction of two major models within Circular Economy: resource sharing and product as a service. It is a very strong interaction, where the strengths of the two models are used to the maximum to minimize waste and increase resource efficiency in creating new value propositions. Each has its own value proposition and advantages; still, while being integrated, it opens new opportunities to derive synergy that propels innovation and sustainability throughout the industries. This section discusses how resource sharing and PaaS can be effectively integrated, provides examples of hybrid business models, and outlines some potential advantages and challenges.

Synergies Between Resource Sharing and PaaS

In the end, resource sharing and PaaS models share a similar underlying focus: access over ownership. These two approaches are meant to maximize the use of resources by making products and services available to as many users as possible—at once decreasing the necessity for further production and minimizing environmental impact. Moreover, if integrated, these models strengthen each other, creating more workable and sustainable business models.

1. Higher Asset Utilization: By integrating resource sharing with PaaS, a company can achieve an even higher level of asset utilization. For instance, a company that leases machinery on an as-needed basis can also support resource sharing among several users, whereby different businesses are provided with the same machinery only at different times. This does not only ensure maximum usage of a given piece of machinery; it also brings down the cost for users by spreading the expense over several parties.

2. More Flexibility and Accessibility: Through integration, businesses can offer a wider range of services, which then can be extended to a greater number of customers. For example, a car-sharing business on a PaaS model would give customers access to vehicles either on a paid subscription model or pay-per-use basis, hence making it easier for a user to select the right level of service. Through this, you can attract more customers from diverse segments of society, be it people who can't afford to own anything fully or who don't like being committed for a long period of time.

3. Extended Product Lifecycles: Resource-sharing and PaaS will present a new incentive to business enterprises for developing products that are readily shared and serviced, both in terms of durability and maintainability, and are viable for many users over time. In so doing, the product lifecycle is prolonged as well—being shared and serviced over and again—leading to a reduction in the sum of total demand for new resources and a reduction in waste.

4. Scalability and Network Effects: When properly done, integrated models can exploit network effects where the value of a service goes up when more people participate. Suppose, for example, a shared workspace offering that uses a PaaS model would be more valuable with increased membership because access to and efficiency of work could increase with more opportunities for collaboration and resource sharing. With one swift move, it easily scales up businesses so that they can, in turn, expand their offerings and reach new markets.

Hybrid Business Models: Integration Examples

1. Shared Mobility Services: Companies like Uber and Lyft have bridged the gap between sharing resources and PaaS by providing ride-hailing services. This way, several customers can share a ride, whereas the latter has the possibility of flexibility and the expense of possessing a car reduced by access to transportation on a per-travel basis. In addition, subscription-based car-sharing models are being

devised wherein customers pay a flat fee for a number of rides, and so, in an even more complete way, blurring resource sharing with PaaS.

2) Tool Libraries with Maintenance Services: Tool libraries that allow members to borrow the tools instead of purchasing can be integrated with PaaS by including services in terms of maintenance and repair in the memberships. This hybrid model not only enables resource sharing but also ensures that the facility is properly maintained, ensuring that the tools are durable and have reduced throughput because newer tools do not have to be produced as often. Finally, the tools with good access and high usability can be much used, and therefore, be bringing in considerable money to the library.

3. Subscription-Based Co-Working Spaces: WeWork Under the subscription model, it is a shared space with elements of both resource sharing and PaaS. Members gain access to shared office spaces and equipment by paying a monthly subscription fee, among other provided amenities. This allows many businesses or freelancers to share the same resources, saving waste in terms of physical space and the natural resources that go into building and maintaining single offices. Being flexible, the subscription model is adopted by start-up organizations and remote workers.

Integration Benefits

1. Better Resource Utilization: Resource sharing, if integrated with PaaS, can help business organizations in better utilization of resources. In that, the assets become more intense and at the same time, the instances of idle time and waste are cut-down. The impacts are in line with eco-friendliness and reduced costs for whole providers and the clients.

2. More Value to Customers: Resource sharing together with PaaS enables customers to get high-quality products and services without having to claim ownership of them, therefore substantially enhancing a value proposition. Increasing value can lead to higher customer satisfaction, loyalty, and retention (Kesavapanikkar et al., 2022).

3. Sustainability and Circularity: Shared models serve the circular economy objective of keeping products and resources in high-value use for a longer time. Through shared access, maintenance, and reutilization of existing assets, they close loops and reduce the extraction of new resources.

4. Market Expansion: The flexibility and access to integrated models can help reach an expanded customer base that possibly includes those in emerging markets or at low income. This opens further business opportunities to scale services touched upon and reaches unserved or underserved populations.

Challenges in Integration

1. Implementation Complexity: Resource sharing has is entangled, integrated with PaaS, as a very complex exercise to be made possible in view of the huge technological infrastructure and seamless coordination between users to use their shared resources most efficiently. Businesses also have to take care of regulatory and legal challenges in shared ownership, liability, and insurance.

2. Supply and Demand Balancing: Making shared resources available only when required but not over or short supply creates a balancing challenge. Businesses need the right handling of inventory, scheduling, and customer expectations for successfully managing this balance between supply and demand.

3. Customer Trust and Adoption: For integrated business models to bear fruit, developing customer trust is key. The businesses have to voice questions of security, privacy, and quality issues of the shared products and services. Customers must equally be made aware of how to assess the value offered by access than ownership.

4. Maintenance and Upkeep: Managing maintenance and upkeep of shared resources across many users could be overwhelming. Companies need to devise effective systems for knowing who is using what, for how long, which items need fixing, when to fix them—in general, overseeing that products are maintained well and in good condition for their entire life cycle.

In conclusion, the integration of Resource Sharing and Product-as-a-Service models opens up powerful space for business to advance further in sustainability, realizing increased value for customers along the way. When the two models are combined, the outcome is innovative, flexible, and can scale in creating solutions that help close a circle-economy loop. There are bound to be challenges, but the potential benefits in terms of resource efficiency and customer and market expansion make this a forceful strategy for the future.

Enablers of Technologies

The setup of circular business models and most especially the scaling of the same on resource sharing and Product-as-a-Service is deeply carried along by technological innovation. This allows them to be managed not only more effectively but also more accessibly and more sustainably. Key technological enablers driving the adoption and growth of circular business models: digital platforms, the Internet of Things (IoT), data analytics, blockchain, and artificial intelligence (AI).

Digital Platforms

Digital platforms are another important facility of resource sharing, as also with the PaaS models which primarily support the networking among providers and users. This allows markets to be established for the real-time offering, access, and trading of services or, in some cases, products. Salient features of such platforms can be summarized as:

1. User Interface and Experience: Digital platforms offer intuitive interfaces that make it easy for users to search for services, book them, and make payments without any hassle. They also have other features, such as reviews, ratings, and customer support, which help build and generate confidence in the user to adopt services.

2. Inventory Management: For businesses offering shared or service-based products, the digital platform aids in effective inventory management in a manner that envisages resources to be at the place of requirement—the least down.

3. Payment Systems: Clearly, payment systems are integral and should incorporate safe and convenient transactions whether in subscription mode, pay as you go, or any other modes of payment. Conveniences are strong pullers for consumers or customers.

4. Scalability: A digital platform can grow with its user base. This helps the business conquer new territories and fresh markets without spending on reinvestment.

Internet of Things (IoT)

The development of Business Models enabled by different types of new technologies, especially those supported by PaaS, consider IoT as one of the most important enablers. IoT is the one that connects physical products to the digital world and enables real-time monitoring, management, and optimization of resources. Important Applications of IoT in a Circular Business Model:

1. Asset Tracking and Monitoring: Embedded throughout the products through IoT sensors, the location, condition, and usage of businesses can track the asset. Real-time data of such nature helps in optimizing asset utilization, scheduling maintenance, and extending product life.

2. Proactive Maintenance: The continuous monitoring of product performance allows IoT systems to predict the necessity for maintenance or repair works, thereby preventing downtime and expensive breakdowns. This capability is especially useful in PaaS models, where the provider has to keep the product updated.

3. Energy Efficiency: IoT devices can be utilized to regulate energy consumption concerning most products and systems to avoid wastage of energy and further decrease the operational cost. For example: Smart lighting can control its brightness

according to occupancy and desired connected appliances and may also possibly operate during off-peak hours.

4. Better User Experience: A user can have a customizd experience when using an IoT-based product because the device may suggest settngs modifation or a change in recommendation according to the user's liking or behavior. Satisfaction can lead to more happy and loyal repeat customers.

Data Analytics

Data analytics is perhaps a function necessary for the optimization of business within a circular model, working on the provision of insights into decision-making and innovation. Huge amounts of data from digital platforms and IoT devices help in the analysis of patterns, which are revealed for predicting trends and optimizing operations. Key areas in which data analytics contribute are:

1. Customer Insights: Further explore available customer data about what users are doing, what they like and need, which is beneficial for customizing services and improving product design in marketing strategies.

2. Operational Efficiency: Data analytics can realize opportunities where there may be inefficiency in resource use, logistics, and inventory management, enhancing operational efficiencies and allowing for additional cost effectiveness. For example, usage data can ensure that shared resources are optimally allocated so they are available at the right time and in the right place (Mei et al., 2012).

3. Product Development: Analytics could also inform design and development processes for new products or services by identifying upcoming trends or unmet customer needs. Such a data-driven approach will ascertain that new offerings are aligned with the needs of the market and sustainability goals.

4. Lifecycle Management: Data analytics could track the lifecycle—the entire period of a product ranging from production to its disposal—of products to give insights on how to extend its useful life and minimum wastage. This information is crucial to a product designed to be durable, repairable, and recyclable.

Blockchain

Blockchain technology ensures secure transparency in transaction management, asset tracking, and information verification, offering valuable support for circular business models. Decentralization and immutability are key when ensuring trust and accountability in resource sharing and PaaS models. Most important applications of blockchain include:

1. Supply Chain Transparency: Blockchain can offer ways to create transparent, traceable supply chains to ensure that products are sourced, produced, and distributed in an ethical and sustainable manner. This cultivates transparency with customers and stakeholders, and fosters the goals of a circular economy.

2. Smart Contracts: Blockchain-based smart contracts are deployable mechanisms through which agreements of parties are automated and enforced, including rental agreements in PaaS models. These contracts assure the conditions are met and payments are cleared, thus automatizing the process, thereby reducing administrative overhead and the potential for disputes.

3. Asset Provenance and Ownership: Blockchain can give a verifiable history of the usage and ownership of an asset, more so in resource sharing models. It is a way to ensure that all of an entity's assets are authentic, well-maintained, and properly managed throughout their lifecycle.

4. Incentivizing Circular Practices: Blockchain can be used to ensure the creation of token-based systems of incentives where users will be awarded progressively for the adoption of circular practices, and the most ordinary examples include returning products for recycling, sharing resources. With the use of such an incentive, more of the business will adopt the circular model.

Artificial Intelligence (AI)

AI is a prime enabler of circular business models, allowing for an increase in process automation, a bettered decision-making process, and experience development. AI is of maximum importance when dealing with complexity in managing big scales of resource sharing and PaaS models. The most important applications of AI include:

1. Demand Forecasting: AI can enable the forecasting of the need for its product and service by supplying deduced data from historical data, market trends, and other affecting factors. This forecasting enables the business organization to optimize their inventory, while they reduce any form of waste while at the same time ensuring that resources are made available whenever called upon.

2. Dynamic Pricing: AI can enable the dynamic pricing that gives real-time price fluctuations based on the need and availability coupled with the behavior of customers. Accordingly, this enables more revenues to accrue while ensuring there is proper allocation of resources.

3. Personalization: There are high levels of intensified personalization in customer data that AI devices can be able to analyze in trying to develop tailor-made recommendations, service packages, and events. The platform could recommend,

for instance, which type of product or service an individual should receive, based on previous behavior and preferences. All these ends in a better way to satisfy customers and retain them.

4. Automated Operations: AI enables the automation of routine functions that involve, for example, scheduling, inventory management, or customer support. It allows the redeployment of human resources to more strategic work. AI in PaaS models is also able to optimize maintenance and repair of assets by attempting to predict problems for pre-emptive maintenance or resource allocation.

Challenges and Future Directions

On the other hand, while technology enablers are a key area for circular business models, the implementation may be challenging. Most of these put up a high upfront investment, a high level of complexity in integrating multiple technologies, and issues of data privacy and security. In addition, while this reliance on digital platforms and data-driven intelligence by business stakeholders continues to grow, there is a need to consider the ethical use of AI to ensure it benefits all stakeholders.

In fact, setting the stage to further increase the potential for circular business models, their development will continue in the future. As the technologies of the IoT, AI, and blockchain-based are increasing their systemic sophistication and performance efficacy, this improvement is facilitated by systemic 5G and edge computing in their support for wide dissemination in practice. As these technologies mature and advance, greater adoption of circular practices by businesses for meeting their sustainability commitments and realizing value accruing from the mechanisms of the circular economy will be observed.

In fact, technology enablers are at the core of shifting business models towards a circular model based on the sharing of resources and towards Product-as-a-Service. IoT with digital platforms, data analytics, blockchain, and AI will not only modify the operation but also place business enterprises in a better position to optimize resource use, derive maximum benefits, and improve customers' experiences for sustainable growth. With time, these technologies will further innovate and open up new vistas of innovation en route to a sustainable economy.

Market Dynamics and Consumer Behavior

The success of circular business models, in particular, those based on resource sharing and product-as-a-service (PaaS), depends highly on the behavior of the market and consumers. Understanding how these factors influence the adoption and growth of circular models is essential for businesses wishing to perform well in this landscape. In this section, we will go deep into some of the key market dynamics that are shaping the environments in which circular business models operate, the trends in consumer behaviour which affect their adoption, and the business strategies to be used to align with the trends.

Shifting Market Dynamics

A multiplicity of market dynamics underpins and reflects wider economic, environmental, and technological changes, all driving the imperative for a transition to circular business models. Such dynamics offer companies ways to grasp new circular practices and yet, with the same token, can represent a challenge on the scale of implementation (Stankevičienė et al., 2020).

1. Sustainability as a Competitive Advantage: There is a growing focus on sustainability by consumers, investors, and regulators; hence, the increased competitiveness of businesses adopting circular models. To consumers and investors concerned with the environment, business patterns like resource sharing and PaaS are seen as the best way to avoid wastage and salvage the environment. This has raised demand for products and services that reduce waste generation, resource consumption, and promote reuse.

2. Regulatory Pressures, and Incentives: World governments are working out policies and regulations that encourage practices of circular economy. Policies range from imposing EPR laws, Waste Reduction targets to granting incentives concerning the use of recycled materials. Firms working in highly regulated sectors like electronics or automotive, therefore find a stronger motivation to develop circular models to comply with such policies and not be penalized. Besides, for circular business models to be economically efficient, there will be a need for provision of incentives by the government in the form of tax breaks or subsidies.

3. Technological Advances: High-speed technological innovation is enabling the implementation of circular business models through the reduction of their related costs and complexities. Enabling technologies in circular practices are transforming business approaches toward optimized resource use, product lifecycle tracking, delivery of service with customization and efficiency, among others. Innovations make circular models accessible and scalable across industries.

4. Economic Shifts and Cost Pressures: With increasing prices for resources and supply chain disruption, global economic changes and mounting uncertainty are driving companies to look for much more flexible and productive business models. Circular business models, focusing on resource efficiency and reuse, provide a way to buffer these pressures, by reducing reliance on raw materials and lowering operating costs. The offerings of PaaS present customers similarly with a minimum upfront cost in times of economic dynamics due to the pay-per-use or subscription-based character of these service models (Bruyne & Verleye, 2022; Deza & Pereira, 2018).

5. Consumer Demand for Flexibility and Convenience:: Today, the consumer trend leans more and more toward flexibility and convenience with access prevailing over ownership. This is very conspicuous in the younger generation's trend towards subscription services, sharing platforms, and other circular models. Therefore, companies that provide easy, flexible access to products or services via a circular landscape are strategically positioned to harness this demand pull and build continuous customer loyalty.

Consumer Behavior Trends

Consumer behavior, therefore, plays a really important role in making a circular business model successful. Businesses can, therefore, conceptualize and market circular offerings to their intended target audiences when they understand what drives, appeals, and raises red flags for consumers.

1. Increasing Environmental Consciousness: There is an increasing awareness of environmental concern that is influencing consumer purchase decisions. At the moment, consumers are becoming more informed about what type of environment their choices or way of life will bring about and seek products and services based on their defined values. This consumer buying trend is forcing an increase in the demand for circular business models that smash wastages and carbon footprints, as well as promoting sustainable consumption. Businesses that are effectively able to communicate, clearly and distinctly, the environmental impacts of adopting circular economy business models are eventually likely to benefit from the increased environmentally conscious customer base (Muhajir, 2024).

2. Preference of Access Over Ownership: There is a general shift from the traditional point of view of ownership to one of access and experience. There is a general inclination that shifts in people, particularly from younger generations, who are now moving towards renting, sharing, or subscribing to a certain product rather than acquiring it fully. It drives the choice towards a PaaS model where people pay for using the utility or outcomes of a product without necessarily buying the product itself. This has also been indicated as a more general trend with popularity for sharing platforms of car-sharing, clothing rental, and tool libraries.

3 Demand for Convenience and Flexibility: With the world moving at such a blistering pace, there is always an increasing demand for ease and flexibility in operations that are consumer-based. In such a setup, it is the circular business model interfaces with low-friction access points, flexible payment options, and a frictionless user experience that does the best. For instance, digital platforms that facilitate consumer booking, subscription management, and real-time tracking of usage are extremely attractive at the time of use. Furthermore, the ability to tailor services or access them on demand increases the value proposition of circular offerings.

4. Trust and Transparency: One of the biggest enablers allowing the consumer to adopt a circular business model is trust. Trust is an enabler, especially in models where there are shared resources and probably long-term service relationships. In this regard, the cases at hand require that the consumer trusts the accessed products for the application of appropriate maintenance measures and the services for the reliability of the products in circulation as well as the safety of their data. Transparency in business practices, including clear communication on product lifecycles, pricing, and sustainability claims, becomes imperative to create and retain this trust with consumers. Blockchain technology has the ability to provide transparent and immutable records.

5. Cost sensitivity: Despite the importance of environmental and ethical considerations, cost remains one of the key influences on customer shopping behavior. Circular business models that generate savings, ideally through lower access costs rather than pay-per-use pricing, can reduce the total cost of ownership and therefore be even more appealing to price-sensitive customers. Moreover, the economic benefits of circular models through the reduction of waste and extension of product life cycles have an ability to materialize into costsaving, which obviously appeals to a broader audience.

Strategies for Aligning with Market Dynamics and Consumer Behavior

The above-discussed strategies will help businesses align better with the changing dynamics of the market as well as the trending behaviors of consumers.

1. Educate and Engage the Customer: Educate consumers on the clear benefits to be realized from circular business models—not just toward the environment but also in their day-to-day lives. This includes how the models work, the value infused through these models, and positive impacts on sustainability. Engage the consumer through storytelling, social media, and influencers so as to build awareness and drive adoption.

2. Personalize with Technology: Customization as a value serves the people longing for flexibility and convenience in what they consume. One can look at data analytics and AI to provide services and recommendations that will be very relevant in enhancing the customer experience. For example, in the PaaS model, you could use AI to make recommendations for subscription plans based on past behavior or recommend maintenance services before something goes wrong.

3. Build Trust Through Transparency: One of the most valuable functions of transparency in business practice is building trust with consumers. A company should be capable of revealing information about its products, services, and operational sustainability clearly and openly to the public. In other words, this stems from the

notion that a company needs to clearly expose the company politicization in the form of pricing, product lifecycle statistics, and eco-impact from product manufacture. Blockchain technology can inherently help and assist with the incorporation of further transparency and building trust by offering genuine records of transactions and product histories.

4. Focus on Cost-Effectiveness: The economic benefits of a circular model are key to attracting cost-sensitive buyers by selling much lower upfront cost, saving from longer product lives, and waste reduction. Flexible payment terms, such as a subscription model or pay-per-use pricing, can make circular offerings accessible to a larger audience.

5. Regulatory Adaptable: The business should be up to date with regulation changes and ready to adapt to new requirements as they come. This would mean that they would have to align their circular business models with government policies and take advantage of incentives promoting sustainably. Complying with the legal scope not only prevents fines for non-compliance but also keeps the company in a good light as a responsible and forward-looking business.

6. Expand Market Reach: Business will expand the market due to their collaborative efforts with other business, industrial groups, and governments, hence helping in accelerating the shift to circular business models. Partnerships will help in reaching the market, sharing resources, and creating synergies out of mutual benefits. An example would be a partnership of a product manufacturer with a sharing platform to create new opportunities and at the same time facilitate the culture of circular practices.

The future of circular business models lies at this intersection of market dynamics and consumer behavior. If sustainability becomes the competitive edge, technology lowers barriers, and the preference of the consumer shifts more toward access and flexibility with transparency, then this period precisely presents business with a one-off opportunity to hitch their wagons on these trends. With alignment to these forces, companies can operate and scale out circular business models within the context of economic and environmental gains in a highly dynamic world.

Policy and Regulatory Considerations

Policy and regulatory frameworks form some of the major drivers that condition the adoption and scaling up of circular business models, including Resource Sharing and Product-as-a-Service (PaaS). Governments and regulatory bodies are an integral part of the environment in which the models will be working, creating opportunities and, at the same time, challenges toward business. This section looks at the key policy and regulatory considerations that determine prevailing circular business models, including waste management regulations, product stewardship requirements, economic incentives, and international standards.

Waste Management Regulations

While waste is a principal concern to a circular business model—most notably, one aiming to drive waste minimization through resource sharing and PaaS—most regulation frameworks today encourage reduction in the generation of waste, mainstreaming the recycling approach and responsible disposal of products. In fact, it is forcing businesses to such practices in circles. Key regulatory areas to focus on include:

1. Extended Producer Responsibility (EPR): EPR is a policy framework that makes the producer responsible for his or her product right from inception to disposal. An EPR is required to force or drive businesses toward designing products that are durable, repairable, and can be recycled. Quite obviously, this is fertile ground for a circular business model. For example, a company offering PaaS has dominion over the product as to its reuse or recycling and does not allow the product to be thrown away.

2. Waste Reduction Targets: Ambitious waste reduction targets set by governments as part of a larger sustainability agenda often overlay requirements for reduced landfill waste and increased recycling along with reduced dependence on singleuse products. Business approaches in the circular economy can contribute to the delivery of these targets in the design of products and services while reducing waste and extending the useful life of resources. Compliance with the rules of reduction of wastes would not only keep a company away from fines but would also a positive impact on the image of a company as an environmentally responsible entity.

3. Recycling and Reuse Mandates: Recycling and reuse mandates have been developed more and more such as in the electronics, automotive, and packaging industry would be requiring a certain business to have a quota for products with recyclable materials or that their design would allow for a product to be easily and quickly maintained. Circular business models, in particular those based on resource sharing, advocate theses imperatives in that products can be designed and remanufactured to give support to these. The adherence to these recycling and reuse demands will also unlock market entry into, for instance, public sector procurement or certifications that may be attractive to green customers.

Product Stewardship Requirements

Product stewardship regulations hold businesses responsible for minimizing the environmental impact of a product from the time it is produced until the time the product is deemed obsolete. A circular business model connotes the new context for the product when the value extracted for all inputs is optimized by the business. Central elements of product stewardship include:

1. Design for Environment (DfE): The DfE principles drive companies to design products taking into account positive environmental attributes through reduction in material usage, use of sustainable materials, and design for repairability and recyclability. In this perspective, a benefit to circular business models, in particular PaaS, is derived from DfE in the creation of products that are easier to maintain, upgrade, and recycle. Regulatory compliance with DfE does not just meet the set legal requirements but also follows consumer preference for products to be sustainable.

2. Take-back Programs: Companies are able to take back their products and recycle them after their useful life has been exhausted. For this purpose, take-back programs can be products, packaging, electronics, and battery-regulated by law to a greater extent. All circular business models consider a form of implementing take-back systems into their operation, whereby goods are taken back for refurbishment, recycle, or reprocessing instead of otherwise wastefully taken into landfills. This strategy not only meets regulatory mandates but also allows for material sourcing to new products with a reduced reliance on virgin resources.

3. Hazardous Materials Regulations: This covers products containing hazardous materials, such as electronics, automotive parts, and some chemicals, which have a high degree of regulation in their usage, disposal, and recycling. Business models in a circular economy need to be highly responsive to these provisions regarding their respective design and use with regard to disposal, to facilitate an approach that assures negligible environmental and health risks. Hazardous materials regulations are at the core of assuring the company's freedom from legal liability and the customer's confidence.

Economic Incentives and Disincentives

Governments use a variety of economic incentives and disincentives to push business towards circular business models. Such financial instruments aim to make circular practices financially rewarding for businesses and consumers, enabling large-scale adoption. The most prominent economic domains are:

1. Tax Incentives: Tax incentives through credits, deductions, or exemptions make circular business models economically more possible. For example, governments can offer tax breaks on the investments carried out by companies in terms of recycling

infrastructure or using greater quantities of recycled materials, besides rewarding effective circular practices. Such discounted costs lower the financial burden on firms with the transition to circular business models and can result in increased profitability. That is why firms must be aware of available fiscal incentives that adjust for financial planning.

2. Subsidies and Grants: Subsidies and grants are yet another policy in the government's armory. Such funds may be given for the research and development of products going in a circular loop, for investing in sustainable technologies, or actual implementation of circular initiatives. Subsidies and grants access can really unlock the required budget for innovating and scaling circular business models. The last line business-wise is that companies should search for potential funding opportunities to apply and provide support for their initiatives.

3. Carbon Pricing and Environmental Taxes: In simple words, carbon pricing is done with mechanisms like carbon taxes or cap-and-trade with financial incentives to companies in order to reduce the extent of their carbon footprint (Chen, 2022). Circular business models, which usually come with a lower carbon footprint due to resource efficiency and waste reduction, will bound to benefit out of such policies. In essence, these environmental taxes on waste generation, single-use plastics, or disposal of waste in landfills add additional business cost to the maintenance of such non-circular practices. By best understanding and harnessing carbon pricing and other policies related to environmental taxes, businesses can craft a view of them as an opportunity for operations in line with ecological imperatives, while their operations are exposed to as little financial risk as possible (Suchek et al., 2021).

4. Green Public Procurement (GPP): GPP is a policy that urges government agencies always to provide preference in purchasing green products and services. Businesses that are implementing circular models will, therefore, have an added advantage over the rest in bidding to win government tenders since they will automatically meet the GPP criteria just by this simple condition of availing their products as recyclable, energy-saving, or made from recycled products. Business will be able to tap into new revenue streams by participating in GPP programs and raising the name of the company as a leader in sustainability.

International Standards and Guidelines

The global nature of supply chains and markets means that businesses have to interact with a complex web of international standards and guidelines on circular economy practices. The document clearly sets a guideline for effective implementation of the circular business models in a manner that is consistent, transparent, and recognized internationally. Key international considerations include:

1. **ISO Standards**: ISO has a series of developed standards in regard to the implementation of practices in the fields of the circular economy, from environmental management to sustainable procurement and product lifecycle assessment. ISO compliance—such as that from certification in ISO 14001 (Environmental Management) or in ISO 20400 (for Sustainable Procurement)—will further provide more credibility for the company achieved and improve its access to international markets. For this, the businesses need to take the process of gaining relevant ISO standards under consideration when fostered toward a circular model.

2. Global Reporting Initiatives (GRI): The GRI standards give guidance to sustainability reports, which cover the way companies report their environmental, social, and governance performance. The circular competent business model reaps the alignment with the GRI guidelines through transparent sustainability impacts, including good notes on resource and energy efficiency, waste reduction, and product stewardship. Such a level of transparency will most likely appeal to socially responsible investors and boost the trust of stakeholders.

3. EU Circular Economy Action Plan: Circular Economy Action Plan of the European Union is a comprehensive circular economy implementation blueprint of the European Union. It includes actions on sustainable product design, waste reduction, and a higher level of resource productivity for this Union. This and more will attach sustainability legislation to companies that are either within the Union or exporting into the Union, covering extensive areas that could include product labeling, recycling, and material use. Explanation and adherence to the EU Circular Economy Action Plan is therefore critical for those businesses that desire to operate or continue to operate in the EU market.

4. UN Sustainable Development Goals (SDGs): At the UN level, the SDGs provide a universal framework for issues on Sustainable Development, which also include responsible consumption and production (SDG 12) and climate action (SDG 13). Circular business models directly contribute to the realization of such targets through resource efficiency, waste minimization, and lowering of carbon footprint. Companies could thus position their circular practices in alignment with SDG targets to uphold their interests under global sustainability agendas and realize dividends tied to their ever-widening CSR chambers.

Challenges and Future Directions

While policy and regulatory frameworks provide important support for circular business models, they also present challenges that businesses must navigate. These include the complexity of complying with multiple regulations across different jurisdictions, the need for significant investment to meet regulatory requirements, and the potential for regulatory changes that could impact business operations. Additionally, the lack of harmonization between national and international standards can create uncertainty and increase compliance costs for businesses operating globally.

In the future, more stringent regulation can be expected, following the increasingly active government and international effort in the area of climate change mitigation policies and sustainable development. Businesses will have to proactively stay in tune with this type of regulation, make compliance investments, and work with policymakers to support the growth of circular business models.

In conclusion, policy and regulatory considerations provide a very critical impetus in how the circular business model environment develops. Based on that framework, firms ensure compliance besides growing into that kind of symbiotic relationship so that they can ingeminate innovation, competitiveness, and sustainability. Businesses that are agile and forward-thinking in their approach to circular practices will thus be easily able to position themselves to mitigate the risks and business challenges associated with such rapidly evolving regulatory environments.

Challenges and Risks

Though the circular business models, such as Resource Sharing and Product-as-a-Service (PaaS), are bound to offer very many advantages environmentally and economically, the implementation journey is not free of challenges and risks. Business enterprises need to weather through these challenges in order to make the introduction and scaling of circular practices successful. This chapter deals with the major challenges and risks associated with the deployment of the circular business model: operational complexities, financial barriers, market acceptance, regulatory uncertainty, and technological constraints.

Operational Complexities

One of the key challenges in making such a transition is that the circular business model is by its nature more operationally complex than any traditional linear model because handling revolves around products at all stages, starting from design, production, and usage to end-of-life management.

1. Supply Chain Integration: Efficient material and product flows within circular business models demand a close supply chain integration. This can be challenging, as it requires orchestration with upstream suppliers, downstream manufacturing, logistics services providers, and customers who make a closed-loop system possible. This entails clear tracking and reverse logistic systems that are attainable to implement and manage.

2. Product Design and Lifecycle Management: Product design involves the design characteristics that are involved in a product to make it circulatory, like durability, repairability, modularity, and recyclability. This generally constitutes a big shift from traditional design practices, which again might lead to a rise in design costs. Moreover, businesses manage the product through its extended life—maintenance, upgrades, and eventual disposal or recycling, which adds more layers of complexity to operations and, in turn, requires new skills, new technologies, and new processes.

3. Inventory and Resource Management: Circular models tend to assume that resources would be available without interruptions through some form of supply, such as recycled or refurbished goods. One major challenge in managing inventory in a circular system is that balancing the inflow of returned products with the demand for new or refurbished products becomes very tough. In other words, either a too-high inflow of used products or too-low inflow, or the quality of returned products might imbalance the demand and supply of flow. These things could lead to significant operational inefficiencies in either part of the loop, potentially breaking the business continuity.

Financial Barriers

Transitioning into a circular business model can be marked with serious financial limitations, especially concerning investment at the initial stage and in terms of recurrent costs, creating low-profit margins, among others.

1. High Level of Initial Investment: Generally, practices in the circular economy are characterized by a need for a high level of up-front investment regarding new technologies, infrastructure, and re-training practices. For example, it requires heavy investment in advanced manufacturing processes for the industries, digital platforms for tracing products, or reverse logistics required for them. These costs are substantial and may amount to a higher entry barrier for small and medium-sized enterprises.

2. Maintenance and Repair Costs: Circular business models, in particular PaaS, bear lifelong maintenance, repair, and after-sale services to customers. This might lead to an overheating operation cost that cannot be any effective cost management for circular models to be profitable.

3. Revenue and Profitability Challenges: Of the circular models, some are definitely less guaranteed in terms of revenue streams in contrast to traditional sales models, or at least stretched over an extended period of time. For instance, PaaS models are commonly monetized through subscription or pay-per-use charges—typically a low initial price that brings in profit over the long term. Companies need to have a high facility in handling the cash flow and strategies of pricing so that they can be financially sustainable in the future. Besides, business models that provide for

relatively reduced potential for profit margins in certain circular models may require companies to identify new revenue streams or otherwise optimize the cost structures.

Market Acceptance

Overall, the success of the circular business models depends on the acceptance in the market. This can be likely to be triggered by one of the three drivers related to consumer behavior, competitive pressure, or other reasons linked to the market environment.

1. Consumer Perception and Education: Consumers may not be aware of circular business models or may be skeptical about them, particularly sharing models or PaaS. Quality and reliability of the product, and perception of ownership, may thus counteract the adoption. It calls for immense business investments in customer education and marketing efforts to build trust and awareness of the circular models that outline advantages in cost savings, convenience, and environmental benefits.

2. Competition with Traditional Models: Customers have much less experience with circular business models than with traditional, linear models. Traditional models often offer less in upfront cost or an easier way to own. This is especially interesting to customers. When this occurs, a circular business will have to deliver on multiple dimensions of value besides delivering on cost reduction, better service, or better sustainability.

3. Market Readiness and Infrastructure: The success of circular models also depends on the readiness of the markets and the infrastructure that supports them. For example, in parts of the world where people are less willing to adopt subscription-based services, the PaaS model will spread more slowly. Similarly, in parts of the world lacking appropriate infrastructure to facilitate returns and recycling of products, this model cannot be as effective as it could be in better-equipped areas. Businesses will need to consider market conditions in order to adjust their strategies for successful implementation.

Regulatory Uncertainties

While related to the potential for driving the adoption of circular business models, the other can just as likely bring uncertainties and challenges facing a business.

1. Evolving Regulatory Landscape: The regulatory landscape for circular economy practices is changing fast with the evolution of new laws and standards at national and international levels. It becomes very difficult to keep these regulations under control in order to guarantee compliance, particularly for companies whose geographic footprint exists in more than one location. Additionally, such regula-

tory changes may further introduce uncertainties in terms of planning long-term investment or strategies.

2. Inconsistent standards across regions: The standards around the activities of the circular economy can vary from region to region—standards are built inconsistently, and such bring challenges to companies that operate across the globe. For instance, the company will have to attempt to find variations in recycling requirements, waste management regulations, or product stewardship obligations in one country from a different country. Navigating through these inconsistencies would require thorough planning and lots of coordination to ensure due compliance and a reduction of legal risks.

3. 3. Potential Regulatory Gaps: There are instances where existing regulation cannot cover the unique challenges posed by circular business models, thus leaving a business open to both legal and operational risks. For example, even related to product liability, data protection, or intellectual property in a circular model, there could be a gap. The business must keep a wide view and its ears open to identify and minimize these risks, which mainly come from working with competitor organizations in situations where regulatory frameworks are unclear.

Technological Constraints

Although technology flowing throughout realization of the circular business models is crucial to it, there are various constraints, where executives need to work on those to realize significant competitive advantage.

1. 1. Limited Technological Maturity: Some of the technologies that would underpin such business models—say, advanced recycling processes, IoT-enabled tracking systems, or even AI-driven platforms for predictive maintenance in the loop—are still in the early phase of development. Their limited maturity can end up with unaffordable levels of costs, unreliability, or underperformance at scales that really make businesses hard to become actually circular.

2. Data Management and Security: Typically, circular business models will be based on optimal operations necessitated by high volumes of data collection and analytics, in-product life cycle tracking, and delivering personalized services. This is data that must be effectively and securely managed, which in itself is a challenge amidst the ever-growing stringent capital requirements. This calls for investment in strong data management and cybersecurity systems for protecting customer information and compliance.

3. Compatibility with Legacy Systems: There are a lot of businesses operating with legacy systems that are not easily compatible with the required technologies for circularity. The integration of old systems with new technological advancements is intricate and expensive. This integration requires a serious amount of investment in

IT infrastructure and man-power. Dealing with this integration headache is crucial to the proper run of business models round.

Strategic Responses to Challenges and Risks

Major strategic responses that businesses can take in order to navigate the identified challenges and risks while circumventing the operations of circular business models include the following:

1. Invest in Innovation and Collaboration: Investment in research and development may help to cross over technological barriers and boost innovation towards circular practices. Collaboration within other company settings, industry groups, or research institutions may merge resources, knowledge, and risks in finding a more effective solution (Schwartz et al., 2022).

2. Flexible and Adaptive Business Models: This flexibility has to relate to the management of the uncertainties in regulations, market dynamicity, and operational complexities. Businesses need to carefully design their delivery of the circular-model essence in such a way as to allow for a necessary degree of adaptability to changes in regulations, consumer behavior, and technological developments.

3. Focus at the Consumer: High consumer awareness and confidence can make the circular business models mainstream. Investment in circular marketing and education campaigns should highlight the benefits of circular practice, dispel consumers' unfavorable notions, and expand the concept of sustainable consumption.

4. Use Financial Incentives and Support: A firm can try removing partial impediments by constructing where possible circular incentives in the form of tax breaks, grants, or subsidies to support their circular initiatives. In addition, a firm can find new revenues through value-added services or develop secondary markets for refurbished products, thus increasing profitability.

5. Strong Implementation of Risk Management and Compliance Strategy: Proactive risk management and adherence to compliance strategy will be needed to navigate uncertainties in regulation and operational risk. Businesses will continuously have to monitor their risk exposures, follow up regulatory developments, and be subject to comprehensive compliance programs that warrant legal and operational resiliencies.

There exist several challenges, risks, and operational complexities of transitioning to circular business models, such as financial barriers and mainstream market acceptance, regulatory uncertainties, and technological constraints. Businesses can effectively address these multiple opportunities in the circular economy through proper planning, strategic investments, and emphasis on innovation in combination with consumer engagement in the area. It is at the heart that the challenges be taken so that the companies can move further towards growth that is sustainable and resilient to achieving a more resource-efficient future.

Future Outlook

Two business models from the circular economy viewpoint show future promise Resource Sharing and PaaS, on grounds that industries and consumers are adopting sustainability and resource efficiency rapidly. With technology continuously evolving, changes in regulatory environments, and shifts in consumer preferences, business will have to respond with appropriate levels of innovation to stay competitive. This section elaborates on the most significant trends and developments that are going to determine the future growth of circular business models and gives a glimpse of the opportunities and challenges these entail.

Trends Shaping the Future

1. Technological Developments: Fast-paced innovations in technologies such as AI, blockchain, and the IoT hold the key to circular business model advancement. Artificial intelligence can be enabling in advanced scenarios for predictive maintenance, resource optimization, and personalized customer experiences. Blockchain technology will play a major role in the transparency and traceability of circular supply chains, making materials and products easier to trace (Nishijima & Oguchi, 2022; Uvarova et al., 2020). The IoT will allow monitoring the performance and usage of products in real time and in an economical way of dealing with resources so that wastage can be reduced.

2. Regulatory Support: Governments and international organizations are expected to develop much more stringent regulations and policies to support the circular economy. This includes an enlargement in EPR requirements with higher goals for recycling and waste reduction and the offering of more incentives to businesses with circular innovation. Those businesses that take an early proactive position toward this regulatory environment and engage in policy discussions are most likely to benefit from the regulatory support to avoid potential penalties.

3. Evolving consumer expectations: This puts a shift on consumer preferences toward sustainable and circular products. Growing consumer concern and knowledge about environmental problems will push consumers into buying differently, seeking services that, perhaps even more than perceived utile features, represent higher efficiency in raw material use. Demands for access-based models, like those for the product, products with long life, repairability, and eventual upcycling through PaaS-like offerings, will be driven. Businesses that will do the best job at marketing these features for the environment and the economy that arise from the usage of such features will be the businesses to capture the new and dynamic market for sustainable goods and services.

4. Applying Circular Practices Throughout All Sectors: Nevertheless, the most important aim will be the main adoption of circular business models in other sectors. This would imply that the level of circularity will grow in sectors such as fashion, electronics, automotive, and construction, probably under regulatory pressure and consumer demand. In an endogenous growth process, these sectors during this transition process will result in more new business opportunities, collaborations, and innovations, thus triggering the shift toward a circular economy.

5. Circular Ecosystems Growth: The creation of circular ecosystems where businesses, consumers, and other array of stakeholders cooperate to create closed-loop systems will define the dominant trend. These ecosystems will require partnerships across business, local government, and local community for purposes of promoting sharing resources, recycling waste, and product refurbishment. Collaborations may be useful for the stakeholders to develop circular systems efficiently and resilient enough to allow value creation and distribution through lifecycle, from primary producers to the final consumers.

Opportunities and Innovations

1. Emerging Business Models: In the following future, business models advancing circularity principles will innovate in the directions of, for example, product-as-platform business models whereby businesses offer comprehensive problems/solutions/services versus discrete products, creating new revenues and value propositions. Further, hybrid models combining the best practices of the circular with linier business models may offer flexible and scalable solutions for both business and consumer.

2. Higher Consumer Engagement: Digital technological advances will also help companies better engage their consumers in circular practices. Digital platforms and apps will make it easier to trace products, facilitate or rent sharing, as well as get access to information regarding repair and recycling options. A higher level of consumer engagement will further boost higher adoption of circular models and lead to sustainability culture.

3. Circular Supply Chain Innovations: Supply chain management innovations, such as advanced recycling technologies, material recovery systems, and closed-loop logistics, will support the growth of a circular business model. Companies investing in these innovations will better position themselves for more effective and sustainable supply chains, reduction of waste, and costs. This also opens opportunities for collaboration and partnerships (Deza & Pérez, 2021; Milios, 2021; Gooijer, 2022).

4. Education and Training: The shift towards the circular business models makes it important to anticipate a rapid increase in the demand for education and training on the principles of the circular economy and related practices. Offering

developments and delivery of programs to build expertise and skills should also centralize education institutions, industry associations, and business on the subject of the circular economy, thus helping accelerate the adoption of circular practices and drive innovation in industries.

5. Global Collaboration and Knowledge Sharing: International collaboration and the sharing of knowledge are important tools in developing modern circular business models. Global networks support industry forums and cross-sector partnerships and foster the sharing of best practices, research, and case studies. Through the establishment of international links, businesses and policymakers will be in a position to learn from each other and work toward driving the global transition to a circular economy.

Challenges and Considerations

1. Scalability and Implementation: This is undoubtedly where a significant challenge will lie in being able to scale up circular business models from what has already been pilot tested and implemented to being largely adopted. Business actors will actually have to bring the solution nearer to supply chain integration, adoption of technology, and consumer behavior for better and improved scalability. Proper implementation will come with the right kind of planning, investments, and collaboration with stakeholders.

2. Balancing Innovation with Practicality: Though innovation is key to the change, companies must balance innovation with practicality. These considerations will include the applicability of new technologies, from a costing perspective, and the concrete difference these circular models will create in front of the end consumer and environment. An approach based on practical and scalable solutions is critical for mass adoption.

3. Regulatory Complexity Adapting: The regulatory landscape for circular economy practices is constantly evolving and businesses need to keep themselves abreast of the changes and the requirements of the laws. Regulatory complexity is a moving target, and for businesses that operate in many jurisdictions, navigating it successfully will require ongoing diligence and adaptation (Milios, 2021; Lestari, 2023; Khan et al., 2020).

4. Meeting Consumer Expectations: Consumers have have multiple and constantly changing expectations, whereby businesses that adopt circular business models will find it hard to comply. Companies have to interact constantly and directly with their consumers, clear their doubts, and deliver transparent value proposals to keep up the customers.

The future of the circular business model is promising in taking the dimensions of the sustainability alongside innovation and economic growth. This will give plenty of opportunities to the businesses to embrace circular ways and drive value for the businesses as technology progresses, regulatory support increases, and consumer preferences change. However, there are challenges and risks that need to be dealt with when scaling and implementing these models. But staying nimble, investing in innovation, and collaborating with stakeholders help business navigate the evolving landscape and make a positive contribution to a more sustainable and resilient circular economy.

CONCLUSION

Circular business models such as Resource Sharing and Product-as-a-Service (PaaS) bring forward a new, transformative role that moves away from the conventional linear economy to a sustainable, resource-effective manner. It impacts largely by extending the life of products, avoiding waste, and optimizing resource utilization, which converges well with global sustainable objectives and creates a resilient economy. Indeed, the incorporation of such practices not only addresses the concerns of most environmental challenges but also paves the way for new opportunities with economic growth and innovation in Europe.

Many of today's technology developments can facilitate or scale up circular business models. Artificial intelligence, blockchain, and, in general, the Internet of Things support mainly the enhancement of operational efficiency and transparency. Through this, they unlock the potential for totally new, even disruptive, solutions managing the life cycle of products and resources. As they develop and mature, they will enhance the progress in the circular practices to be more effective and accessible to the business at large and across other sectors.

Regulatory and policy frameworks play a critical role in supporting the transition to circular business models. In a conducive economic environment, effective regulation concerning waste management, product stewardship, and economic incentives should motivate businesses to take up such practices, in line with stated sustainability goals. Business must be sensitive to regulatory change and become compliant with it and take part in policy discussions and be part of the fighters for conditions supporting circular development.

Understanding market dynamics and consumer behavior lies at the core of the implementation of circular models. In a shifting landscape of consumption preferences toward sustainability, businesses should attune their strategies to these increasing expectations and communicate the value essence of offerings modeled under circularity. Consumers will develop an awareness and gain confidence that is required to increase adoption and entry into a loyal customer base.

The above benefits from circular business models are met, but several challenges tend to emerge: operational complexities, financial barriers, and regulatory uncertainties. In this view, the above challenges require a coordinated response that includes not only strategic and innovative planning, but also collaboration with relevant stakeholders. Such tools as investment in research and development, enhanced consumer engagement, alignment with regulatory frameworks, optimization of operation, and collaboration would have been used by the companies to help in overcoming the presented challenges on the way to success within the circular economy.

Circular business models are, thus, set to receive a new horizon of expanded possibilities, driven by technology innovations, regulatory support, and evolving consumer expectations. Businesses that continue to be agile and proactive in their adaptive ability to be scaled in solutions and risk management will be best positioned to survive in this new future. Companies will continue to build a more sustainable, resource-efficient, and resilient economy through circular practices, realizing at the same time economic success and value creation for future generations.

REFERENCES

Bocken, N., & Ritala, P. (2021). Six ways to build circular business models. *The Journal of Business Strategy*, 43(3), 184–192. DOI: 10.1108/JBS-11-2020-0258

Bocken, N., Strupeit, L., Whalen, K., & Nußholz, J. (2019). A review and evaluation of circular business model innovation tools. *Sustainability (Basel)*, 11(8), 2210. DOI: 10.3390/su11082210

Bruyne, M., & Verleye, K. (2022). Realizing the economic and circular potential of sharing business models by engaging consumers. *Journal of Service Management*, 34(3), 493–519. DOI: 10.1108/JOSM-08-2021-0318

Chen, P. (2022). The spatial impacts of the circular economy on carbon intensity - new evidence from the super-efficient sbm-dea model. *Energy & Environment*, 35(1), 47–63. DOI: 10.1177/0958305X221125125

Deza, X., & Pereira, Á. (2018). Eco-innovation and circular business models as drivers for a circular economy. *Contaduría y Administración*, 64(1), 64. DOI: 10.22201/fca.24488410e.2019.1806

Deza, X., & Pérez, S. (2021). Taxation for a circular economy: New instruments, reforms, and architectural changes in the fiscal system. *Sustainability (Basel)*, 13(8), 4581. DOI: 10.3390/su13084581

Giessmann, A., & Legner, C. (2016). Designing business models for cloud platforms. *Information Systems Journal*, 26(5), 551–579. DOI: 10.1111/isj.12107

Gooijer, J. (2022). Corporate taxation in a circular economy., 53-61. DOI: 10.1007/978-3-030-85322-8_6

Han, J., Heshmati, A., & Rashidghalam, M. (2020). Circular economy business models with a focus on servitization. *Sustainability (Basel)*, 12(21), 8799. DOI: 10.3390/su12218799

Kesavapanikkar, P., Amit, R., & Ramu, P. (2022). Product as a service (paas) for traditional product companies: An automotive lease practice evaluation. *Journal of Indian Business Research*, 15(1), 40–54. DOI: 10.1108/JIBR-04-2022-0107

Khan, S., Haleem, A., & Khan, M. (2020). Enablers to implement circular initiatives in the supply chain: A grey dematel method. *Global Business Review*, 25(1), 68–84. DOI: 10.1177/0972150920929484

Lestari, E. (2023). Tax policy reconstruction toward implementation of circular economy in indonesia.. DOI: 10.3390/proceedings2022083068

Mei, H., Shao, J., & Wang, Q. (2012). Model based monitoring and controlling for platform-as-a-service (paas). *International Journal of Cloud Applications and Computing*, 2(1), 1–15. DOI: 10.4018/ijcac.2012010101

Milios, L. (2021). Towards a circular economy taxation framework: Expectations and challenges of implementation. *Circular Economy and Sustainability*, 1(2), 477–498. DOI: 10.1007/s43615-020-00002-z

Muhajir, A. (2024). Sustainable marketing model: Market research, marketing capability and entrepreneurial orientation in indonesia. *International Journal of Business Law and Education*, 5(1), 1007–1020. DOI: 10.56442/ijble.v5i1.497

Nishijima, D., & Oguchi, M. (2022). Measuring product lifetime extension potential by increasing the expected product lifetime: Methodology and case study. *Business Strategy and the Environment*, 32(4), 1218–1231. DOI: 10.1002/bse.3183

Özdemir, C., Sandikkaya, M., & Yaslan, Y. (2018). Classifying malicious thread behavior in paas web services.. DOI: 10.5220/0006688204180425

Raj, K. and Aithal, P. (2020). A new concept of circular model of management for achieving sustainable success and growth. International Journal of Management Technology and Social Sciences, 1-17. https://doi.org/DOI: 10.47992/IJMTS.2581.6012.0079

Schwartz, H., Solakivi, T., & Gustafsson, M. (2022). Is there business potential for sustainable shipping? price premiums needed to cover decarbonized transportation. *Sustainability (Basel)*, 14(10), 5888. DOI: 10.3390/su14105888

Sehnem, S., Campos, L., Julkovski, D., & Cazella, C. (2019). Circular business models: Level of maturity. *Management Decision*, 57(4), 1043–1066. DOI: 10.1108/MD-07-2018-0844

Stankevičienė, J., Nikanorova, M., & Çera, G. (2020). Analysis of green economy dimension in the context of circular economy: The case of baltic sea region. *E+M. Ekonomie a Management*, 23(1), 4–18. DOI: 10.15240/tul/001/2020-1-001

Suchek, N., Fernandes, C., Kraus, S., Filser, M., & Sjögrén, H. (2021). Innovation and the circular economy: A systematic literature review. *Business Strategy and the Environment*, 30(8), 3686–3702. DOI: 10.1002/bse.2834

Swaroop, K. and Gade, S. (2023). Sustainable marketing and people behavior for enhanced governance., 242-262. DOI: 10.4018/978-1-6684-9711-1.ch013

Uvarova, I., Atstāja, D., Korpa, V., Avena, L., & Erdmanis, M. (2020). End-of-life tyre recycling: going beyond to new circular business models in latvia.. DOI: 10.22616/ERDev.2020.19.TF435

Chapter 9
Social Impact of Circular Economy Startups

Preet Kanwal
https://orcid.org/0009-0006-5114-8381
Lovely Professional University, India

Majdi Anwar Quttainah
https://orcid.org/0000-0002-6280-1060
College of Business Administration, Kuwait University, Kuwait

Anish Kumar
https://orcid.org/0000-0002-8047-4227
O.P. Jindal Global University, India

ABSTRACT

Circular economy startups are pivotal in advancing sustainable and equitable economic models. This chapter explores their social impact, focusing on key metrics that highlight their contributions to environmental sustainability, economic development, social equity, and consumer engagement. By examining environmental benefits, job creation, inclusion practices, and supply chain sustainability, the chapter provides a comprehensive analysis of how these startups drive positive societal change. Challenges in measuring social impact are also discussed, emphasizing the need for standardized indicators and robust data collection. The findings underscore the importance of effective metrics in demonstrating the value of circular economy practices and guiding future developments. This exploration is crucial for stakeholders aiming to understand and enhance the role of circular startups in fostering a more sustainable and equitable future.

DOI: 10.4018/979-8-3693-9241-6.ch009

1. INTRODUCTION

1.1 Circular Economy Concept

The circular economy is a very disruptive model of the economy dependent on overcoming the conventional linear approach of "take, make, dispose." In its place is an insistence on continued use of resources, by closing product, material, and resource loops in use for as long as possible in a bid to avert waste generation and source extraction thus promoting sustainability (Barna et al., 2023).

In the last few decades, the concept of a circular economy has gained a significant foothold as a response to growing environmental concerns regarding resource depletion, climate change, and waste generation. Linear models should be done away with and replaced by circular ones; this is what governments, corporations, and CSOs are increasingly becoming aware of as a must for a more sustainable and resilient economy.

1.2 The Role of Startups in the Circular Economy

In the circular economy, startups play a critical role because they represent new innovation and change. Unlike established firms that have to bear all the burdens of legacy, startups are innately flexible to test out business models and technologies by design, which can point them toward circularity. That is, their agility empowers them to be disruptors of conventional industries with innovative solutions—that have the potential for really large-scale scaling (Opstal & Borms, 2022).

More often than not, the circular economy startups are pioneers in developing and implementing business models with resource efficiency, product longevity, and waste reduction. Quite often, those startups deal in the areas of recycling, upcycling, remanufacturing, and sharing economies, which create new value out of what has previously been treated as waste. By doing so, they not only contribute to environmental sustainability but also create new economic opportunities (Redko, 2024).

1.3 The social impact of startup in the circular economy

The circular economy has been repeatedly recited to have positively influenced the environment, but not too often the social benefits that are attributed to it. Social impact, in its broader sense, refers to business activities' influence on society is, therefore comes naturally to mind as regards developing the idea of social impact like the employment, development of community, social equity, and better quality life (Gao & Chen, 2013).

Circular economy startups may be high-impact social enterprises that help in the solution of wider societal problems—unemployment, social inequality, access to resources. For example, startup companies that offer jobs within the cycle of waste management not only reduce the negative social consequences related to too high an environmental burden but support local economic development through the recycling and remanufacturing chain, reducing social disparities through newly created opportunities for employment. Moreover, with sharing models for resources, they facilitate access to products and services for low-income classes (Suchek et al., 2021).

In this chapter, we will take a look at how circular economy startups make a social difference, what kinds of metrics are used to measure this impact, and what challenges exist around maximizing the inputs they could make into society. We will further utilize examples drawn from the case studies of some successful circular start-ups that have made a real difference in their communities and beyond.

1.4 Purpose and Scope of the Chapter

The purpose of this chapter is to analyze in a more comprehensive way the social impact of circular economy startups. We will, therefore, discuss the theoretical underpinnings of the circular economy and social entrepreneurship, ways how startups contribute to social well-being, and find out the main factors influencing their ability to create social impact.

The challenges and barriers to attaining social impact for circular startups are also addressed in this chapter, together with strategies that can help overcome such obstacles. We close by elaborating on the role of policy and regulation in supporting the social impact of circular economy startups and provide insights into future trends and opportunities.

The end of this chapter will provide more insight into what critical role circular economy startups play in driving not only sustainability but also social change.

2. THEORETICAL BACKGROUND

2.1 Definition and Principles of the Circular Economy

The circular economy is the transformation from the conventional linear economy and traveling down the road of "take, make, dispose." There are three principles at the heart of any circular economy:

1. Design out waste and pollution: This implies that products are designed to begin tackling waste and pollution right from the beginning of their life cycle. These include easily re-used, easily-recycled, or compostable materials, followed by durable and easily repairable or upgradable products.
2. Product and material use assurance: The circular economy keeps strong focus on making a product last longer in its life cycle, with options for sharing, leasing, reuse, repair, refurbishment, remanufacturing, and recycling. This is premised on designing for long life and sounding material circulation rather than landfilling after one cycle of use (Bocken & Coffay, 2022).
3. Restoring and regenerating natural systems: The circular economy also looks into a positive environmental impact through the restoration or regeneration of natural systems, as opposed to just harm reduction. This may include practices for regenerative agriculture that help in restoring soil health, among other factors, up to the use of renewable energy sources (Rok & Kulik, 2020).

Such precepts mark the contours of a more resourceful and absorptive economy of resources with waste not being a drag, but an input for the system.

2.2 Social Entrepreneurship and the Circular Economy Concept

Social entrepreneurship is the process of creating and running a business to solve emergent social issues and create social value. Social entrepreneurship is a mission-driven cause, striving to solve such problems in society that include poverty, inequality, and environmental degradation. It very often operates in those spaces in which traditional market mechanisms fail to address the needs of society (Giesen et al., 2010).

Social entrepreneurship is very close to the goals of a circular economy. Both concepts deal with value creation much more broadly, far beyond financial profit, and with systemic change. Social entrepreneurship is thus crucial in boosting the innovations of a circular economy that diminishes the ecological footprint while harnessing welfare. They create shared value for society and the environment in the field of business model innovations, including such aspects as participation in local communities, job creation, and stimulation of inclusive growth (Genet, 2023).

2.3 Where Circular Economy Meets Social Impact

This social impact is manifest in the interplay of the circular economy space. The social impact in the context of the circular economy means positive change in the direction of individuals, communities, and society at large through circular business practices. These may be either direct impacts, such as generation of employment and skill development, or indirect ones manifested in public health improvement due to the cleaner environment arising from reduced pollutants.

Circular economy startups are especially well-placed to engender social impact because they work at the very nexus of environmental sustainability and social responsibility. By adopting circular business models, circular economy startups act on the most acute social problems and massively contribute to the achievement of environmental goals. For example, upcycling startups working with waste materials often get into collaboration with local craftsmen, thereby providing them with income-opportunity frameworks and preserving traditional handicrafts. Similarly, sharing economy startups are reducing resource-intensive production, increasing access to goods and services for lower-income communities.

2.4 Role of Innovation in Circular Economy Startups

Circular economy startups mean a lot of innovation. In most cases, these startups are distinguished by creative thinking about the transformation of waste into value, extension of the life cycle of a product, and business model design that is sustainable and socially impactful. Several types of innovation are specifically applicable to a circular economy startup:

1. Product innovation: Developing products for acceptance having long life, modularity, and recyclability, using materials that are sustainable and including design principles for products that can be easily maintained or even upgraded.

2. Process Innovation: Introduction of new modes of production such that the amount of waste generation is low or less in the manner in which they have been produced, ensuring better efficiency of resources. This may count in closed-loop manufacturing systems whereby there is a guarantee that waste by-products are fed back into the processing cycle.

3. Business Model Innovation: Developing new business models that emphasize access over ownership, such as product-as-a-service models—consumers pay for product use rather than product ownership. This limits demand for new products and stimulates existing ones to be maintained and re-used.

4. Social Innovation: Innovations addressing both environmental and social issues. Circular Economy startups involved in sorting and recycling solid waste from municipal, for instance, can also become a source of employment for people

belonging to socially excluded segments of society or their end products can support specific social needs, including affordable housing or the social end of clean energy (Bifaretti et al., 2023).

2.5 Key Theoretical Frameworks and Models

A number of theoretical frameworks and models can be applied to understand better the social impact of circular economy startups:

1. TBL (Triple Bottom Line): TBL extends the conventional reporting framework to include those related to social and environmental performance in conjunction with performance that is related to financial outcomes. Circular economy startups are usually aimed at balancing these three dimensions that create value for people, planet, and profit (Aspara et al., 2010).

2. Shared Value: This concept, according to Michael Porter and Mark Kramer, captures the point that business can bring economic value in a way that also creates value for society by helping it meet some needs or problems. This is best demonstrated by startups within business activity in a circular economy.

3. Systems Thinking: It is the holistic approach toward the analysis of a system, considering the relativity between the parts, how the system works over time, and within the context of larger systems. In a circular economy startup scenario, systems thinking fits in well with the understanding of how elements of the business and its environment interact to deliver social impact.

4. Theory of Change: This is a framework that states how organizations' activities connect with the social change they want to achieve. It describes what the end goal is and works backward to identify precondition for that to be possible and further backward to find the activities that would lead to these outcomes. The startups in the circular economy can use this framework to state how their operations end up in social impact.

The theoretical background is the foundation of the explanation between the complex interplay of the circular economy, social entrepreneurship, and social impact. The following of these concepts and their relations will yet to show the uniqueness of the position of circular economy startups in driving not only environmental sustainability but serious social change. This sets the scene for a deeper journey into how these start-ups actually operate in practice and what is the effect on society, which is realized in the subsequent sections of the chapter.

3. CASE STUDIES OF CIRCULAR ECONOMY STARTUPS

3.1 Introduction to Case Studies

Case studies make the illustration real with respect to how circular economy startups drive social impact. From these examples of existing applications, we can derive valuable lessons from the strategies, challenges, and successes of circular economy startups in creating value for society and the environment. The case studies represent a wide array of circular economy startups in different sectors and regions that have come up with fresh approaches in solving social and environmental problems.

3.2 Case Study 1: Waste Ventures India

- Overview: Waste Ventures India is a social enterprise whose work centers on transforming municipal solid waste handling. This 2011 birthed startup aims at reducing landfill waste through the promotion of collection and recycling of organic and inorganic waste.
- Circular Economy Model: Waste Ventures India operates a decentralized waste management system in which the waste collectors are trained to segregate organic and recyclable waste at source. The degradable waste, collected and transported to the processing sites, is converted into compost, while the inorganic and non-biodegradable waste are sold to recycling industries for processing.
- Employment Generation: Waste Ventures India has provided steady employment and a living wage to a significant number of waste pickers, most of them from the underprivileged sections and laboring in dangerous working conditions. It enhanced their health, safety, and earnings through the formalization of their operations and provision of safety gear and training.
- Community Health: Lessening of landfills supports improved public health resulting from the limited potential for pollution and disease spreading.
- Women empowerment: Most of the waste pickers who work for Waste Ventures India are women. This empowers them economically and in turn boosts gender equality in the engagements of the communities involved.
- Challenges and Lessons Learned: Perhaps the greatest challenge Waste Ventures India has faced is raising public awareness and changing household behavior to segregate waste at source. It has met this challenge with extensive community education campaigns, driven by the startup, with the support of local governments.

3.3 Case Study 2: Fairphone

• Overview: Fairphone is a Dutch social enterprise designing and producing environmentally friendly, ethically sourced smartphones. Created in 2013, this enterprise works for a more sustainable and socially responsible electronics industry.

• Understanding that Fairphone designs modular smartphones that are easily repaired or upgraded affordably, and have the capability to be recycled. Also, it sources minerals absent of conflicts and uses used materials in its design. To ensure that old phones are responsibly recycled, there is a take-back program.

• Ethical Supply Chains: Working conditions in the supply chain of Fairphone have been upgraded with a special focus on the conflict regions from where minerals are sourced. This is not only to ensure fair trade with miners—a good price is paid to them—but also the absence of child labor.

• Consumer Awareness: Fairphone increased the capability of customers to understand the environmental and social consequences of electronic production. This way, a startup company empowers customers to make situational choices and ethical purchasing decisions by being aware of transparent information on the lifecycle of purchased products.

• E-Waste Reduction: Through the use of modularity within its products, Fairphone increases the life span of smartphones, which in turn reduces demand for new devices and subsequent electronic waste.

• Challenges and Lessons Learnt: Challenges faced by Fairphone include scaling up production while ensuring adherence to ethical standards. Treading an appropriate middle path between commercial viability and socio-economic goals needed careful management of innovation in design and practices in the supply chain.

3.4 Case Study 3: Rubicon Global

• Overview: Rubicon Global is a technology firm of US origin. It helps with waste management and recycling through a cloud-based platform. Started in 2008, Rubicon works to create a waste-free world through building data-informed solutions that promote recycling and a circular economy (Rachinger et al., 2019).

• Circular Economy Model: The model optimizes routes of collection for waste generators connected to a network of haulers and recyclers on the platform to guarantee that materials are moving out of landfills and into recycling centers. It also gives analytics to enable businesses to reduce waste generation and increase recycling rates.

•Social Impact:

• Environmental Stewardship: The technology employed by Rubicon has managed to up the recycling rates of businesses and municipalities, hence cutting on the quantity of landfill wastes in addition to GHG emissions.

• Economic Opportunities: By providing small, independent haulers access to larger clients, Rubicon has helped fuel the success of local businesses and, therefore, job creation in the recycling sector.

• Community Engagement: Rubicon collaborates with cities and schools in an effort to engage communities in learning about the benefits related to recycling and waste reduction for the sake of living a sustainability culture.

• Challenges and Lessons Learned: Rubicon has faced problems with data accuracy and integrations with existing waste management systems. The startup has been able to address such issues by continuously innovating its technology and building meaningful partnerships with key influencers in the waste management industry.

3.5 Case Study 4: Toast Ale

•Overview: Toast Ale is a UK-based brewery that makes beer out of surplus bread, fighting food waste. Having been founded in 2015, it pursues a mission of tasty beer with great purpose: reducing food waste markedly and supporting environmental charities.

• Circular Economy Model – Used unsold bread from bakeries and sandwich manufacturers, collected, to be included in the brewing process which would otherwise go to landfill sites.

More so, the startup donates all their profits to the charities working towards the reduction of food waste.

Social Impact:

• Food Wastage Reduction: Till now Toast Ale has saved tremendous amounts of bread from being dumped into landfills by turning the waste into something meaningful and having some value.

• Charitable Contributions: Toast Ale has donated its profits to environmental charities involved in initiatives focused on food waste reduction and the shaping of sustainable food systems.

• Consumer Engagement: This startup was able to drive full consumer engagement towards food waste by employing the product to raise awareness and change behaviors.

• Challenges and Lessons Learned: Toast Ale has wrestled with growing the production of its beers while at the same time keeping the supply of surplus bread constant. The startup has created strong relationships with suppliers, like large commercial bakeries and industrial sandwich makers, from which they source this surplus bread. It is looking at new markets for expansion.

3.6 Case Study 5: The Renewal Workshop

• Summary: Based in the USA, The Renewal Workshop partners with clothing brands to collect damaged or other apparel that would have otherwise been thrown away. Afterwards, the firm repairs, cleans and re-sells the same to ensure that the garments live longer while reducing the wastes from textiles.

• Circular Economy Model: The Renewal Workshop is operated as a zero-waste facility, repurposing apparel that would have gone to landfill. The startup utilizes advanced cleaning and repair methods to bring the garment to sellable condition and sells them on their own platform, or returns them to the brand for resale.

Social Impact:

• Employment Opportunities: It has established an advanced workforce in garment repairs and sustainable fashion, thus providing local economic development.

• Waste Reduction: The company has diverted thousands of tons of textile from landfills, hence reducing environmental impacts from fashion—being one of the major industry generators of global waste.

• Change in Consumer Behavior: The Renewal Workshop has made consumers change their behaviors and adopt a sustainable lifestyle in fashion by changing purchasing behaviors to replacements.

• Challenges and Lessons Learnt: Renewal Workshop: Renewal Workshop has had to deal with challenges relating to consumer perception of secondhand clothing and logistics of processing high volumes of garments. This startup has resolved such challenges by developing methods of assuring quality and establishing a brand reputation of being sustainable.

3.7 Conclusion of Case Studies

The three case studies provided in this section represent different ways in which circular economy startups contribute to social impact. Each of these startups has found environmentally innovative solutions while creating tremendous social value—job creation, community development, or the fostering of good, ethical consumer behavior. In the same way, these business innovations show the potential of the circular economy startup to lead systemic change: it can be realized that there is an alternative sustainable state without trade-off in social goods.

These case studies further convey very useful lessons to aspiring entrepreneurs and policy makers on why integrating circular principles with social impact goals require collaboration, innovation and perseverance in overcoming challenges.

4. SOCIAL IMPACT METRICS FOR CIRCULAR STARTUPS

4.1 Introduction to Social Impact Metrics

It is, therefore, a need to measure social impact from startups in the circular economy to establish the contributions they help make towards societal and environmental goals. Metrics for social impact framework how such startups create value beyond financial performance, including impacts on communities, workers, and the environment. By developing and applying such metrics, therefore, startups will be in a position to not only trace their progress and communicate their achievement but also learn how to make improvements.

4.2 Key Metrics for Social Impact Evaluation

1. Environmental Improvement and Resource Efficiency

The primary social impact metric of circular startup is their environmental performance. This can measure by the extent the startup can efficiently reduce its waste, conserve the resource and emit a low level of greenhouse gases. Circular practice would reflect environmental benefits—e.g., metrics on utilizing recycled materials or minimizing landfills, having a general carbon footprint for the products and operations. These factors become measurable, indicating the level of demonstrating a commitment to sustainability on the startup's end and the contribution of eliminating environmental challenges.

2. Economic Impact and Job Creation

Overall, new job creation by circular economy startups and further strengthening of local economies bring forth economic growth. Job creation metrics—measured by numbers of full-time and part-time jobs, but also quality of jobs, such as good wages, benefit packages, and working conditions—seek to measure this area. Furthermore, for startups, being responsible for the number of contributions to local supply chains and the economic value in which they are taking part through circular business model implementation can be tracked. These show the way that startups can eventually be able to leverage economic growth and resilience for their community.

3. Social Equity and Inclusion

Assessing social equity and inclusion is vital for understanding how circular economy startups address social justice issues. Metrics related to diversity and inclusion within the workforce, community engagement, and support for marginalized groups provide insights into the social impact of these startups. Evaluating practices such as fair labor standards, equal opportunities for underrepresented groups, and community outreach initiatives helps measure how startups contribute to social equity and foster inclusive growth (Ostermann et al., 2021; Mederake, 2022).

4. Consumer Engagement and Education

In this way, circular start-ups educate the consumer about sustainable practices, causing changes in behavior. Metrics for consumer engagement could include the number of consumers contacted after educational campaigns, the impact of outreach on changing consumer attitudes to sustainability, and the level of product labeling and transparency. Therefore, it is important to know what type of consumer behavioral change is reached at this startup level, in view of how the consumer becomes more aware of the principles underpinned by the circular economy.

5. How It Affects Supply Chain Sustainability

By the very nature of the circular startup, it often tends to take the lead by partnering with one's own supply chains toward sustainability and ethical practices. The metrics for supply chain sustainability usually involve the adoption of circular practices by the suppliers, the transparency of the supply chain, and the general reduction of environmental and social impacts within the supply chain. These processes will allow startups to understand how their practices of production influence and foster the sustainability of the broader supply chain with an impact on environmental and social goals.

4.3 Problems of Measuring Social Impact

There are problems like how to measure a number of diverse yet interconnected metrics of social impact; a clamor for standardized indicators; and quantification of qualitative results. For instance, it's challenging for a startup to get reliable data on the measurement of long-term impacts or the broader social implications from their practices. Only confirmed strong methods in data collection, working with external evaluators, and standardized metrics for use in comparative and evaluative capacities can ensure these challenges are properly met.

Social impact metrics will let one realize how a startup of a circular economy can contribute to the betterment of the environment and the people in it. Startups will be able to prove their worth, with the betterment of continuous processes inducing effective tracking of key metrics associated with environmental benefits, economic impact, social fairness, consumer engagement, and supply chain sustainability. While the social impact is difficult to measure, appropriate effective metrics are developed to display the benefits of circular practices in driving and creating a more sustainable and equitable future.

5. CHALLENGES AND BARRIERS

5.1 Regulatory and Compliance Issues

Circular economy start-ups are often hammered by labyrinthine and complicated regulatory and compliance hurdles; this can slow down its growth dynamics and operational productivity. Often, it's difficult to keep up with fragmented and inconsistent regulations of most countries on the globe. The start-ups may find difficult to synch with various waste management, recycling, and product design standards. Moreover, austere regulations without flexibility may hinder the ability to experiment or try original business models, thereby negatively impacting innovation. The impediment from the regulation can only be overcome by an up-to-date start-up that knows the changes in the regulation, and through interaction with the policymakers, the result may be clear guidelines and adjustment of practices to ensure innovation without noncompliance.

5.2 Market Acceptance and Consumer Behavior

Another big challenge is how to get acceptance in the markets their target market will react to the circular product. It might be that consumers simply do not want to change their buying behavior, or else the message about the benefits of circular products and services has not clearly reached them. Addressing such mistrust and building trust requires consumer awareness of the value behind circular economy principles, among which the tangible benefits generated for the consumer. Some of the variables for which startups really have to invest, then, if intending to effectively change perceptions and thereby spur adoption on the market, are: effective communication, transparency in operations, and compelling value propositions.

5.3 Financial and Resource Constraints

Strong financial and resource constraints are among the top challenges that most circular economy startups face. The initial investment in the development of circular products, the adoption of practices, and the required scaling of operations are huge. Again, financial assistance is hard to procure for startup companies, and more so for early-stage companies with little record of performance. Resource constraints in terms of accessing raw materials from recycling, or for that matter, building any kind of infrastructure to that end—such a thing in itself further throttles progress. Start-ups have to explore any possible source of funding including grants, impact investors and how to establish partnerships as well as other innovative means of management and optimization of resources

5.4 Hurdles Securing Supply Chain

Implemented correctly and efficient circular economy works only if there is a sufficient and sustainable supply chain however this is generally one of the commonest challenges the start-ups face Periodic unreliable for recycling materials, difficulties in setting up circular supply networks as well as suppliers needing much cooperation and supply in sectors. Further, circular start-ups need to invest in building resilient and sustainable supply chains by nurturing relationships with suppliers, developing strategies for material recover and recycling and getting flexible in the complex area of reversible logistic. Supply chain sustainability and efficiency continue to take the center juncture since the goals of a circular economy can only be achieved by such proper and working systems

5.5 Scalability and Growth

The concept of expanding startups involved in the circular economy comes with. As start-ups scale, they need to balance the need for increased production and market expansion with the commitment to circular practices, maintaining the quality of scaling sustainable processes and not letting growth compromise environmental and social goals. Build scalable models that can adapt with larger volumes and broader markets while maintaining the integrity of circular practices in order for long-term success and impact.

5.6 Limits of Technology

A large share of the effectiveness that can be demonstrated by the circular economy startup is based on the availability or maturity of these technologies. This might include existing limitations in recycling technologies, material innovations, or digital tools for circular practices, among others, that would support the practice of circles. These technological constraints may influence the effectiveness of circular processes and the possibility to implement innovative solutions. One of the most critical investments in the circular business remains to be research and innovation, technology providers' interaction, keenly monitoring technological changes with inquisitive strategic flows is a step for increased benefits and efficacy of the circular practices.

A strategy towards overcoming the outlined challenges is necessary for success of the startups and ultimately the diffusion of the circular economy (Holm & Günzel-Jensen, 2017). That way, startups will be able to navigate regulatory complexities, stimulate market acceptance, overcome financial constraints, solve supply chain issues to stimulate growth, level the playing field, and overcome technological limitations in pursuit of better impact in an economy that is sustainable in its development. The realization of meaningful social and environmental outcomes depends on how effective different stakeholders collaborate and help the circular startups to overcome such challenges: policymakers, investors, and industry partners.

6. STRATEGIES FOR CREATING SOCIAL IMPACT

6.1. Social and Environmental Objectives Merged Together

A way to make an improved social effect effective is the merging of social and environmental objectives within the core business model. Circular economy startups can do this in practices that fit in the orbit of the bigger sustainability goals and principles of social equity. By establishing clear and measurable goals that work toward the reduction of environmental footprints with social outcomes that are positive, those startups with a frame that is more comprehensive for the creation of impact include practices of ethical sourcing, waste reduction, and helping out local communities in a positive manner concerning society and the environment.

6.2. Building Strong Community Relationships

Engage and support local communities for a stronger social impact. A way to do this is for startups to develop these strong relationships by involving community members in the decision-making process and supporting localized initiatives and needs within the community. Examples include creating job opportunities for a community resident, working with organizations, and investing in the improvement of local infrastructure. Partnerships and working on mutual benefit with communities enable startups to foster co-benefits in enhancing social impact.

6.3. Promoting Transparency and Accountability

Finally, transparency and accountability build trust and show social impact. The information regarding practices should highlight the goals and impacts of the circular economy practices for startups. This would entail regular reports on environmental performance, social contributions, and challenges of the practice. With the implementation of third-party certifications and audits, transparency and accountability of startups will become credible and assure the stakeholders. Startups become more credible and increase their ability to engage stakeholders with transparency and accountability of performance in implementation.

6.4. Technology-enabled Impact

Technology can be used to increase the social effect of CE start-ups through digital tools and platforms that enable operations, optimize resource efficiency, and make useful data available for impact assessment. These ways might include blockchain for the sake of the supply chain's visibility, IoT for the monitoring of resource usage, and data analytics for processes. Investment in and adoption of relevant technologies will increase the effectiveness of circular practices toward better decision-making and higher impact.

6.5. Develop Inclusive Business Models

Inclusive business models that prioritize social equity, in fact, vastly enhance the potential of impact from circular economy startups. It could be done in the manner of designing products or services that are user friendly to diverse populations, which could include the poor or a marginalized community. They may also target fair labor practices where their workforce is diversified equally. Business models that contain inclusivity will tend to bring about both social equality and broad, general social advantages.

6.6. Entering into Strategic Partnerships

Strategic partnerships with other organizations can multiply the social impact created by circular economy startups. Such organizational settings can provide additional resources, expertise, and reach, allowing the startup to access these through partnerships and collaboration. This means that collaboration can be a way for the startup to use complementary strengths for the attainment of new markets opened up at the same time that challenges are being met with increased effectiveness. Co-joined initiatives and mutual goals will give a better result and more room for a more substantial systemic change.

6.7. Educating and Empowering Consumers

Consumer education and empowerment are the most important points toward the eventual behavior change and improvement of social impact. Circular economy-driven startups should fuel their mission with the support of consumer education regarding the benefits of circularity, making consumers champions for sustainable consumption. This includes organizing workshops, campaigns, or educative content that diffuses information to consumers and creates added awareness as to why they should be a part of the circular economy and through what avenues they can do it. By teaching the consumers, and respectively, providing the consumers with knowledge and tools, startups can empower a better-informed customer base, making it more sustainable and cooperative towards the circular practices.

6.8. Measuring and Communicating Impact

Indeed, effective measurement and communication of impact are crucial to proving the value of practices adopted in the circular economy. The startup needs to evolve some robust metrics and methodologies for assessing all associated social and environmental impacts through quantitative as well as qualitative indicators. Such metrics can be reported consistently while sharing leading practices and in building credibility with and engaging various stakeholders. Only then can a startup measure and communicate the impact effectively, attract support, secure funding, and incite other organizations to follow the virtuous circle practices.

Social impact needs to be increased multifariously and delivered through integrated and infused goals related to social and environmental priorities. Public engagement, transparency, use of technology, and fostering inclusiveness need to be accomplished through inclusive business models, strategic partnership, customer education, proper measurement, and communication for social and environmental impact for circular economy start-ups to veer positive change, reach their objectives of overt change. These are strategies applied for the success of an individual startup and to offer support for the greater transition to a circular economy and a sustainable future.

7. POLICY AND REGULATORY ENVIRONMENT

7.1. Creation of a Conducive Regulatory Environment

Policies and regulations are an important aspect of the ecosystem in which circular economy startups operate. A supportive regulatory regime can provide clear guiding principles, incentives, and support mechanisms for the adoption and scaling of circular practices. Governments can set in place regulations that liven the pace of resource efficiency, waste reduction, and circular product design. Willingness from the policy makers to set those standards and conditions for a more circular economy will require startup business models to make that shift from linear interventions to a more circular economy approach and, in turn, help them clear the bottlenecks in terms of implementation (Gupta, 2024; Rakesh, 2023).

7.2. Incentives and Funding Opportunities

This growth and innovation of circular economy startups can be encouraged by policy makers through an array of incentives and funding opportunities. The financial incentives in the form of tax breaks, grants, and subsidies could remove the huge upfront costs associated with adopting circular practices and thus provide support for research and development. Apart from that, funding opportunities for scaling up operations towards sustaining impact could be given to startups that work on sustainability. These incentives reduce the financial barriers and enhance the attractiveness of startups to invest in circular solutions.

7.3. Addressing market failures and externalities

Quite frequently, circular economy startups are involved in markets with an inherent inefficiency or even externality that traditional models cannot correct. Therefore, policy interventions can also help correct market failures through internalization. For instance, the setup of extended producer responsibility programs empowers the latter with end-of-life management of products; hence, producers are motivated to design for circularity. carbon pricing policies and waste levies reflect avoided cost for waste and greenhouse gas emissions. These policies address these failures in the market and enable a more level playing field for circular economy startups.

7.4. Streamlining Regulations and Reducing Complexity

Circular economy startups often operate in very complex and fragmented regulatory settings that hinder their operations. This is where policymakers can help: simplify the regulation and provide clear compliance guidance. Simplification and harmonization of regulations across regions can reduce the administrative burden on startups so they can operate more smoothly. Having a one-stop-shop on regulatory information and offering support on compliance helps startups comply with regulations while staying focused on their core activities.

7.5. Balancing Regulation and Innovation

One of the most important questions for policymakers is finding the right balance between regulation and the need for innovation. Too strict or prescriptive regulations hinder creativity and limit the possibility for new, circular solutions to arise. Instead, flexible, performance-based regulation should be put in place by policymakers, articulating clear environmental and social goals that are not combined with specifications of particular methods and technologies. The approach will allow innovation and the development of new solutions while achieving regulatory objectives. Pilot projects and experimentation can be encouraged under the umbrella of such regulatory provisions so that innovation in circular practices is fostered.

7.6. Assuring Policy Coherence and Coordination

This policy coherence can be offered across multiple sectors and levels of government, hence developing an enabling framework for circular economy start-ups. This calls for alignment and coherence among policymakers at all levels to ensure that policies relating to waste, product design, trade, and other relevant policy areas are mutually supportive. This can be further enhanced by strengthening intergovernmental coordination among national, regional, and local governments, which would help in lessening the possibility of regulatory duplication and increasing the general effectiveness of policy. Therefore, policy coherence would create a more predictable and stable environment for circular startups to operate and flourish.

7.7. Assistance to International Collaboration and Standards

Transition toward a circular economy is a frontal international collaboration subject to standard harmonization. Policymakers can work at the international front through international collaboration in global initiatives, agreements, and in standard-setting bodies. The alignment with international standards and best practices will bring immense benefits to circular economy startups for scaling up globally and multiplying their impact. Close collaboration with international organizations will also help in knowledge exchange and the furtherance of policies at the global level in favor of circular practices.

7.8. Public Awareness and Participation

Public awareness and participation are a necessity for securing the required impact of circular economy initiatives. This might also involve policymakers undertaking and encouraging public awareness campaigns regarding the benefits of circular economy practices, responsible consumption, and changing attitudes in favour of sustainability. Consultation with stakeholders—including consumers, business, and community organizations—can build support for circular initiatives and engender a culture of sustainability. In its broadest sense, awareness and education, enabled by raising public awareness on a more macro level, provide an enabling environment in which circular economy startups can become more established, thus driving wider adoption of circular practices.

The role of policy and regulation is core to the success of circular economy startups. It means that making a supportive regulatory framework, offering incentives, addressing market failures, smoothing regulations, balancing innovation with regulation, ensuring coherence of policies, supporting international collaboration, and promoting public engagement—so the best possible conditions are set for the development and flourish of circular startups. Good policies and regulations can hence act as an accelerator of the shift towards a circular economy and increase the positive social and environmental impact that startups can generate, thereby contributing to a more sustainable and resilient future.

8. FUTURE DIRECTIONS

8.1. Technology and Innovation

The future of circular economy startups is as bright as the future of technological development and innovation. New technologies that will emerge, from artificial intelligence and blockchain to advanced materials science, will further open more opportunities in enhancing circular practices. AI can improve the optimality of resource management and enhance waste sorting by offering better designs for products. Blockchain offers transparency into and traceability of supply chains. Further investment and development are necessary if these technologies are to support innovation in circular business models. Startups that can leverage these developments will continue to have a competitive advantage in developing more efficient and effective circular systems (Payne et al., 2021; Tashtamirov, 2023; Rakesh, 2023).

8.2. Evolving Consumer Preferences and Behavior

Consumer preferences and behaviours constantly keep changing, which impacts the success and growth of circular economy startups. Growing awareness about the environment and rising demand for sustainable products drive customers toward circular solutions. Most probably, future directions will be characterized by a deeper integration of circular principles into mainstream consumer behavior with a stronger focus on ethical consumption and sustainable lifestyles. It is upon startups to keep up with these shifts and adapt their offerings accordingly to the changing expectations from consumers. By way of anticipating and adapting to evolving trends, startups can help their market fit better and increase their impact (Lin et al., 2023).

8.3. Circular Business Models Scale Beyond Traditional Sectors

The scaling potential of circular business models is high in new sectors beyond traditional circles. While current circular activity in fashion and electronics has reached visible milestones, construction, agriculture, and health are among the industries holding huge potential for circular innovation. Future developments will likely see the circular principles widespread in a much larger suite of sectors, with new business models and opportunities. Startups that embrace and innovate circular approaches in those emerging sectors can lead the way in creating comprehensive, sector-wide, circular systems.

8.4. Integration of Circular Economy into Policy and Regulation

The future landscape will prominently be driven by the integration of the circular economy into policy and regulation. As circular practices continue to build in momentum, there will likely be an increased demand from policymakers to quickly develop and implement enabling frameworks. This may include future directions that better harmonize and integrate policies to incentivize circularity, countervail market failures, and promote sustainable practices. Start-ups and stakeholders will be actively engaged in ensuring the regulations are aligned with circular economy goals and supporting advocacy. This calls for developing new metrics and standards in measurement and communication of impact.

8.5. Development of New Metrics and Standards

As the Circular Economy progresses, it becomes imperative to create new measurement metrics and standards for the right communication of defined impact. In the future, developing standardized indicators that more precisely capture social, environmental, and economic benefits of circular practices will not only be important in measuring performance but also for purposes of improvement. Industry-wide standards and benchmarks on the level of circularity can be made by which consistent and more transparent reporting will be possible. The more startups contribute to these new metrics and adopt them, the better it will be for improving their credibility and demonstrating their commitment to circular principles.

8.6. Scaling and Replicating Successful Models

Moreover, for the full-scale impact and wide adoption, the scaling and replication of proven business models are necessary. Start-ups that have succeeded in some markets or regions should consider scaling models to some new geographies and sectors. This may involve modifications in practices to cater to different regulatory environments, consumer preferences, and supply chain conditions. Scaling should be done together with other businesses, investors, and stakeholders so successful models are replicated in largely differing contexts (Dunford et al., 2010).

8.7. Emphasis on Collaboration and Ecosystem Development

Thus, the way forward for every future circular economy startup is going to be strongly anchored towards collaboration and the development of its ecosystem. It will require the formation of a strong supplier partnership, customer collaboration, and other stakeholder relationships to build up effective circular systems. These efforts can foster innovation, exchanging best practices, and wrestling with joint challenges. Circular economies that englobe business, governments, NGOs, and consumers in circular practices are more effective and can easily scale. Startups participating and contributing much to these ecosystems will be better placed to drive systemic change.

8.8. Promoting Social Equity and Inclusion

That the practices of circular economy are useful to social equity and inclusion will be a necessary consideration for future developments. While these are all essential elements of the Circular Economy, one emerging trend is that with its ongoing maturation, greater attention will be paid to how such practices can positively shape the lives of diverse communities and address social justice. It may involve a bigger emphasis, further down the line, on the creation of opportunities that are more equitable, fair labor practices, and protection of the most marginalized groups within the circulatory system. Startups focused on social equity and inclusion will not only bring enormous improvement to their social impact but also contribute to a more just and inclusive circular economy.

The future for circular startups will be filled with opportunities and challenges as they manoeuvre among fast technology development, new consumer behavior, new business models, and the main circular principles that should be anchored in policies developed with new metrics, scaled-up successful models, collaboration generated, and more focus by startups on social equities to drive the shift toward a circular economy. Embracing these future directions will enable startups to maximize their impact, be supportive of sustainable development, and create a resilient and equitable economic system.

9. CONCLUSION

The rise of circular economy startups signals a transformational shift toward more sustainable and more equitable economic models. A whole new generation of circular economy startups is opening up new pathways in resource efficiency, waste reduction, and social impact—providing new solutions to some of the most serious environmental and social problems of our times. This chapter has explored the multi-faceted social impact of circular economy startups: role modeling in the creation of economic opportunities, driving innovation, and fostering community resilience.

The social impact of circular economy startups reaches further than the mitigation of environmental impacts, entailing even larger societal issues. They generate jobs, ensure labor fairness, and foster local communities through stakeholder inclusiveness and transparency. It caters to the growing consumer demand for responsible consumption and ethical business conduct. By applying circular principles, startups will not only be able to reduce their ecological footprint but at the same time exert positive spill-overs on the economy and society.

Although circularity is an incremental path toward a more regenerative and distributive economic model, it faces a number of barriers: regulatory complexity, market acceptance, and resource constraints. Multi-stakeholder engagement, therefore, calls for top policymakers, investors, and industry leaders to pave the way. To create an enabling environment in which circular startups can thrive, effective policy frameworks, enabling regulations, and dedicated incentives are crucial. In other words, if stakeholders address these challenges and offer the required support, that would be the way to make a leap toward accelerating a shift in the linear economy and maximizing the socio-economic impact of these new ventures.

The angle is that there is huge potential for startups in the circular economy. Such changes will create the right platform on which these startups can now learn and orient to changes in trends for justifiable improvement in innovations. Key themes of the future will be the use of new technologies, global sustainability goals, and embedding circular economy principles in larger economic and societal frameworks.

In other words, circular economy startups are part of everyday social impact under the umbrella of sustainability and resilience. In other words, value created from these startups by circular practices not only solves environmental challenges but also includes social well-being and economic stability. Building the path toward a more sustainable and inclusive future, in an evolving circular economy, the efforts sped up by startups with support from effective policy and collaborative partnership will be outstanding.

REFERENCES

Aspara, J., Hietanen, J., & Tikkanen, H. (2010). Business model innovation vs replication: Financial performance implications of strategic emphases. *Journal of Strategic Marketing*, 18(1), 39–56. DOI: 10.1080/09652540903511290

Barna, C., Zbuchea, A., & Stănescu, S. (2023). Social economy enterprises contributing to the circular economy and the green transition in romania. Ciriec-España. *C.I.R.I.E.C. España*, 47(107), 47–69. DOI: 10.7203/CIRIEC-E.107.21738

Bifaretti, A., Paván, E., & Grigioni, G. (2023). Consumer attitudes and concerns about beef consumption in argentina and other south american countries. *Agriculture*, 13(3), 560. DOI: 10.3390/agriculture13030560

Bocken, N., & Coffay, M. (2022). The circular experimentation workbench – a lean and effectual process. *Circular Economy and Sustainability*, 3(3), 1361–1383. DOI: 10.1007/s43615-022-00239-w PMID: 36531657

Dunford, R., Palmer, I., & Benveniste, J. (2010). Business model replication for early and rapid internationalisation. *Long Range Planning*, 43(5-6), 655–674. DOI: 10.1016/j.lrp.2010.06.004

Gao, J., & Chen, W. (2013). Research on collaborative mechanism in large and complex business process modeling. *Advanced Materials Research*, 850-851, 1012–1015. . DOI: 10.4028/www.scientific.net/AMR.850-851.1012

Genet, C., Gandia, R., & Colombero, S. (2023). Simultaneous management of business model innovation and replication processes. *Journal of Business Models*, 11(2). Advance online publication. DOI: 10.54337/jbm.v11i2.7427

Giesen, E., Riddleberger, E., Christner, R., & Bell, R. (2010). When and how to innovate your business model. *Strategy and Leadership*, 38(4), 17–26. DOI: 10.1108/10878571011059700

Gupta, P., Singh, S., Ghosh, R., Kumar, S., & Jain, C. (2024). Regulatory framework on governing equity crowdfunding: A systematic literature review and future directions. *Journal of Financial Regulation and Compliance*, 32(4), 421–444. DOI: 10.1108/JFRC-10-2023-0160

Holm, A., & Günzel-Jensen, F. (2017). Succeeding with freemium: Strategies for implementation. *The Journal of Business Strategy*, 38(2), 16–24. DOI: 10.1108/JBS-09-2016-0096

Lin, C., Wang, X., & Yang, Y. (2023). Sustainable apparel consumption: Personal norms, csr expectations, and hedonic vs. utilitarian shopping value. *Sustainability (Basel)*, 15(11), 9116. DOI: 10.3390/su15119116

Mederake, L. (2022). Without a debate on sufficiency, a circular plastics economy will remain an illusion. *Circular Economy and Sustainability*, 3(3), 1425–1439. DOI: 10.1007/s43615-022-00240-3 PMID: 36531658

Opstal, W., & Borms, L. (2022). Startups and circular economy strategies: profile differences, barriers and enablers. SSRN Electronic Journal. DOI: 10.2139/ssrn.4244706

Ostermann, C., Nascimento, L., & Zen, A. (2021). Business model innovation for circular economy in fashion industry: A startups' perspective. *Frontiers in Sustainability*, 2, 766614. Advance online publication. DOI: 10.3389/frsus.2021.766614

Payne, A., Nay, Z., & Maguire, R. (2021). Regulating a circular economy for textiles in australia.. DOI: 10.31880/10344/10245

Rachinger, M., Rauter, R., Müller, C., Vorraber, W., & Eva, S. (2019). Digitalization and its influence on business model innovation. *Journal of Manufacturing Technology Management*, 30(8), 1143–1160. DOI: 10.1108/JMTM-01-2018-0020

Rakesh, C. (2023). Towards a circular economy: challenges and opportunities for recycling and re-manufacturing of materials and components. E3s Web of Conferences, 430, 01129. DOI: 10.1051/e3sconf/202343001129

Redko, K. (2024). Circular economy and ai empowerment in social entrepreneurship: A path to sustainability. *International Science Journal of Management Economics & Finance*, 3(3), 27–35. DOI: 10.46299/j.isjmef.20240303.04

Rok, B., & Kulik, M. (2020). Circular start-up development: The case of positive impact entrepreneurship in poland. *Corporate Governance (Bradford)*, 21(2), 339–358. DOI: 10.1108/CG-01-2020-0043

Suchek, N., Fernandes, C., Kraus, S., Filser, M., & Sjögrén, H. (2021). Innovation and the circular economy: A systematic literature review. *Business Strategy and the Environment*, 30(8), 3686–3702. DOI: 10.1002/bse.2834

Tashtamirov, M. (2023). The circular economy and regional economic development. E3s Web of Conferences, 431, 07003. DOI: 10.1051/e3sconf/202343107003

Chapter 10

Driving Small and Medium Enterprise Success:
Exploring Entrepreneurial Spirit, Novelty, and Gender Perspectives

Pooja Sharma
https://orcid.org/0000-0002-6874-5901
Tecnia Institute of Advanced Studies, India

ABSTRACT

Entrepreneurial Spirit and novelty are crucial for small and medium enterprises (SMEs) aiming to thrive, especially during economic crises. Gender differences among entrepreneurs may influence these dynamics. The present study investigates potential differences in the five aspects of individual entrepreneurial orientation and their impact on performance amongst 352 SME owners, analyzing male and female entrepreneurs. Using structural equation modeling (SEM) and multi-group analysis, the study finds that while all dimensions of Entrepreneurial Spirit are significant, risk-taking stands out as notably different between genders, with male entrepreneurs generally displaying a greater propensity for risk. Additionally, Entrepreneurial Spirit significantly enhances performance through novelty, with no substantial difference observed between male and female entrepreneurs in this regard. These insights contribute to understanding gender's role in entrepreneurial behavior and the relationship between novelty and SME performance.

DOI: 10.4018/979-8-3693-9241-6.ch010

INTRODUCTION

Many economies around the world rely heavily on small and medium-sized enterprises (SMEs). This type of enterprises are especially vulnerable during external crises such as the COVID-19 epidemic. According to research, entrepreneurial approach and novelty are major determinants of business performance (Dewi Astuti et al., 2024). Yet, research suggests that male and female owners' Entrepreneurial Spirits may differ (de Almeida & Silva, 2023). Furthermore, the effect of an entrepreneurial mindset on success differs by the gender, as seen in hotels and familial businesses in the country.

Previous studies have examined how Entrepreneurial Spirit, novelty, and performance are interrelated. They have also explored gender differences in Entrepreneurial Spirit and how gender moderates the relationship between Entrepreneurial Spirit and performance. It is crucial to thoroughly examine the impact of gender on the performance of SMEs during pandemic. By comprehensively examining how gender affects the association between Entrepreneurial Spirit, potentially mediated by novelty, and business performance.

In India, SMEs have usually demonstrated resilience in previous economic crises, but they encountered extraordinary hurdles during the COVID-19 pandemic, with almost 98% affected and major sales declines reported. Women own nearly 60% of India's SMEs, which contribute 9.17% of GDP and 5% of exports. Since the epidemic began, many women entrepreneurs have evolved by adopting digital business methods, diversifying their businesses, and exploring new opportunities. Despite these efforts, female SME owners in India face obstacles such as self-doubt about their entrepreneurial ability, limited business networks, trouble getting funding, and lower levels of creativity when compared to their male peers.

Past study has looked into the links between Entrepreneurial Spirit, novelty, and performance, as well as gender differences in the entrepreneurial mindset along with how gender influences the connection between Entrepreneurial Spirit and efficiency. There is a need for a thorough investigation into gender's involvement in determining the relationship across Entrepreneurial Spirit, maybe mediated by novelty and overall success. This is critical for understanding how gender effects SME performance, particularly in light of the Covid 19.

LITERATURE REVIEW

Women entrepreneurs support their family members by offering additional income streams and improve their communities by leveraging valued assets (Markman et al., 2005). During the COVID-19 epidemic, some female entrepreneurs evolved by adjusting their business models to reflect shifting customer patterns and worldwide demands. However, female SME entrepreneurs continue to face numerous challenges, such as a dearth of education, experience, and training; insufficient innovative skills; inadequate access to capital, awareness, and technology; operational inadequacies; a lack of close support from family members; and other challenges

Entrepreneurial Spirit, which included innovativeness, proactiveness, and risk-taking, was critical in assisting SMEs to effectively traverse crises (Mohammadi, 2021). Finding creative solutions that differ from typical ways, which may require the use of new technology, processes, or products/services. Risk-taking means allocating resources despite potential, managed uncertainty. Proactiveness entails grabbing chances while displaying resilience, adaptation, and accountability (Engidaw, 2022). SME owners that are inventive, capable of satisfying consumer wants through new services, and skilled at managing business risks are better positioned to ensure their companies survive crises. This approach has been crucial in improving SME performance during previous financial and global economic downturns (Abu-Rumman et al., 2022; Soininen et al., 2012). During economic downturns, while innovativeness and proactiveness positively influenced SME performance, risk-taking had negative impacts.

Entrepreneurial Spirit is strategic at both the corporate and personal level (Ferreira, 2016) stressed the significance of an individual entrepreneurial mindset in an international setting. Employees, who generate novel thoughts, embrace possibilities, take risks, or demonstrate initiative and competence are entrepreneurial (Lee & Peterson, 2000). Thus, individual entrepreneurial mindset refers to an individual's proclivity within a business to act creatively, actively, and risk-taking (Wales et al., 2021). Personal traits and beliefs including willingness to take risks, creativeness, independence, and assertiveness are critical for developing a mindset of entrepreneurship and attaining success (Bolton & Lane, 2012).

Individual entrepreneurial mindset, which includes characteristics such as innovativeness, proactiveness, and risk-taking, matches corporate Entrepreneurial Spirit (Soininen et al., 2012; Wales et al., 2020). Creative thinking comprises developing new ideas; being proactive comprises capitalizing on opportunities to generate value; and taking risks has evolved entails making decisions in the face of uncertainty. Furthermore, Santos et al. (2020) emphasize tenacity and entrepreneurial drive as critical for success, which necessitates specialized talents (Ferreira, 2016; Lee & Peterson, 2000).

Research on the association between an entrepreneurial mindset and SME success yields conflicting results regarding gender. According to some study, female-led SMEs function well because they are regarded to be more entrepreneurial in nature (Ferreira, 2016). In contrast, research findings from Europe show that male-led SMEs outperform their female counterparts (Wales et al., 2021). Other study, however, shows that gender has no major influence on the association among entrepreneurial mindset and performance, despite varying assessments of entrepreneurial attributes among entrepreneurs (Brownhilder Ngek Neneh et al., 2017; Fellnhofer, 2018). Further investigation of the role of gender in business performance is an important subject of further study.

According to Gunjati and Adake (2020), small and medium companies (SMEs) rely heavily on craetivity for growth and resilience. This includes both incremental enhancements to existing items and originality that introduce new offerings to the market. SMEs use innovatoveness to improve product originality, fulfill evolving customer needs, and eventually boost business success (Fellnhofer, 2018). Studies have shown that developments in corporate structures can have a beneficial effect on female entrepreneurship, implying that variables such as educational background, age, and type of enterprise have a major effect on female entrepreneurs' abilities to innovate as opposed to their male colleagues (Mohammadi, 2021).

Hypothesis

The purpose of this study is to investigate gender differences in individual Entrepreneurial Spirit among SME owners, as well as how gender influences the links between individual Entrepreneurial Spirit, novelty, and performance. Hypotheses proposed are as follows:

H1: Gender disparities exist in the characters of the five aspects that define individual Entrepreneurial Spirit.

H2: Male and female entrepreneurs have different levels of beneficial impact on SME performance due to their entrepreneurial mindset.

H3: The facilitation role of novelty in the link between individual Entrepreneurial Spirit and performance differs between male and female entrepreneurs.

Figure 1. Conceptual Model

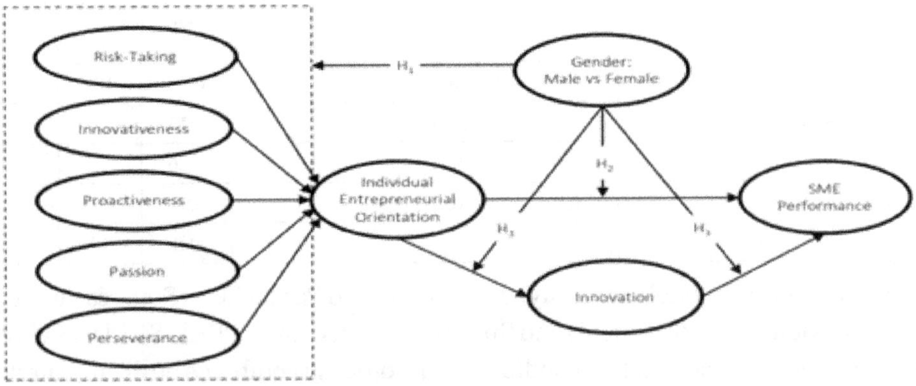

Figure 1 in the research model depicts how these engines—Entrepreneurial Spirit and novelty—have a direct impact on the entire performance of small and medium-sized businesses. It's like figuring out how each of these critical aspects collaborates to generate achievement in an environment of business competition.

The research questionnaire consisted of 34 questions covering three important categories. It featured a part on individual Entrepreneurial Spirit, which contained 17 questions organized into categories such as taking risks, creativity, being proactive, enthusiasm, and persistence, as adapted from (Franco-Santos et al., 2022). Other factors were evaluated as reflective latent variables, including the novelty variable with six questions from Chege and Wang (2020) and SME performance with four modified questions from (Wales et al., 2021). Each question used a five-point Likert scale (1 = strongly disagree, 5 = strongly agree), with specific question content available in Appendix A of the study.

Table 1. General Information

Indicator		**Male**		**Female**	
		N	%	N	%
Age	≤ 41 years	132	0.73	113	65.7
	> 41 years	48	0.27	59	34.3
Education	No university degree	75	0.42	78	45.3
	University degree	105	0.58	94	54.7

continued on following page

Table 1. Continued

Indicator		Male		Female	
		N	%	N	%
Industry sector	Primary	103	0.57	109	63.4
	Manufacturing	30	0.17	35	20.3
	Services	47	0.26	28	16.3
Number of employees	≤ 10	173	0.96	159	92.4
	> 10	7	0.0	13	7.6

To examine our model and test hypotheses, we used Partial Least Squares Structural Equation Modeling (PLS-SEM) and Smart-PLS 3.0 software. PLS-SEM was chosen precisely because it adequately handles second-order structures (Abu-Rumman et al., 2021). Following that, we did a multi-group analysis, comparing male and female entrepreneurs. Our respondents were the proprietors of small and medium-sized enterprises (SMEs).We collected data by email from all 1600 platform members, receiving 372 replies, or a 23.25% response rate. After validation and purification, 352 replies remained legitimate, with 180 males (51%) and 172 females (49%).

Table 2. Reliability and convergent validity

Variable/ Dimension	Item	Male				Female			
		Outer Loading	AVE	Cronbach's Alpha	CR	Outer Loading	AVE	Cronbach's Alpha	CR
Individual Entrepreneurial Orientation				**0.891**	**0.907**			**0.878**	**0.898**
Risk-taking	IEO1	0.779	0.639	0.731	0.853	0.591	0.517	0.728	0.839
	IEO2	0.810				0.837			
	IEO3	0.823				0.711			
Innovativeness	IEO4	0.789	0.613	0.663	0.823	0.783	0.581	0.827	0.889
	IEO5	0.789				0.769			
	IEO6	0.739				0.738			
Proactiveness	IEO7	0.829	0.644	0.711	0.829	0.816	0.63	0.779	0.859
	IEO8	0.813				0.728			
	IEO9	0.751				0.850			
Passion	IEO10	0.714	0.579	0.649	0.809	0.736	0.639	0.881	0.923
	IEO11	0.767				0.814			
	IEO12	0.821				0.836			

continued on following page

Table 2. Continued

Variable/ Dimension	Item	Male				Female			
		Outer Loading	AVE	Cronbach's Alpha	CR	Outer Loading	AVE	Cronbach's Alpha	CR
Individual Entrepreneurial Orientation				**0.891**	**0.907**			**0.878**	**0.898**
Perseverance	IEO13	0.609	0.531	0.793	0.837	0.683	0.529	0.713	0.841
	IEO14	0.669				0.751			
	IEO15	0.821				0.768			
	IEO16	0.789				0.739			
	IEO17	0.779				0.768			
Novelty	INO1	0.643	0.519	0.821	0.859	0.749	0.539	0.848	0.881
	INO2	0.689				0.649			
	INO3	0.719				0.768			
	INO4	0.773				0.850			
	INO5	0.723				0.769			
	INO6	0.749				0.718			
SME Performance	PER1	0.821	0.789	0.927	0.939	0.831	0.738	0.641	0.779
	PER2	0.937				0.869			
	PER3	0.910				0.871			
	PER4	0.910				0.849			

Table 3. Discriminant validity

Dimensions	Male					Female				
	1	2	3	4	5	1	2	3	4	5
Risk-taking	0.813					0.721				
Innovativeness		0.769					0.759			
Proactiveness			0.789					0.799		
Passion				0.771					0.789	
Perseverance					0.741					0.741

Table 4. Individual Entrepreneurial Spirit as the second-order construct

Dimension	Male		Female	
	ß	t-value	ß	t-value
Risk-taking	0.229	11.698	0.151	6.879

continued on following page

Table 4. Continued

Dimension	Male		Female	
	ß	t-value	ß	t-value
Innovativeness	0.239	13.661	0.215	9.688
Proactiveness	0.251	14.871	0.256	14.221
Passion	0.179	10.863	0.243	12.489
Perseverance	0.358	15.836	0.409	16.499

Table 5. Descriptive mean difference t-test

Indicator	Mean		T-test	
	Male	Female	t-value	t-table
Risk-taking	3.78	3.69	1.39	1.89
Innovativeness	4.13	3.89	1.08	
Proactiveness	4.41	4.29	0.59	
Passion	4.63	4.39	1.79	
Perseverance	4.32	4.09	1.02	
Noveltys	3.79	3.89	–0.67	
Performance	3.49	3.46	–0.61	

Novelty strongly impacted the pathway from individual Entrepreneurial Spirit to SME performance in both male and female entrepreneurs. The projected β value suggests that female entrepreneurs have a larger mediation effect than their male counterparts. Thus, novelty has a greater impact on moderating the association between individual Entrepreneurial Spirit and SME performance for female entrepreneurs than for male entrepreneurs.

The study highlights disparities in the trajectories of the model. To verify the statistical significance of these differences and test the hypotheses, a multi-group analysis comparing male and female groups was conducted.

CONCLUSION

Across both male and female groups, all five factors contribute considerably to the formation of an individual Entrepreneurial Spirit. Notably, perseverance emerges as the key driver of this construct for both genders, demonstrating its association with tenacity in the face of obstacles to success (Markman et al., 2005). Male entrepreneurs rank proactiveness and innovativeness as the second and third most influential aspects, respectively, whereas female entrepreneurs rank proactiveness and passion. These findings highlight the importance of all five characteristics in influencing individual entrepreneurial inclination across genders.

During current circumstances such as the outbreak, the dimension of risk-taking appears as a significant discriminator in the Entrepreneurial Spirits of male and female SME owners, with males generally displaying higher risk tolerance. Despite this difference, female entrepreneurs in the sample have a larger preference for the perseverance dimension, demonstrating their resilience despite a potentially lower risk appetite. While there are no substantial variations in mean scores between male and female entrepreneurs across all dimensions, male entrepreneurs tend to score higher on individual Entrepreneurial Spirit variables. This study mirrors earlier studies showing that male entrepreneurs tend to demonstrate higher degrees of an entrepreneurship inclination than their female counterparts.

Recent research calls into question prior findings that directly connected individual Entrepreneurial Spirit to SME performance, arguing that such attributes may not be sufficient during disruptive periods such as a pandemic. The study emphasizes that, while Entrepreneurial Spirit is important, the impact on SME performance is heavily reliant on novelty. Novelty in the technological, product, marketing, and managerial domains emerges as critical for improving SME performance, since it not solely directly effects results but also mediates the effect of entrepreneurial mindset. This emphasizes novelty's dual role: as a direct stimulant of business performance and as a facilitator of the relationship among Entrepreneurial Spirit and performance, which is especially important during economic crises.

REFERENCES

Abu-Rumman, A., Al Shraah, A., Al-Madi, F., & Alfalah, T. (2021). Entrepreneurial networks, entrepreneurial orientation, and performance of small and medium enterprises: Are dynamic capabilities the missing link? *Journal of Innovation and Entrepreneurship*, 10(1), 29. Advance online publication. DOI: 10.1186/s13731-021-00170-8

Abu-Rumman, A., Al Shraah, A., AlSha'ar, H., & Alqhaiwi, L. A. (2022). Innovation and Entrepreneurship: Attitudes and intentions of undergraduates in a developing country. *Res. Sq.*, 1, 1–21. DOI: 10.21203/rs.3.rs-1369010/v1

Bolton, D. L., & Lane, M. D. (2012). Individual entrepreneurial orientation: Development of a measurement instrument. *Education + Training*, 54(2/3), 219–233. DOI: 10.1108/00400911211210314

Brownhilder Ngek Neneh, A., van Zyl, J., & Ngek Neneh, B. (2017). Entrepreneurial orientation and its impact on firm growth amongst SMEs in South Africa. Problems and Perspectives in Management, 15, 166.

de Almeida, R. G., & Silva, H. (2023). the Entrepreneur Between Two Circuits: The Critical Contribution of Milton Santos To Entrepreneurship Studies. *Res. Hist. Econ. Thought Methodol.*, 41B, 49–66. DOI: 10.1108/S0743-41542023000041B003

Dewi Astuti, R., Ezni Balqiah, T., & Yuliati, E. (2024). Role of individual entrepreneurial orientation and innovation in SME performance: Gender perspectives. *Problems and Perspectives in Management*, 22(2), 365–378. DOI: 10.21511/ppm.22(2).2024.28

Engidaw, A. E. (2022). Small businesses and their challenges during COVID-19 pandemic in developing countries: In the case of Ethiopia. *Journal of Innovation and Entrepreneurship*, 11(1), 1–14. DOI: 10.1186/s13731-021-00191-3 PMID: 35036286

Fellnhofer, K. (2018). Narratives boost entrepreneurial attitudes: Making an entrepreneurial career attractive? *European Journal of Education*, 53(2), 218–237. DOI: 10.1111/ejed.12274 PMID: 29863170

Ferreira. (2016). CThe advertisement call and geographic distribution of Proceratophrys dibernardoi Zootaxa. *Zootaxa*, 4205, 480–482.

Franco-Santos, M., Stull, D., & Bourne, M. (2022). Performance Management and Wellbeing at the Workplace. DOI: 10.1007/978-3-030-29010-8_42

Lee, S. M., & Peterson, S. J. (2000). Culture, entrepreneurial orientation, and global competitiveness. *Journal of World Business*, 35(4), 401–416. DOI: 10.1016/S1090-9516(00)00045-6

Markman, G. D., Baron, R. A., & Balkin, D. B. (2005). Are perseverance and self-efficacy costless? Assessing entrepreneurs' regretful thinking. *Journal of Organizational Behavior*, 26(1), 1–19. DOI: 10.1002/job.305

Mohammadi, S. (2021). The relationship between individual entrepreneurial orientation (IEO) and entrepreneurial bricolage: Exploring passion and perseverance. *Asia Pacific J. Innov. Entrep.*, 15(1), 75–86. DOI: 10.1108/APJIE-01-2021-0002

Soininen, J., Puumalainen, K., Sjögrén, H., & Syrjä, P. (2012). The impact of global economic crisis on SMEs: Does entrepreneurial orientation matter? *Management Research Review*, 35(10), 927–944. DOI: 10.1108/01409171211272660

Wales, W. J., Covin, J. G., & Monsen, E. (2020). Entrepreneurial orientation: The necessity of a multilevel conceptualization. *Strategic Entrepreneurship Journal*, 14(4), 639–660. DOI: 10.1002/sej.1344

Wales, W. J., Kraus, S., Filser, M., Stöckmann, C., & Covin, J. G. (2021). The status quo of research on entrepreneurial orientation: Conversational landmarks and theoretical scaffolding. *Journal of Business Research*, 128, 564–577. DOI: 10.1016/j.jbusres.2020.10.046

Chapter 11
Business Strategies for Navigating Environmental Pressures and Global Challenges:
A Case-Based Perspective

Yang Sihan
Graduate Business School, UCSI University, Malaysia

Mustafa Rehman Khan
https://orcid.org/0000-0002-0250-9092
Graduate Business School, UCSI University, Pakistan

Haseeb Rehman Khan
Solace Sleep, Australia

Akhtiar Ali
University of Sufism and Modern Sciences, Pakistan

ABSTRACT

Our chapter explores the operational management challenges and strategic responses of Shell Company, particularly in the face of increasing environmental pressures and global competition. The first section provides an overview of Shell's background and operational management issues. The second section discusses Shell's key operational strategies, including infrastructure location analysis, factor rating, cost-return analysis, product and process layout, and both internal and external system reforms. The third section identifies current management challenges and offers detailed suggestions for improving Shell's operational management. These

DOI: 10.4018/979-8-3693-9241-6.ch011

suggestions include developing clear sustainable development goals, investing in green technologies, promoting carbon neutrality, enhancing stakeholder cooperation, improving employee environmental awareness, strengthening transparency and accountability, and establishing crisis response capabilities.

INTRODUCTION

Operation management and logistics are becoming increasingly important in modern society, which have a significant impact on the production efficiency, cost control, product quality, customer satisfaction and other aspects of the enterprise (Christopher, 2016: Masood, Khan & Khan, 2024). With the development of economic globalization and the increasing demand for resources closely related to human survival, the import and export orders of large multinational enterprises, especially energy enterprises, have surged, leading to the expansion of production categories and the diversification of investment types in energy enterprises. A large amount of greenhouse gases produced by industrial products and their derivative services have been emitted into the atmosphere, affecting the carbon and oxygen balance in the atmosphere and exacerbating the global environmental crisis. Adhering to achieving sustainable development goals for all mankind, the international community has called for innovation to reduce environmental degradation, as emphasized in SDG 9. In recent years, countries have actively formulated carbon neutrality goals based on the emission reduction model independently contributed by countries under the Paris Agreement (Ali, Khan & Ghouri, 2023).

As one of the leading companies in the global energy industry, Shell has taken on important responsibilities in sustainable development and environmental protection. Royal Dutch Shell plc is a globally renowned integrated energy company headquartered in the Netherlands and the United Kingdom. Shell is one of the world's largest oil companies, with operations in multiple countries and regions around the world. Shell was founded in 1907 through the merger of Royal Dutch and Shell Transport and Trading. The company mainly engages in exploration, production, processing, sales, and distribution businesses in the fields of oil, natural gas, chemical, and new energy, covering the entire energy value chain.

The company is committed to promoting the development and application of clean energy technology, while striving to reduce carbon emissions, improve energy efficiency, and develop renewable energy projects (Uralovich et al., 2023). Shell has strong technological capabilities and a global operational network, providing important support for global energy supply and demand. The company has business presence in various countries and regions, and works closely with governments, partners, customers, and stakeholders to jointly address the challenges and opportunities faced by the energy industry. Shell as an energy company with a long history and global influence, is committed to continuous innovation and development to meet global energy needs, advocate for sustainable development concepts, and promote the development of the energy industry towards a cleaner, more efficient, and sustainable direction (Sluyterman, 2010).

Although, Shell as an established industry giant, ranks among the top in the world in terms of wealth, it still has some operational management issues. Based on public platform data, there are mainly the following operational management data points. According to the financial reports of 2019 and 2020, Shell's revenue and profit have both decreased. Data shows that Shell achieved a revenue of $352.5 billion in 2019, but by 2020 this number had dropped to $244.9 billion, a 30% year-on-year decrease. There has also been a significant decline in profits, from $15.7 billion in 2019 to only $4.4 billion in 2020, a year-on-year decrease of 72%. This indicates the challenges Shell faces in market competition and the instability of the industry environment (Chrascina, Vaněk & Pekarčíková, 2024).

Shell's global market share has also declined, with data showing a decrease from 4.5% in 2019 to 3.9% in 2020. This includes factors such as fierce market competition and rapid development of emerging energy technologies. Recently, with the increasingly serious global climate change problem, Shell has been under increasing pressure in environmental protection. For example, in Canada, Shell's oil sands project faced resistance from environmental organizations and civil society groups, resulting in slow progress of the project. In addition, as an industry giant, Shell's carbon emissions have also become a focus of attention for environmental organizations and regulatory agencies (Topić et al., 2023).

Further, Shell also has some problems in terms of production efficiency, such as insufficient maintenance capabilities for facilities and equipment, as well as insufficient ability to respond to emergency problems. For example, a refinery located in Texas, USA, experienced a power outage and a burst water pipe during extremely cold weather in 2021, resulting in the factory shutting down for a month. This also reflects Shell's shortcomings in equipment and production management (Abdellatif et al., 2024)

Among these operational management issues, this study focuses on exploring the increasing environmental pressure in Shell's operational management. As a global energy giant, reducing carbon emissions has been one of the main challenges faced by Shell in recent years. Not only does it bear external supervision pressure, but it must also face economic efficiency issues. They must develop and implement effective carbon emission management strategies, which include not only controlling greenhouse gas emissions, optimizing energy efficiency, but also promoting low-carbon technologies and transitioning to clean energy. They must open up sources and reduce costs, and comprehensively manage carbon emissions from the source (Ali et al., 2023).

In order to reduce environmental impact and reduce the pressure of environmental protection, Shell needs to optimize its production and operation processes to improve energy utilization efficiency (Li, Li & Ge, 2023). This not only involves monitoring and managing energy consumption, adopting energy-saving measures, improving process flow, but also requires increasing investment proportion and using advanced energy management technologies to achieve continuous improvement of energy efficiency. Shell needs to address environmental risks, comply with environmental regulations, and establish corresponding management systems. This includes assessing and managing environmental risks, developing emergency plans, ensuring safe operations, and collaborating with relevant stakeholders to jointly reduce environmental risks and improve response capabilities (Mumfrd, 2003). During the construction of Shell's facilities and energy extraction process, Shell faces the problem of ecosystem damage and biodiversity loss. They need to take measures to protect the natural environment, including reducing land development, protecting critical ecosystems and habitats, and promoting sustainable land management (Chavan & Chondekar, 2023). With the increasing demand of society for sustainable development of enterprises, Shell needs to strengthen its social responsibility management. This includes close cooperation with stakeholders, promoting community participation, carrying out social projects and public welfare activities to enhance the social recognition and sustainable development performance of enterprises. At the same time, it is necessary to enhance the positive influence of the brand and maintain a positive image under the pressure of environmental protection. Faced with the trend of global energy transformation, Shell needs to actively invest in and develop clean energy technologies to promote an increase in the proportion of clean energy in its energy product portfolio. This may involve challenges in investment risks, market competition, and the adoption of new technologies.

The above are some specific operational management issues that Shell faces when environmental protection pressure increases. To address these issues, Shell needs to develop corresponding strategies and policies, and collaborate with stakeholders to jointly promote the achievement of sustainable development and environmental protection goals. The company's awareness of such problems and describes its efforts to contain potential damage to the degree permitted by existing technological and economic constraints (Sluyterman, 2010).

Operational Management Strategies for Dealing With Environmental Stress Issues

According to Shell's official website and various platforms, Shell has adopted multiple operational management strategies in response to the increasing pressure of environmental protection, and some achievements and benefits achieved. These measures not only help reduce the environmental impact of the company, but also lay a solid foundation for its sustainable and future development. The following are some prominent key strategies:

First, Shell has set carbon neutrality targets and plans to reduce its carbon emissions by 50% by 2030. By optimizing production processes and promoting clean energy technologies, Shell has successfully reduced carbon emissions per barrel of oil production, from 25 kilograms in 2010 to 15 kilograms in 2023 (López et al., 2023). Second, Shell has implemented an energy management system to improve energy utilization efficiency. According to internal data, Shell's annual energy consumption efficiency has increased by an average of 3% over the past five years. By introducing energy-saving equipment and technological innovation, Shell has successfully reduced energy consumption during operation, lowered production costs, and achieved considerable economic benefits. At the same time, in order to address environmental challenges, Shell may increase its investment in environmental technology innovation. They may strengthen their research and development capabilities, develop more environmentally friendly production processes and products, promote the application of clean energy technologies, improve resource utilization efficiency, and reduce carbon emissions (Ali et al., 2024).

Further, Shell emphasize sustainable development strategy, incorporating environmental protection and social responsibility into its core values. They may set specific environmental goals and indicators, incorporate environmental performance into the performance evaluation system, to ensure that environmental protection work becomes an important component of enterprise development (Quayson et al., 2023). At the same time, Shell actively participates in community environmental protection projects and public welfare activities, investing funds for environmental protection and social development. According to the latest publicly available data, Shell invested as much as $100 million in social responsibility in 2023. In collaboration with local governments and NGOs, Shell has carried out multiple ecological conservation projects to help restore damaged ecosystems and promote the increase of local biodiversity. In addition, Shell also conducts green supply chain management, requiring suppliers and partners to comply with environmental standards and prioritize environmentally friendly products and services. They may establish an environmental audit mechanism to monitor the environmental performance of the supply chain and ensure that all links meet environmental requirements. Shell also strengthens environmental governance and information disclosure, improves transparency, and responds to the concerns of stakeholders regarding environmental issues. They will regularly release environmental reports, publicly disclose environmental data and information, share environmental achievements and challenges with stakeholders, and enhance trust and cooperation. Shell has increased investment in renewable energy and clean technology. As of the end of 2023, the company has built 10 solar and wind energy projects worldwide, with a total installed capacity of 5GW. Through cooperation with new energy companies, Shell has successfully launched multiple clean energy products and achieved good sales results in the market. (Minghui, 2024). Shell also consciously strengthens employee environmental awareness education and training, and increases employee awareness and participation in environmental protection work. Encourage employees to actively participate in environmental protection actions and jointly promote environmental awareness through training courses, internal publicity, and other means (Emeka-Okoli et al., 2024).

Analysis of the Impact of Environmental Pressures on Infrastructure Location

Firstly, when considering the location of Shell's operational infrastructure, environmental pressure becomes an important factor. In recent years, facing increasing environmental pressure, Shell has made many operational strategic changes in infrastructure selection, mainly including the following aspects: First, different countries and regions have established a series of environmental regulations to restrict the construction and operation of industrial facilities. Shell must comply with these regulations and reasonably select locations that meet environmental standards to reduce environmental risks and potential fines.

In recent years, carbon emissions have become a focus of global environmental protection, and Shell must consider the impact of infrastructure construction and site selection on carbon emissions. When selecting the location of these facilities, more consideration should be given to factors such as energy, energy efficiency, and carbon capture technology to reduce carbon footprint and address climate change risks. Water resources have always been the top priority of environmental protection. Shell's infrastructure usually requires a large amount of water resources, so when selecting a site, environmental issues such as water sustainability, supply stability, and water pollution prevention must be considered.

Shell's infrastructure sites should be selected as much as possible to avoid negative impacts on sensitive ecosystems and important biodiversity areas. At the same time, Shell must fully evaluate the potential impact of site selection on the local ecosystem and take corresponding protection measures strategically. When facing environmental pressure, the part of social concern and public opposition is an important part, which largely determines Shell's brand acceptance. Shell needs to consider the opinions and interests of local communities to ensure that the selection of infrastructure locations is widely accepted and supported by society. Therefore, as mentioned earlier, Shell needs to comprehensively consider factors such as environmental regulations, carbon emissions and climate change, water resource management, ecosystem protection, and social acceptance to ensure that site selection complies with sustainable development principles, reduces environmental risks, and enhances corporate image. This reflects Shell's specific requirements for infrastructure location in considering environmental pressure operation strategies.

Factor Rating Analysis and Calculation of Shell's Site Selection

When evaluating the factors of Shell's site selection, weight allocation can be applied to each factor and rating scores for each site selection factor can be given. Based on the table 1, it can be seen that Location 2 has a higher total score compared to Location 1, indicating that Location 2 may be a better site selection based on these factors. This score can help Shell make a more informed site selection decision (Joel & Oguanobi, 2024). The following is a sample table format to display the rating analysis and calculation of Shell's site selection factors:

Table 1. Location Analysis

Factors	Weight	Location 1 Rating (1-10)	Location 2 Rating (1-10)	Location 1 Weighted Score	Location 2 Weighted Score
Environmental Regulations	0.15	8	7	1.2	1.05
Carbon Emissions and Climate Change	0.1	7	6	0.7	0.6
Water Resource Management	0.1	6	8	0.6	0.8
Ecosystem Protection	0.2	9	8	1.8	1.6
Social Acceptance	0.15	8	7	1.2	1.05
Resource Distribution	0.1	7	9	0.7	0.9
Transportation Accessibility	0.1	8	7	0.8	0.7
Market Demand	0.1	7	8	0.7	0.8
Total Score				7.7	7.5

Break-Even Analysis

With the increasing pressure of environmental protection, Shell has adopted a series of operational management strategies to reduce its environmental impact and improve sustainability. The implementation of these strategies not only helps promote environmental protection and sustainable development, but may also have a certain impact on the company's profitability. Table 2 provide break-even analyses of Shell's operational management strategy changes in response to increasing environmental pressures. By implementing energy-saving and emission reduction measures, Shell can reduce its operating costs and achieve higher economic benefits. Shell actively carries out social responsibility projects to enhance its social recognition and bring better brand image and business opportunities to the company. The transition to clean energy will help Shell meet consumer demand for clean energy, expand its product portfolio, and enhance market competitiveness. Shell needs to invest a large amount of funds to cope with environmental protection pressures, such as introducing new technologies and constructing new projects, which will lead to short-term losses for the company. The reduction in carbon emissions by Shell may have a certain impact on its production efficiency, increase its operating costs, and thus reduce its profits.

Overall, the operational management strategies adopted by Shell in response to environmental protection pressures may have a certain impact on its profitability. However, in the long run, these strategies will help improve Shell's sustainability and social recognition, bringing greater opportunities and potential for its future development. The financial reports and annual reports of Shell on public platforms can confirm this viewpoint (Christophers, 2022).

Table 2. Break-even analysis

Time	Environmental investment (million $)	Production cost change (%)	Sales growth (%)	Profit change (%)	Break-even analysis
2022	50	+5	+3	-2	Profit decline, but still maintaining profitability
2023	55	+7	+2	-4	Profit decline, loss
2024	60	+8	+1	-5	Profit decline, loss

Product and Process Layout Under Environmental Pressure

The overall design of facility layout should include the entire strategies and objectives that are set by the organization. In this context, there is a need for optimum space for being allocated for the technology and process. In addition, the overall policies and direction for future empowerment are two crucial factors for facility layout of an organization (Bodrožić & Adler, 2022). Shell has adjusted its product and process layout to adapt to more environmentally friendly and sustainable development trends under environmental pressure. The following are some product and process layout adjustments taken by Shell under environmental pressure:

First, faced with increasingly strict environmental regulations and emission reduction requirements, Shell has increased investment and development in clean energy products (such as natural gas, biofuels, electric vehicle charging services, etc.) to reduce the use of fossil fuels and carbon emissions. Second, Shell has increased investment in renewable energy projects (such as wind and solar energy) to increase the proportion of renewable energy in its energy portfolio and reduce dependence on traditional fossil fuels. Third, Shell reduces energy consumption and waste emissions, improves resource utilization efficiency, and reduces the impact of production processes on the environment by optimizing production processes. Fourth, Shell has introduced more green technologies (such as carbon capture and storage technology, energy storage technology, etc.) to reduce carbon emissions and improve environmental performance. Fifth, Shell strengthens the application of the concept of circular economy in product and process design, promotes waste resource utilization, and reduces environmental burden (Midttun et al., 2022).

Inbound and Outbound System Reform

In the face of environmental pressure reform, Shell has reformed its inbound and outbound systems by optimizing raw material selection, strengthening supply chain management, introducing energy-saving and emission reduction technologies, adjusting product structure, and promoting green supply chain cooperation, in order to achieve more environmentally friendly and sustainable development (Christopher, 2016; Gul, Raziq & Khan, 2024). Shell has optimized the selection of raw materials, such as choosing more environmentally friendly raw materials, renewable energy raw materials that replace traditional fuels, etc. Shell has implemented advanced energy technologies to save energy and reduce emissions, such as improving energy efficiency, carbon capture and storage technology, thereby reducing energy consumption and emissions during the product delivery process. Moreover, Shell collaborate with suppliers and partners to promote green supply chain cooperation, ensuring the environmental quality and sustainability of products shipped out and utilized digital technologies to increase environmental information disclosure for outbound products, which provides more environmental performance indicators and lifecycle information about products, and enhance consumer awareness and choice of environmentally friendly products (Khan et al., 2024a; Sotoodeh, 2024).

Operational Management of Storage Systems

Shell has taken a series of effective measures in the operation and management of storage systems. Inaccurate inventory counts have the potential to cause stock outs, in which products are unavailable when consumers need them, or overstock situations, which can occasionally result in the wasteful accumulation of capital and storage space. Putting resources into cutting-edge stock global positioning framework empowers exact stock counts while upgrading perceivability across distribution centers and satisfaction focuses further develops responsiveness to changes in demand and inventory levels. In this regard, Shell has taken some measures in the operation and management of storage systems to cope with environmental pressure. The following is an analysis based on relevant facts:

Shell widely uses various environmental protection technologies in its industrial projects, such as carbon capture and storage technology, wastewater treatment technology, etc. For example, at a chemical production site in Fort Saskatchewan, Alberta, Canada, Shell has adopted an advanced wastewater treatment system to treat the generated wastewater into a reusable water source. In addition, Shell has launched a renewable energy plan for its fuel stations, promoting solar charging stations to reduce reliance on traditional energy. Shell regularly inspects and maintains its storage system to ensure the normal operation of the facility. For example, in a fuel storage facility in Arizona, Shell conducts a comprehensive safety inspection once a week and develops emergency plans to address potential environmental risks. Shell has also developed a comprehensive emergency plan to address environmental risks. For example, in the 2010 Gulf of Mexico oil spill, Shell actively assisted in responding to the incident and assumed corresponding responsibilities and compensation.

Further, Shell has established a comprehensive environmental monitoring system, regularly monitoring the surrounding environment of the storage system, and disclosing information to relevant departments and the public. For example, in an oil storage facility in the UK, Shell records and publishes the quantity and type of all pollutants generated by the facility on a daily basis. Shell promotes sustainable management practices, including measures for effective resource utilization, waste reduction, energy conservation etc., to reduce negative impacts on the environment. For example, in a natural gas project in Algeria, Shell successfully reduced carbon dioxide emissions by over 90% by improving production processes and technology (Armour, Enriques & Wetzer, 2023). Therefore, Shell has huge investment in green energy applications, energy-saving technology improvements, waste management and recycling, environmental risk assessment and control, technology monitoring and data analysis, participation in environmental protection initiatives, public communication and information transparency, and continuously optimize the operation and management of storage systems to achieve sustainable development (Christopher, 2016).

Transportation and Operational Management

The supply chain is becoming more complicated due to transportation-related problems. Costs are further increased by human involvement brought on by bad weather, heavy traffic on the road, or logistical changes that impact delivery times (Kim, Kim & Park, 2022). Shell has taken a series of measures in operational management to address environmental pressure and transportation issues to achieve sustainable development (Park et al., 2024). Shell actively promotes the application of clean energy in transportation, such as increasing the proportion of using liquefied natural gas (LNG) or biofuels to replace traditional petroleum fuels. Shell has already used LNG powered trucks and ships in some areas to reduce carbon emissions during transportation (Simpa et al., 2024). Shell is committed to optimizing logistics management to reduce energy consumption and carbon emissions during transportation. For example, optimizing the route planning of ships and trucks, improving cargo loading rates, and reducing empty container transportation can effectively reduce energy consumption and adverse environmental impacts during transportation. Shell continuously updates transportation equipment and introduces more energy-efficient, environmentally friendly, and energy-efficient vehicles, ships, and other transportation equipment. For example, Shell uses an electric truck called "Ecorunner" in the Netherlands, which features a lightweight design and an efficient energy recovery system to reduce energy consumption and carbon emissions. Shell widely uses environmental protection technologies in the transportation process, such as waste gas and wastewater treatment technologies. These technologies can effectively reduce the impact of exhaust emissions and ship emissions on marine ecosystems.

Contemporary Challenges

Shell has established a relatively complete operational management strategy and system, and has responded to the increasing pressure of environmental protection to some extent. However, it is also evident that the company's breakeven situation is not optimistic, especially the loss situation that has occurred in the past two years. Firstly, we can analyze the shortcomings of Shell's existing operational management strategies in response to the surge in environmental pressure, in order to improve and supplement them. Shell has encountered the several issues in its operational management strategy in the face of environmental pressure. Despite Shell's efforts in renewable energy investment, there is still a dependence on traditional petroleum fuels. This may lead to slow progress in achieving environmental goals and risks in energy transformation for the company. Although Shell promotes the development of green logistics, it may face some difficulties in the actual promotion process. For example, the high cost of electric trucks and inadequate charging infrastructure may limit their large-scale application, thereby affecting the effectiveness of green logistics. Further, Shell needs to establish close cooperation with suppliers to improve supply chain transparency. However, in the face of environmental pressure, the complexity and dispersion of the supply chain may lead to difficulties in information collection and regulation, which may make ensuring the effective implementation of supply chain environmental standards more complex, making it difficult to ensure the transparency of the supply chain (Christopher, 2016)

Although Shell has strengthened its assessment of environmental risks in recent years, the assessment results will inevitably have some inaccuracies objectively due to the influence of technical factors and the complex and ever-changing environment. In addition, identifying and assessing environmental risks requires complex data collection and analysis, which may result in insufficient information acquisition or limited methods for assessing environmental risks, all of which may lead to potential environmental issues not being detected and resolved in a timely manner (Hua & Ye, 2023). Due to fact that Shell's active participation in environmental initiatives in recent years, they have invested a lot of resources and energy, and their capital flow and profits have been affected to varying degrees, facing various challenges in different dimensions. For example, comprehensive consideration and management are required in areas such as collaboration with other stakeholders, project feasibility assessment, and promotional effectiveness, which may increase the management complexity and operational costs of the company (Sotoodeh, 2024). Additionally, Shell is committed to technological innovation and adopted a series of operational management strategies in the face of environmental pressure, there are still some problems and challenges that require further efforts and improvement by the company (Sluyterman, 2010). For example, technological feasibility, market acceptance, and capital investment may all have an impact on the success of technological innovation, which may limit the company's progress in environmental protection technology.

Recommendations

When confronted with escalating environmental pressures, Shell can implement targeted strategies to effectively manage and mitigate these challenges. Based on literature, this chapter provides several recommendations for Shell to navigate future environmental pressures. Firstly, Shell should establish clear and sustainable development goals integrated into its strategic planning and business decisions. These goals should be specific, measurable, and traceable, encompassing areas such as carbon emission reduction, energy conservation, water resource management, waste treatment, and recycling (Shan et al., 2024). By setting robust environmental targets, Shell can ensure steady progress towards sustainable development objectives. Secondly, Shell needs to significantly increase its investment in green technology and innovation. This includes expanding investments in renewable energy projects, energy storage technologies, carbon capture and storage, and electric vehicle infrastructure (Bhardwaj et al., 2024; Mumfrd, 2003). Collaborating with research institutions and universities under an open innovation framework will accelerate the development and application of these technologies, thereby reducing environmental impact and fostering industry-wide transformation.

Furthermore, Shell should actively promote carbon neutrality and adopt circular economy principles. Developing a comprehensive carbon neutrality plan and maximizing resource utilization through circular economy practices will minimize waste emissions and enhance environmental sustainability (Mumfrd, 2003; Khan et al., 2024a; Khan et al., 2024b). To strengthen its environmental stewardship, Shell should forge closer partnerships with stakeholders including governments, NGOs, customers, suppliers, and communities. Collaborative efforts will facilitate knowledge sharing, innovative solution development, and collective action on environmental challenges, thereby enhancing Shell's social responsibility and corporate image. Employee environmental awareness should also be prioritized through comprehensive training programs and incentives. By fostering a culture of environmental responsibility and ensuring alignment with corporate environmental policies, Shell can mobilize its workforce to actively participate in environmental protection efforts (Sluyterman, 2010).

Moreover, Shell should enhance transparency and accountability by regularly disclosing environmental performance data to the public. Strengthening environmental data transparency and accountability mechanisms will build trust, enhance corporate reputation, and demonstrate commitment to sustainable practices (Sluyterman, 2010). Additionally, Shell must develop robust crisis management capabilities to swiftly respond to potential environmental incidents and public opinion crises. This involves creating and regularly updating emergency response and crisis communication plans, conducting drills, and training employees to mitigate environmental risks effectively (Paiement, 2023). Lastly, Shell should remain attentive to evolving social expectations and investor demands related to environmental, social, and governance (ESG) standards. By aligning with these standards, Shell can bolster investor confidence, secure financing, and reinforce its commitment to sustainable development (Chou et al., 2023). Therefore, by adopting these strategies such as focused on technological innovation, stakeholder collaboration, transparency, crisis preparedness, employee engagement, and adherence to ESG standards, Shell can effectively navigate environmental pressures, achieve sustainable development goals, and strengthen its competitive position in the global market (Luo, 2024). These measures will not only enhance Shell's resilience to environmental challenges but also contribute positively to the environment and society at large.

CONCLUSION

This article mainly focuses on the operational management issues of Shell Company and is divided into three parts. The first part introduces the background and operational management issues of Shell Company; The second part introduces Shell's important operational management strategies in dealing with environmental pressure, including infrastructure location analysis, factor rating analysis and calculation, cost return analysis, product and process layout, internal and external system reform, storage system and transportation issues. The third part analyzes the current management problems of Shell and proposes suggestions for improving operational management strategies, reducing environmental pressure, and addressing future global challenges and competition. Finally, on basis of prior literature, this chapter provide suggestion that allow organization to effectively adapt to global challenges and competition, achieve sustainable development and long-term growth, maintain competitiveness, and seize more business opportunities. These measures will help enhance the company's comprehensive strength and market competitiveness, laying a solid foundation for future development.

REFERENCES

Abdellatif, H. H., Bhowmik, P. K., Arcilesi, D., & Sabharwall, P. (2024). Accident event progression, gaps, and key performance indicators for steam generator tube rupture events in water-cooled SMRs: A review. *Progress in Nuclear Energy*, 168, 105021. DOI: 10.1016/j.pnucene.2023.105021

Ali, A., Khan, M. R., & Ghouri, A. M. (2023). Carbon neutrality concept and progress. In *Recent Developments in Green Finance, Green Growth and Carbon Neutrality* (pp. 85-108). Elsevier. DOI: 10.1016/B978-0-443-15936-7.00003-7

Ali, A. M., Bagdanavicius, A., Barbour, E. R., Pottie, D. L., Garvey, S., Rouse, J., & Baniamerian, Z. (2024). Improving the performance of a shell and tube latent heat thermal energy storage through modifications of heat transfer pipes: A comprehensive investigation on various configurations. *Journal of Energy Storage*, 96, 112678. DOI: 10.1016/j.est.2024.112678

Armour, J., Enriques, L., & Wetzer, T. (2023). Green Pills: Making Corporate Climate Commitments Credible. *Arizona Law Review*, 65, 285.

Bhardwaj, C., Kishwar, S. D., Khurana, B., Vatsa, K., & Manderna, M. K. (2024). Contextualizing the application of the Milieudefensie v. Royal Dutch Shell decision in Indian climate change litigation: Possibilities and challenges. *Sustainability and Climate Change*, 17(1), 77–90. DOI: 10.1089/scc.2023.0137

Bodrožić, Z., & Adler, S., P. (. (2022). Alternative futures for the digital transformation: A macro-level Schumpeterian perspective. *Organization Science*, 33(1), 105–125. DOI: 10.1287/orsc.2021.1558

Chavan, A. S., & Chondekar, R. P. (2023). Overexploitation of Cowrie Shells: Future threats to the Marine Ecosystem. *International Journal of Zoology Studies*, 8(3), 8–10.

Chou, C. C., Hwang, N. C. R., Li, C. W., Wang, T., & Wang, Y. Y. (2023). Implementing a multichain framework using hyperledger for supply chain transparency in a dynamic partnership: A feasibility study. *Computers & Industrial Engineering*, 175, 108906. DOI: 10.1016/j.cie.2022.108906

Chrascina, M., Vaněk, M., & Pekarčíková, K. (2024). Intrinsic Value of Stocks of "Big Oil" Companies. *GeoScience Engineering*, 70(1), 67–77. DOI: 10.35180/gse-2024-0107

Christophers, B. (2022). Fossilised capital: Price and profit in the energy transition. *New Political Economy*, 27(1), 146–159. DOI: 10.1080/13563467.2021.1926957

Emeka-Okoli, S., Otonnah, C. A., Nwankwo, T. C., & Nwankwo, E. E. (2024). Internal and external communication in oil & gas for enhancing CSR implementation: A review. *World Journal of Advanced Research and Reviews*, 21(3), 109–118. DOI: 10.30574/wjarr.2024.21.3.0665

Gul, I., Raziq, A., & Khan, M. R. (2024). Towards Sustainable Supply Chains with Blockchain. In *Achieving Secure and Transparent Supply Chains With Blockchain Technology* (pp. 18–37). IGI Global. DOI: 10.4018/979-8-3693-0482-2.ch002

Hua, W., & Ye, J. (2023). Seismic risk assessment of reticulated shell structures considering multiple uncertainties. *Thin-walled Structures*, 185, 110618. DOI: 10.1016/j.tws.2023.110618

Joel, O. T., & Oguanobi, V. U. (2024). Geological survey techniques and carbon storage: optimizing renewable energy site selection and carbon sequestration. *Open Access Research Journal of Science and Technology, 11*(1), 039-051.

Khan, M. I., Haq, M. A. U., Khan, M. R., Ghouri, A. M., & Farooqui, R. (2024b). Industry 4.0 or Pharma 4.0?: Assessing Suitability, Benefits, Challenges, and Opportunities for Healthcare Supply Chains. *Convergence of Industry 4.0 and Supply Chain Sustainability*, (pp. 319-341). IGI Global.

Khan, M. R., Masood, F., Gul, I., & Khan, M. R. (2024a). Blockchain Technology in Supply Chain Management: Opportunities and Challenges. *Convergence of Industry 4.0 and Supply Chain Sustainability*, (pp. 275-295). IGI Global.

Kim, E., Kim, Y., & Park, J. (2022). The necessity of introducing autonomous trucks in logistics 4.0. *Sustainability (Basel)*, 14(7), 3978. DOI: 10.3390/su14073978

Li, C., Li, Q., & Ge, R. (2023). Comparison of performance enhancement in a shell and tube based latent heat thermal energy storage device containing different structured fins. *Renewable Energy*, 206, 994–1006. DOI: 10.1016/j.renene.2023.02.087

Luo, Q. (2024, May). Financial Characteristics and Risk Strategy Analysis of Oil Giant Companies under The Background of Global Economic Recession. In *9th International Conference on Financial Innovation and Economic Development (ICFIED 2024)* (pp. 442-449). Atlantis Press. DOI: 10.2991/978-94-6463-408-2_50

Masood, F., Khan, N. R., & Khan, M. R. (2024). Blockchain-based supply chain management: A challenge yet an opportunity to gauge. In *Achieving Secure and Transparent Supply Chains With Blockchain Technology* (pp. 267–285). IGI Global. DOI: 10.4018/979-8-3693-0482-2.ch015

Midttun, A., Khanieva, M., Lia, M., & Wenner, E. (2022). The greening of the European petroleum industry. *Energy Policy*, 167, 112964. DOI: 10.1016/j.enpol.2022.112964

Mumford, E. (2003). Quality and Environmental Issues in Shell International. In *Redesigning Human Systems* (pp. 210–232). IGI Global. DOI: 10.4018/978-1-59140-118-6.ch012

Paiement, P. (2023). Reimagining the energy corporation: Milieudefensie and others v Royal Dutch Shell Plc. In *Netherlands Yearbook of International Law 2021: A Greener International Law—International Legal Responses to the Global Environmental Crisis* (pp. 281–299). TMC Asser Press. DOI: 10.1007/978-94-6265-587-4_11

Quayson, M., Bai, C., Mahmoudi, A., Hu, W., Chen, W., & Omoruyi, O. (2023). Designing a decision support tool for integrating ESG into the natural resource extraction industry for sustainable development using the ordinal priority approach. *Resources Policy*, 85, 103988. DOI: 10.1016/j.resourpol.2023.103988

Shan, C., Sun, J., Jia, X., Wu, R., & Lu, X. (2024). The mechanical behavior of cylindrical shell with composite corrugations under uniform and concentrated pressure. *Ocean Engineering*, 298, 117148. DOI: 10.1016/j.oceaneng.2024.117148

Simpa, P., Solomon, N. O., Adenekan, O. A., & Obasi, S. C. (2024). Sustainability and environmental impact in the LNG value chain: Current trends and future opportunities.

Sluyterman, K. (2010). Royal Dutch Shell: Company strategies for dealing with environmental issues. *Business History Review*, 84(2), 203–226. DOI: 10.1017/S0007680500002580

Sotoodeh, K. (2024). *Storage Tanks Selection, Design, Testing, Inspection, and Maintenance: Emission Management and Environmental Protection: Emission Management and Environmental Protection*. Elsevier.

Topić Popović, N., Lorencin, V., Strunjak-Perović, I., & Čož-Rakovac, R. (2023). Shell waste management and utilization: Mitigating organic pollution and enhancing sustainability. *Applied Sciences (Basel, Switzerland)*, 13(1), 623. DOI: 10.3390/app13010623

Uralovich, K. S., Toshmamatovich, T. U., Kubayevich, K. F., Sapaev, I. B., Saylaubaevna, S. S., Beknazarova, Z. F., & Khurramov, A. (2023). A primary factor in sustainable development and environmental sustainability is environmental education. *Caspian Journal of Environmental Sciences*, 21(4), 965–975.

Chapter 12
Application of fsQCA Method in Operations Management Area:
Systematic Literature Review

Molk Oukili Garti
Sidi Mohamed Ben Abdellah University, Fez, Morocco

Jabir Arif
https://orcid.org/0000-0002-5285-7976
Sidi Mohamed Ben Abdellah University, Fez, Morocco

Fouad Jawab
https://orcid.org/0000-0002-0508-7278
Sidi Mohamed Ben Abdellah University, Fez, Morocco

ABSTRACT

Fuzzy-set Qualitative Comparative Analysis (fsQCA) is a configurational method used in fields like business, marketing, and supply chain management. Despite its utility, its role in supply chain operations has been underexplored. This research aims to investigate fsQCA's application in these areas. The study includes a comprehensive literature review and a systematic and bibliometric analysis of 75 publications from 19 leading journals (2015-2024). The findings offer new insights into fsQCA's potential in various research areas and suggest future research directions. The study also identifies significant research challenges and highlights key perspectives for advancing this critical field.

Supply chain management has always held a significant place in scientific inquiry (Arif et al., 2023), especially in the aftermath of various crises following the COVID-19 crisis, resulting in significant disruptions in most supply chains and

DOI: 10.4018/979-8-3693-9241-6.ch012

temporary production halts (Farooq et al., 2021). In a report published by the McKinsey Global Institute (MGI), it is stated that COVID-19 has affected all business operations in every sector, such as airlines experiencing a 60% drop in revenues in 2020, with air travel and tourism not expected to return to 2019 levels before 2024 (McKinsey, 2022). In another statement by (McKinsey, 2022), "The COVID-19 pandemic created short-term disruptions and provoked long-term changes in how the world lives and does business."

Therefore, and following the critical situations experienced by industries, there is a transition towards a new generation of industry bringing with it new strategies, known as Industry 5.0, which is primarily based on the three fundamental concepts of "sustainability, resilience, and human-centricity" (Garrido et al., 2024). These new concepts have started to gain more importance both among industrialists and theorists because it has become essential to ensure rigorous management of all supply chains while applying various methods and technologies that contribute to the robustness of different operations management systems describing logistics management. In this context, competition has increased in this research domain, aiming to outline sustainable and robust management of supply chains (El Jaouhari et al., 2022), based on both macro and micro aspects of the term.

This is very apparent in the latest reports published by various companies. For instance, in a recent report by (Deloitte, 2021), it is stated that the company is committed to integrating sustainability into all operations related to organizational policies and practices, as well as empowering its employees to make climate-friendly decisions and influence others to do the same. As a future strategy, it commits to achieving net-zero greenhouse gas emissions by 2030 for all its operations. In another example cited by (Deloitte, 2021), it describes that when the COVID-19 pandemic disrupted business activities three weeks before client annual filing deadlines, Deloitte practitioners using Deloitte Omnia were able to continue executing their audits both virtually and digitally, for the first time, while maintaining high-quality audit standards without compromising deadlines. This also aligns with actions contributing to the sustainability and resilience of logistics management operations.

On the other hand, in the research domain, various studies have been provided by theorists, while advocating for the implementation of methods examining the various disruptions experienced by these supply chains in a market that is never constant and constantly evolving (Woodside, 2018). However, management studies relying on linear statistical analysis with finite contextual factors may no longer guarantee prediction accuracy because the environment in which various supply chains currently operate is quite complex and leads to contradictory paths (Woodside, 2018). For this reason, recent research has begun to focus on applying analyses based on complex adaptive systems while applying complexity theory to scientific investigation, such as the Fuzzy Qualitative Comparative Analysis (fsQCA) method (Kumar et al., 2022), which offer new perspectives on the management of complex systems and the enhancement of operations resilience (Kumar et al., 2022).

However, despite the use of this method in several studies related to logistics management and supply chains, it was rarely exploited and explored in operations related to supply chain management, which created a significant gap in the research field and provided us with a new field of research and study to explore. However, the objective of our study is to shed light on a new research avenue while leveraging the fsQCA method in supply chain management through the application of a systematic literature review (Kumar et al., 2022). A bibliographic and content analysis of previously published research on this subject was part of our two-tiered SLR. Drawing on previous studies conducted in other research domains, we were able to conduct a systematic review of existing literature in a fair, rigorous, and reproducible manner (El Jaouhari et al., 2023). We used bibliometric analysis to identify the literature on the relationship between fsQCA and supply chain management, in order to examine everything reported on this subject so far. A bibliographic analysis of previously published research on this topic was part of our two-tiered systematic literature review (SLR). We used bibliometric analysis to identify the literature on the relationship between the fsQCA method and supply chain management, in order to examine everything reported on this subject so far. Our bibliometric analyses contributed to providing a solid foundation for identifying key components following the application of the fsQCA method in supply chain management, as well as offering new and holistic perspectives on future studies.

Furthermore, the objective of this study is to present a literature review that can be utilized in future research perspectives to determine the extent to which the application of this method can contribute to achieving sustainable supply chain management. This is well established by addressing the following three research questions, which will be central to this systematic and bibliometric study:

RQ1: How has previous literature represented the fsQCA method?

RQ2: Who are the most impactful contributors (e.g., source title, articles, authors, country)?

RQ3: What are the recommendations for advancing research in sustainable supply chain management by applying the fsQCA method?

Moreover, to effectively structure the response to the research questions, the chapter is organized into five main sections. After introducing the research topic, it begins with a literature review to explore how previous studies have described the fsQCA method and the domains in which it has been applied. Next, the chapter presents the methodology through the application of the systematic literature review (SLR), followed by bibliometric results. Subsequently, it moves to the discussion, where it presents recommendations and new perspectives to follow, before concluding.

LITERATURE REVIEW

Exploration of the fsQCA Method in the Existing Literature

The fsQCA Method has gained importance in various research domains such as commerce and management because it is based on Boolean algebra and configurational relationship (Di Paola, 2021), leading to a negative result and a positive result (Huarng & Yu, 2017), distinguishing it from other analytical methods as it combines matrix algebra with statistical methods that describe the asymmetrical thinking of complexity theory (Llopis-Albert et al., 2021). It thus combines the reasoning and methodological robustness of qualitative case-oriented methods to create propositions that determine membership in certain configurations (Kumar et al., 2022). The utility of fsQCA is evident in creating results that indicate notions of complexity theory focused on three types (Prentice, 2019): firstly, fsQCA presents variables that are causally and asymmetrically associated within a configuration (Gligor et al., 2022; Lee, 2022); secondly, fsQCA identifies multiple alternatives for the same outcome while revealing equifinality (Kopplin & Rosch, 2021); and thirdly, it indicates complex or conjunctural causality through the reasoning that the impact of predecessors on an event is determined by how the predecessors are integrated (Romero-Castro et al., 2021).

In this regard, it is evident to confirm that the fsQCA method is the most optimal method, which, through its application, guarantees the sustainability and resilience of supply chains (Farooq et al., 2021). In recent research conducted in SCOPUS, on the application of the fsQCA method in the field of logistics chain management, the results showed that most research contributions have utilized the fsQCA method in management, aiming to extract the various possible configurations of managing complex systems and reflect an aspect of robust management in different sectors of activity. This demonstrates the massive influence this new method has had in various research domains (Table 1).

Table 1. Prominent review studies on fsQCA and operations of management

S. No.	Author (s)	Article Title	Supply chain domain/Activity	Theme	Year of publication	Research contribution to litterature
1	Innocent Senyo Kwasi Acquah	"Unravelling the asymmetric effects of procurement practices on firm performance: A complexity theory approach to complementing fsQCA with NCA"	Purchasing and procurement management	Utilization of the fsQCA method in procurement practices	2024	Application of both fsQCA and NCA methods to enhance firm performance in procurement practices.
2	Md. Mominur Rahman et al	"Unveiling the link between environmental management accounting, energy efficiency, and accountability in state-owned enterprises: An integrated analysis using PLS-SEM and fsQCA"	Environmental management and energy efficiency.	Using fsQCA to identify practices that enhance transparency, accountability, and reporting.	2024	Combining the two methods fsQCA and PLS-SEM to enhance the company's performance in terms of transparency, accountability, and reporting, with the aim of integrating these practices into overall sustainability strategies.
3	Stefano Armenia et al	"Identifying policy options and responses to water management issues through System Dynamics and fsQCA"	Sustainable water resources management	The application of fsQCA in water management	2023	The article as a whole elaborates on water management issues and examines, through the application of fsQCA, the conditions that contribute to sustainable water management.

continued on following page

Table 1. Continued

S. No.	Author (s)	Article Title	Supply chain domain/Activity	Theme	Year of publication	Research contribution to litterature
4	Silvia Cantele et al	"Supply chain agility and sustainability performance: A configurational approach to sustainable supply chain management practices"	Sustainable supply chain management.	Application of fsQCA in describing a configuration of sustainable supply chain management practices.	2023	The article elaborates on a study that relies on the theoretical framework of Resource Orchestration Theory (ROT) while applying the fsQCA method to explore the various potential combinations of sustainability practices within firms and the supply chain.
5	Xiu-Ming Loh al	"Understanding consumers' resistance to pay with cryptocurrency in the sharing economy: A hybrid SEM-fsQCA approach"	Transaction management and sharing economy	Utilization of the combined fsQCA-SEM method to understand consumer behavior	2023	Utilizing the combination of the two methods fsQCA-SEM in analyzing consumer behavior towards their resistance to paying with cryptocurrencies in the sharing economy, the study provided new insights into the fields of cryptocurrency, consumer behavior, the sharing economy, and innovation resistance.
6	Satish Kumar et al	"Fuzzy-set qualitative comparative analysis (fsQCA) in business and management research: A contemporary overview"	Business and management research	Application of fsQCA in business and management	2022	The article revolves around the application of fsQCA to examine business and management phenomena.
7	Jan Dul	"Problematic applications of Necessary Condition Analysis (NCA) in tourism and hospitality research"	Tourism and hospitality management	The utility of applying condition analysis in the field of tourism and hospitality	2022	Comparison between NCA and fsQCA to enhance research in the field of tourism and hospitality

continued on following page

Table 1. Continued

S. No.	Author (s)	Article Title	Supply chain domain/Activity	Theme	Year of publication	Research contribution to litterature
8	Sara J. Marks et al	"Pathways to sustainability: A fuzzy-set qualitative comparative analysis of rural water supply programs"	Management of rural water supply infrastructure.	Application of fsQCA in water supply programs	2018	The article examines different approaches to achieve sustainable water supply distribution using the fsQCA method.

Review Methodology

The present research employs the Systematic Literature Review (SLR) as a methodology recommended by several experienced researchers who have adopted SLR to determine the status of a specific field and reach clear conclusions. According to (Liliani et al.,2020), In his article where he applied this approach effectively, he considered SLR as a process that enables robust evaluation to optimize researchers' work and maintain the independence of the research process while enhancing discovery and exploration that contribute to the development of understanding. In another sense of this context, the SLR is an approach that relies on a review strategy to guide and account for the decisions made in the literature review, making them transparent and reproducible compared to traditional approaches (Lim et al., 2022; El Jaouhari et al., 2023). The current study is inspired by other review articles that have already highlighted the usefulness of employing the SLR approach in their research through various forms (e.g., narrative, thematic, systematic, bibliographic) (Kumar et al., 2022; El Jaouhari et al., 2024). In our case, the SLR is applied in both systematic and bibliographic forms, based on the exploitation of data from SCOPUS, which provides a broad field of scientific research and facilitates information collection (Kumar et al., 2022). Furthermore, this database was selected because it provides an interface allowing simultaneous searching across different sources using a common set of search fields to obtain comprehensive results. It covers studies from ACM, EBSCOhost, Elsevier, Emerald, IEEE, INFORMS, MDPI, ProQuest, SAGE, Springer, Taylor and Francis, and Wiley, among many other publishers (Franco et al., 2018). The use of other tools (such as Excel in analysis) has also helped in tracing the results. Figure 1 depicts the methodology followed for the present review.

Assembling

The initial stage of our methodology, “Assembling,” is applied in two phases (Kumar et al., 2022). The first phase, “Identification,” involves preparing the search steps and points, while highlighting the research objective aimed at addressing the three questions RQ1, RQ2, and RQ3, and establishing the general theme of the research (El Jaouhari et al., 2023). The second stage, “Acquisition,” first involves selecting the most appropriate database for our research. Scopus was chosen because it covers numerous journals meeting stringent quality criteria and indexed.

The second step in the “Acquisition” section was to accurately define the established research period. In our case, the search encompassed all years of research up to the date of conducting the search (02/05/24) to ensure that all relevant articles were included in the scope of the review. The final step was to carefully select appropriate search keywords capable of capturing all research, using Boolean operations in the following form: ("fsQCA" OR "fuzzy set qualitative comparative analysis" OR "qualitative comparative analysis" OR "QCA") AND ("Supply Chain Management" OR "Supply Chain" OR "Management" OR "Logistics" OR "Management of Logistics"). The final result yielded 2698 documents selected within the scope of the research.

Arranging

The second stage, "Arrangement," also consists of two steps based on organization and purification (Kumar et al., 2022). The 2698 articles already selected must be sorted and filtered to extract the most relevant articles for the objectives of the current review. The organization activity involves determining the necessary criteria for extraction. For this reason, we chose "supply chain management" to highlight the objective of our research, which focuses on the applicability of fsQCA in the field of supply chain management. The chosen source type is "Journal," and the document type is "Article," providing a more rigorous and targeted inclusion criterion, resulting in 1993 articles while excluding other documents such as books, editorials, notes, and conference proceedings. Subsequently, the final filter includes the language "English" to simplify the reliability of the established SLR. The result encompassed 1993 articles.

The second part, "Purification," is utilized as a more focused second filter, which involves searching for keywords "fsQCA and supply chain," "fsQCA and management," "fsQCA and supply chain management," "fsQCA and sustainable supply chain management," or "fsQCA and sustainable supply chain" within any element of the selected articles, including the journal title, article title, abstract, or even keywords used in the articles. The result yielded 76 articles, while excluding 1917 articles. A second check was conducted to eliminate duplicates. The final selection comprised 75 articles.

Assessing

The third stage of this research involves evaluating the research outcomes based on the analysis of bibliographic data and the presentation of results (Kumar et al., 2022). The current review examines 75 articles selected through a bibliometric procedure using an analytical framework centered on addressing the three well-defined questions at the outset, RQ1, RQ2, and RQ3. The initial analysis regarding the response to question RQ1 is based on a bibliometric review concerning the input elements of this research. This includes presenting the profile of participants in empirical research, the geographical location (region) of research expertise in the studied field, as well as the underdeveloped regions in this field. Additionally, it considers the types of journals with more article publications in this field.

To address RQ2, a classification analysis was conducted on the entire selected articles, based on the PARETO analysis, to assess the extent to which the fsQCA method is applied in supply chain management, which process has been primarily based on in the study of supply chain management, and at what level the fsQCA method is involved in achieving sustainable supply chain management. This aimed to identify the different clusters that form the basis of a new framework to be presented subsequently. For RQ3, the results provided by this analysis can be considered as new orientations and directions for further future research and case applications (Kumar et al., 2022) in the context of implementing sustainable supply chain management.

Figure 1. Review methodology: "SLR Method"

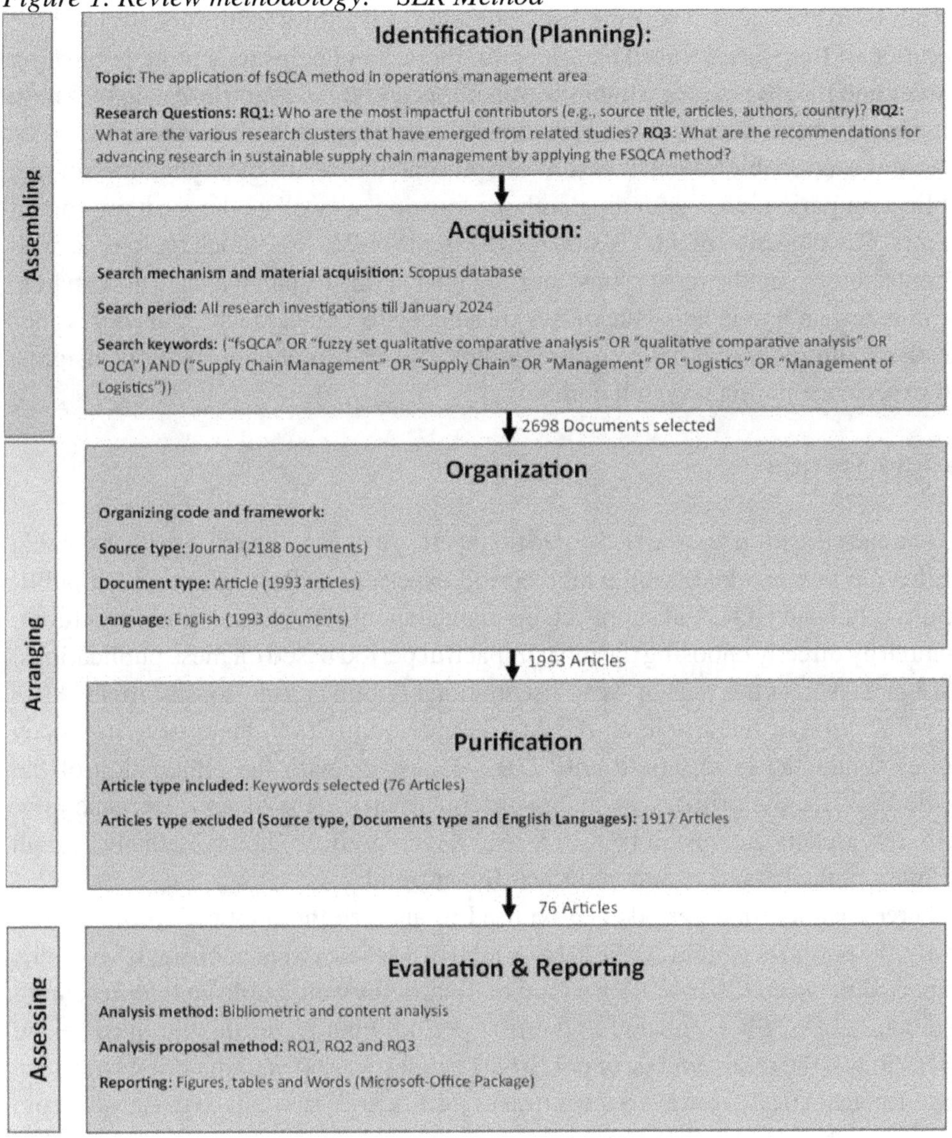

Bibliometric Findings

Bibliometric analysis represents a comprehensive evaluation of the state within a specific research domain through the examination of existing publications encompassing authors, publishing locations, sources, and countries. This analytical approach facilitates an assessment of the developmental trajectory and potential of a designated topic. Moreover, the use of bibliometric analysis is considered fundamental and has been exploited in various research fields as it allows for the discovery of the evolution of literature focused on a specific theme, and helps to explore publishing sources and the diverse contributions of authors and their countries/regions. These components were valuable for addressing all pertinent research questions.

In this section, bibliometric results are presented in terms of publication source, publication period, corresponding author's location, as well as the most prominent authors. The objective of this session is to examine and assess which regions, as well as contributors, are the most robust and engaged in this research area. This can help in future research to identify the most experienced researchers who can address our questions, future surveys, or even case studies, and draw more information, insights, and experience in this research domain.

Article Trends

The classification was carried out in this section by year with the aim of observing publication trends, identifying which period experienced the highest rate of publications related to fsQCA in supply chain management. This can also assist in future research by directly choosing the most impactful period based on these publications.

Figure 2 shows the year-by-year distribution of publications in our sample. After the publication of the article on the fsQCA method in 2009, there were not many studies conducted in this field until 2015. However, with the publication of the article in 2015, the primary focus in subsequent articles is clearer. Because after 2015, researchers' interest in fsQCA research increased, as shown by the bar graph in Figure 6, the bars have a more or less linear trend.

Three distinct time periods can be used to analyze the publication of articles. Firstly, the period between (2009-2015), a total of 3 articles were published. Secondly, the period between (2016-2019), a total of 13 articles were published, representing an increase of 62.5% compared to the first period. Finally, during the third period (2016-2024), the total number of published articles was 60, and the rate of increase was once again 62%. However, the ultimate significance that can be discerned from Figure 2 is the significant increase in the number of published articles on fsQCA and supply chain management in recent years.

Figure 2. Publications on the fsQCA method and supply chain management

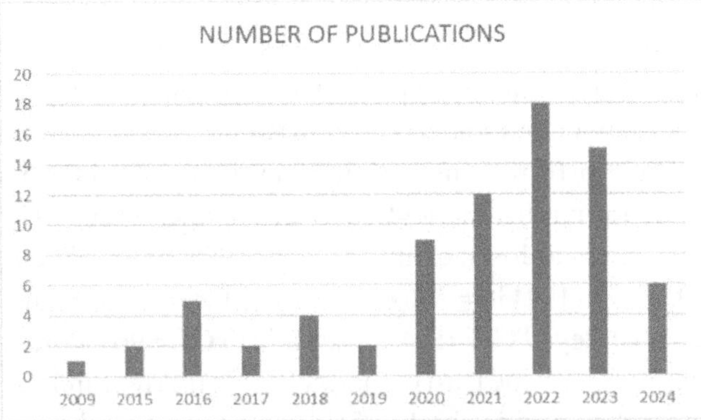

Publishing Source

In this section, articles are checked for trends by journal, revealing that publication in this field is scattered. Articles are found in a wide variety of journals and are not limited to specific ones; they explore various management, economics, business, engineering, and commerce journals. This journal trend can also help provide insight into which journals might be suitable for publishing our future research articles.

The number of articles published between 2009 and 2024 in various journals is presented in Figure 3. The six journals that publish the most articles in the field of fsQCA and supply chain management are respectively: "Journal of Business Research" (15), "Computers & Industrial Engineering" (10), "Technological Forecasting and Social Change" (9), "International Journal of Information Management" (6), "International Journal of Production Economics" (5), and "Journal of Cleaner Production" (5). Additionally, there are other journals that can be consulted due to their contributions of between 2 and 3 articles in the studied research domain such as "Tourism Management Perspectives" (3), "European Management Journal" (2), "Long Range Planning" (2).

Local Citations

In this section, the aim of the analysis is to pinpoint the region with the highest number of citations drawn present in other articles, reflecting that the most impacted and influential articles globally are located in the region with the highest total global citation count (Satish Kumar et al., 2022). Thus, the calculation is performed on the 75 articles from our research to extract the Total Global Citation (TGC) per article, then extract the region to which each publication belongs. This allowed us to determine which region is most interested in conducting research and publishing articles (with the highest number of citations) in the field of fsQCA and supply chain management. The results were presented in ascending order in Figure 4 and also illustrated through the graphical representation of these localization results on a map Figure 5. The top 10 regions contributing the most, in terms of the highest number of citations for publishing and conducting research in fsQCA and supply chain management, are as follows: China (TGC=1099), India (TGC=295), Switzerland (TGC=287), Finland (TGC=266), Norway (TGC=179), France (TGC=146), Spain (TGC=129), Turkey (TGC=124), Australia (TGC=96), Portugal (TGC=93). Conversely, the regions with the least exploitability in this research, and which could improve their research capacities in this field, are those with the lowest number of publications with a low TGC, such as United Arab Emirates (TGC=2), Belgium (TGC=2), and Monaco (TGC=4).

Figure 3. Most productive journals for research using fsQCA method and supply chain management

Figure 4. Most impactful countries for research using fsQCA and supply chain management

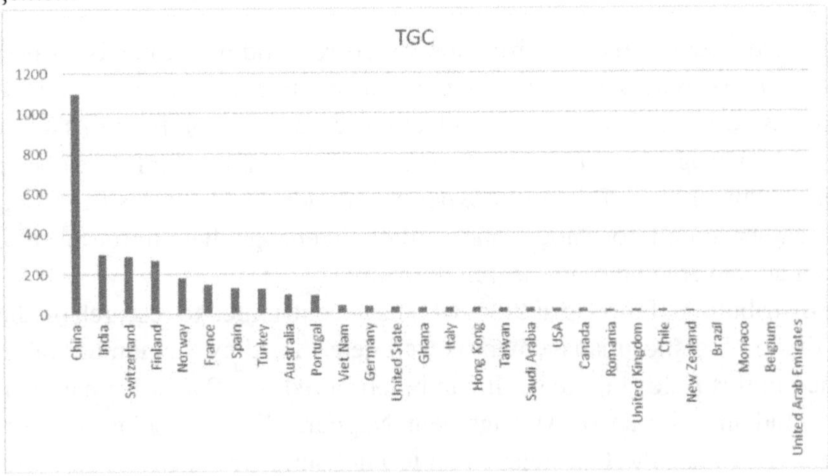

Figure 5. Most impactful countries for research using fsQCA and supply chain management

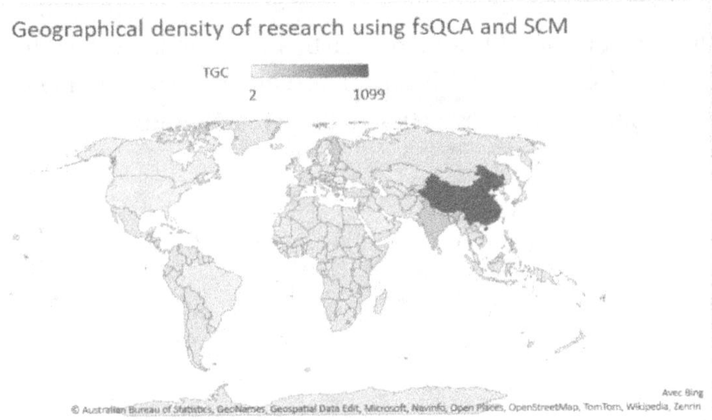

Publications by Corresponding and First Authors Throughout the World

The reason behind the classification by corresponding author is to precisely target which researchers are the most experienced in this research domain and are most interested in publishing and conducting research in the field of fsQCA and supply chain management. This can serve as a reference guide for future researchers by giving them an idea of the most experienced individuals in this field, enabling them to gather more information, and potentially engage them in future studies or surveys that converge on this research domain.

The distribution of the top authors who have contributed to research on the fsQCA method in logistics management is well determined by the number of articles published in this field (Figure 6). It can be observed that Satish Kumar, affiliated with the Indian Institute of Management Nagpur, Nagpur, India, is one of the leading researchers who has contributed to publishing 257 articles with a total of 9783 citations in other research articles. Similarly, Mikalef, Patrick, affiliated with the Norges Teknisk-Naturvitenskapelige Universitet, Trondheim, Norway, has also contributed to publishing 139 articles in this regard, with 5883 citations in other articles. Additionally, Pappas, Ilias O., affiliated with the Universitetet i Agder, Kristiansand, Norway, has contributed 126 published articles, of which 5231 have been cited in other publications (Table 2). These results highlight the significance of research in the field of fsQCA and logistics management, which has emerged particularly in specific regions, with certain researchers being highly recommended to follow and consult for their expertise in this area of study.

Table 2. TOP Most impactful and recent articles according to total publications and citations for research using fsQCA and supply chain management

S. No.	Article	Author(s)	TC	TP	Institution	Journal	Year of Publication
1	Fuzzy-set qualitative comparative analysis (fsQCA) in business and management research: A contemporary overview,	Satish Kumar	9783	257	Indian Institute of Management Nagpur, Nagpur, India	Technological Forecasting and Social Change	2022
2	Understanding gender differences in logistics innovation: A complexity theory perspective	Gligor, David Marius	3460	96	Florida Gulf Coast University, Fort Myers, United States	International Journal of Production Economics	2022
3	International trade resilience and the Covid-19 pandemic	Mena, Carlos	2805	51	Portland State University, Portland, United States	Journal of Business Research	2022
4	A contingency perspective on manufacturing configurations for the circular economy: Insights from successful start-ups	Cagliano, Raffaella	2443	60	Politecnico di Milano, Milan, Italy	International Journal of Production Economics	2022
5	Water and waste management strategies as drivers of the financial performance of food companies	López-Cabarcos, María Ángeles	964	53	Universidad de Santiago de Compostela, Santiago de Compostela, Spain	Technological Forecasting and Social Change	2024

continued on following page

Table 2. Continued

S. No.	Article	Author(s)	TC	TP	Institution	Journal	Year of Publication
6	A framework for determining the impacts of a multiple relationship network on green innovation,	Bai, Yu	865	23	Hefei University of Technology, Hefei, China	Sustainable Production and Consumption	2021
7	Impact of digital transformation on the automotive industry	Rubio, Francisco J.	825	31	Universitat Politècnica de València, Valencia, Spain	Technological Forecasting and Social Change	2021
8	Supply chain collaboration in the petroleum sector of an emerging economy: Comparing results from symmetrical and asymmetrical approaches	Acquah, Innocent Senyo Kwasi	683	26	University of Cape Coast Ghana, Cape Coast, Ghana	Technological Forecasting and Social Change	2021
9	The impact of supply chain social responsibility on sustainable performance	Yu, Yubing	660	33	Zhejiang Wanli University, Ningbo, China	Journal of Cleaner Production	2023
10	Transformation strategies connected to carbon capture and utilization: A cross-sectoral configurational study,	Naims, Henriette	589	10	Research Institute for Sustainability – Helmholtz Centre Potsdam (RIFS), Potsdam, Germany	Journal of Cleaner Production	2022

continued on following page

Table 2. Continued

S. No.	Article	Author(s)	TC	TP	Institution	Journal	Year of Publication
11	Bricolage as an effective tool for the survival of owner-managed SMEs during crises	Baier-Fuentes, Hugo	566	14	Universidad Catolica de la Santisima Concepcion, Concepcion, Chile	Journal of Business Research	2023
12	The empirical study of digital marketing strategy and performance in small and medium-sized enterprises (SMEs),	Wu, Chih Wen	525	17	National Chung Hsing University, Taichung, Taiwan	Technological Forecasting and Social Change	2024
13	Green supply chain management practices and third-party logistics providers' performances: A fuzzy-set approach,	Stekelorum, Rébecca	467	29	ICN Business School, Nancy, France	International Journal of Production Economics	2021
14	Exploring the relationship between quality ambidexterity and sustainable production	Gomes, Paulo J.	339	15	Florida International University College of Business, Miami, United States	International Journal of Production Economics	2020
15	Time-to-unicorn and digital entrepreneurial ecosystems	Venâncio, Ana	211	16	Universidade de Lisboa, Lisbon, Portugal	Technological Forecasting and Social Change	2023

continued on following page

Table 2. Continued

S. No.	Article	Author(s)	TC	TP	Institution	Journal	Year of Publication
16	Relation between managerial cognition and industrial performance: An assessment with strategic cognitive maps using fuzzy-set qualitative comparative analysis	Kumbure, Mahinda Mailagaha	184	9	LUT University, Lappeenranta, Finland	Journal of Business Research	2020
17	Supplier selection, control mechanisms, and firm innovation: Configuration analysis based on fsQCA	Lou, Zhukun	131	6	Shanghai University, Shanghai, China	Journal of Business Research	2022
18	Can digital transformation improve market and ESG performance? Evidence from Chinese SMEs	Wang, Shaofeng	119	12	Zhejiang Wanli University, Ningbo, China	Journal of Cleaner Production	2023
19	Home country and firm-specific advantage influences on HRM replication versus adaptation in EMNEs operating in advanced economies: A qualitative comparative analysis,	Patel, Parth	110	27	Australian Institute of Business, Adelaide, Australia	Journal of Business Research	2024

continued on following page

Table 2. Continued

S. No.	Article	Author(s)	TC	TP	Institution	Journal	Year of Publication
20	Path selection of lean digitalization for traditional manufacturing industry under heterogeneous competitive position	Jing, Shuwei	98	17	Shanxi University of Finance and EcoNomics, Taiyuan, China	Computers & Industrial Engineering	2021

TC: Total citation ; TP: Total publication

Figure 6. Most productive authors for research using fsQCA and supply chain management

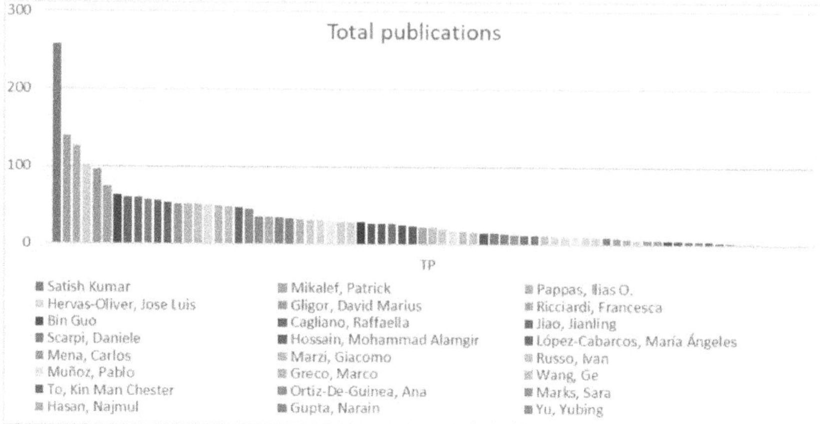

DISCUSSION

The current study represents a literature review that explores the fsQCA method in the field of logistics operations management. To achieve this, the study aimed to address the following three research questions:

Firstly, to answer the question: RQ1, "How has previous literature represented the fsQCA method?" A literature review was initially conducted to provide a theoretical definition of the fsQCA method based on existing literature. This involved examining various significant review studies on fsQCA and management operations, with the aim of building an understanding of the most extensively studied domain using this method. Additionally, the review sought to identify the gap that will be the focus of our next study, confirming that previous research has not sufficiently highlighted the role of fsQCA in supply chain management operations. Nevertheless, the objective of our research is to explore the role of the fsQCA method in operations and supply chain management.

Secondly, to address the question RQ2, "Who are the most impactful contributors (e.g., source title, articles, authors, country)?" The study employs an SLR methodology to analyze the research domain involving the application of the fsQCA method in supply chain management operations. It presented an overview of 75 articles targeting the studied domain, supplemented by bibliometric analysis. To the best of our knowledge, this review is the first of its kind to report on the evolution of research related to the application of fsQCA in supply chain operations management.

According to the analysis results, the number of published articles has steadily increased over the past few years, with the majority originating from China and India. These findings suggest that an increasing number of researchers from these regions are inclined to use the fsQCA method in studies related to logistics operations management, aiming to determine solutions related to the sustainable management of logistics operations.

And finally, for the last research question RQ3, "What are the recommendations for advancing research in sustainable supply chain management by applying the fsQCA method?" The present research serves both as an initial investigation and an invitation for future studies to build upon the detected findings. This includes conducting content analysis in future studies, extracting the most emerging clusters from this study to develop a conceptual framework that could be adopted in practice by industries across various sectors. Furthermore, it is crucial to measure the impact of these methods in resolving challenges related to various global crises, as we are all faced with the challenge of achieving sustainability in our production systems.

CONCLUSION

The present chapter constitutes a literature review that only describes the first part of a work, which also includes a conceptual framework that will be addressed based on this initial research in a subsequent chapter. However, to complete the literature review on the fsQCA method and its application in the field of logistics operations management, this study addressed three research questions. It utilized the SLR method and a bibliometric analysis of data collected from 75 publications. This review, to the best of our knowledge, is the first of its kind to report on the evolution of research related to the application of fsQCA in supply chain operations management.

According to the results of the analysis conducted, the number of published articles has steadily increased over the past few years, with the majority originating from China and India. These findings suggest that an increasing number of researchers in these regions are inclined to use the fsQCA method in studies related to logistics operations management, aiming to determine solutions related to sustainable management of logistics operations elements.

This review serves as an invitation to encourage aspiring researchers to adopt the fsQCA method to study various case scenarios related to sustainable management within supply chains. The aim is to shed more light on all aspects of supply chain management operations, thereby advancing sustainability practices in logistic management.

On the other hand, as the second part of this work, based on the research findings of this chapter, a potential study will be conducted. The first part of this study will involve a content analysis targeting the different clusters identified based on the findings from the previously applied SLR. In the second part, a conceptual framework will be developed with the aim of assessing its impact on resolving constraints related to various global crises, specifically those associated with sustainability within production systems and supply chain management. Additionally, this research will highlight the practical and theoretical implications it has contributed to.

REFERENCES

Acquah, I. S. K., Naude, M. J., & Sendra-García, J. (2021). Supply chain collaboration in the petroleum sector of an emerging economy: Comparing results from symmetrical and asymmetrical approaches. *Technological Forecasting and Social Change*, 166, 120568. DOI: 10.1016/j.techfore.2020.120568

Alsuwaidi, M., Eid, R., & Agag, G. (2022). Tackling the complexity of guests' food waste reduction behaviour in the hospitality industry. *Tourism Management Perspectives*, 42, 100963. DOI: 10.1016/j.tmp.2022.100963

Ambroise, L., Prim-Allaz, I., & Teyssier, C. (2018). Financial performance of servitized manufacturing firms: A configuration issue between servitization strategies and customer-oriented organizational design. *Industrial Marketing Management*, 71, 54–68. DOI: 10.1016/j.indmarman.2017.11.007

Armenia, S., Barnabè, F., Franco, E., Iandolo, F., Pompei, A., & Tsaples, G. (2023). Identifying policy options and responses to water management issues through System Dynamics and fsQCA. *Technological Forecasting and Social Change*, 194, 122737. DOI: 10.1016/j.techfore.2023.122737

Bai, Y., Wang, J., & Jiao, J. (2021). A framework for determining the impacts of a multiple relationship network on green innovation. *Sustainable Production and Consumption*, 27, 471–484. DOI: 10.1016/j.spc.2021.01.014

Baier-Fuentes, H., Andrade-Valbuena, N. A., Huertas Gonzalez-Serrano, M., & Gaviria-Marin, M. (2023). Bricolage as an effective tool for the survival of owner-managed SMEs during crises. *Journal of Business Research*, 157, 113608. DOI: 10.1016/j.jbusres.2022.113608

Bergmann, A., Stechemesser, K., & Guenther, E. (2016). Natural resource dependence theory: Impacts of extreme weather events on organizations. *Journal of Business Research*, 69(4), 1361–1366. DOI: 10.1016/j.jbusres.2015.10.108

Cantele, S., Russo, I., Kirchoff, J. F., & Valcozzena, S. (2023). Supply chain agility and sustainability performance: A configurational approach to sustainable supply chain management practices. *Journal of Cleaner Production*, 414, 137493. DOI: 10.1016/j.jclepro.2023.137493

Castka, P. (2018). Modelling firms' interventions in ISO 9001 certification: A configurational approach. *International Journal of Production Economics*, 201, 163–172. DOI: 10.1016/j.ijpe.2018.05.005

Deloitte. (2021). A year of connection, action and impact, 2021 GLOBAL IMPACT REPORT. 98. gx-about-deloitte-global-report-full-version-2021.pdf

Di Paola, N. (2021). Pathways to academic entrepreneurship: The determinants of female scholars' entrepreneurial intentions. *The Journal of Technology Transfer*, 46(5), 1417–1441. DOI: 10.1007/s10961-020-09824-3

Dul, J. (2022). Problematic applications of Necessary Condition Analysis (NCA) in tourism and hospitality research. *Tourism Management*, 93, 104616. DOI: 10.1016/j.tourman.2022.104616

Efendigil, T., Önüt, S., & Kahraman, C. (2009). A decision support system for demand forecasting with artificial neural networks and neuro-fuzzy models: A comparative analysis. *Expert Systems with Applications*, 36(3), 6697–6707. DOI: 10.1016/j.eswa.2008.08.058

El Jaouhari, A., Arif, J., Samadhiya, A., & Kumar, A. (2023). Net zero supply chain performance and industry 4.0 technologies: Past review and present introspective analysis for future research directions. *Heliyon*, 9(11), e21525. DOI: 10.1016/j.heliyon.2023.e21525 PMID: 38027864

El Jaouhari, A., Arif, J., Samadhiya, A., Kumar, A., & Garza-Reyes, J. A. (2023). An environmental-based perspective framework: Integrating IoT technology into a sustainable automotive supply chain. *Benchmarking*. Advance online publication. DOI: 10.1108/BIJ-05-2023-0322

El Jaouhari, A., Arif, J., Samadhiya, A., Kumar, A., Jain, V., & Agrawal, R. (2023). Are metaverse applications in quality 4.0 enablers of manufacturing resiliency? An exploratory review under disruption impressions and future research. *The TQM Journal*.

El Jaouhari, A., Arif, J., Samadhiya, A., Naz, F., & Kumar, A. (2024). Exploring the application of ICTs in decarbonizing the agriculture supply chain: A literature review and research agenda. *Heliyon*, 10(8), e29564. DOI: 10.1016/j.heliyon.2024.e29564 PMID: 38665579

El Jaouhari, A., Azari, M., Arif, J., El Farouk, I. I., Jawab, F., & Moufad, I. "IoT for the future of sustainable supply chain management in Industry 4.0: A Systematic Literature Review," *2022 14th International Colloquium of Logistics and Supply Chain Management (LOGISTIQUA)*, EL JADIDA, Morocco, 2022, pp. 1-6, DOI: 10.1109/LOGISTIQUA55056.2022.9938123

El Jaouhari, A., Fellaki, S., Amejwal, M., & Arif, J. (2023). Industry 4.0 Implementation in Lean Supply Chain Management: A Systematic Literature Review. *Statistics, Optimization & Information Computing*, 11(1), 178–185. DOI: 10.19139/soic-2310-5070-1539

Farooq, M. U., Hussain, A., Masood, T., & Habib, M. S. (2021). Supply Chain Operations Management in Pandemics: A State-of-the-Art Review Inspired by COVID-19. *Sustainability (Basel)*, 13(5), 2504. DOI: 10.3390/su13052504

Franco, E. F., Hirama, K., & Carvalho, M. M. (2018). Applying system dynamics approach in software and information system projects: A mapping study. *Information and Software Technology*, 93, 58–73. DOI: 10.1016/j.infsof.2017.08.013

Garrido, S., Muniz, J.Jr, & Batista Ribeiro, V. (2024). Operations Management, Sustainability & Industry 5.0: A critical analysis and future agenda. *Cleaner Logistics and Supply Chain*, 10, 100141. DOI: 10.1016/j.clscn.2024.100141

Gligor, D. M., Golgeci, I., Rego, C., Russo, I., Bozkurt, S., Pohlen, T., Hiatt, B., & Garg, V. (2022). Examining the use of fsQCA in B2B marketing research: Benefits, current state and agenda for future research. *Journal of Business and Industrial Marketing*, 37(7), 1542–1552. DOI: 10.1108/JBIM-09-2020-0436

Gomes, P. J., Silva, G. M., & Sarkis, J. (2020). Exploring the relationship between quality ambidexterity and sustainable production. *International Journal of Production Economics*, 224, 107560. DOI: 10.1016/j.ijpe.2019.107560

Greco, M., Campagna, M., Cricelli, L., Grimaldi, M., & Strazzullo, S. (2022). COVID-19-related innovations: A study on underlying motivations and inter-organizational collaboration. *Industrial Marketing Management*, 106, 58–70. DOI: 10.1016/j.indmarman.2022.07.014

Gupta, N., Sardana, D., & Lee, R. (2024). Dynamic capabilities that matter for business failure versus survival. *Industrial Marketing Management*, 116, 40–50. DOI: 10.1016/j.indmarman.2023.11.004

Habib, F., Bastl, M., Karatzas, A., & Mena, C. (2020). Treat me well and I may leave you kindly: A configurational approach to a buyer's relationship exit strategy. *Industrial Marketing Management*, 84, 237–250. DOI: 10.1016/j.indmarman.2019.07.008

Han, B., Zheng, M., Fan, L., & Shi, W. (2022). Mechanism of governance pressures, green production and collaboration on the performance of maritime supply chain: Evidence from the moderating effect of government subsidies. *Research in Transportation Business & Management*, 43, 100820. DOI: 10.1016/j.rtbm.2022.100820

Huang, G., Tong, Y., Ye, F., & Li, J. (2020). Extending social responsibility to small and medium-sized suppliers in supply chains: A fuzzy-set qualitative comparative analysis. *Applied Soft Computing*, 88, 105899. DOI: 10.1016/j.asoc.2019.105899

Huarng, K.-H., & Yu, T. H.-K. (2017). Using qualitative approach to forecasting regime switches. *Quality & Quantity*, 51(5), 2035–2048. DOI: 10.1007/s11135-016-0338-x

Jiao, J., Zhang, X., & Tang, Y. (2020). What factors determine the survival of green innovative enterprises in China? — A method based on fsQCA. *Technology in Society*, 62, 101314. DOI: 10.1016/j.techsoc.2020.101314 PMID: 32834233

Jing, S., Feng, Y., & Yan, J. (2021). Path selection of lean digitalization for traditional manufacturing industry under heterogeneous competitive position. *Computers & Industrial Engineering*, 161, 107631. DOI: 10.1016/j.cie.2021.107631

Jovanovic, J., & Morschett, D. (2022). Under which conditions do manufacturing companies choose FDI for service provision in foreign markets? An investigation using fsQCA. *Industrial Marketing Management*, 104, 38–50. DOI: 10.1016/j.indmarman.2022.03.018

Kopplin, C. S., & Rösch, S. F. (2021). Equifinal causes of sustainable clothing purchase behavior: An fsQCA analysis among generation Y. *Journal of Retailing and Consumer Services*, 63, 102692. DOI: 10.1016/j.jretconser.2021.102692

Kosmol, T., Reimann, F., & Kaufmann, L. (2018). Co-alignment of supplier quality management practices and cognitive maps – A neo-configurational perspective. *Journal of Purchasing and Supply Management*, 24(1), 1–20. DOI: 10.1016/j.pursup.2017.11.002

Kumar, S., Sahoo, S., Lim, W. M., Kraus, S., & Bamel, U. (2022). Fuzzy-set qualitative comparative analysis (fsQCA) in business and management research: A contemporary overview. *Technological Forecasting and Social Change*, 178, 121599. DOI: 10.1016/j.techfore.2022.121599

Kumbure, M. M., Tarkiainen, A., Luukka, P., Stoklasa, J., & Jantunen, A. (2020). Relation between managerial cognition and industrial performance: An assessment with strategic cognitive maps using fuzzy-set qualitative comparative analysis. *Journal of Business Research*, 114, 160–172. DOI: 10.1016/j.jbusres.2020.04.001

Lee, C. K. H. (2022). How guest-host interactions affect consumer experiences in the sharing economy: New evidence from a configurational analysis based on consumer reviews. *Decision Support Systems*, 152, 113634. DOI: 10.1016/j.dss.2021.113634

Liliani, T., Tjahjono, B., & Cao, D. (2020). Advancing bioplastic packaging products through co-innovation: A conceptual framework for supplier-customer collaboration. *Journal of Cleaner Production*, 252, 119861. DOI: 10.1016/j.jclepro.2019.119861

Lim, W. M., Rasul, T., Kumar, S., & Ala, M. (2022). Past, present, and future of customer engagement. *Journal of Business Research*, 140, 439–458. DOI: 10.1016/j.jbusres.2021.11.014

Llopis-Albert, C., Palacios-Marqués, D., & Simón-Moya, V. (2021). Fuzzy set qualitative comparative analysis (fsQCA) applied to the adaptation of the automobile industry to meet the emission standards of climate change policies via the deployment of electric vehicles (EVs). *Technological Forecasting and Social Change*, 169, 120843. DOI: 10.1016/j.techfore.2021.120843

Llopis-Albert, C., Rubio, F., & Valero, F. (2021). Impact of digital transformation on the automotive industry. *Technological Forecasting and Social Change*, 162, 120343. DOI: 10.1016/j.techfore.2020.120343 PMID: 33052150

Loh, X.-M., Lee, V.-H., Leong, L.-Y., Aw, E. C.-X., Cham, T.-H., Tang, Y.-C., & Hew, J.-J. (2023). Understanding consumers' resistance to pay with cryptocurrency in the sharing economy: A hybrid SEM-fsQCA approach. *Journal of Business Research*, 159, 113726. DOI: 10.1016/j.jbusres.2023.113726

López-Cabarcos, M. Á., Piñeiro-Chousa, J., Quiñoá-Piñeiro, L., & López-Pérez, M. L. (2024). Water and waste management strategies as drivers of the financial performance of food companies. *Technological Forecasting and Social Change*, 200, 123138. DOI: 10.1016/j.techfore.2023.123138

Lou, Z., Ye, A., Mao, J., & Zhang, C. (2022). Supplier selection, control mechanisms, and firm innovation: Configuration analysis based on fsQCA. *Journal of Business Research*, 139, 81–89. DOI: 10.1016/j.jbusres.2021.09.045

Marks, S. J., Kumpel, E., Guo, J., Bartram, J., & Davis, J. (2018). Pathways to sustainability: A fuzzy-set qualitative comparative analysis of rural water supply programs. *Journal of Cleaner Production*, 205, 789–798. DOI: 10.1016/j.jclepro.2018.09.029

Marzi, G., Marrucci, A., Vianelli, D., & Ciappei, C. (2023). B2B digital platform adoption by SMEs and large firms: Pathways and pitfalls. *Industrial Marketing Management*, 114, 80–93. DOI: 10.1016/j.indmarman.2023.08.002

Mazumder, S., & Garg, S. (2021). Decoding digital transformational outsourcing: The role of service providers' capabilities. *International Journal of Information Management*, 58, 102295. DOI: 10.1016/j.ijinfomgt.2020.102295

McKinsey. (2022). Coronavirus' business impact: Evolving perspective | McKinsey

Mena, C., Karatzas, A., & Hansen, C. (2022). International trade resilience and the Covid-19 pandemic. *Journal of Business Research*, 138, 77–91. DOI: 10.1016/j.jbusres.2021.08.064 PMID: 34538982

Meneses, R., Quelhas Brito, P., & Coelho Gomes, P. (2016). From offshore-provider to brand creator: fsQCA of footwear industry. *Journal of Business Research*, 69(11), 5540–5546. DOI: 10.1016/j.jbusres.2016.04.168

Minerbo, C., Kleinaltenkamp, M., & Brito, L. A. L. (2021). Unpacking value creation and capture in B2B relationships. *Industrial Marketing Management*, 92, 163–177. DOI: 10.1016/j.indmarman.2020.11.011

Mühlbacher, H., & Böbel, I. (2019). From zero-sum to win-win—Organisational conditions for successful shared value strategy implementation. *European Management Journal*, 37(3), 313–324. DOI: 10.1016/j.emj.2018.10.007

Muñoz, P., & Cohen, B. (2017). Mapping out the sharing economy: A configurational approach to sharing business modeling. *Technological Forecasting and Social Change*, 125, 21–37. DOI: 10.1016/j.techfore.2017.03.035

Naims, H., & Eppinger, E. (2022). Transformation strategies connected to carbon capture and utilization: A cross-sectoral configurational study. *Journal of Cleaner Production*, 351, 131391. DOI: 10.1016/j.jclepro.2022.131391

Patel, P., Bhanugopan, R., Sinha, P., Prikshat, V., & Boyle, B. (2024). Home country and firm-specific advantage influences on HRM replication versus adaptation in EMNEs operating in advanced economies: A qualitative comparative analysis. *Journal of Business Research*, 170, 114335. DOI: 10.1016/j.jbusres.2023.114335

Prentice, C. (2019). Testing complexity theory in service research. *Journal of Services Marketing*, 34(2), 149–162. DOI: 10.1108/JSM-09-2019-0353

Prosman, E. J., & Cagliano, R. (2022). A contingency perspective on manufacturing configurations for the circular economy: Insights from successful start-ups. *International Journal of Production Economics*, 249, 108519. DOI: 10.1016/j.ijpe.2022.108519

Rahman, M., Saha, S., & Hoque, M. (2024). Unveiling the link between environmental management accounting, energy efficiency, and accountability in state-owned enterprises: An integrated analysis using PLS-SEM and fsQCA. *Environmental Challenges*, 14, 100832. DOI: 10.1016/j.envc.2023.100832

Romero-Castro, N., Piñeiro-Chousa, J., & Pérez-Pico, A. (2021). Dealing with heterogeneity and complexity in the analysis of the willingness to invest in community renewable energy in rural areas. *Technological Forecasting and Social Change*, 173, 121165. DOI: 10.1016/j.techfore.2021.121165

Russo, I., Confente, I., Gligor, D. M., & Autry, C. W. (2016). To be or not to be (loyal): Is there a recipe for customer loyalty in the B2B context? *Journal of Business Research*, 69(2), 888–896. DOI: 10.1016/j.jbusres.2015.07.002

Sandra, M., Narayanamoorthy, S., Ferrara, M., Innab, N., Ahmadian, A., & Kang, D. (2024). A novel decision support system for the appraisal and selection of green warehouses. *Socio-Economic Planning Sciences*, 91, 101782. DOI: 10.1016/j.seps.2023.101782

Scarpi, D., Raggiotto, F., & Visentin, M. (2022). Untying the knot: Drivers of the intention to downgrade the relationship in B2B service contexts. *Industrial Marketing Management*, 105, 200–210. DOI: 10.1016/j.indmarman.2022.06.005

Stekelorum, R., Laguir, I., Gupta, S., & Kumar, S. (2021). Green supply chain management practices and third-party logistics providers' performances: A fuzzy-set approach. *International Journal of Production Economics*, 235, 108093. DOI: 10.1016/j.ijpe.2021.108093

Sun, S., Hall, D. J., & Cegielski, C. G. (2020). Organizational intention to adopt big data in the B2B context: An integrated view. *Industrial Marketing Management*, 86, 109–121. DOI: 10.1016/j.indmarman.2019.09.003

Tran, P. N. T., Gorton, M., & Lemke, F. (2021). When supplier development initiatives fail: Identifying the causes of opportunism and unexpected outcomes. *Journal of Business Research*, 127, 277–289. DOI: 10.1016/j.jbusres.2021.01.009

Venâncio, A., Picoto, W., & Pinto, I. (2023). Time-to-unicorn and digital entrepreneurial ecosystems. *Technological Forecasting and Social Change*, 190, 122425. DOI: 10.1016/j.techfore.2023.122425

Wang, S., & Esperança, J. P. (2023). Can digital transformation improve market and ESG performance? Evidence from Chinese SMEs. *Journal of Cleaner Production*, 419, 137980. DOI: 10.1016/j.jclepro.2023.137980

Wang, X., Zhang, T., Luo, S., & Abedin, M. Z. (2023). Pathways to improve energy efficiency under carbon emission constraints in iron and steel industry: Using EBM, NCA and QCA approaches. *Journal of Environmental Management*, 348, 119206. DOI: 10.1016/j.jenvman.2023.119206 PMID: 37898049

Woodside, A. G. (2018). Have your cake and eat it too: Achieving scientific legitimacy. *Industrial Marketing Management*, 69, 53–61. DOI: 10.1016/j.indmarman.2018.01.028

Wu, C.-W., Botella-Carrubi, D., & Blanco-González-Tejero, C. (2024). The empirical study of digital marketing strategy and performance in small and medium-sized enterprises (SMEs). *Technological Forecasting and Social Change*, 200, 123142. DOI: 10.1016/j.techfore.2023.123142

Yin, Q., Song, D., Lai, F., Collins, B. J., & Dogru, A. K. (2023). Customizing governance mechanisms to reduce opportunism in buyer–supplier relationships in the digital economy. *Technological Forecasting and Social Change*, 190, 122411. DOI: 10.1016/j.techfore.2023.122411

Yu, Y., Xu, J., Huo, B., Zhang, J. Z., & Cao, Y. (2023). The impact of supply chain social responsibility on sustainable performance. *Journal of Cleaner Production*, 385, 135666. DOI: 10.1016/j.jclepro.2022.135666

Compilation of References

Abdellatif, H. H., Bhowmik, P. K., Arcilesi, D., & Sabharwall, P. (2024). Accident event progression, gaps, and key performance indicators for steam generator tube rupture events in water-cooled SMRs: A review. *Progress in Nuclear Energy*, 168, 105021. DOI: 10.1016/j.pnucene.2023.105021

Abir, M. (1968). Caravan Trade and History in the Northern Parts of East Africa. *Paideuma*, 14, 103–120. https://www.jstor.org/stable/40341453

Abu-Rumman, A., Al Shraah, A., Al-Madi, F., & Alfalah, T. (2021). Entrepreneurial networks, entrepreneurial orientation, and performance of small and medium enterprises: Are dynamic capabilities the missing link? *Journal of Innovation and Entrepreneurship*, 10(1), 29. Advance online publication. DOI: 10.1186/s13731-021-00170-8

Abu-Rumman, A., Al Shraah, A., AlSha'ar, H., & Alqhaiwi, L. A. (2022). Innovation and Entrepreneurship: Attitudes and intentions of undergraduates in a developing country. *Res. Sq.*, 1, 1–21. DOI: 10.21203/rs.3.rs-1369010/v1

Acquah, I. S. K., Naude, M. J., & Sendra-García, J. (2021). Supply chain collaboration in the petroleum sector of an emerging economy: Comparing results from symmetrical and asymmetrical approaches. *Technological Forecasting and Social Change*, 166, 120568. DOI: 10.1016/j.techfore.2020.120568

Acs, Z. J., & Audretsch, D. B. (2003). Innovation and Technological Change. In Acs, Z. J., & Audretsch, D. B. (Eds.), *Handbook of Entrepreneurship Research* (pp. 55–79). Kluwer Academic Publishers. DOI: 10.1007/0-387-24519-7_4

Aday, S., & Aday, M. S. (2020). Impact of COVID-19 on the food supply chain. *Food Quality and Safety*, 4(4), 167–180. DOI: 10.1093/fqsafe/fyaa024

Adidas. (2024). Sustainability Supply Chain. https://www.adidas-group.com/en/sustainability/social-impacts/supply-chain/#/training-and-empowering-suppliers/

Ahi, P., & Searcy, C. (2013). A comparative literature analysis of definitions for green and sustainable supply chain management. *Journal of Cleaner Production*, 52, 329–341. DOI: 10.1016/j.jclepro.2013.02.018

Ait-Kadi, D., Chouinard, M., Marcotte, S., Riopel, D. (2012). "Sustainable Reverse Logistics Network: Engineering and Management" Wiley-ISTE: 35-87.

Ajzen, I. (1991). The theory of planned behavior. *Organizational Behavior and Human Decision Processes*, 50(2), 1–63. DOI: 10.1016/0749-5978(91)90020-T

Akima, H., Goto, H., & Yamamura, T. (2015). Toukyou seibu ni okeru animeshon sangyou no ricchi senkou to sono hensen: Dejitaruka ni tomonau sagyou koutei no henka ni tsuite [Location preferences and changes of the animation industry in Western Tokyo: Changes in work processes due to digitalization]. *Urban Planning Papers*, 50(3), 644–649.

Ali, A., Khan, M. R., & Ghouri, A. M. (2023). Carbon neutrality concept and progress. In *Recent Developments in Green Finance, Green Growth and Carbon Neutrality* (pp. 85-108). Elsevier. DOI: 10.1016/B978-0-443-15936-7.00003-7

Ali, A. M., Bagdanavicius, A., Barbour, E. R., Pottie, D. L., Garvey, S., Rouse, J., & Baniamerian, Z. (2024). Improving the performance of a shell and tube latent heat thermal energy storage through modifications of heat transfer pipes: A comprehensive investigation on various configurations. *Journal of Energy Storage*, 96, 112678. DOI: 10.1016/j.est.2024.112678

Ali, S. I., Ali, A., AlKilabi, M., & Christie, M. (2021). Optimal supply chain design with product family: A cloud-based framework with real-time data consideration. *Computers & Operations Research*, 126, 105112. Advance online publication. DOI: 10.1016/j.cor.2020.105112

Alizon, F., Shooter, S., & Simpson, T. (2009). Henry Ford and the Model T: Lessons for Product Platforming and Mass Customization. *Design Studies*, 30(5), 588–605. DOI: 10.1016/j.destud.2009.03.003

Almond, G., & Verba, S. (1965) The civic culture. Little, Brown and Company(Inc.), Boston: MASS, 1965.

Almond, G., & Verba, S. (Eds.). (1989), The Civic Culture revisited. Political Attitudes and Democracy in Five Nations, California, sage Publications Inc.

Almond, G., & Verba, S. (2001). La cultura política. In Batlle, A. (Ed.), *Diez textos básicos de ciencia política* (pp. 171–201). Ariel.

Alsuwaidi, M., Eid, R., & Agag, G. (2022). Tackling the complexity of guests' food waste reduction behaviour in the hospitality industry. *Tourism Management Perspectives*, 42, 100963. DOI: 10.1016/j.tmp.2022.100963

Ambroise, L., Prim-Allaz, I., & Teyssier, C. (2018). Financial performance of servitized manufacturing firms: A configuration issue between servitization strategies and customer-oriented organizational design. *Industrial Marketing Management*, 71, 54–68. DOI: 10.1016/j.indmarman.2017.11.007

American Psychological Association. (2019). *Stress in America 2019.* Retrieved February 18th, 2020, from https://www.apa.org/images/stress-america-2019_tcm7-264533.pdf

Angwin, D., & Sammut-Bonnici, T. (2015): *Strategic Alliances*, in: Cooper (ed): Wiley Encyclopedia of Management, John Wiley & Sons, Ltd. DOI: 10.1002/9781118785317.weom120047

Aragon-Sanchez, A., Baixauli-Soler, S., & Carrasco-Hernandez, A. J. (2017). A missing link: The behavioral mediators between resources and entrepreneurial intentions. *International Journal of Entrepreneurial Behaviour & Research*, 23(5), 752–768. Advance online publication. DOI: 10.1108/IJEBR-06-2016-0172

Armenia, S., Barnabé, F., Franco, E., Iandolo, F., Pompei, A., & Tsaples, G. (2023). Identifying policy options and responses to water management issues through System Dynamics and fsQCA. *Technological Forecasting and Social Change*, 194, 122737. DOI: 10.1016/j.techfore.2023.122737

Armitage, C. J., & Conner, M. (2001). Efficacy of the theory of planned behavior: A meta-analytic review. *British Journal of Social Psychology*, 40(4), 471–499. DOI: 10.1348/014466601164939 PMID: 11795063

Armour, J., Enriques, L., & Wetzer, T. (2023). Green Pills: Making Corporate Climate Commitments Credible. *Arizona Law Review*, 65, 285.

Artner, A. (1995). Vállalati együttműködés a mai világgazdaságban (Corporate cooperation in today's global economy). *Közgazdasági Szemle*, XLLII(1), 104–115.

Aspara, J., Hietanen, J., & Tikkanen, H. (2010). Business model innovation vs replication: Financial performance implications of strategic emphases. *Journal of Strategic Marketing*, 18(1), 39–56. DOI: 10.1080/09652540903511290

Ayuntamiento de Tlajomulco de Zúñiga. Jalisco (2015). *Caracterización del subsistema social*. Retrieved from https://tlajomulco.gob.mx/sites/default/files/documentos/poel/poet_tlj_1.3_caracterizacion_subsistema_social.pdf

Baier-Fuentes, H., Andrade-Valbuena, N. A., Huertas Gonzalez-Serrano, M., & Gaviria-Marin, M. (2023). Bricolage as an effective tool for the survival of owner-managed SMEs during crises. *Journal of Business Research*, 157, 113608. DOI: 10.1016/j.jbusres.2022.113608

Bai, Y., Wang, J., & Jiao, J. (2021). A framework for determining the impacts of a multiple relationship network on green innovation. *Sustainable Production and Consumption*, 27, 471–484. DOI: 10.1016/j.spc.2021.01.014

Bakos, G. (1996). Magyar Suzuki and the Emergence of Japanese Direct Investmen in Central Europe. In Darby, J. (Ed.), *Japan and the European Periphery* (pp. 244–253). Palgrave Macmillian. DOI: 10.1007/978-1-349-25196-4_15

Ballou, R. H. (2004). *Business Lojistik / Supply Chain Management* (5th ed.). Pearson Education.

Bandura, A. (1991). Social cognitive theory of self-regulation. *Organizational Behavior and Human Decision Processes*, 50(2), 248–287. DOI: 10.1016/0749-5978(91)90022-L

Baptista, R., Escária, V., & Madruga, P. (2017). *Entrepreneurship, regional development and job creation: The case of Portugal. Discussion papers on entrepreneurship, growth and public policy*. Max Planck Institute for Research in Economic Systems.

Barna, C., Zbuchea, A., & Stănescu, S. (2023). Social economy enterprises contributing to the circular economy and the green transition in romania. Ciriec-España. *C.I.R.I.E.C. España*, 47(107), 47–69. DOI: 10.7203/CIRIEC-E.107.21738

Barney, J. (2001). Is the resource-based “view” a useful perspective for strategic management research? *Academy of Management Review*, 26(1), •••.

Beazley, R. (1913). The Early History of the Compass and the First Scientific Maps. *History (London)*, 2(1), 46–52. https://www.jstor.org/stable/44991448

Bergmann, A., Stechemesser, K., & Guenther, E. (2016). Natural resource dependence theory: Impacts of extreme weather events on organizations. *Journal of Business Research*, 69(4), 1361–1366. DOI: 10.1016/j.jbusres.2015.10.108

Bernardi, R. A. (2011). The Relationships among locus of control, perceptions of stress and performance. *Journal of Applied Business Research*, 13(4), 1. Advance online publication. DOI: 10.19030/jabr.v13i4.5736

Besanko, D., Dranove, D., Shanley, M., & Schaefer, S. (2004). *Economics of strategy*. John Wiley & Sons Inc.

Bhardwaj, C., Kishwar, S. D., Khurana, B., Vatsa, K., & Manderna, M. K. (2024). Contextualizing the application of the Milieudefensie v. Royal Dutch Shell decision in Indian climate change litigation: Possibilities and challenges. *Sustainability and Climate Change*, 17(1), 77–90. DOI: 10.1089/scc.2023.0137

Bianco, D., Bueno, A., Filho, M. G., Lata, H., Ganga, G. M. D., Frank, A. G., & Jabbour, C. J. C. (2023). The role of Industry 4.0 in feveloping resilience for manufacturing companies during COVID-19. *International Journal of Production Economics*, 256, 108728. Advance online publication. DOI: 10.1016/j.ijpe.2022.108728

Bifaretti, A., Paván, E., & Grigioni, G. (2023). Consumer attitudes and concerns about beef consumption in argentina and other south american countries. *Agriculture*, 13(3), 560. DOI: 10.3390/agriculture13030560

Blaikie, N. (2007). *Approaches to Social Inquiry*. Polity Press.

Bocken, N., & Coffay, M. (2022). The circular experimentation workbench – a lean and effectual process. *Circular Economy and Sustainability*, 3(3), 1361–1383. DOI: 10.1007/s43615-022-00239-w PMID: 36531657

Bocken, N., & Ritala, P. (2021). Six ways to build circular business models. *The Journal of Business Strategy*, 43(3), 184–192. DOI: 10.1108/JBS-11-2020-0258

Bocken, N., Strupeit, L., Whalen, K., & Nußholz, J. (2019). A review and evaluation of circular business model innovation tools. *Sustainability (Basel)*, 11(8), 2210. DOI: 10.3390/su11082210

Bodrožić, Z., & Adler, S., P. (. (2022). Alternative futures for the digital transformation: A macro-level Schumpeterian perspective. *Organization Science*, 33(1), 105–125. DOI: 10.1287/orsc.2021.1558

Bolton, D. L., & Lane, M. D. (2012). Individual entrepreneurial orientation: Development of a measurement instrument. *Education + Training*, 54(2/3), 219–233. DOI: 10.1108/00400911211210314

Bonadio, B., Huo, Z., Levchenko, A. A., & Pandalai-Nayar, N. (2021). Global supply chains in the pandemic. *Journal of International Economics*, 133, 103534. Advance online publication. DOI: 10.1016/j.jinteco.2021.103534 PMID: 34866652

Boone, J. (2000). Competitive Pressure: The Effects on Investments in Product and Process Innovation. *The RAND Journal of Economics*, 31(3), 549–569. DOI: 10.2307/2601000

Bowersox, D. J. & Closs, D.J. (1996). *Lojistical Management: The Integrated Supply Chain Process.* McGraw-Hill Companies. 88-100.

Brownhilder Ngek Neneh, A., van Zyl, J., & Ngek Neneh, B. (2017). Entrepreneurial orientation and its impact on firm growth amongst SMEs in South Africa. Problems and Perspectives in Management, 15, 166.

Bruyne, M., & Verleye, K. (2022). Realizing the economic and circular potential of sharing business models by engaging consumers. *Journal of Service Management*, 34(3), 493–519. DOI: 10.1108/JOSM-08-2021-0318

Burgueño Salas, E. (25 Sept. 2020). *Volumen de producción mensual de fertilizantes fosfatados en México de enero de 2019 a julio de 2020 (en toneladas métricas).* Statista. Retrieve on the 2 of July 2021 from https://es.statista.com/estadisticas/594554/volumen-de-produccion-de-fertilizantes-superfosfatados-en-mexico/

Cabinet Office. (2024). Nenji GDP seichouritsu [Annual GDP growth rate]. *Kokumin keizai keisan* (GDP toukei) [National Economic Accounts (GDP Statistics)]. https://www.esri.cao.go.jp/jp/sna/menu.html

Cai, J., Sharkawi, I., & Taasim, S. I. (2024). How does digital transformation promote supply chain deversification? From the perspective of supply chain transaction costs. *Finance Research Letters*, 63, 105399. Advance online publication. DOI: 10.1016/j.frl.2024.105399

Campagna, K., Wilson, R., Callahan, S., & Jason, L. A. (2015). Women in recovery: Predictors of internal and external work locus of control. *Journal of Psychological Issues in Organizational Culture*, 6(1), 7–15. Advance online publication. DOI: 10.1002/jpoc.21169

Cantele, S., Russo, I., Kirchoff, J. F., & Valcozzena, S. (2023). Supply chain agility and sustainability performance: A configurational approach to sustainable supply chain management practices. *Journal of Cleaner Production*, 414, 137493. DOI: 10.1016/j.jclepro.2023.137493

Cantú, P. (2008). Desarrollo sustentable: conceptos y reflexiones. *Universidad Autónoma de Nuevo León*. Colección: *Tendencias Científicas. ISBN: 978-607- 433-117-2*

Cantwell, J., & Sanna Randaccio, F. (1990). The Growth of Multinationals and the Cathing up Effect. *Economic Notes*, (1), 1–23.

Carissimi, M. C., Creazza, A., & Colicchia, C. (2023). Crossing the chasm: Investigating the relationship between sustainability and resilience in supply chain management. *Cleaner Logistics and Suppyl Chain*, 7, 100098. Advance online publication. DOI: 10.1016/j.clscn.2023.100098

Carree, M. A., & Thurik, A. R. (2010). The impact of entrepreneurship on economic growth. In Zoltan, J., & Audretsch, D. (Eds.), *Handbook of entrepreneurship research*. Springer. DOI: 10.1007/978-1-4419-1191-9_20

Castka, P. (2018). Modelling firms' interventions in ISO 9001 certification: A configurational approach. *International Journal of Production Economics*, 201, 163–172. DOI: 10.1016/j.ijpe.2018.05.005

Castro, A. (Julio de 1998). *Hacia el desarrollo sostenible y la ecoeficiencia: integración de las normas ISO 9000, ISO 14000 e ISO 18000 diseño de un sistema de gestión ambiental certificable. (Tesis de maestría inédita).* Obtenido de Facultad Regional de Buenos Aires: http://posgrado.frba.utn.edu.ar/investigacion/tesis/MIA-1998-Castro.pdf

Charmaz, K. (2000). Constructivist and objectivist grounded theory. In Denzin, N. K., & Lincoln, Y. (Eds.), *Handbook of qualitative research* (pp. 509–535). Sage.

Charmaz, K. (2008). Constructionism and the Grounded Theory Method. In Holstein, J. A., & Gubrium, F. J. (Eds.), *Handbook of Constructionist Research* (pp. 397–412). The Guilford Press.

Chavan, A. S., & Chondekar, R. P. (2023). Overexploitation of Cowrie Shells: Future threats to the Marine Ecosystem. *International Journal of Zoology Studies*, 8(3), 8–10.

Chen, G., Goddard, T. G., & Casper, W. J. (2004). Examination of the relationship among general and work-specific self-evaluations, work-related control beliefs, and job attitudes. *Applied Psychology*, 53(3), 349–370. DOI: 10.1111/j.1464-0597.2004.00175.x

Chen, P. (2022). The spatial impacts of the circular economy on carbon intensity - new evidence from the super-efficient sbm-dea model. *Energy & Environment*, 35(1), 47–63. DOI: 10.1177/0958305X221125125

Chiu, C. K., Lin, C. P., Tsai, Y. H., & Hsiao, C. Y. (2005). Modelling turnover incidents and their antecedents using the locus of control as a moderator: A case of customer service employees. *Human Resource Development Quarterly*, 16(4), 481–499. DOI: 10.1002/hrdq.1152

Chopra, S., & Meindl, P. (2004). *Supply Chain Management Strategy, Planning, and Operation* (2nd ed.). Pearson Education International.

Chou, C. C., Hwang, N. C. R., Li, C. W., Wang, T., & Wang, Y. Y. (2023). Implementing a multichain framework using hyperledger for supply chain transparency in a dynamic partnership: A feasibility study. *Computers & Industrial Engineering*, 175, 108906. DOI: 10.1016/j.cie.2022.108906

Chowdhury, P., Paul, S. K., Kaisar, S., & Moktadir, Md. A. (2021). COVID-19 pandemic relatd supply chain studies: A systematic review. *Transportation Research Part E, Logistics and Transportation Review*, 148(April). Advance online publication. 102271 PMID: 33613082

Chrascina, M., Vaněk, M., & Pekarčíková, K. (2024). Intrinsic Value of Stocks of "Big Oil" Companies. *GeoScience Engineering*, 70(1), 67–77. DOI: 10.35180/gse-2024-0107

Christophers, B. (2022). Fossilised capital: Price and profit in the energy transition. *New Political Economy*, 27(1), 146–159. DOI: 10.1080/13563467.2021.1926957

Churchill, S. A., Munyanyi, M. E., Prakash, K., & Smyth, R. (2020). Locus of control and the gender gap in mental health. *Journal of Economic Behavior & Organization*, 178, 740–758. DOI: 10.1016/j.jebo.2020.08.013

Cobb-Clark, D. (2015). Locus of control and the labor market. *IZA Journal of Labor Economics*, 4(1), 3. DOI: 10.1186/s40172-014-0017-x

Coclanis, P. A. (Ed.). (2005). *The Atlantic Economy during the Seventeenth and Eighteenth Centuries: Organization, Operation, Practice, and Personnel*. University of South Carolina Press., DOI: 10.2307/j.ctv1169bdh

Cohen, M. (1979). *La Contaminación Atmosférica y la Salud*. IGE. UdeG. México.

Cohen, S., & Roussel, J. (2005). *Strategic supply chain management: the five disciplines for top performance*. McGraw-Hill.

Coltman, T., Bru, K., Perm-Ajchariyawong, N., Devinney, T. M., & Benito, G. R. (2009). Supply Chain Contract Evolution. *European Management Journal*, 27(6), 388–401. DOI: 10.1016/j.emj.2008.11.005

CONAPO. (2017). *Estimación de la mortalidad infantil para México, las entidades federativas y los municipios 2005*. Retrieved from http://www.conapo.gob.mx/es/CONAPO/Base_de_datos

Consejo Mundial Empresarial para el Desarrollo Sostenible. (1991). Ecoeficiencia y sustentabilidad. *Ciencia* UANL, 35.

Coyle, J. J., Bardi, E. J., Langley, C. J. (2003). *The Management of Business Logistics, A Supply Chain Perspective*. South-Western, Thomson Learning. 13-174.

Creswell, J. W. (2013). *Qualitative Inquiry and Research Design: Choosing among five approaches*. SAGE Publication.

Czakó, K. (2014): Az Audi Hungaria Motor Kft. hatása a helyi gazdasági és társadalmi folyamatokra (The Impact of Audi Hungaria Motor Ltd on Local Economic and Social Processes), *Tér és Társadalom, 28(2)*, pp. 188–198.

Daniels, K., & Guppy, A. (1992). Control, information-seeking preferences, occupational stressors, and psychological wellbeing. *Work and Stress*, 6(4), 347–353. DOI: 10.1080/02678379208259965

de Almeida, R. G., & Silva, H. (2023). the Entrepreneur Between Two Circuits: The Critical Contribution of Milton Santos To Entrepreneurship Studies. *Res. Hist. Econ. Thought Methodol.*, 41B, 49–66. DOI: 10.1108/S0743-41542023000041B003

Deloitte 2022. Save & Close Corporate Research & Development Report 2022 (deloitte.com)

Deloitte. (2021). A year of connection, action and impact, 2021 GLOBAL IMPACT REPORT. 98. gx-about-deloitte-global-report-full-version-2021.pdf

Demirel, G. (2022): Network science for the supply chain: theory, methods, and empirical results, *The Digital Supply Chain*, pp. 343-359.

Dewi Astuti, R., Ezni Balqiah, T., & Yuliati, E. (2024). Role of individual entrepreneurial orientation and innovation in SME performance: Gender perspectives. *Problems and Perspectives in Management*, 22(2), 365–378. DOI: 10.21511/ppm.22(2).2024.28

Deza, X., & Pereira, Á. (2018). Eco-innovation and circular business models as drivers for a circular economy. *Contaduría y Administración*, 64(1), 64. DOI: 10.22201/fca.24488410e.2019.1806

Deza, X., & Pérez, S. (2021). Taxation for a circular economy: New instruments, reforms, and architectural changes in the fiscal system. *Sustainability (Basel)*, 13(8), 4581. DOI: 10.3390/su13084581

Dffreight. (2024). An Insight into Starbucks Supply Chain Strategy, https://dfreight.org/blog/an-insight-into-starbucks-supply-chain-strategy/

Di Paola, N. (2021). Pathways to academic entrepreneurship: The determinants of female scholars' entrepreneurial intentions. *The Journal of Technology Transfer*, 46(5), 1417–1441. DOI: 10.1007/s10961-020-09824-3

Dirección de Estadística. (2013). *Secretaría de Educación de Jalisco, México 2013.* Retrieved from http://www.informador.com.mx/jalisco/2017/699906/6/zapopan-proyecta-red-de-parques-agroecologicos.htm

Do Paço, F., Arminda, M., Ferreira, J. M., Raposo, M., Gouveia, R., & Dinis, A. (2011). Behaviours and entrepreneurial intention: Empirical findings about secondary students. *Journal of International Entrepreneurship*, 9(1), 20–38. DOI: 10.1007/s10843-010-0071-9

Dobos, I., Pintér, M. (2010): *Cooperation in supply chains: A cooperative game theoretic analysis*, working paper in: Corvinus University of Budapest

Doz, Y. L., Bartlett, C. A., & Prahalad, C. K. (1981). Global Competitive Pressures and Host Country Demands Managing Tensions in MNCs. *California Management Review*, 23(3), 63–74. DOI: 10.2307/41172603

Dul, J. (2022). Problematic applications of Necessary Condition Analysis (NCA) in tourism and hospitality research. *Tourism Management*, 93, 104616. DOI: 10.1016/j.tourman.2022.104616

Dunford, R., Palmer, I., & Benveniste, J. (2010). Business model replication for early and rapid internationalisation. *Long Range Planning*, 43(5-6), 655–674. DOI: 10.1016/j.lrp.2010.06.004

Efendigil, T., Önüt, S., & Kahraman, C. (2009). A decision support system for demand forecasting with artificial neural networks and neuro-fuzzy models: A comparative analysis. *Expert Systems with Applications*, 36(3), 6697–6707. DOI: 10.1016/j.eswa.2008.08.058

El Jaouhari, A., Azari, M., Arif, J., El Farouk, I. I., Jawab, F., & Moufad, I. "IoT for the future of sustainable supply chain management in Industry 4.0: A Systematic Literature Review," *2022 14th International Colloquium of Logistics and Supply Chain Management (LOGISTIQUA)*, EL JADIDA, Morocco, 2022, pp. 1-6, DOI: 10.1109/LOGISTIQUA55056.2022.9938123

El Jaouhari, A., Arif, J., Samadhiya, A., & Kumar, A. (2023). Net zero supply chain performance and industry 4.0 technologies: Past review and present introspective analysis for future research directions. *Heliyon*, 9(11), e21525. DOI: 10.1016/j.heliyon.2023.e21525 PMID: 38027864

El Jaouhari, A., Arif, J., Samadhiya, A., Kumar, A., & Garza-Reyes, J. A. (2023). An environmental-based perspective framework: Integrating IoT technology into a sustainable automotive supply chain. *Benchmarking*. Advance online publication. DOI: 10.1108/BIJ-05-2023-0322

El Jaouhari, A., Arif, J., Samadhiya, A., Kumar, A., Jain, V., & Agrawal, R. (2023). Are metaverse applications in quality 4.0 enablers of manufacturing resiliency? An exploratory review under disruption impressions and future research. *The TQM Journal*.

El Jaouhari, A., Arif, J., Samadhiya, A., Naz, F., & Kumar, A. (2024). Exploring the application of ICTs in decarbonizing the agriculture supply chain: A literature review and research agenda. *Heliyon*, 10(8), e29564. DOI: 10.1016/j.heliyon.2024.e29564 PMID: 38665579

El Jaouhari, A., Fellaki, S., Amejwal, M., & Arif, J. (2023). Industry 4.0 Implementation in Lean Supply Chain Management: A Systematic Literature Review. *Statistics, Optimization & Information Computing*, 11(1), 178–185. DOI: 10.19139/soic-2310-5070-1539

Emeka-Okoli, S., Otonnah, C. A., Nwankwo, T. C., & Nwankwo, E. E. (2024). Internal and external communication in oil & gas for enhancing CSR implementation: A review. *World Journal of Advanced Research and Reviews*, 21(3), 109–118. DOI: 10.30574/wjarr.2024.21.3.0665

Encyclopædia Britannica, Inc. n.d. https://www.britannica.com/money/Fordism

Engidaw, A. E. (2022). Small businesses and their challenges during COVID-19 pandemic in developing countries: In the case of Ethiopia. *Journal of Innovation and Entrepreneurship*, 11(1), 1–14. DOI: 10.1186/s13731-021-00191-3 PMID: 35036286

Evans, B. J., & Coman, G. J. (1993). General versus specific measures of occupational stress: An Australian police survey. *Stress Medicine*, 9(1), 11–20. DOI: 10.1002/smi.2460090105

Evans, D. S., & Leighton, L. S. (1989). Some empirical aspects of entrepreneurship. *The American Economic Review*, 79, 519–535.

Farooq, M. U., Hussain, A., Masood, T., & Habib, M. S. (2021). Supply Chain Operations Management in Pandemics: A State-of-the-Art Review Inspired by COVID-19. *Sustainability (Basel)*, 13(5), 2504. DOI: 10.3390/su13052504

Fellnhofer, K. (2018). Narratives boost entrepreneurial attitudes: Making an entrepreneurial career attractive? *European Journal of Education*, 53(2), 218–237. DOI: 10.1111/ejed.12274 PMID: 29863170

Fernandez, R. (2016). How to boost your resilience at work. Retrieved from https://hbr.org/2016/06/627-building-resilience-ic-5-ways-to-build-your-personal-resilience-at-work

Ferreira. (2016). CThe advertisement call and geographic distribution of Proceratophrys dibernardoi Zootaxa. *Zootaxa*, 4205, 480–482.

FIRA (2020). Reporte trimestral de fertilizantes, Dirección de Investigación y Evaluación Económica del Fideicomisos Instituidos en relación con la Agricultura. Diciembre 2020.

Franco, E. F., Hirama, K., & Carvalho, M. M. (2018). Applying system dynamics approach in software and information system projects: A mapping study. *Information and Software Technology*, 93, 58–73. DOI: 10.1016/j.infsof.2017.08.013

Franco-Santos, M., Stull, D., & Bourne, M. (2022). Performance Management and Wellbeing at the Workplace. DOI: 10.1007/978-3-030-29010-8_42

Frazelle, E. (2002). *Supply Chain Strategy, the Logistics of Supply Chain Management.* McGraw-Hill; 145-166.

Galka, S., & Wappler, M. (2023). Integration of cash flow management and further aspects of the supply chain management in production system design. *IFAC-PapersOnLine*, 56(2), 947–952. DOI: 10.1016/j.ifacol.2023.10.1687

Gallegos Cedillo, G. (2021). Interview to a specialist of FIRA conducted on January 13th, 2021.

Gallegos Cedillo, G. (2021). Working paper Agronegocios FIRA.

Galor, S. (2014). Stress - An overview and the start of a few articles on the phenomenon. Retrieved from https://drsharongalor.wordpress.com/2014/11/02/stress-an-overview-and-the-start-of-a-few-articles-on-the-phenomenon/

Gao, J., & Chen, W. (2013). Research on collaborative mechanism in large and complex business process modeling. *Advanced Materials Research*, 850-851, 1012–1015. . DOI: 10.4028/www.scientific.net/AMR.850-851.1012

Garrido, S., Muniz, J.Jr, & Ribeiro, V. B. (2024). Operations Management, Sustainability & Industry 5.0: A critical analysis and future agenda. *Cleaner Logistics and Supply Chain*, 10, 100141. Advance online publication. DOI: 10.1016/j.clscn.2024.100141

Gáspár, T., Sass, M., Koppány, K., & Bi, S. (2023). Foreign trade relations of Hungary with China: A global value chain perspective. *Society and Economy*, 45(3), 229–249. DOI: 10.1556/204.2023.00018

Gelderblom, O., & Trivellato, F. (2019). The business history of the preindustrial world: Towards a comparative historical analysis. *Business History*, 61(2), 225–259. DOI: 10.1080/00076791.2018.1426750

Gelei, A. (2014). Az üzleti kapcsolatok irányítása – fókuszban a bizalom (Managing business relationships – focus on trust). *Köz-gazdaság*, 9(2), 85–99.

Gelei, A., & Dobos, I. (2016). Bizalom az üzleti kapcsolatokban (Trust in business relationships). *Közgazdasági Szemle*, 63(3), 330–349. DOI: 10.18414/KSZ.2016.3.330

Genet, C., Gandia, R., & Colombero, S. (2023). Simultaneous management of business model innovation and replication processes. *Journal of Business Models*, 11(2). Advance online publication. DOI: 10.54337/jbm.v11i2.7427

Geography of Transport Systems. n.d. https://transportgeography.org/contents/chapter5/maritime-transportation/evolution-containerships-classes/

Giannoccaro, I. (2018). Centralized vs. decentralized supply chains: The improtance of decision maker's cognitive ability and resistance to change. *Industrial Marketing Management*, 73, 59–69. DOI: 10.1016/j.indmarman.2018.01.034

Giesen, E., Riddleberger, E., Christner, R., & Bell, R. (2010). When and how to innovate your business model. *Strategy and Leadership*, 38(4), 17–26. DOI: 10.1108/10878571011059700

Giessmann, A., & Legner, C. (2016). Designing business models for cloud platforms. *Information Systems Journal*, 26(5), 551–579. DOI: 10.1111/isj.12107

Ginn, W. (2024). Global supply chain disruptions and financial conditions. *Economics Letters*, 239, 111739. Advance online publication. DOI: 10.1016/j.econlet.2024.111739

Gligor, D. M., Golgeci, I., Rego, C., Russo, I., Bozkurt, S., Pohlen, T., Hiatt, B., & Garg, V. (2022). Examining the use of fsQCA in B2B marketing research: Benefits, current state and agenda for future research. *Journal of Business and Industrial Marketing*, 37(7), 1542–1552. DOI: 10.1108/JBIM-09-2020-0436

Gobierno de Jalisco (2010). *Desarrollo humano y demografía de grupos vulnerables en Jalisco.*

Gobierno de Jalisco. (2013). *Equidad de oportunidades 16 Educación. Un plan de Todos para un futuro compartido*. Retrieved from https://transparencia.info.jalisco.gob.mx/sites/default/files/PED%20-%20Educaci%C3%B3n.pdf

Gobierno de Zapopan. (2015). *Zapopan estrena parque agroecológico*. Retrieved from: https://www.zapopan.gob.mx/zapopan-estrena-parque-agroecologico/

Gobierno de Zapopan. (2016). *Parque Agroecológico de Zapopan: Un modelo de Agricultura Urbana Sustentable*. Retrieved from: https://www.zapopan.gob.mx/parque-agroecologico-de-zapopan-un-modelo-de-agricultura-urbana-sustentable/

Gobierno de Zapopan. (2016). *Proyecto de presupuesto 2016. Diagnóstico del municipio para la elaboración del proyecto de presupuesto para el ejercicio fiscal 2016*. Retrieved from https://www.zapopan.gob.mx/wp-content/uploads/2016/01/Anexo4de12_DiagnosticoDelMunicipio.pdf

Gomes, P. J., Silva, G. M., & Sarkis, J. (2020). Exploring the relationship between quality ambidexterity and sustainable production. *International Journal of Production Economics*, 224, 107560. DOI: 10.1016/j.ijpe.2019.107560

Gooijer, J. (2022). Corporate taxation in a circular economy., 53-61. DOI: 10.1007/978-3-030-85322-8_6

Greco, M., Campagna, M., Cricelli, L., Grimaldi, M., & Strazzullo, S. (2022). COVID-19-related innovations: A study on underlying motivations and inter-organizational collaboration. *Industrial Marketing Management*, 106, 58–70. DOI: 10.1016/j.indmarman.2022.07.014

Grosser, P. (2010). The Fall of the Berlin Wall: The Revolutionary Legacy of 1989. *Cold War History*, 10(4), 578–579. DOI: 10.1080/14682745.2010.513513

Gul, I., Raziq, A., & Khan, M. R. (2024). Towards Sustainable Supply Chains with Blockchain. In *Achieving Secure and Transparent Supply Chains With Blockchain Technology* (pp. 18–37). IGI Global. DOI: 10.4018/979-8-3693-0482-2.ch002

Gupta, N., Sardana, D., & Lee, R. (2024). Dynamic capabilities that matter for business failure versus survival. *Industrial Marketing Management*, 116, 40–50. DOI: 10.1016/j.indmarman.2023.11.004

Gupta, P., Singh, S., Ghosh, R., Kumar, S., & Jain, C. (2024). Regulatory framework on governing equity crowdfunding: A systematic literature review and future directions. *Journal of Financial Regulation and Compliance*, 32(4), 421–444. DOI: 10.1108/JFRC-10-2023-0160

Habib, F., Bastl, M., Karatzas, A., & Mena, C. (2020). Treat me well and I may leave you kindly: A configurational approach to a buyer's relationship exit strategy. *Industrial Marketing Management*, 84, 237–250. DOI: 10.1016/j.indmarman.2019.07.008

Han, B., Zheng, M., Fan, L., & Shi, W. (2022). Mechanism of governance pressures, green production and collaboration on the performance of maritime supply chain: Evidence from the moderating effect of government subsidies. *Research in Transportation Business & Management*, 43, 100820. DOI: 10.1016/j.rtbm.2022.100820

Han, J., Heshmati, A., & Rashidghalam, M. (2020). Circular economy business models with a focus on servitization. *Sustainability (Basel)*, 12(21), 8799. DOI: 10.3390/su12218799

Hanzawa, S. (2013). Animeshon sangyou ni okeru bungyou taisei no henyou [Transformation of the division of labor in the animation industry]. *Cultural Economics*, 10(1), 20–33.

Heckhausen, J., & Schulz, R. (1995). A life-span theory of control. *Psychological Review*, 102(2), 284–304. DOI: 10.1037/0033-295X.102.2.284 PMID: 7740091

Hietala, H., & Päivärinta, T. (2021). Benefits Realisation in Post-Implementation Development of ERP Systems: A Case Study. *Procedia Computer Science*, 181, 419–426. DOI: 10.1016/j.procs.2021.01.186

HIPA. (2018). *Automotive Industry in Hungary*. Hungarian Investment Promotion Agency.

Holm, A., & Günzel-Jensen, F. (2017). Succeeding with freemium: Strategies for implementation. *The Journal of Business Strategy*, 38(2), 16–24. DOI: 10.1108/JBS-09-2016-0096

Holmes, T. J., & Schmitz, J. A.Jr. (1990). A theory of entrepreneurship and its application to the study of business transfers. *Journal of Political Economy*, 98(2), 265–294. DOI: 10.1086/261678

Ho, W., Zheng, T., Yildiz, H., & Talluri, S. (2015). Supply chain risk management: A literature review. *International Journal of Production Research*, 53(16), 5031–5069. DOI: 10.1080/00207543.2015.1030467

Huang, G., Tong, Y., Ye, F., & Li, J. (2020). Extending social responsibility to small and medium-sized suppliers in supply chains: A fuzzy-set qualitative comparative analysis. *Applied Soft Computing*, 88, 105899. DOI: 10.1016/j.asoc.2019.105899

Huang, K., Wang, K., Lee, P. K. C., & Yeung, A. C. L. (2023). The impact of industry 4.0 on supply chain capability and supply chain resilience: A dynamic resource-based view. *International Journal of Production Economics*, 262, 108913. Advance online publication. DOI: 10.1016/j.ijpe.2023.108913

Huarng, K.-H., & Yu, T. H.-K. (2017). Using qualitative approach to forecasting regime switches. *Quality & Quantity*, 51(5), 2035–2048. DOI: 10.1007/s11135-016-0338-x

Hua, W., & Ye, J. (2023). Seismic risk assessment of reticulated shell structures considering multiple uncertainties. *Thin-walled Structures*, 185, 110618. DOI: 10.1016/j.tws.2023.110618

Huyghebaert, N. (2004). *Comportamiento estratégico de los titulares en los mercados financieros y la salida de los arranques empresariales.*

Hwang, J., & Kim, Y. J. (2023). Challenges of Dark Stores and Urban Planning: A Case Study of B-Mart, *Seoul.* DOI:DOI: 10.20944/preprints202305.0084.v1

Hwarng, H. B., & Xie, N. (2008). Understanding supply chain dynamics: A chaos perspective. *European Journal of Operational Research*, 184(3), 1163–1178. DOI: 10.1016/j.ejor.2006.12.014

Ibsen, C. L., Sezer, L., & Doellgast, V. (2022). Coordination versus organization: Diverging logics of firm cooperation in Denmark and Sweden. *British Journal of Industrial Relations*, 61(3), 526–549. DOI: 10.1111/bjir.12704

Ichifuji, H. (2022). *(Gakui ronbun youyaku) Seizougyouteki kanten kara mita animeshon seisaku: Seisaku genba no bunka ni chuumoku shite* [(Thesis summary) Animation production from a manufacturing perspective: Focusing on the culture of the production site], Graduate School of Education, Hiroshima University. https://ir.lib.hiroshima-u.ac.jp/54233/files/46207

IIEG (2015). *Nota Técnica Jalisco registra 7.8 millones de pobladores al inicio de 2015. Instituto de Información Estadística y Geográfica Guadalajara.*

IIEG (2016). *Diagnóstico municipal Septiembre 2016. Instituto de Información Estadíastica y Geografía.*

IIEG (2016a). *Instituto de Información Estadística y Geográfica del Estado de Jalisco con base en INEGI, censos y conteos nacionales, 2010-2015.*

IIEG (2016b). *Instituto de Información Estadística y Geográfica del Estado de Jalisco; con información de INEGI, DENUE.*

INEGI. (2011). Censo General de Población y Vivienda 2010. Retrieved from http://www.inegi.org.mx

Information-technology Promotion Agency, Social Infrastructure Center (IPA-SIC) (Ed.). (2020). IT jinzai doukou chousa [IT Human Resources Trends Survey]. *IT Jinzai Hakusho 2020* [IT Human Resources White Paper 2020]. https://www.ipa.go.jp/archive/publish/hjuojm0000007e6n-att/000085255.pdf

Ivanov, D. & Sokolov, B. (2010). *Adaptive Supply Chain Management.* Springer.

Ivanov, D., Dolgui, A., & Sokolov, B. (2022). Cloud supply chain: Integrating Industry 4.0 and digital platforms in the „Supply Chain-as-a-Service. *Transportation Research Part E, Logistics and Transportation Review*, 160, 102676. Advance online publication. DOI: 10.1016/j.tre.2022.102676

Jackson, I., Ivanov, D., Dolgui, A., & Namdar, J. (2024). Generative artificial intelligence in supply chain and operations management: A capability-based framework for analysis and implementation. *International Journal of Production Research*, •••, 1–26. DOI: 10.1080/00207543.2024.2398583

Jagtap, S., Trollman, H., Trollman, F., Garcia-Garcia, G., Parra-López, C., Duong, L., Martindale, W., Munekata, P. E. S., Lorenzo, J. M., Hdaifeh, A., Hassoun, A., Salonitis, K. (2022): The Russia-Ukraine Conflict: Its Implications for the Global Food Chains, *Foods, 11(14)*, doi: 2098

James, R. (2001). *Stock, Douglas M. Lambert, "Strategic Logistics Management"* (4th ed.). McGraw Hill.

Jamil, M., Mustofa, R., Hossain, N. U. I., Rahman, S. M. A., & Chowdhury, S. (2024). A structural equation modeling framework for exploring the industry 5.0 and sustainable supply chain determinants. *Supply Chain Analytcs*, 6, 100060. Advance online publication. DOI: 10.1016/j.sca.2024.100060

Japan Student Services Organization (JASSO). (2023). "2022 (Reiwa 4) nendo gaikokujin ryuugakusei zaisekijoukyou chousa" nado kekka no kouhyou [Publication of the results of the 2022 (Reiwa 4) survey on the enrollment status of international students]. *Press release*. https://www.jasso.go.jp/about/press/__icsFiles/afieldfile/2023/03/01/jp2023030701.pdf

Jennings, B. M. (1990). Stress, locus of control, and psychological symptoms among head nurses. *Research in Nursing & Health*, 13(6), 393–401. DOI: 10.1002/nur.4770130607 PMID: 2270304

Jiao, J., Zhang, X., & Tang, Y. (2020). What factors determine the survival of green innovative enterprises in China? — A method based on fsQCA. *Technology in Society*, 62, 101314. DOI: 10.1016/j.techsoc.2020.101314 PMID: 32834233

Jing, S., Feng, Y., & Yan, J. (2021). Path selection of lean digitalization for traditional manufacturing industry under heterogeneous competitive position. *Computers & Industrial Engineering*, 161, 107631. DOI: 10.1016/j.cie.2021.107631

Joel, O. T., & Oguanobi, V. U. (2024). Geological survey techniques and carbon storage: optimizing renewable energy site selection and carbon sequestration. *Open Access Research Journal of Science and Technology, 11*(1), 039-051.

Joe, V. C. (1971). Review of the internal-external control construct as a personality variable. *Psychological Reports*, 28(2), 619–640. DOI: 10.2466/pr0.1971.28.2.619 PMID: 4932156

Johanson, J., Vahlne, JE. (1977): The Internationalization Process of the Firm – A Model of Knowledge Development and Increasing Foreign Market Commitments

Jovanovic, J., & Morschett, D. (2022). Under which conditions do manufacturing companies choose FDI for service provision in foreign markets? An investigation using fsQCA. *Industrial Marketing Management*, 104, 38–50. DOI: 10.1016/j.indmarman.2022.03.018

Judge, T. A., & Bono, J. E. (2001). Relationship of core self-evaluations traits—self-esteem, generalized self-efficacy, locus of control, and emotional stability—with job satisfaction and job performance: A meta-analysis. *The Journal of Applied Psychology*, 86(1), 80–92. DOI: 10.1037/0021-9010.86.1.80 PMID: 11302235

Kacz, K. (2019). Local Product Within Short Food Supply Chains in Hungary. *Annals PAAAE*, XXI(4), 172–181. DOI: 10.5604/01.3001.0013.5952

Kalpana, P. (2023). Factors influencing proactiveness in supply chain risk identification: A fuzzy-set qualitative comparative analysis. *International Journal of Disaster Risk Reduction*, 88, 103614.

Kee-hung Lai and T.C.E. Cheng, "Just-in-Time, Logistics", Gower: 47-108, 2009.

Kelman, H. C. (1958). Compliance, identification, and internalization three processes of attitude change. *The Journal of Conflict Resolution*, 2(1), 51–60. DOI: 10.1177/002200275800200106

Kendall, R., & Tatiana, K. (2003). The Use of the Multinational Corporation as a Research Context. *Journal of Management*, 29(6), 883–902. DOI: 10.1016/S0149-2063(03)00083-7

Kesavapanikkar, P., Amit, R., & Ramu, P. (2022). Product as a service (paas) for traditional product companies: An automotive lease practice evaluation. *Journal of Indian Business Research*, 15(1), 40–54. DOI: 10.1108/JIBR-04-2022-0107

Keskin, M. H. (2018a). *Tedarik Zinciri Yönetimi* (Vol. II). Baskı, Nobel Yayın Dağıtım.

Keskin, M. H. (2018b). *Lojistik El Kitabı* (Vol. III). Baskı, Nobel Yayın Dağıtım.

Keskin, M. H. (2020). *Warehousing, Explained for Making Money, Principles, Policies and Practices*. Sharp and Sharp Publishing.

Ketchen, D. J.Jr, & Craighead, C. W. (2020). Research at the intersection of entrepreneurship, supply chain management, and strategic management: Opportunities highlighted by COVID-19. *Journal of Management*, 46(8), 1330–1341. DOI: 10.1177/0149206320945028

Khan, M. I., Haq, M. A. U., Khan, M. R., Ghouri, A. M., & Farooqui, R. (2024b). Industry 4.0 or Pharma 4.0?: Assessing Suitability, Benefits, Challenges, and Opportunities for Healthcare Supply Chains. *Convergence of Industry 4.0 and Supply Chain Sustainability*, (pp. 319-341). IGI Global.

Khan, M. R., Masood, F., Gul, I., & Khan, M. R. (2024a). Blockchain Technology in Supply Chain Management: Opportunities and Challenges. *Convergence of Industry 4.0 and Supply Chain Sustainability*, (pp. 275-295). IGI Global.

Khan, S., Haleem, A., & Khan, M. (2020). Enablers to implement circular initiatives in the supply chain: A grey dematel method. *Global Business Review*, 25(1), 68–84. DOI: 10.1177/0972150920929484

Kiechel, W.III. (1988). Corporate Strategy for the 1990s. *Fortune*, 117(5), 34–42.

Kildow, B. A. (2011). *A Supply Chain Management Guide to Business Continuity*. AMACOM Division of American Management Association International. https://www.jstor.org/stable/j.ctt1d2qzhb

Kim, E., Kim, Y., & Park, J. (2022). The necessity of introducing autonomous trucks in logistics 4.0. *Sustainability (Basel)*, 14(7), 3978. DOI: 10.3390/su14073978

Kopplin, C. S., & Rösch, S. F. (2021). Equifinal causes of sustainable clothing purchase behavior: An fsQCA analysis among generation Y. *Journal of Retailing and Consumer Services*, 63, 102692. DOI: 10.1016/j.jretconser.2021.102692

Kormanik, M. B., & Rocco, T. S. (2009). Internal versus external control of reinforcement: Q review of the locus of control construct. *Human Resource Development Review*, 8(4), 463–483. DOI: 10.1177/1534484309342080

Kosmol, T., Reimann, F., & Kaufmann, L. (2018). Co-alignment of supplier quality management practices and cognitive maps – A neo-configurational perspective. *Journal of Purchasing and Supply Management*, 24(1), 1–20. DOI: 10.1016/j.pursup.2017.11.002

Krause, N., & Stryker, S. (1984). Stress and well-being: The buffering role of locus of control beliefs. *Social Science & Medicine*, 18(9), 783–790. Advance online publication. DOI: 10.1016/0277-9536(84)90105-9 PMID: 6729538

Krueger, N. F.Jr, Reilly, M. D., & Carsrud, A. L. (2000). Competing models of entrepreneurial intentions. *Journal of Business Venturing*, 15(5-6), 411–432. DOI: 10.1016/S0883-9026(98)00033-0

Kuglin, F.A. (1998). *Customer-Centered Supply Chain Management (A link-by-link guide)*. American Management Assosication. 226-247.

Kumar, S., Sahoo, S., Lim, W. M., Kraus, S., & Bamel, U. (2022). Fuzzy-set qualitative comparative analysis (fsQCA) in business and management research: A contemporary overview. *Technological Forecasting and Social Change*, 178, 121599. DOI: 10.1016/j.techfore.2022.121599

Kumar, S., Tiwari, P., & Zymbler, M. (2019). Internet of Things is a Revolutionary Approach for Future Technology Enhancement: A Review. *Journal of Big Data*, 6(111), 111. Advance online publication. DOI: 10.1186/s40537-019-0268-2

Kumbure, M. M., Tarkiainen, A., Luukka, P., Stoklasa, J., & Jantunen, A. (2020). Relation between managerial cognition and industrial performance: An assessment with strategic cognitive maps using fuzzy-set qualitative comparative analysis. *Journal of Business Research*, 114, 160–172. DOI: 10.1016/j.jbusres.2020.04.001

Larson, P. D., & Rogers, D. S. (1998). Supply Chain Management: Definition, Growth, and Approaches. *Journal of Marketing Theory and Practice*, 6(4), 1–5. DOI: 10.1080/10696679.1998.11501805

Lazarus, R. S. (1990). Theory-based stress measurement. *Psychological Inquiry*, 1(1), 3–13. DOI: 10.1207/s15327965pli0101_1

Lee, C. K. H. (2022). How guest-host interactions affect consumer experiences in the sharing economy: New evidence from a configurational analysis based on consumer reviews. *Decision Support Systems*, 152, 113634. DOI: 10.1016/j.dss.2021.113634

Lee, S. M., & Peterson, S. J. (2000). Culture, entrepreneurial orientation, and global competitiveness. *Journal of World Business*, 35(4), 401–416. DOI: 10.1016/S1090-9516(00)00045-6

Lefcout, R. S. (2014). *Locus of Control: Current trends in theory and research.* Psychology Press. DOI: 10.4324/9781315798813

Leng, J., Sha, W., Wang, B., Zheng, P., Zhuang, C., Liu, Q., Wuest, T., Mourtzis, D., & Wang, L. (2022). Industry 5.0: Prospect and retrospect. *Journal of Manufacturing Systems*, 65, 279–295. DOI: 10.1016/j.jmsy.2022.09.017

Lestari, E. (2023). Tax policy reconstruction toward implementation of circular economy in indonesia.. DOI: 10.3390/proceedings2022083068

Levenson, H. (1981). Differentiating among internality, powerful others, and chance. In Lefcourt, H. M. (Ed.), Research with the locus of control construct. vol. I: *Assessment methods* (pp. 15-63). New York: Academic Press. DOI: 10.1016/B978-0-12-443201-7.50006-3

Liang, M., Yang, L., Li, K., & Zhai, H. (2024). Improved collaborative filtering for cross-store demand forecasting. *Computers & Industrial Engineering*, 190, 110067. DOI: 10.1016/j.cie.2024.110067

Li, C., Li, Q., & Ge, R. (2023). Comparison of performance enhancement in a shell and tube based latent heat thermal energy storage device containing different structured fins. *Renewable Energy*, 206, 994–1006. DOI: 10.1016/j.renene.2023.02.087

Li, H., Chai, J., Qian, Z.-F., & Chen, H. (2022). Cooperation strategies when leading firms compete with small and medium-sized enterprises in a potentially competitive market. *Journal of Management Science and Engineering*, 7(3), 489–509. DOI: 10.1016/j.jmse.2022.02.003

Li, J., Wang, H., Qu, Q., Zhu, J., & Wang, J. (2024). Actors' interactions in the evolution of service supply networks of manufacturing firms. *International Journal of Production Economics*, 272, 109224. Advance online publication. DOI: 10.1016/j.ijpe.2024.109224

Liliani, T., Tjahjono, B., & Cao, D. (2020). Advancing bioplastic packaging products through co-innovation: A conceptual framework for supplier-customer collaboration. *Journal of Cleaner Production*, 252, 119861. DOI: 10.1016/j.jclepro.2019.119861

Lim, W. M., Rasul, T., Kumar, S., & Ala, M. (2022). Past, present, and future of customer engagement. *Journal of Business Research*, 140, 439–458. DOI: 10.1016/j.jbusres.2021.11.014

Lin, C., Wang, X., & Yang, Y. (2023). Sustainable apparel consumption: Personal norms, csr expectations, and hedonic vs. utilitarian shopping value. *Sustainability (Basel)*, 15(11), 9116. DOI: 10.3390/su15119116

Lin, Z., Manser, M. E., & Picot, G. (1998), The Role of Self-Employment in Job Creation in Canada and the U.S., *OECD-CERF-CILN International Conference on Self-Employment*, Burlington, Ontario, Canada.

Lin, Z., Manser, M. E., & Picot, G. (1998), The Role of Self-Employment in Job Creation In Canada and the U.S., *OECD-CERF-CILN International Conference on Self-Employment*, Burlington, Ontario, Canada.

Liu, S., Han, W., Zhang, Z., & Chan, F. T. S. (2024). An analysis of performance, pricing, and coordination in a supply chain with cloud services: The impact of data security. *Computers & Industrial Engineering*, 192, 110237. Advance online publication. DOI: 10.1016/j.cie.2024.110237

Liu, W., Bai, E., Liu, L., & Wei, W. (2017). A Framework of Sustainable Service Supply Chain Management: A Literature Review and Research Agenda. *Sustainability (Basel)*, 9(3), 421. DOI: 10.3390/su9030421

Li, Y., Wei, F., Ren, S., & Di, Y. (2015). Locus of control, psychological empowerment and intrinsic motivation relation to performance. *Journal of Managerial Psychology*, 20(4), 422–438. DOI: 10.1108/JMP-10-2012-0318

Llopis-Albert, C., Palacios-Marqués, D., & Simón-Moya, V. (2021). Fuzzy set qualitative comparative analysis (fsQCA) applied to the adaptation of the automobile industry to meet the emission standards of climate change policies via the deployment of electric vehicles (EVs). *Technological Forecasting and Social Change*, 169, 120843. DOI: 10.1016/j.techfore.2021.120843

Llopis-Albert, C., Rubio, F., & Valero, F. (2021). Impact of digital transformation on the automotive industry. *Technological Forecasting and Social Change*, 162, 120343. DOI: 10.1016/j.techfore.2020.120343 PMID: 33052150

Loh, X.-M., Lee, V.-H., Leong, L.-Y., Aw, E. C.-X., Cham, T.-H., Tang, Y.-C., & Hew, J.-J. (2023). Understanding consumers' resistance to pay with cryptocurrency in the sharing economy: A hybrid SEM-fsQCA approach. *Journal of Business Research*, 159, 113726. DOI: 10.1016/j.jbusres.2023.113726

López-Cabarcos, M. Á., Piñeiro-Chousa, J., Quiñoá-Piñeiro, L., & López-Pérez, M. L. (2024). Water and waste management strategies as drivers of the financial performance of food companies. *Technological Forecasting and Social Change*, 200, 123138. DOI: 10.1016/j.techfore.2023.123138

Lőrincz, N. (2017). Main Characteristics of Nowadays' Global Value Chains and their Relevance to the Hungarian Automotive Manufacturing Industry, *Vezetéstudomány – Budapest. Management Review*, 48(5), 35–48.

Lou, Z., Ye, A., Mao, J., & Zhang, C. (2022). Supplier selection, control mechanisms, and firm innovation: Configuration analysis based on fsQCA. *Journal of Business Research*, 139, 81–89. DOI: 10.1016/j.jbusres.2021.09.045

Luo, Q. (2024, May). Financial Characteristics and Risk Strategy Analysis of Oil Giant Companies under The Background of Global Economic Recession. In *9th International Conference on Financial Innovation and Economic Development (ICFIED 2024)* (pp. 442-449). Atlantis Press. DOI: 10.2991/978-94-6463-408-2_50

Lyons, A. C., Mondragon, A. E. C., Piller, F., Poler, R. (2012). *Customer-Driven Supply Chains from Glass Pipelines to Open Innovation Networks*. Springer, 113-130.

Magistretti, S., Dell'Era, C., & Verganti, R. (2020). Searching for the Right Application: A Technology Development Review and Research Agenda. *Technological Forecasting and Social Change*, 151(119879), 119879. Advance online publication. DOI: 10.1016/j.techfore.2019.119879

Malik, A. K., Singh, A., Jit, S., & Garg, C. P. (2010). Supply Chain Management: An Overview. *International Journal of Logistics and Supply Chain Management*, 2(2), 97–101.

Manichander, T. (2014). Locus of Control and Performance: Widening Applications. *Indian Journal of Research*, 3(2).

Manzhynski, S., & Biedenbach, G. (2023). The knotted paradox of coopetition for sustainability: Investigating the interplay between core paradox properties. *Industrial Marketing Management*, 110, 31–45. DOI: 10.1016/j.indmarman.2023.02.013

Markman, G. D., Baron, R. A., & Balkin, D. B. (2005). Are perseverance and self-efficacy costless? Assessing entrepreneurs' regretful thinking. *Journal of Organizational Behavior*, 26(1), 1–19. DOI: 10.1002/job.305

Marks, S. J., Kumpel, E., Guo, J., Bartram, J., & Davis, J. (2018). Pathways to sustainability: A fuzzy-set qualitative comparative analysis of rural water supply programs. *Journal of Cleaner Production*, 205, 789–798. DOI: 10.1016/j.jclepro.2018.09.029

Martínez, I. (2016). *Zapopan busca ser Ciudad Amiga de la Infancia*. Retrieved from http://www.informador.com.mx/jalisco/2016/693500/6/zapopan-busca-ser-ciudad-amiga-de-la-infancia.htm

Martin, R., Thomas, G., Charles, K., Epitropaki, O., & McNamara, R. (2005). The role of leader-memberexchanges in mediating the relationship between locus of control and work reactions. *Journal of Occupational and Organizational Psychology*, 78(1), 141–147. DOI: 10.1348/096317904X23763

Marzi, G., Marrucci, A., Vianelli, D., & Ciappei, C. (2023). B2B digital platform adoption by SMEs and large firms: Pathways and pitfalls. *Industrial Marketing Management*, 114, 80–93. DOI: 10.1016/j.indmarman.2023.08.002

Masoomi, B., Sahebi, I. G., Ghobakhloo, M., & Mosayebi, A. (2023). Do industry 5.0 advantages address the sustainable development challenges of the renewable energy supply chain? *Sustainable Production and Consumption*, 43, 94–112. DOI: 10.1016/j.spc.2023.10.018

Mazumder, S., & Garg, S. (2021). Decoding digital transformational outsourcing: The role of service providers' capabilities. *International Journal of Information Management*, 58, 102295. DOI: 10.1016/j.ijinfomgt.2020.102295

McCarthy, A., & Garavan, T. (2006). Post-feedback development perceptions: Applying the theory of planned behavior. *Human Resource Development Quarterly*, 17(3), 245–267. DOI: 10.1002/hrdq.1173

McDougall, P. (2000). *International entrepreneurship*. AMJ.

McKinsey. (2022). Coronavirus' business impact: Evolving perspective | McKinsey

Mederake, L. (2022). Without a debate on sufficiency, a circular plastics economy will remain an illusion. *Circular Economy and Sustainability*, 3(3), 1425–1439. DOI: 10.1007/s43615-022-00240-3 PMID: 36531658

Medina, C. (2016). The role of innovation in green areas for the revitalization of German and Mexican Cities.

Mei, H., Shao, J., & Wang, Q. (2012). Model based monitoring and controlling for platform-as-a-service (paas). *International Journal of Cloud Applications and Computing*, 2(1), 1–15. DOI: 10.4018/ijcac.2012010101

Mena, C., Karatzas, A., & Hansen, C. (2022). International trade resilience and the Covid-19 pandemic. *Journal of Business Research*, 138, 77–91. DOI: 10.1016/j.jbusres.2021.08.064 PMID: 34538982

Meneses, R., Quelhas Brito, P., & Coelho Gomes, P. (2016). From offshore-provider to brand creator: fsQCA of footwear industry. *Journal of Business Research*, 69(11), 5540–5546. DOI: 10.1016/j.jbusres.2016.04.168

Mentzer, J. T., DeWitt, W., Keebler, J. S., Min, S., Nix, N. W., Smith, C. D., & Zacharia, Z. G. (2001). Defining Supply Chain Management. *Journal of Business Logistics*, 22(2), 1–25. DOI: 10.1002/j.2158-1592.2001.tb00001.x

Micheli, P., Johnson, M., & Godsell, J. (2021). Editorial How the Covid-19 pandemic has affected, and will affect, operations and supply chain management research and practice. International Journal of Operations &amp. *International Journal of Operations & Production Management*, 41(6), 773–780. DOI: 10.1108/IJOPM-06-2021-902

Michelon, P. (2016, December 18). What are Cognitive Abilities and Skills, and how to boost them? Retrieved from https://sharpbrains.com/blog/2006/12/18/what-are-cognitive-abilities/

Midttun, A., Khanieva, M., Lia, M., & Wenner, E. (2022). The greening of the European petroleum industry. *Energy Policy*, 167, 112964. DOI: 10.1016/j.enpol.2022.112964

Milios, L. (2021). Towards a circular economy taxation framework: Expectations and challenges of implementation. *Circular Economy and Sustainability*, 1(2), 477–498. DOI: 10.1007/s43615-020-00002-z

Minerbo, C., Kleinaltenkamp, M., & Brito, L. A. L. (2021). Unpacking value creation and capture in B2B relationships. *Industrial Marketing Management*, 92, 163–177. DOI: 10.1016/j.indmarman.2020.11.011

Ministry of Economy, Trade and Industry (METI). (2019). IT jinzai jyukyuu ni kansuru chousa (gaiyo) [Survey on IT human resources supply and demand (summary)]. *Dejitaru jinzai no ikusei* [Developing Digital Human Resources]. https://www.meti.go.jp/policy/it_policy/jinzai/gaiyou.pdf

Ministry of Economy, Trade and Industry (METI). (2024). Jouhou saabisu gyoukai [Information services industry]. *Tokutei saabisu sangyou doutai toukei chousa* [Statistical Survey of Specific Service Industries]. https://www.meti.go.jp/statistics/tyo/tokusabido/result-2.html

Ministry of Foreign Affairs (MOFA). (2024). Betonamu kiso deeta [Basic data on Vietnam]. *Socialist Republic of Viet Nam*. https://www.mofa.go.jp/mofaj/area/vietnam/data.html

Ministry of Internal Affairs and Communications (MIC). (2021). (3) ICT jinzai no fusoku, henzai [(3) Shortage and uneven distribution of ICT human resources]. *Jouhou tsuushin hakusho 2021* [Information and Communications White Paper 2021]. https://www.soumu.go.jp/johotsusintokei/whitepaper/ja/r03/html/nd104300.html

Mitchell, T. R., Smyser, C. M., & Weed, S. E. (1975). Locus of Control: Supervision and work satisfaction. *Academy of Management Journal*, 18(3), 623–631. DOI: 10.2307/255692

Mohammadi, S. (2021). The relationship between individual entrepreneurial orientation (IEO) and entrepreneurial bricolage: Exploring passion and perseverance. *Asia Pacific J. Innov. Entrep.*, 15(1), 75–86. DOI: 10.1108/APJIE-01-2021-0002

Moraga, C. (2005). Introduction to Fuzzy Logic. *Facta universitatis - series. Electronics and Energetics*, 18(2), 319–328. DOI: 10.2298/FUEE0502319M

Muhajir, A. (2024). Sustainable marketing model: Market research, marketing capability and entrepreneurial orientation in indonesia. *International Journal of Business Law and Education*, 5(1), 1007–1020. DOI: 10.56442/ijble.v5i1.497

Mühlbacher, H., & Böbel, I. (2019). From zero-sum to win-win—Organisational conditions for successful shared value strategy implementation. *European Management Journal*, 37(3), 313–324. DOI: 10.1016/j.emj.2018.10.007

Mumford, E. (2003). Quality and Environmental Issues in Shell International. In *Redesigning Human Systems* (pp. 210–232). IGI Global. DOI: 10.4018/978-1-59140-118-6.ch012

Muñoz, P., & Cohen, B. (2017). Mapping out the sharing economy: A configurational approach to sharing business modeling. *Technological Forecasting and Social Change*, 125, 21–37. DOI: 10.1016/j.techfore.2017.03.035

Murphy, P. R., Jr., & Wood, D. F. (2004). "Contemporary Logistics", Eight Edition, Pearson Education International, Prentice Hall: 35-49.

Nagy-Bota, S., & Moldovan, L. (2022). Key Differences and Common Aspects of Logistics and Supply Chain Management. *Acta Marisiensis Seria Technologica*, 19(1), 42–46. DOI: 10.2478/amset-2022-0008

Naims, H., & Eppinger, E. (2022). Transformation strategies connected to carbon capture and utilization: A cross-sectoral configurational study. *Journal of Cleaner Production*, 351, 131391. DOI: 10.1016/j.jclepro.2022.131391

National Geographic. (2024). Encyclopedic Entry: The Silk Road. https://education.nationalgeographic.org/resource/silk-road/

Natsuda, K., Sass, M., & Csonka, L. (2022). Developing a local supply chain network: The case of Magyar Suzuku in Hungary. *Acta Oeconomica*, 72(4), 531–552. DOI: 10.1556/032.2022.00034

Ng, T. W. H., Sorensen, K. L., & Eby, L. (2006). Locus of control at work: A meta-analysis. *Journal of Organizational Behavior*, 27(8), 1057–1087. DOI: 10.1002/job.416

Nikookar, E., Gligor, D., & Russo, I. (2024). Supply chain resilience: When the recipe is more important than the ingredients for managing supply chain disruptions. *International Journal of Production Economics*, 272, 109236. Advance online publication. DOI: 10.1016/j.ijpe.2024.109236

Nishijima, D., & Oguchi, M. (2022). Measuring product lifetime extension potential by increasing the expected product lifetime: Methodology and case study. *Business Strategy and the Environment*, 32(4), 1218–1231. DOI: 10.1002/bse.3183

Nwankpa, J. K. (2015). ERP system usage and benefit: A model of antecedents and outcomes. *Computers in Human Behavior*, 45, 335–344. DOI: 10.1016/j.chb.2014.12.019

Opstal, W., & Borms, L. (2022). Startups and circular economy strategies: profile differences, barriers and enablers. SSRN Electronic Journal. DOI: 10.2139/ssrn.4244706

Ortega-Anderezand, D., & Lai, E. (2017, February). The Main Factors Influencing Entrepreneurial Activities and Intentions within a Country—A Case Study of Spain. *International Journal of Innovation, Management and Technology*, 8(1), •••.

Ostermann, C., Nascimento, L., & Zen, A. (2021). Business model innovation for circular economy in fashion industry: A startups' perspective. *Frontiers in Sustainability*, 2, 766614. Advance online publication. DOI: 10.3389/frsus.2021.766614

Özdemir, C., Sandikkaya, M., & Yaslan, Y. (2018). Classifying malicious thread behavior in paas web services.. DOI: 10.5220/0006688204180425

Padmanabhan, S. (2021). The impact of locus of control on workplace stress and job satisfaction: A pilot study on private-sector employees. *Current Research in Behavioral Sciences*, 2, 100026. DOI: 10.1016/j.crbeha.2021.100026

Paiement, P. (2023). Reimagining the energy corporation: Milieudefensie and others v Royal Dutch Shell Plc. In *Netherlands Yearbook of International Law 2021: A Greener International Law—International Legal Responses to the Global Environmental Crisis* (pp. 281–299). TMC Asser Press. DOI: 10.1007/978-94-6265-587-4_11

Pásztor, Sz. (2022): A külpiacra lépés kezdetei néhány hazai vállalat szemszögéből (The beginnings of foreign market entry from the perspective of some domestic companies), Oecaonomus Gazdaságkutató Alapítvány, online: https://www.oeconomus.hu/irasok/a-kulpiacra-lepes-kezdetei-nehany-hazai-vallalat-szemszogebol/ (download: 03. 01. 2024.)

Patel, P., Bhanugopan, R., Sinha, P., Prikshat, V., & Boyle, B. (2024). Home country and firm-specific advantage influences on HRM replication versus adaptation in EMNEs operating in advanced economies: A qualitative comparative analysis. *Journal of Business Research*, 170, 114335. DOI: 10.1016/j.jbusres.2023.114335

Payne, A., Nay, Z., & Maguire, R. (2021). Regulating a circular economy for textiles in australia.. DOI: 10.31880/10344/10245

Pellegrino, R., & Gaudenzi, B. (2023). Impacts and Supply Chain Resilience Strategies to Cope with COVID-19 Pandemic: A Literature Review. *Springer Series in Supply Chain Management*, 21, 5–18. DOI: 10.1007/978-3-031-16489-7_1

Peng, M. (2012). *Global Strategy*. Thomsom South-Western.

Peters, M. A. (2021). The ancient Silk Road and the birth of merchant capitalism. *Educational Philosophy and Theory*, 53(10), 955–961. DOI: 10.1080/00131857.2019.1691481

Petit, P. (1999). Structural Forms and Growth Regimes of the Post-Fordist Era. *Review of Social Economy*, 57(2), 220–243. DOI: 10.1080/00346769900000037

Pfeiffer, F., & Reize, F. (2000). Business Start-ups by the Unemployed - an Econometric Analysis Based on Firm Data. *Labour Economics*, 7(5), 629–663. DOI: 10.1016/S0927-5371(00)00016-6

Piekkari, R., Welch, C., & Westney, D. E. (2022). The Challenge of the Multinational Corporation to Organization Theory: Contextualizing Theory. *Organization Theory*, 3(2). Advance online publication. DOI: 10.1177/26317877221098766

Piricz, N. (2017): The Role and Impact of Fairness on Cooperation in Hungarian Metal and Machinery Supply Chains, *Management, Enterprise and Benchmarking in the 21st Century, pp. 312-322.*

Porter, M. (1980). *Competitive Strategy*. Free Press.

Porter, M. E. (1991). *Strategy: Seeking and Securing Competitive Advantage*. HBR Book Series.

Prentice, C. (2019). Testing complexity theory in service research. *Journal of Services Marketing*, 34(2), 149–162. DOI: 10.1108/JSM-09-2019-0353

Prosman, E. J., & Cagliano, R. (2022). A contingency perspective on manufacturing configurations for the circular economy: Insights from successful start-ups. *International Journal of Production Economics*, 249, 108519. DOI: 10.1016/j.ijpe.2022.108519

Pryer, M. W., & Distefano, M. K.Jr. (1971). Perceptions of leadership behaviour, job satisfaction, and internal-external control across three nursing levels. *Nursing Research*, 20(6), 534–537. DOI: 10.1097/00006199-197111000-00014 PMID: 5210833

Putnam, D., Pharr, S. J., & Dalton, R. J. (2000). Introduction: What's troubling the trilateral democracies. In Pharr, S. J., & Putnam, R. D. (Eds.), *Disaffected democracies* (pp. 3–27). Princeton University Press. DOI: 10.1515/9780691186849-005

Putnam, R. (1993). *Making democracy work*. Princeton University Press.

Putnam, R. (2000). *Bowling alone*. Simon & Schuster.

Putnam, R. (Ed.). (2002). *Democracies in flux*. Oxford University Press. DOI: 10.1093/0195150899.001.0001

Qi, R., Ma, G., Liu, C., Zhang, Q., & Wang, Q. (2024). Enterprise digital transformation and supply chain resilience. *Finance Research Letters*, 66, 105564. Advance online publication. DOI: 10.1016/j.frl.2024.105564

Quayson, M., Bai, C., Mahmoudi, A., Hu, W., Chen, W., & Omoruyi, O. (2023). Designing a decision support tool for integrating ESG into the natural resource extraction industry for sustainable development using the ordinal priority approach. *Resources Policy*, 85, 103988. DOI: 10.1016/j.resourpol.2023.103988

Rachinger, M., Rauter, R., Müller, C., Vorraber, W., & Eva, S. (2019). Digitalization and its influence on business model innovation. *Journal of Manufacturing Technology Management*, 30(8), 1143–1160. DOI: 10.1108/JMTM-01-2018-0020

Ragin, C., & Davey, S. (2014). fsQCA (Version 2.5) [Computer software]. University of California.

Rahman, M., Saha, S., & Hoque, M. (2024). Unveiling the link between environmental management accounting, energy efficiency, and accountability in state-owned enterprises: An integrated analysis using PLS-SEM and fsQCA. *Environmental Challenges*, 14, 100832. DOI: 10.1016/j.envc.2023.100832

Raj, K. and Aithal, P. (2020). A new concept of circular model of management for achieving sustainable success and growth. International Journal of Management Technology and Social Sciences, 1-17. https://doi.org/DOI: 10.47992/IJMTS.2581.6012.0079

Raj, A., Mukherjee, A. A., de Sousa Jabbour, A. B. L., & Srivastava, S. K. (2022). Supply chain management during and post-COVID-19 pandemic: Mitigation strategies and practical lessons learned. *Journal of Business Research*, 142, 1125–1139. DOI: 10.1016/j.jbusres.2022.01.037 PMID: 35079190

Rakesh, C. (2023). Towards a circular economy: challenges and opportunities for recycling and re-manufacturing of materials and components. E3s Web of Conferences, 430, 01129. DOI: 10.1051/e3sconf/202343001129

Redko, K. (2024). Circular economy and ai empowerment in social entrepreneurship: A path to sustainability. *International Science Journal of Management Economics & Finance*, 3(3), 27–35. DOI: 10.46299/j.isjmef.20240303.04

Reyes, R., Castellanos, T., & Curiel, F. (2009). *La calidad del aire en Zapopan*. Editorial Páramo.

Reynolds, C. H. (1976). Correlational findings, educational implications, and criticisms of locus of control research. *Journal of Black Studies*, 6(3), 221–256. DOI: 10.1177/002193477600600301

Roberts, J. A., Lapidus, R. S., & Chonko, L. B. (1997). Salespeople and Stress : The Moderating Role of Locus of Control on Work Stressors and Felt Stress. *Journal of Marketing Theory and Practice*, 5(3), 93–108. DOI: 10.1080/10696679.1997.11501773

Roberts, K. (2011). *The Origins of Business, Money, and Markets*. Columbia University Press., DOI: 10.7312/robe15326

Rocha, A. (2016). *El Espejo: Parque Agroecológico Zapopan, zona de cultivo en la metrópoli.* Retrieved from http://www.cronicajalisco.com/notas/2016/60254.html

Roddenberry, A., & Renk, K. (2010). Locus of control and self-efficacy: Potential mediators of stress, illness, and utilization of health services in college students. *Child Psychiatry and Human Development*, 41(4), 353–370. DOI: 10.1007/s10578-010-0173-6 PMID: 20204497

Rojas. H (2012) *Una década de participación del Producto Interno Bruto de Puerto Vallarta al estado de Jalisco, 2000-2009*. Investigación y Ciencia de la Universidad Autónoma de Aguascalientes, *vol* (54), pp. 30-39.

Rok, B., & Kulik, M. (2020). Circular start-up development: The case of positive impact entrepreneurship in poland. *Corporate Governance (Bradford)*, 21(2), 339–358. DOI: 10.1108/CG-01-2020-0043

Romero-Castro, N., Piñeiro-Chousa, J., & Pérez-Pico, A. (2021). Dealing with heterogeneity and complexity in the analysis of the willingness to invest in community renewable energy in rural areas. *Technological Forecasting and Social Change*, 173, 121165. DOI: 10.1016/j.techfore.2021.121165

Rothbaum, F., Weisz, J. R., & Snyder, S. S. (1982). Changing the world and changing the self: A two-process model of perceived control. *Journal of Personality and Social Psychology*, 42(1), 5–37. DOI: 10.1037/0022-3514.42.1.5 PMID: 7108745

Rotter, J. B. (1954). *Social learning and clinical psychology*. Prentice Hall. DOI: 10.1037/10788-000

Rotter, J. B. (1975). Some problems and misconceptions related to the construct of internal versus external control of reinforcement. *Journal of Consulting and Clinical Psychology*, 43(1), 56–67. DOI: 10.1037/h0076301

Rotter, J. B. (2021). Internal versus external control of reinforcement: A case history of a variable. *The American Psychologist*, 45(4), 489–493. DOI: 10.1037/0003-066X.45.4.489

Runyon, K. E. (1973). Some interactions between personality variables and management styles. *The Journal of Applied Psychology*, 57(3), 288–294. DOI: 10.1037/h0034723

Russo, I., Confente, I., Gligor, D. M., & Autry, C. W. (2016). To be or not to be (loyal): Is there a recipe for customer loyalty in the B2B context? *Journal of Business Research*, 69(2), 888–896. DOI: 10.1016/j.jbusres.2015.07.002

Saha, S., Jana, B., & Poray, J. (2019). A Study on Blockchain Technology, *SSRN*, DOI: 10.2139/ssrn.3477373

Saisho, T. (2014). *Chuugoku to betonamu no inobeeshon shisutemu [Dai 2 han]* [Innovation systems in China and Vietnam [2nd edition]]. Hakuto-Shobo.

Saisho, T. (2024a), A study on the actual situation of global supply chains in ASEAN: Focusing on the case of Japanese auto parts Company A. *Kokushikan University bulletin of the Research Institute of Business*, March 2024, 1-21.

Saisho, T. (2024b). Shikisha ni kiku: Shikisha ga shimesu sofuto kaihatsu no "guroobaru sapurai cheen" gijutsu busoku to guroobaruka, futatsu no keieikadai wo kaiketsu suru hinto towa [Ask the experts: Experts' hints for solving two management issues, shortage of engineers in the global supply chain for software development and globalization]. *Global Vision 2024 Handout*. FPT Japan Holdings.

Saisho, T. (2010). Chuugoku no dejitaru kontentsu bunya ni okeru sangyou kurasutaa senryaku [Industrial cluster strategy in China's digital content sector]. *Kanto Gakuin University Research Institute for Economics and Business Management Annual Report*, 32, 162–178.

Saisho, T. (2024c). Ajia ni okeru guroobaru sapurai cheen ni kansuru kousatu [A study on global supply chains in Asia: A case study of global supply chains in the IT service Sector]. *Globalization Research*, 21(1), 61–80.

Saisho, T. (2024d). Waga kuni no jouhouka shakai no shinten ni okeru jouhourenkei to jouhoutougou ni kansuru kousatsu [A study on the progress of Japan's information society and information collaboration: Focusing on the current status and possibilities of information collaboration]. *Kokushikan Business Review*, 14(1), 1–22.

Sambasivan, M., Siew-Phaik, L., Mohamed, Z. A., & Leong, Y. C. (2013). Factors influencing strategic alliance outcomes in a manufacturing supply chain: Role of alliance motives, interdependence, asset specificity and relational capital. *International Journal of Production Economics*, 141(1), 339–351. DOI: 10.1016/j.ijpe.2012.08.016

Sammut-Bonnici, T., & McGee, J. (2002). Network Strategies for the New Economy. *European Business Journal*, 14(4), 174–185.

Samsung. (2024). Shaping the Future Together: We Aim for a Sustainable Supply Chain, https://www.samsung.com/us/aboutsamsung/sustainability/environment/sustainable-supply-chain/

Samuelson, R. J. (2012). Revisiting the Great Depression. *The Wilson Quarterly*, 36(1), 36–43. https://www.jstor.org/stable/41484425

Sandra, M., Narayanamoorthy, S., Ferrara, M., Innab, N., Ahmadian, A., & Kang, D. (2024). A novel decision support system for the appraisal and selection of green warehouses. *Socio-Economic Planning Sciences*, 91, 101782. DOI: 10.1016/j.seps.2023.101782

Sandro, N., Petar, Š., Diego, L. I. G. A., & Luigi, P. (2020). Internet of Things (IoT): Opportunities, Issues and Challenges towards a Smart and Sustainable Future. *Journal of Cleaner Production*, 274(22877), 122877. Advance online publication. DOI: 10.1016/j.jclepro.2020.122877 PMID: 32834567

Sarker, M. N. I., Hossin, M., Yin, X., & Sarkar, M. (2018). One Belt One Road Initiative of China: Implication for Future of Global Development. *Modern Economy*, 09(4), 623–638. DOI: 10.4236/me.2018.94040

Scarpi, D., Raggiotto, F., & Visentin, M. (2022). Untying the knot: Drivers of the intention to downgrade the relationship in B2B service contexts. *Industrial Marketing Management*, 105, 200–210. DOI: 10.1016/j.indmarman.2022.06.005

Schafer, W. E., & McKenna, J. F. (1991). Perceived energy and stress resistance: A study of city managers. *Journal of Social Behavior and Personality*, •••, 271–282.

Schwartz, H., Solakivi, T., & Gustafsson, M. (2022). Is there business potential for sustainable shipping? price premiums needed to cover decarbonized transportation. *Sustainability (Basel)*, 14(10), 5888. DOI: 10.3390/su14105888

Sehnem, S., Campos, L., Julkovski, D., & Cazella, C. (2019). Circular business models: Level of maturity. *Management Decision*, 57(4), 1043–1066. DOI: 10.1108/MD-07-2018-0844

Selimović, I. (2022). Advantages and Disadvantages of Principles of Scientific Management and Lean Organisation. *Izzivi prihodnost*, 7. DOI: DOI: 10.37886/ip.2022.001

Serin, N. B., Serin, O., & Şahin, F. S. (2010). Factors affecting the locus of control of the university students. *Procedia: Social and Behavioral Sciences*, 2(2), 449–452. DOI: 10.1016/j.sbspro.2010.03.041

Shan, C., Sun, J., Jia, X., Wu, R., & Lu, X. (2024). The mechanical behavior of cylindrical shell with composite corrugations under uniform and concentrated pressure. *Ocean Engineering*, 298, 117148. DOI: 10.1016/j.oceaneng.2024.117148

Shannak, R. O., & Al-Taher, A. (2012). Factors affecting Work Locus of Control : An Analytical and Comparative Study. *Jordan Journal of Business Administration*, 8(2), 373–389.

Shapero, A., & Sokol, L. (1982). The social dimensions of entrepreneurship. In Kent, C. A., Sexton, D. L., & Vesper, K. H. (Eds.), *Encyclopedia of Entrepreneurship* (pp. 72–90). Prentice Hall.

Shapiro, J. F. (2001). *Modeling the Supply Chain.* Thomson Learning. 3-23.

Shea, E. (2024). The Silk Roads. https://smarthistory.org/reframing-art-history/the-silk-roads/

Shi, X., Liu, W., & Zhang, J. (2023). Present and future trends of supply chain management in the presence of COVID-19: A structured literature review. *International Journal of Logistics*, 26(7), 813–842. DOI: 10.1080/13675567.2021.1988909

Shook, C. L., Priem, R. L., & McGee, J. E. (2003). Venture creation and the enterprising individual: A review and synthesis. *Journal ofManagement*, 29(3), 379–399. DOI: 10.1016/S0149-2063(03)00016-3

Siegrist, J. (1996). Adverse health effects of high-effort/low-reward conditions. *Journal of Occupational Health Psychology*, 1(1), 27–41. DOI: 10.1037/1076-8998.1.1.27 PMID: 9547031

Siegrist, J., Wege, N., Pühlhofer, F., & Wahrendorf, M. (2009). A short generic measure of work stress in the era of globalization: Effort–reward imbalance. *International Archives of Occupational and Environmental Health*, 82(8), 1005–1013. DOI: 10.1007/s00420-008-0384-3 PMID: 19018554

Simpa, P., Solomon, N. O., Adenekan, O. A., & Obasi, S. C. (2024). Sustainability and environmental impact in the LNG value chain: Current trends and future opportunities.

Sluis, S., & De Giovanni, P. (2016). The selection of contracts in supply chains: An empirical analysis. *Journal of Operations Management*, 41(1), 1–11. DOI: 10.1016/j.jom.2015.10.002

Sluyterman, K. (2010). Royal Dutch Shell: Company strategies for dealing with environmental issues. *Business History Review*, 84(2), 203–226. DOI: 10.1017/S0007680500002580

Smith, A. (2018). *The Wealth of Nations*. CreateSpace Independent Publishing Platform.

Sodhi, M. S., & Tang, C. S. (2021). Supply Chain Management for Extreme Conditions: Research Opportunities. *The Journal of Supply Chain Management*, 57(1), 7–16. DOI: 10.1111/jscm.12255

Soininen, J., Puumalainen, K., Sjögrén, H., & Syrjä, P. (2012). The impact of global economic crisis on SMEs: Does entrepreneurial orientation matter? *Management Research Review*, 35(10), 927–944. DOI: 10.1108/01409171211272660

Soonhong, M., Zach, G. Z., & Carlo, D. S. (2019). Defining Supply Chain Management: In the Past, Present, and Future. *Journal of Business Logistics*, 40(1), 44–55. Advance online publication. DOI: 10.1111/jbl.12201

Sotoodeh, K. (2024). *Storage Tanks Selection, Design, Testing, Inspection, and Maintenance: Emission Management and Environmental Protection: Emission Management and Environmental Protection*. Elsevier.

Souitaris, V., Zerbinatib, S., & Al-Lahamc, A. (2007). Do entrepreneurship programmes raise entrepreneurial intention of science and engineering students? The effect of learning, inspiration and resources. *Journal of Business Venturing*, 22(4), 566–591. DOI: 10.1016/j.jbusvent.2006.05.002

Spalding, M. J. (1997). Lessons of NAFTA for APEC. *Journal of Environment & Development*, 6(3), 252–275. https://www.jstor.org/stable/44319277. DOI: 10.1177/107049659700600303

Spector, P. E. (1982). Behavior of organizations as a function of employee's locus of control. *Psychological Bulletin*, 91(3), 482–497. DOI: 10.1037/0033-2909.91.3.482

Spector, P. E. (1988). Development of the work locus of control scale. *Journal of Occupational Psychology*, 61(4), 335–340. DOI: 10.1111/j.2044-8325.1988.tb00470.x

Srinivas, R. E., & Sanjeev, G. (2023). Review article: The Emerging Drone Technology and the Advancement of the Indian Drone Business Industry. *The Journal of High Technology Management Research*, 34(2), 100464. Advance online publication. DOI: 10.1016/j.hitech.2023.100464

Stadtler, H. (2002). *Christoph Kilger, "Supply Chain Management and Advance Planning, Concepts, models Software and Case Studies"* (2nd ed.). Springer.

Stankevičienė, J., Nikanorova, M., & Çera, G. (2020). Analysis of green economy dimension in the context of circular economy: The case of baltic sea region. *E+M. Ekonomie a Management*, 23(1), 4–18. DOI: 10.15240/tul/001/2020-1-001

Stekelorum, R., Laguir, I., Gupta, S., & Kumar, S. (2021). Green supply chain management practices and third-party logistics providers' performances: A fuzzy-set approach. *International Journal of Production Economics*, 235, 108093. DOI: 10.1016/j.ijpe.2021.108093

Stress. (2023, February 21). World Health Organization (WHO). Retrieved January 29, 2024, from https://www.who.int//news-room/questions-and-answers/item/stress/?gclid=EAIaIQobChMI5Yzj2feBhAMVc6hoCR25mAVSEAAYASAAEgISFvD_BwE

Study Group on Advanced Global Supply Chains in the Digital Era (SGAGSC). (2023). *Dejitaru jidai ni okeru guroobaru sapurai cheen koudoka kenkyukai* [Report of study group on advanced global supply chains in the digital era, Asia and Oceania division]. https://www.meti.go.jp/shingikai/external_economy/global_supply_chain/pdf/20230331_1.pdf

Suchek, N., Fernandes, C., Kraus, S., Filser, M., & Sjögrén, H. (2021). Innovation and the circular economy: A systematic literature review. *Business Strategy and the Environment*, 30(8), 3686–3702. DOI: 10.1002/bse.2834

Sun, S., Hall, D. J., & Cegielski, C. G. (2020). Organizational intention to adopt big data in the B2B context: An integrated view. *Industrial Marketing Management*, 86, 109–121. DOI: 10.1016/j.indmarman.2019.09.003

Susan, F. (1984). Personal control and stress and coping processes: A theoretical analysis. *Journal of Personality and Social Psychology*, 46(4), 893–852. DOI: 10.1037/0022-3514.46.4.839 PMID: 6737195

Swaroop, K. and Gade, S. (2023). Sustainable marketing and people behavior for enhanced governance., 242-262. DOI: 10.4018/978-1-6684-9711-1.ch013

Szentes, T. (1976). A Few Thoughts on the Problem of Hungarian Cooperation With Developing Countries. *Acta Oeconomica*, 17(2), 145–158.

Taj, S., Imran, A. S., Kastrati, Z., Daudpota, S. M., Memon, R. A., & Ahmed, J. (2023). IoT-based supply chain management: A systematic literature review. *Internet of Things : Engineering Cyber Physical Human Systems*, 24, 100982. Advance online publication. DOI: 10.1016/j.iot.2023.100982

Tashtamirov, M. (2023). The circular economy and regional economic development. E3s Web of Conferences, 431, 07003. DOI: 10.1051/e3sconf/202343107003

Taylor, F. (2006). *The Principles of Scientific Management*. Cosimo Classics.

The Japan Foundation (JF). (2023). *Betonamu (2022): Nihongo kyouiku kuni chiiki betsu jouhou* [Vietnam (2022): Japanese language education country/region information]. https://www.jpf.go.jp/j/project/japanese/survey/area/country/2022/vietnam.html

Tjahjono, B., Esplugues, C., Ares, E., & Pelaez, G. (2017). What does Industry 4.0 mean to Supply Chain? *Procedia Manufacturing*, 13, 1175–1182. DOI: 10.1016/j.promfg.2017.09.191

Tliche, Y., Taghipour, A., & Canel-Depitre, B. (2018). Downstream Demand Inference in decentralized supply chains. *European Journal of Operational Research*, 274(1), 65–77. DOI: 10.1016/j.ejor.2018.09.034

Topić Popović, N., Lorencin, V., Strunjak-Perović, I., & Čož-Rakovac, R. (2023). Shell waste management and utilization: Mitigating organic pollution and enhancing sustainability. *Applied Sciences (Basel, Switzerland)*, 13(1), 623. DOI: 10.3390/app13010623

Trafico, Z. M. G. (2016). *El Parque Agroecológico de Zapopan celebra la autosustentabilidad*. Retrieved from http://traficozmg.com/parque-agroecologico-zapopan-celebra-la-autosustentabilidad/

Tran, P. N. T., Gorton, M., & Lemke, F. (2021). When supplier development initiatives fail: Identifying the causes of opportunism and unexpected outcomes. *Journal of Business Research*, 127, 277–289. DOI: 10.1016/j.jbusres.2021.01.009

Uralovich, K. S., Toshmamatovich, T. U., Kubayevich, K. F., Sapaev, I. B., Saylaubaevna, S. S., Beknazarova, Z. F., & Khurramov, A. (2023). A primary factor in sustainable development and environmental sustainability is environmental education. *Caspian Journal of Environmental Sciences*, 21(4), 965–975.

Uvarova, I., Atstāja, D., Korpa, V., Avena, L., & Erdmanis, M. (2020). End-of-life tyre recycling: going beyond to new circular business models in latvia.. DOI: 10.22616/ERDev.2020.19.TF435

Uysal, Ş. K., Karadağ, H., Tuncer, B., & Şahin, F. (2022). Locus of control, need for achievement, and entrepreneurial intention: A moderated mediation model. *International Journal of Management Education*, 20(2), 100560. DOI: 10.1016/j.ijme.2021.100560

Van Stel, A., & Suddle, K. (2007). The Impact of New Firm Formation on Regional Development in the Netherlands. *Small Business Economics*.

Vandchali, H. R., Cahoon, S., & Chen, S.-L. (2021). The impact of supply chain network structure on relationship management strategies: An empirical investigation of sustainability practices in retailers. *Sustainable Production and Consumption*, 28, 281–299. DOI: 10.1016/j.spc.2021.04.016

Veciana, J. M., Aponte, M., & Urbano, D. (2005). University students' attitudes towards entrepreneurship: A two countries comparison. *The International Entrepreneurship and Management Journal*, 1(2), 165–182. DOI: 10.1007/s11365-005-1127-5

Venâncio, A., Picoto, W., & Pinto, I. (2023). Time-to-unicorn and digital entrepreneurial ecosystems. *Technological Forecasting and Social Change*, 190, 122425. DOI: 10.1016/j.techfore.2023.122425

Villa, R. A., & Thousand, J. S. (2000). Collaborative teaming: A powerful tool in school restructuring. In Villa, R. A., & Thousand, J. S. (Eds.), *Restructuring for caring and effective education: Piecing the puzzle together* (2nd ed.). Paul H. Brookes Publishing Co.

Wales, W. J., Covin, J. G., & Monsen, E. (2020). Entrepreneurial orientation: The necessity of a multilevel conceptualization. *Strategic Entrepreneurship Journal*, 14(4), 639–660. DOI: 10.1002/sej.1344

Wales, W. J., Kraus, S., Filser, M., Stöckmann, C., & Covin, J. G. (2021). The status quo of research on entrepreneurial orientation: Conversational landmarks and theoretical scaffolding. *Journal of Business Research*, 128, 564–577. DOI: 10.1016/j.jbusres.2020.10.046

Wang, Q., Bowling, N. A., & Eschleman, K. J. (2010). A meta-analytic examination of work and general locus of control. *The Journal of Applied Psychology*, 95(4), 761–768. DOI: 10.1037/a0017707 PMID: 20604595

Wang, S., & Esperança, J. P. (2023). Can digital transformation improve market and ESG performance? Evidence from Chinese SMEs. *Journal of Cleaner Production*, 419, 137980. DOI: 10.1016/j.jclepro.2023.137980

Wang, X., Zhang, T., Luo, S., & Abedin, M. Z. (2023). Pathways to improve energy efficiency under carbon emission constraints in iron and steel industry: Using EBM, NCA and QCA approaches. *Journal of Environmental Management*, 348, 119206. DOI: 10.1016/j.jenvman.2023.119206 PMID: 37898049

Waters, D. (2003). *Logistics: An Introduction to Supply Chain Management*. Palgrave MacMillan, 27-54.

Wennekers, A. R. M., & Thurik, A. R. (1999). Linking entrepreneurship and economic growth. *Small Business Economics*, 13(1), 27–55. DOI: 10.1023/A:1008063200484

Wennekers, A. R. M., Thurik, A. R., & Uhlaner, L. (2002). Conditions, entrepreneurship and economic performance: The macro view. *International Journal for Entrepreneurship Education*, 1(2), 157–179.

Wilde, A. (2000). *The East India Company: Trade and Conquest*. The Lyons Press.

Woodside, A. G. (2018). Have your cake and eat it too: Achieving scientific legitimacy. *Industrial Marketing Management*, 69, 53–61. DOI: 10.1016/j.indmarman.2018.01.028

Wu, C.-W., Botella-Carrubi, D., & Blanco-González-Tejero, C. (2024). The empirical study of digital marketing strategy and performance in small and medium-sized enterprises (SMEs). *Technological Forecasting and Social Change*, 200, 123142. DOI: 10.1016/j.techfore.2023.123142

Wu, M., Fu, C., Holguin-veras, J., Enz, M. G., & Mondy, C. (2024). The impact of digital technology deployment on mitigating supply chain disruptions: Evidence from Chinese automotive manufacturers during the COVID-19 crisis. *Journal of Purchasing and Supply Management*, 30(3), 100936. Advance online publication. DOI: 10.1016/j.pursup.2024.100936

Wuni, I. Y. (2022). Mapping the barriers to circular economy adoption in the construction industry: A systematic review, Pareto analysis, and mitigation strategy map. *Building and Environment*, 223, 109453. DOI: 10.1016/j.buildenv.2022.109453

Xin, B., Zhang, F., Hu, Z., Yang, Y., & Ma, X. (2021). Complex Dynamics Analysis of Closed-Loop Supply Chain considering CSR and Fairness Concerns. *Discrete Dynamics in Nature and Society*, 2021, 1–23. Advance online publication. DOI: 10.1155/2021/7787420

Yamaguchi, Y. (Ed.). (2004). *Nihon no anime zenshi: Sekai wo seishita nihon anime no kiseki* [The complete history of Japanese anime: The miracle of Japanese anime that conquered the world]. Ten Books.

Ye, Y., Wang, H., Tian, K., Li, M. (2024): Supply chain risks and the cost of debt: Evidence from the COVID-19 pandemic, *Research in International Business and Finance, 70(B)*, DOI: 10.1016/j.ribaf.2024.102399

Yin, Q., Song, D., Lai, F., Collins, B. J., & Dogru, A. K. (2023). Customizing governance mechanisms to reduce opportunism in buyer–supplier relationships in the digital economy. *Technological Forecasting and Social Change*, 190, 122411. DOI: 10.1016/j.techfore.2023.122411

Yu, Y., Xu, J., Huo, B., Zhang, J. Z., & Cao, Y. (2023). The impact of supply chain social responsibility on sustainable performance. *Journal of Cleaner Production*, 385, 135666. DOI: 10.1016/j.jclepro.2022.135666

Zaretsky, L. (2005). From Practice to Theory: Inclusive Models Require Inclusive Theories. American Secondary Education, Summer 2005, Vol. 33, No. 3 (Summer 2005), pp. 65-86

Zhang, N., Guo, M., Bu, X., & Jin, C. (2023). Understanding green loyalty: A literature review based on bibliometric-content analysis. *Heliyon*, 9(7), e18029. DOI: 10.1016/j.heliyon.2023.e18029 PMID: 37483765

Zona Guadalajara. (2017). *Zapopan*. Retrieved from https://zonaguadalajara.com/zapopan/

Zouaghi, I., & Laghouag, A. (2021). A Research Note on Defining the Concept of Supply Chain. *International Journal of Scientific Engineering and Science*, 5(9), 6–10.

About the Contributors

Muhammad Nawaz Tunio is Assistant Professor at the Department of Business Administration, University of Sufism and Modern Sciences, Bhitshah, Pakistan. Dr. Tunio has prior working experience at Mohammad Ali Jinnah University, Karachi, Pakistan as Assistant Professor; Greenwich University, Karachi, Pakistan as Assistant Professor, In-charge Director ORIC, and Editor of the biannual Journal of Business Strategy (JBS). Dr. Tunio is Ph.D. in Entrepreneurship, Innovation, and Economic Development, Alpen Adria University, Klagenfurt, Austria. He was awarded government scholarship by the Higher Education Commission of Pakistan. He was awarded a young scientist research fellowship for Kent State University, Ohio. His fields of research interest are entrepreneurship, CSR, Careers, Youth Development, and Self-employment. He has publications in top-notch research journals, and he has presented papers at international conferences and conducted research workshops. Dr. Tunio has edited several books, contributed chapters in different book published by reputable publishers, and edited special issues of the impact factor, and Scopus indexed journals in the field of entrepreneurship. He has conducted several sessions, and workshops.

Aamir Rashid is an Assistant Professor of Supply Chain Management (SCM), bridging the gap between academic excellence and industry expertise. He has thrived in York College (YC)'s supportive academic environment and actively shaped it. Among his key accomplishments is securing the prestigious "Career Success Fellowship 2024-25," sponsored by the Centre of Transformation, CUNY. He is also engaged in the "Getting Started with ACUE Teaching with AI Programme,". Moreover, the current year brought several notable highlights. Dr. Rashid was honoured to be invited by the School Dean to deliver a lecture on "Global Production and Supply Chain Management" at Universiti Sultan Zainal Abidin (UniSZA), Malaysia. Likewise, he hosts the "Business and Economics Talk" that engages the experts globally. His dedication to research excellence is demonstrated through more than fifty research publications in the field of expertise in top-tier journals. Beyond publishing, he has also actively shared his research on academic platforms, including presenting at the "2024 Spring Symposium" YC, City University of New York.

Rizwana Rasheed has a Ph.D. in Management from France. She is a Doctoral Lecturer at the College of Staten Island, City University of New York (CUNY), USA. Her research interests are related to strategic human resource management, human capital development, stress and social support, organizational culture, leadership roles in an organization, diversity management, organizational justice, employee empowerment, psychological capital, performance management, E-HRM and their different aspects. She is actively pursuing various research projects. Likewise, she is an expert in qualitative and quantitative methods. In recent months, she has published multiple papers in top-tier journals. Dr. Rasheed goes beyond her research by influencing the field through editorial work and rigorous peer review, ensuring high research standards

***

Ambreen Ahmed is a seasoned professional with a demonstrated history of working in the higher education sector and conducting corporate training. She is skilled in basic and applied research, and creative and technical writing. Currently, she is the Cluster Head of the Management, HR & Humanities cluster in SZABIST University Karachi.

Akhtiar Ali is an Associate Professor and the Director of Academics at USMS, where he also serves as the Head of the Department of Business Administration and Commerce. With a strong commitment to academic excellence and innovative teaching, Dr. Ali plays a crucial role in shaping the educational landscape of the department. His expertise and leadership are integral to fostering a robust academic environment.

Jabir Arif received the M.Sc., Engineering, Ph.D., HdR degrees in Industrial Engineering and Logistics from the National School of Applied Sciences Tangier, Faculty of Sciences and Technologies Fez, in 2008, 2010, 2016, and 2020 respectively. He is currently serving as an Associate Professor at Sidi Mohamed Ben Abdellah University, Morocco. He began his career as a Production Planner within a multinational company operating in the automotive wiring harness. Afterward, he was appointed as State Engineer at the Ministry of Public Services and Modernization of Administration where he was in charge of the national major projects. Jabir Arif's main research area is Supply Chain Management & Logistics,

Outsourcing of Logistic Activities, Risk Assessment, IoT, Artificial Intelligence, and Industrial engineering. Apart from teaching and research, he is acting as a reviewer in many ranked journals and conferences. He served as a Technical Committee member of several international conferences, tracks, and workshops.

Kürşad Derinkuyu, Ph.D., earned his B.S. from Bilkent University and completed M.Sc. degrees at Lehigh University and The University of Texas at Austin, achieving his Ph.D. in Operations Research and Industrial Engineering in 2011. He held positions at Hacettepe University, University of Turkish Aeronautical Association (UTAA), and TOBB University of Economics and Technology. He co-founded departments and research centers, notably at UTAA and Energy Exchange Istanbul. He developed software for supply chain management, logistics planning, and forecasting for companies like AMD, BNSF Railway, Enexis, and Aselsan. He led EU and TUBITAK projects and advised companies including ILBANK, EnerjiSA, and Gama. In 2023, he became a Full Professor at Istanbul Aydin University, focusing his research on energy markets, data science, supply chain management and healthcare systems.

|**Narayanage Jayantha Dewasiri**, Ph.D., is a Chartered Manager at the Chartered Management Institute, UK. He conducts research at the Open University of Sri Lanka and the Sri Lanka Institute of Marketing. He is the founding Editor-in-Chief of the South Asian Journal of Marketing. His research interests are in corporate social responsibility, corporate governance, marketing and sales, management, and finance. He is working as the Head of Field Force at the HMD Global Inc., Sri Lanka. He also serves as a senior lecturer at University of Sabaragamuwa, Sri Lanka. He can be reached at dnjay@ou.ac.lk

Tamás Faludi is working for the hungarian University of Miskolc, Faculty of Economics, Institute of Management Science since 2017 as PhD student, researcher, and teacher. His research topic is focused on the supply chain management, especially on the coordination with contracts. The list of his publication can be found on the following site: https://m2.mtmt.hu/gui2/?type=authors&mode=browse&sel=10062698 The educational experience contains hungarian and english courses, as well, which is including but not limited to supply chain management, organizing and managing, human resource management, strategic management, logistics, etc. In 2019, he graduated in pedagogy, as a Master of Education in Economics. In 2016, he finished of logistics management in master degree. His bachelor's degree is Economist in Business Administration and Management. He obtained his PhD in 2023 with a dissertation on supply chain management.

Jawab Fouad is a Full Professor at the Higher School of Technology of the Sidi Mohamed Ben Abdellah University in Fez, Morocco. He is responsible for the research team "Industrial Management and Logistics" (MILOG), vice-director of the "Industrial Technologies and Services" (IST) laboratory and former director of the laboratory "International Management, Decision Techniques and Logistics" (MIDLOG). He has directed the Department of Science and Management Techniques (STG) as well as the University Diploma of Technology (DUT) "Logistics and Transport Management (GLT)" and currently directs the Professional License "LOGISTICS". He is the Founder of the international conference on logistics and supply chain management (LOGISTIQUA).

Preet Kanwal is an academician and researcher with over 20 years of experience in the field of Human Resource Management. She holds a Ph.D. in Human Resource Management from I.K. Gujral Punjab Technical University, Punjab, where she conducted an empirical study on the quality of work life in the textile industry of Punjab. Dr. Kanwal completed her Post-Doctoral Fellowship at the ESG, University of Quebec in Montreal, Canada, furthering her expertise in her field. She has also an international experience of teaching to students of MBA from Victoria University, Australia, and Sunway University, Malaysia. Dr. Kanwal's research interests revolve around the quality of work-life, industrial relations, labour laws, social security and labour welfare, organizational stress, and behaviour, particularly in the context of the textile industry. She has presented her research at numerous national and international conferences and published her work in reputed journals. Additionally, she has authored several book chapters on related topics, underscoring her commitment to advancing knowledge in her field. Her contributions extend beyond teaching and research; she has been actively involved in organizing and leading training sessions, workshops, and conferences, both as a participant and as a session chair.

Ercan Kaya completed her master's degree in economics at Hacettepe University in 1996, and received his doctorate in economics from Selçuk University in 2006. For nearly 20 years, he lectured financial management and economic policies undergrad and master programs at the Military Academy, which trains officers for the Turkish army. Kaya held academic and administrative positions. He lectured on international economics, macro and micro economy and international trade at many other universities and educational institutions, penned many articles as well. He is currently responsible for the financial management of OYAK, one of Turkey's most important commercial organizations.

M. Keskin is a distinguished luminary within the Association for Research and Diplomacy, having formerly held the position of vice-rector. With authorship credited to seven books and a plethora of articles, he has graced the lecterns of numerous esteemed universities and academic institutions. He earned his doctoral degree from Dokuz Eylül University in 2008 and the title of Professor from Nişantaşı University in 2014. His scholarly pursuits predominantly orbit around the realms of logistics and supply chains. Additionally, he wielded executive authority as the Chief Executive Officer of OMSAN, a leading logistics enterprise specializing in multi-modal and global logistics operations.

Mustafa Khan has been associated with UCSI University, Malaysia. He received PhD in Management Sciences from Universiti Pendidikan Sultan Idris, Malaysia. He has published in several esteemed international journals such as the IEEE Transactions on Engineering Management, Management of Environmental Quality, and the International Journal of Productivity and Performance Management.

Ferhat Kökyay received his master's degree in the History of the Republic of Turkey from Fırat University in 2004 and his doctorate in the History of the Revolution from Hacettepe University in 2008. He has been working as a faculty member at Istanbul Nişantaşı University, Faculty of Economics, Administrative and Social Sciences since 2015. He has been focusing on studies in the field of International relations since 2015. He has numerous books and articles on his work in energy policies, the Antarctic Treaty system and global governance.

Molk Oukili Garti received her Engineering degree in Engineering & Industrial field from ENSA Fez in 2020. She is currently a PhD candidate in the Laboratory of Technologies and Industrial Services at the Higher School of Technology, Sidi Mohamed Ben Abdellah University, Morocco. She started out in the automobile industry as a Production Planner for a large international company. After that, she was employed by a multinational corporation in the same industry as a Project Leader.

Majdi Anwar Quttainah earned his Ph.D. degree in Management from Rensselaer Polytechnic Institute, Lally School of Management & Technology (USA); MBA degree with merits from the Business School & Entrepreneurship at Newcastle University (UK), and bachelor's degree in International Business from the American International University in London (UK). Dr. Quttainah is an associate professor of management in the College of Business Administration at Kuwait University. His research and teaching interests are corporate governance and strategies, entrepreneurship & small businesses, and organizational development. In addition, as a recognition of his research, he was awarded the Best Young Researcher academic year 2016/2017 Kuwait University. He is an active scholar, presently working as senior editor of FIIB Business Review (Scopus, WoS, Published by the Sage Publishing). His research won several recognition and awards including the Best Paper Award at the 76th Annual Meeting of the Academy of Management Anaheim, CA, the Best Paper Award at the AGBA's 12th Annual World Congress, Kuantan City (State of Pahang), Malaysia, and the Best Paper Award of the Gorontalo International Conference of Project Management (ICPM) - Gorontalo/Indonesia. Also, at the home country level the best paper award for the Kuwait Economic Researcher Award by the Central Bank of Kuwait; May 2019 and 2022.

Index

A

B

C

D

E

G

I

J

L

M

www.ingramcontent.com/pod-product-compliance
Lightning Source LLC
LaVergne TN
LVHW081349300926
849161LV00008B/2108